To Arnold,
    Happy birthday.
        With all my love,
            Marian

# 'If Only My People. . . .'

By the same author:

*Jewish Medical Ethics*
*Journal of a Rabbi*
*The Timely and the Timeless*

# 'If Only My People. . . .'
## Zionism in My Life

### Sir Immanuel Jakobovits
#### With a Foreword by Sir Isaiah Berlin

Weidenfeld and Nicolson
London

Dedicated to Amélie –

Precious helpmeet and ideal partner,
without whose inspiration, encouragement
and criticism the contents of this book
could not have been experienced or recorded

'If only My People would hearken unto Me,
and Israel walk in My ways,
I would soon subdue their enemies
and turn My hand against their adversaries'
Psalm 81 : 14–15

# Contents

# Foreword

The Jewish community of Great Britain, and, indeed, that of the Common-wealth, can feel justified pride in having as their spiritual leader a scholar of the first water, a man of deeply civilized mind and feeling, unswerving integrity and, above all, moving faith and exemplary courage in inter-preting the traditional values of Judaism in their application to the spiritual and political problems which today beset Jews individually and collectively. Example is better than precept: Sir Immanuel Jakobovits has shown admir-able independence, wisdom and moral strength in resisting the forces of fanaticism and extremism, both theological and political, which threaten the future both of Israel and of the Diaspora.

I feel deeply honoured, unqualified as I am to deal with religious issues, to be invited to testify to the respect which I, and all those who have the cause of the Jewish destiny at heart, feel for his views; and to the admiration which all who know him, far beyond the confines of the Jewish community, must feel for one of the most truly impressive incumbents of his high and responsible office.

*Isaiah Berlin*
OXFORD
MARCH 1984

# Preface

This book, urged upon me by my friend Lord Weidenfeld, is in a sense the product of a compromise, a natural reflection of my penchant for the Maimonidean 'Golden Mean' which has characterized so many of my attitudes and principles.

It was originally suggested that I write about my life, my rabbinic activities on both sides of the Atlantic, my experiences with the most diverse people and leaders of men, my interests especially in medical ethics, and my travels in five continents and on both sides of the Iron Curtain – in a word, an autobiography.

By contrast, I had myself intended to compile a collection of my writings and studies on Zionism in book form. But it was put to me, I suspect quite rightly, that such a compilation would lack reader-appeal. And so a compromise emerged, an autobiographical book on 'Zionism in My Life'.

I chose to limit this self-portrayal to my Zionism in action and thought, although in fact Zionism has been neither the major dynamic nor the principal pursuit of my life, except in the sense that Israel has made greater demands on my time, and prompted more of my published utterances, than any other single subject. For instance, I would describe the areas of Jewish education and medical ethics as typifying my personal specialized interests and contributions far more characteristically. Furthermore, the choice was not dictated by an admitted discomfort at my continuing to be so widely misunderstood, or misrepresented, in my attitude to Zionism, anxious though I obviously am in my own undoctored version to set the record straight. I have learned to live with this criticism, just as others have learned to live with mine.

My reason for focusing on Zionism in the only autobiographical work I am likely to write is the recognition of its centrality in Jewish life today. The kind of Zionism we teach and practise will govern the future of Israel, its security, its character and its image in the world. It will also determine for Jews everywhere their fate, their security and the Jewish quality of their lives. But what is even more important to me, Zionism and Jewish statehood will have a major, if not decisive, effect on the content and the observance of Judaism, on Jewish self-identification, and on the role of the Jewish people in human history in the future. It is to this aspect of Zionism that I have primarily addressed myself, fearful lest a falsified vision or revision of the Zionist dream, wrested from its prophetic definition, may cause infinite grief to Jews and Judaism alike. By the same token, I am convinced that a return to authentic Zionism, rooted in the Jewish tradition, will prove a source of infinite pride to the Jewish people, as a supreme manifestation of Judaism's glory and its contribution to human advancement. Moreover, it is my understanding of Zionism that Israel's physical security depends primarily on its spiritual health, in accordance with Jewish teachings and the lessons of Jewish history.

In assembling the material for this volume, I have had to wade through an enormous mass of writings, and select from statements, reports and correspondence accumulated over nearly four decades. In my autobiographical narrative in Part I and also in my exposition of Zionist thought in Part II, I have incorporated frequent quotations from these sources, some quite lengthy, but all of them I have endeavoured to weave into the fabric of the text in a presentation structured chronologically or by subject matter in the two parts respectively. Without these selections, the work would lack much of its basic substance. As far as possible, especially in the longer quotations, I have given preference to material not previously published, including some from my personal letter-files. To round off the account of my encounter with Zionism I have also added two of my more substantial Zionist studies, duly documented in extensive notes. These two chapters are reproduced, respectively, from a paper published by the Jewish Historical Society of England in 1982, and from an article in *Tradition* (1982).

Apart from my debt to the distinguished publisher and his assistants for their encouragement and help, I owe much to several friends who have read the original draft with painstaking care and a profound concern to ensure that the book will strike the right balance between intended challenge and unintended provocation, between what the writer seeks to convey and what the reader is likely to receive with an open mind, perhaps even with conviction. Some thus rendered me invaluable assistance by revisions, clarifications and sometimes omissions that they suggested. Most of their careful amendments – ranging from stylistic to quite substantial changes – I readily accepted, though the final responsibility for the text as it appears is mine alone. For such demonstration of real friendship, I am particularly grateful to Mr Norman Cohen, Rabbi Maurice Unterman, Judge Israel Finestein and Mr Geoffrey Paul, editor of the *Jewish Chronicle* whom, together with editors of several other journals, I also thank for permission to reproduce parts of articles and statements. Dr Geoffrey Wigoder and Mr Bill Wilson have helped me by finding and checking historical data and with other very useful suggestions. The preparation of this book placed many extra burdens on my office staff, especially my secretary, Mrs Norma Pearlman, without whose patience and skill in producing reams of text and corrections from countless tapes and constantly revised typescripts, this volume would never have seen the light of day.

Above all, I wish to express my very special indebtedness to Sir Isaiah Berlin, ОМ, for gracing this book with his touching Foreword. I feel greatly enriched by enjoying the friendship and support of a personality of his rare distinction, and I hope the book thus enhanced will promote the ideals which we both hold so dear.

# Part One:

# Zionism in Action

# 1

# Conversion to Zionism –
# My First Visit to Palestine

My conscious Zionism is about as old as the State of Israel. To be more precise, it is a year older, and dates back to my first visit to the Holy Land. I was then twenty-six years old, and had just been appointed to my third ministerial position in London as Minister of the Great Synagogue, Duke's Place.

From my earliest recollection, the Jewish national struggle had been a major topic with my friends and the subject was often raised in heated discussions with my fellow-students, especially during my rabbinic studies and degree courses at Jews' College and at the Yeshiva (Talmudical college) Etz Chaim. My closest friend at the Yeshiva happened to be a passionate follower of Jabotinsky's Revisionism, and our positions were poles apart. I had occasion to listen to Chaim Weizmann, and to several other prominent Zionist leaders, speaking at various public meetings, but I was impressed more by their oratory than by their policies.

A major stimulus to my Zionist interests was the result of my encounter with the Torah Va'Avodah movement from the early years of the Second World War. Whilst my parents lived in Bedford, where my father was Rabbi of the evacuee Jewish community for a few years during the war, I had quite by chance 'discovered' a nearby kibbutz of the Bachad, the movement for the training of agricultural settlers in Israel, which was closely linked to Torah Va'Avodah and its junior section, B'nei Akivah. There were then about half-a-dozen such kibbutzim in various parts of England, mostly made up of refugees from Germany. Fascinated by their religious and Zionist idealism, I visited all these centres and before long I was conducting regular study sessions in several of them. The sessions were followed by animated discussions, often into the early hours of the morning, on the intense 'religious socialism' of these pioneers. For many years I retained my active association with the movement. But, keenly interested as I was, I definitely would not have labelled myself a Zionist, least of all in a political sense.

My aversion to political identification was bequeathed me by my revered father. In 1936 I arrived in London as a teenage refugee from Nazi oppression, followed in 1938 by my father and our immediate family. Membership of any political grouping, even that of Agudat Israel, which was probably closest to him ideologically, was simply taboo to him as a rabbi, whether in my native Königsberg, or later in Berlin where we moved in 1928 and where he became the senior communal Dayan, or finally in England where he served on the London Beth Din (ecclesiastical court) for two years until his passing in 1946. Emigration to Palestine had never been considered as an option in our family. The German-Jewish tradition of Orthodoxy in which I was raised – following the teachings of what became known as 'Neo-Orthodoxy' pioneered by Samson Raphael Hirsch, Ezriel Hildesheimer and David Hoffmann – was distinctly lukewarm towards Jewish nationalism.

For me, Zionism was the object of intense interest and agitated debates, but I personally remained independent and non-conformist, and found myself a critic of its right and left wings alike ; even for the policies advocated by the religious faction, the Mizrachi, I had but qualified sympathies.

My visit in 1947 began to change all this. It was the first of over a hundred visits, but that visit remains the incomparable experience of a lifetime. I had joined a teachers' group, sailing from London on the maiden voyage of the first Jewish boat, the *Kedmah*. Ten days later we received a boisterous welcome on our arrival in Tel Aviv, given preference over Haifa to mark the Jewish significance of the event. The following three weeks were spent in a busy programme of travels and activities, largely with the group but often with members of my own family, of whom many had already settled there some years earlier.

Predominantly the country still reflected its Biblical image. It was a vast monument to its inspired and inspiring history, even more than to the enterprise of its modern pioneers. The 'Kotel' was still the Wailing Wall with its narrow access and mournful memories, Rachel's Tomb and the Cave of Machpela almost brought the Patriarchs to life again, Beer Sheva appeared little different from what it must have been in Abraham's day, and Jericho with its flat walls shown to tourists had hardly changed since Joshua brought them down. Little did I realize then that these time-hallowed places would for the next twenty years be out of bounds to us and would never be the same again.

The tour of course also included exciting encounters with the idealistic builders of the modern Yishuv, witnessing as we did their wondrous achievements – from the bustling life of Tel Aviv and Haifa to the imposing Hebrew University campus on Mount Scopus, from the clusters of new religious kibbutzim in the Gush Etzion and the Bet Shean valley to the much older and rabidly secularist settlements dotting the still largely barren landscape from the Galilee to the Negev. It seemed to me that in the country as a whole, religious stirrings were evoked rather by history than by contemporary life.

It was the time when the violent struggle against the British was at its height. Since the bomb attack wrecking the British headquarters in the King David Hotel a year earlier, the violence had escalated, culminating in the hanging of two British sergeants by the Irgun just before I arrived, in reprisal for the execution of several Irgun men. Curfews were imposed almost every night, and as a visitor from Britain I was chilled by the hatred the Jewish population had of the British.

I vividly recall spending one Shabbat with my cousin at Kibbutz Masuot Yitzchak in the Gush Etzion, named after the Chief Rabbi of the Holy Land, Dr Yitzchak Halevi Herzog. It was my good fortune to find the Chief Rabbi at the kibbutz on that Shabbat. After the Friday evening service, he was pre-vailed upon to say a few words to the members of the kibbutz. Known as a staunch Anglophile, he made reference to the current situation by relating the Biblical prediction that the Messiah would arrive riding on a donkey, adding 'and I believe Britain is the donkey'. By this he implied that salvation might well be at hand.

While there was no love among the Jews for the British, there was wide-spread contempt for the Arabs. The prevailing opinion of Palestinian Jews everywhere, my relatives included, was that the British were the only real enemy; once they were driven out, the Arabs would present no problem, as they would soon and easily come to terms with Jewish rule. I found it difficult to follow and accept this line of thinking.

It was this experience which planted the seeds of the principal attitudes which I hold to the present day. My love at first sight of the Holy Land deepened into an ever-growing commitment to the cause of Zionism. In the relative comfort and safety of my life in London, I felt humbled by the idealism, the valour, the hardship and the intense Jewish purpose of my brethren in the Land. A longing to join them one day was sparked in my heart.

But at the same time, the visit reinforced my innate abhorrence of violence, and my profound belief in its futility. I could not share the unquestioning confidence of the Yishuv that the moment the struggle against the British was over, the Zionist dream would become a radiant reality, the State to be born thriving in peace as a haven for the Jewish people, so many of whom were still languishing in refugee camps in Europe and suffering various degrees of discrimination in Arab countries. To me it appeared that the fierce hatred and bitterness of the Palestinian Arabs and their neighbours would not just go away, or be suppressed, with the departure of the British; and I could not dismiss from my mind the ceaseless Arab riots to which the Yishuv had been exposed in unremitting acts of terror and sabotage for decades past. I missed sustained efforts to replace, or at least to accompany, the show of strength by goodwill and reassurance. The cocksure manner in which my friends pooh-poohed the threat from the Arabs worried me. Yet any mention of my anxieties was curtly dismissed as defeatist and condemned as almost heretical. As I was to hear over and over again in the years and decades ahead – as an outsider I could not judge the situation, I did not understand the real character of the Arabs and their submissiveness in the face of force, and I had therefore neither the moral right nor the competence to express opinions in these matters, which were the sole province of Jews living in Palestine.

Under the pressure of such attitudes, if not their logic, my arguments were gradually reduced to a whisper, and in the end faded out altogether. The claim that only they knew the facts and what promoted their best interests was certainly plausible, and I accepted it, even though I remained unconvinced.

Another impression which left an indelible imprint upon me was the extraordinary social polarization within the Yishuv, most markedly between the religious and non-religious segments. I had never seen such her-metically-sealed divisions among Jews, inhibiting even some geographical cohesion between them. They mostly lived in separated – segregated may be the better word – quarters, and there was neither communication nor under-standing between them. For instance, members of a non-religious kibbutz, or certainly their children, had never seen Jews at prayer, or a *tallit*, or a Torah scroll. For them the Jewish belief in God was merely an archaic matter of ancient history, and they did not even know that there were still Jews who professed it. These were no longer the victims of assimilation, but rather of a new creed which deliberately sought to eradicate any trace of our religious heritage.

Equally, the comparatively small religious element also seemed completely insulated from the rest of society, relating to it with a mixture of indifference and hostility. Thus, the Land of Israel became the home of two Jewish peoples, divided almost like the ancient Kingdoms of Judah and Israel. The only common denominator, apart from some joint self-defence activities, was the intolerance of each towards the other. Coming from England, with its flair for compromise and middle-of-the-road tradi-tionalism, I found this acute form of polarization particularly striking – and disturbing.

One further impression had a formative influence upon my subsequent thinking. Although the British were still in occupation, and the United Nations had not yet voted for the partition of the country authorizing the establishment of the Jewish State, there was already a feeling of inevitability in the air. Underlying this feeling was the conviction, held and fostered especially by some religious leaders and their followers, that the convulsive events unfolding in the Holy Land were of Messianic, or at least pre-Messianic, dimensions. Of course, religious Zionism had always been inspired by Messianic hopes and visions. Some had already hailed the Balfour Declaration as the imminent dawn of the Messianic era. Later the Holocaust catastrophe of the Final Solution inevitably intensified speculation that the Final Redemption was at hand. The whole drama of the Jewish return to the Land and the mighty struggle to regain Jewish national independence was seen as the realization of Biblical prophecies.

For me such reliance on imminent deliverance always evoked haunting memories of the many pseudo-Messianic disasters in our history, and I was troubled by the incipient signs of identifying contemporary events, however hopeful or even promising, with Messianic certainties.

I came back from my visit with much exhilaration. It did indeed convert me to Zionism, but not to Zionist policies. I was entranced by the loveliness of the Land and the pioneering spirit of its builders. But I was estranged by some features and disconcerted by others. Most of the fears then planted in my mind were only seminal and for long remained latent. I returned, as a young rabbi, to minister in London's East End for the next two years, to become absorbed mostly in youth and social work. But in retrospect, I can see that my stance in later years was moulded by this visit, and it has consistently guided my thinking and my public statements over the years to the present day.

The year following my visit was to prove the most momentous in the history of modern Zionism. On 29 November 1947 the United Nations General Assembly passed a resolution on the partition of Palestine by more than a two-thirds majority in a rare convergence of views between East and West, and on 14 May 1948 the State of Israel was proclaimed and established. This act precipitated an attack by Israel's Arab neighbours and created tensions which have persisted, in sometimes more and sometimes less violent form, to the present day. These almost apocalyptic events, profoundly stirring as they were, did not at the time affect the routine of Jewish life and sentiment as acutely as they did decades later. Perhaps the reaction to the Holocaust, at the opposite extreme in the Jewish experience, showed a similar slow transformation from initial numbness to increasing awareness and identification.

Just one example will illustrate this. Only six weeks after the inauguration of the Jewish State, Israel Brodie was installed as the new Chief Rabbi at an imposing ceremony in the New Synagogue in North London. He had been my tutor at Jews' College for several years, and as minister of the oldest synagogue under his jurisdiction, I was entitled to lead the procession of ministers on that occasion. Though a life-long Zionist, the new Chief Rabbi made no reference to Israel in his Installation Address on 28 June 1948, just as his predecessor, Joseph Herman Hertz – also a passionate Zionist – had not mentioned Zionism from the pulpit when he was installed in office in 1913. In 1948 and the years immediately following, however intense the political activity in support of the new-born State, Israel was still very remote from the religious concerns of Anglo-Jewry. It was not until Israel's seventh birthday in 1955 that the first Israel Independence Day service was held in London, though a Prayer for the State of Israel had been introduced earlier into the Sabbath and Festival services.

My own work and interests during the two years of my ministry at the Great Synagogue reflected this remoteness. Here and there my sermons at the time would mention Israel, especially its tribulations in resisting the invading Arab armies in the War of Liberation and the feverish but unavailing efforts to win some international support for the embattled Yishuv. But all these references were only relatively cursory, and nowhere near the centre of concern to which they gradually moved in later years. Compared to my many other religious, educational and social activities, Zionism and Israel featured only somewhat peripherally during my tenure of service in London's East End. They had undergone little change from what they had been in my two previous positions with the Brondesbury and South-East London synagogues, with the exception of my continuous involvement with the Zionist youth movement, Torah Va'Avodah, and its Bachad agricultural training centres of future Chalutzim who eventually pioneered several Mizrachi kibbutzim in Israel, and whose early members were mostly known to me. They included my youngest brother, Manfred, who settled in Kibbutz Lavi.

At that time, I could hardly foresee that just over forty years later I would have three Jerusalem-born grandchildren, be actively associated with quite a few institutions in Israel, and involved as a principal protagonist in several worldwide controversies regarding Israel.

# 2

# Ireland and America –
# Zion Rises and Recedes

My involvement in Zionist affairs, both ideological and practical, increased significantly on my move to Dublin as Chief Rabbi of Ireland early in 1949. Though geographically further away from Israel, spiritually I became much closer. There were two principal reasons for this. Firstly, the Irish-Jewish community, led and inspired for seventeen years by Chief Rabbi Dr Isaac Herzog, my immediate predecessor who had left Ireland to become Chief Rabbi of the Holy Land in 1936, had always been staunchly Zionist. It never counted anti-Zionists among its members as did other communities, and its Aliyah rate before my appointment and subsequently was the best, in size and quality, of any Western country, approximating to perhaps as much as one-third of the 5,400 Jews I found in Ireland on my arrival. Zionist societies flourished, and the *per capita* contributions to numerous Israeli causes were appreciably higher than elsewhere.

The second reason lay in the nature of my new office. I was now the religious spokesman for an entire community. As Chief Rabbi, I was called upon to pronounce on issues which had been far beyond my ken in London. The pressures to make statements bearing on Israel were all the greater in the absence of diplomatic relations between Ireland and Israel throughout my ten-year tenure, especially in a country as devoutly Catholic and as closely tied to the Vatican as the Republic of Ireland. Incidentally, Ireland was proclaimed a republic in the same year as the State of Israel was established, and the two countries were admitted simultaneously to the United Nations on 11 May 1949.

I was proud when the Irish Prime Minister announced his government's *de facto* recognition of Israel at the dinner to celebrate my installation in office. This constituted and was intended to be a gesture to Ireland's Jewish community rather than to Israel, and the occasion provided me with my first

9

little niche in the consolidation of the Jewish State. My next encounter over Israel, soon after, was rather less pleasant. There had been some mild anti-Jewish demonstrations in Dublin in response to the worldwide Catholic agitation on the 'Holy Places'. I went to see Archbishop McQuaid of Dublin, the Primate of Ireland, to reassure him of the protection of Catholic rights and property in Israel and to request his assistance in preserving the happy relations between Jews and Catholics in Ireland. In reply, he asked me to secure for him an official declaration on the safety of the 'Holy Places' from the government of Israel. Nothing less would do. He subsequently put his request to me in a personal letter dated 26 May 1949:

> ... Such a declaration would greatly assist, too, in preventing unfortunate reper-
> cussions such as you stated you fear may arise in Dublin .... It would indeed be a
> grievous pity if after having safely traversed a period of worldwide and unexampled
> crisis, innocent people of your Community should now suffer hurt, by reason of the
> attitude and actions of irreligious members of Israel whose merely political or
> commercial aims would never be countenanced by the peaceful members of your
> Community in Dublin.

This extraordinary and hardly veiled threat was my first taste of the adverse effect on Diaspora Jews of events in Israel. Here was a Jewish community being held accountable and threatened with reprisals for the actions of an independent country thousands of miles away, for whose policies this community could not be held responsible and in whose affairs it had no say. It was one of those experiences which multiplied and intensified with the years, and which rendered rather hollow, in my view, the argument that Diaspora Jews had no right to express critical views on Israel since their fate was not at stake. Often it clearly was, and continues to be.

As Chief Rabbi, I had also assumed responsibility for religious decisions relating to Israel. Among the first of these was a directive to all synagogues to discontinue singing the *Hatikvah* at the end of each Sabbath service, as had been done since the proclamation of the Jewish State two years earlier. The community had simply forgotten that Israel was now a fact and no longer required a weekly affirmation of Zionist patriotism in regular acts of worship. My order at first met with some hostility, but it soon became the accepted norm. I had a similar experience some ten years later when, at the Fifth Avenue Synagogue, as at most other American synagogues, I found the American and Israeli flags flanking the Holy Ark at all times – a practice I also stopped as being incongruent with the spirit of the synagogue.

There were other religious rulings relating to Israel that I felt I could not give in isolation from other communities, especially from Israel itself. I have always held that innovations affecting religious traditions require universal agreement and implementation, and cannot be limited to a single community within the House of Israel. So when the local JNF Commission approached me with a proposal to celebrate Israel Independence Day on the anniversary date of 5 Iyar with musical entertainment – that is, during the Sephirah mourning period when music is normally banned – I turned to Chief Rabbi Herzog for a ruling, 'so as to ensure that we act in conformity with the other communities in world Jewry'. I received the following reply dated 22 October 1950:

Your letter has been considered at a meeting of the Chief Rabbinate of Israel, and in accordance with its decision we are to inform you that we are unable to sanction instrumental music and dances on this day which occurs during the Sephirah period.

I acted accordingly, and, when the matter was raised again, published this reply in a letter to the *Jewish Chronicle* on 1 May 1953.

Services for Israel of an unusual nature presented themselves when El Al began its transatlantic flights in 1950. The company asked the rabbinate in Dublin to arrange the supply of kosher meals, under its supervision, for the three-score Constellation passengers during their stop-over at Shannon about once a week, usually on forty-eight-hours' notice. We soon found ourselves involved not only in a somewhat erratic catering service three-quarters of an hour's flying time away from Dublin, but in arguments with the Jewish crews who refused to sit down at the kosher tables, and on occasional Sabbath flights, in breach of promises we had been given. Then there was trouble over payments for the whole operation, for which El Al had engaged another non-Jewish airline, which eventually turned to us for help to recoup its money. In my first encounter with Israeli officialdom to avoid a *Chillul Hashem*, I went on a futile mission to London to discuss the predicament with Ambassador Mordecai Eliash, who clearly had more important business to attend to, and did not secure a settlement until I intervened directly with the Ministry of Transport in Israel. That episode was a long, long way from the beautiful £100,000 kosher catering centre of El Al, under the supervision of the London Beth Din, that I was to consecrate at Heathrow airport over twenty years later.

In Ireland I led or supported every Zionist campaign and rally, and I willingly encouraged an Israel orientation in our schools and youth movements, particularly among my own disciples, many of whom now occupy leading posts in Israel. This strong commitment to Israel was equally shared by my wife, whom I married in Paris a few months after taking up office in Ireland. She had grown up in a circle of friends most of whom later settled in Israel. At our home we entertained a ceaseless flow of visitors, emissaries and delegations on Zionist missions from Britain as well as from Israel for whom the Dublin Jewish community, despite its relatively small size, remained a Zionist stronghold. Among the numerous dignitaries we received with special pleasure were Chaim Herzog, now President of Israel, and his late lamented brother Jacob with whom I had shared a year at London's Yeshiva Etz Chaim. Both had spent their childhood and early youth in the very home in Dublin which we then occupied. We thus lived in an intensely Zionist atmosphere and fully identified with it.

Of course, I had my reservations, but these were still generally muted. Despite my penchant for political non-conformity and independence, my Zionist credentials were well established. Whatever doubts I occasionally entertained as to the wisdom of certain Israeli policies, I did not as a rule express them in public. I regarded these criticisms as being outside my rabbinic competence and provenance, since they did not strike me as being the religious challenges which they turned out to be in later years. Even in those early days I felt assailed by anxiety over the indifference to the Arab refugee problem, the solution to which I regarded as a humanitarian impera- tive and as the principal key to peace. The massive retaliation raids following Arab terrorist attacks in Israel, in a cycle of escalating terror, I believed could never achieve their objective of 'teaching the Arabs a lesson in the only language they would understand'. After thirty-five years of persistent instruction, they still do not seem to understand either the language or the lesson! The whole stance of militancy, which has hardly changed over the decades, simply did not appeal to my Jewish conscience or my human reason.

But with Israel's spectacular development proving a source of immense pride to Jews everywhere, and the triumphs of military prowess notably in the Sinai campaign of 1956, I reluctantly had to acknowledge the efficacy of might in an unrighteous world, just as in the preceding decade I had to admit grudgingly that force had worked where diplomacy had failed. However, I certainly never gloried in military strength, and in all my public references to Israel, whatever the occasion, I would always emphasize our spiritual aspirations as our national goal and true source of pride.

Late in 1948, when I accepted my Irish assignment, I had given myself ten years for service in this outpost, somewhat removed from the heartland of Jewish life; and ten years it was almost to the day when I accepted a call to become the first Rabbi of New York's Fifth Avenue Synagogue – officiating at its opening for Rosh Hashanah in 1958. My American experience, which was to last for eight years, coincided with the longest spell of relative peace in Israel's history – between the Sinai campaign of 1956 and the Six Day War of 1967. It was a period of low-key lobbying by American Jews when, following the retreat from Sinai imposed by President Eisenhower on Prime Minister Ben-Gurion in 1956, Israel enjoyed its heyday of sympathy in the world, including much of Africa. When I joined a delegation of Orthodox leaders to meet President Johnson in the White House, the subject of our representations had nothing to do with political support for Israel, as would become so common after I left America early in 1967, but rather with the allocation of funds for some Jewish religious causes.

Other factors, too, accounted for my lesser involvement in Zionist affairs. As a congregational rabbi I had dropped the 'Chief' from my title and represented no one except a small community of some 200 members, although quite a few of them were personalities of considerable distinction and influence. I never shared the predilection of the American rabbinate for turning sermons into political commentaries or for aspiring to a press mention on the front page of the *New York Times*. I was attracted neither to holding office in the Rabbinical Council of America to which I belonged, nor to participating in the high politics of the New York Board of Rabbis, to which I did not belong – organizations which might have provided platforms for articulating widely reported views on Zionism and Israel. True, I was the guest speaker at many national conventions, I spoke at numerous fund-raising dinners and I lectured widely, addressing Jewish leaders and Jewish communities large and small throughout America and Canada. But, my subject usually dealt with Jewish education, or Jewish values generally, and particularly my specialized field of Jewish medical ethics. In fact, much of the time I could spare from my somewhat limited congregational duties I spent conducting seminars for doctors, speaking at medical schools and presiding over a joint committee of rabbis and physicians, which advised New York's large hospitals on medico-halachic questions, particularly autopsies. I eventually published the *Jewish Hospital Compendium*, the first practical guide of its kind, later revised in many editions.

Israel was no longer at the top of my extra-congregational agenda, as it had been in Ireland. This did not reflect any lessened commitment on my part, but rather the relationship of American Jews with Israel which I found more distant than in Ireland or even Britain. During my sojourn in America, and on my frequent regular visits there, I have always found that, passionate as American Jews may be in their political agitation for Israel, they are far more remote from identifying with it than are their transatlantic brethren. Their Aliyah rate is proportionally only one-sixth of the corresponding figure in Britain, and an even smaller fraction of the Irish counterpart. The ratio of American Jews who have visited Israel is likewise much smaller. As the only Jewish community in history to have settled as equals – as immigrants like all other Americans – American Jews feel that they have arrived at their final destination. They seek equality not just as individual citizens but as a group, quite unlike Jews anywhere else in the Diaspora. Hence their obsession with the separation of state and church. The non-denominational character of America was to be preserved. This precluded America's being a specifically Christian country; for that would mean inequality. Jews and Jewish money therefore pioneered the Supreme Court rulings against prayers at public (national) schools and against Federal aid for parochial schools – a stand quite unthinkable among Jews in Europe or elsewhere. Even the issue of a Christmas postage stamp aroused the annual ire and protest of American-Jewish leaders and organizations as an intolerable breach of the wall between religion and state!

This mentality profoundly affected attitudes to Israel. Two experiences gave me striking illustrations which I have never forgotten. A Conservative rabbi, editor of a series of prayer-books and similar texts, proudly presented me with his latest *Hagadah* for Passover. The Hebrew text was left unchanged, since it was not suspected that the average American Jew might detect anything objectionable in it. But in the English rendering, I discovered a few subtle revisions. The text naturally included the Grace-after-Meals, with the prayer: 'May the All-merciful break the yoke of oppression from off our necks and may He lead *us* upright into our Land.' The translation reads: '. . . and may He lead the *homeless of our people* in dignity to our Homeland.' Israel is not for 'us' but for 'the homeless of our people'. It is a land for refugees, a shelter for people without a haven, not for Americans!

My second discovery of American-Jewish idiosyncrasies was rather less benign. I had been invited to be the principal guest speaker at an Orthodox Synagogue convention in the Midwest. Dealing in passing with relations between Israel and the Diaspora, I quite innocently referred to us as being 'in exile'. For such an unpardonable slight to the status of American Jewry I was severely taken to task. It was quite 'un-American' to think and speak in these terms – even in the eyes of my own fraternity who thrice daily prayed with me, 'And raise the banner to gather our exiles, and gather us from the four corners of the earth.' Israel had still not made any difference to the self-identification of American Jews, however traditional their daily discipline of life, and to challenge their philosophy of national complacency was a cause for censure.

Zionist fund-raising had of course by then become big business as a central feature of Jewish communal life in America, and I played my modest part in helping to turn the wheels of the production line which in the end brought forth the pledges for the UJA (United Jewish Appeal) and Israel Bonds in a continual sequence of breakfasts and dinners together with other arm-twisting and stomach-filling exercises, usually culminating in the wholesale award of plaques and other honorific gestures. But even in these campaigns, Israel generally featured only as the principal beneficiary together with domestic causes and contributions to the Joint Distribution Committee for the alleviation of Jews in need in many parts of the world. The community chest in America run on these lines was thus quite different from the virtual monopoly of big fund-raising for Israel as established in Britain and Ireland. And this difference in the allocation of communal resources reflected a corresponding difference in outlook and commitment.

In noting this relative distance of American Jewry from Zionism, I was certainly not alone. Avraham Harman, who was Israel's Ambassador to the United States at the time, expressed a similar view in a paper prepared for the 1983 President's International Seminar on World Jewry and the State of Israel:

If we once had as our goal, when we [Zionists] were a minority movement, the 'conquest of the communities', then we must admit that after 1947–8, the Zionist Movement failed completely in this task in the United States. It did not conquer the communities. Instead, it became distanced from the communities.

That judgement would definitely not apply to Britain and Ireland, or to most other parts of the Diaspora.

Occupying a back seat in the Jewish national arena, I had no occasion to be particularly involved in any celebrated Zionist controversies. Nor did I feel any special urge to rock the boat of Israeli policies which was then sailing in comparatively calm waters, though I still had the gnawing feeling that it was heading in the direction of dangerous rocks rather than towards a safe haven. Much to the irritation of my listeners, and sometimes evoking their angry protests, I did occasionally mention in my speeches, as later recorded in my books *Journal of a Rabbi* and *The Timely and the Timeless*, such taboo subjects as the plight of the Arab refugees and the pursuit of peace through the efforts of the Jewish side.

Meanwhile, the continued state of war and the intermittent fedayeen raids wreaking terror inside Israel had become virtually an accepted fact of life. But there was hardly any Jewish challenge to Israeli policies, consisting of a mixture of defiance and massive retaliation as the unquestioned norm. I felt uneasy about these policies. They seemed to me counter-productive as they fed Arab hatred and resentment, thus making the prospect of ultimate peace ever more remote. I had never doubted that in the *creation* of the Arab refugee problem justice was entirely on the Israeli side and that the blame lay solely with the Arabs who, during the War of Liberation, had urged their own people to leave the country for what they claimed would be a short period, and then return to reclaim their – and the Jews' – possessions upon the anticipated Arab victory.

But whatever the origins, the Palestinians had become a fact, and I feared that Israeli policies, instead of reducing the tensions – still confined to a refugee problem – aggravated them, both by nursing the Palestinians' sense of national identity and by allowing decades of wretched existence in refugee camps to turn them into the world's worst breeding-grounds of implacable hate and terror, born of humiliation and despair. In my still inchoate thinking, the promotion of Israel's peace and security demanded neither ignoring the Palestinian refugees as simply a problem of the Arabs, nor further inflaming Arab vengeance by ever-escalating retaliation. The key to the solution of Israel's predicament, as I saw it, lay in reassuring the Arabs, not in intimidating them. They had to be convinced that Israel shared their concern over the future of the refugees, that they had nothing to fear from a Zionist state, and that such a state would not be an outpost of Western colonialism threatening to dominate the whole region, but would gradually integrate harmoniously into its Semitic environment. My feeling at that time was the same as expressed many years later by the distinguished Israeli Sephardi leader Elie Eliachar, who died in 1981, in his book *Living with Jews* which was published posthumously in 1983:

> I am well aware that if the Arabs, the Palestinians and other Moslems should ever have the military power and the historical opportunity to annihilate Israel, they would do so without any qualms. For we have persistently chosen to be an alien element in the Middle East, instead of returning to our heritage as members of the Semitic family. Therefore, until such time as we learn to live together, we shall have to maintain a deterrent military force.

Political expediency apart, my Jewish conscience also told me that reliance on power alone and disregard for the sufferings of others were incompatible with our moral commitment and could not prevail in the long run. But all these gnawing doubts, completely outweighed as they were by Israel's colossal accomplishments, were still on the whole low-key, and so was the degree of agitation within me.

What exercised me a little more were the religious controversies erupting within Israel with increasing frequency and intensity. But even here I did not feel disposed towards, and indeed resisted considerable pressure to join, the orchestrated agitation of protests and denunciation by Orthodox leaders and parties. When an Israeli cabinet crisis in 1958 – over the registration as 'Jews' of people who without conversion simply affirmed their national identification with the Jewish people – led Ben-Gurion to elicit responses on this question from some seventy rabbinical and lay scholars in Israel and the Diaspora, the overwhelming consensus of opinion insisted that Israel should follow the rules of Halachah in this matter. I was not among them, but I did publish a lengthy article supporting the halachic stand on what was later to become an entirely different argument in the fierce and still-unresolved 'Who is a Jew?' controversy. In this latter phase I was subsequently to take a singularly lonely stand within the Orthodox establishment, though not because of any lesser commitment to the norms of Halachah and the unity of the Jewish people than that claimed by the zealous protagonists in the furore.

There were other battles over religious issues which occasionally prompted me to support Orthodox protests publicly. Such an occasion was the bitter controversy aroused over the proposal in 1958 to establish a mixed public swimming-pool in Jerusalem, and I published a letter in the *Jewish Chronicle* challenging an editorial which had rather intemperately denounced a protest signed by sixty-three rabbis who considered the proposal incompatible with the sanctity of Jerusalem.

But on the whole, I tried to steer clear of involvement in the many collisions on religious legislation in Israel, always believing that the secular majority in Israel would become amenable to religious influences more through education and persuasion than through coercion by legislation. Even on the vexed problem of autopsies in Israel, though within my specialized sphere of medical ethics, I only rarely added my voice to the Orthodox protests against the widespread abuses in Israel which erupted in such frequent and sometimes violent clashes as a major *casus belli* between the rabbinical and medical fraternities, spilling over into bitter civil and parliamentary strife. I was to make some efforts later to find and promote a formula to narrow the gap between medical needs and halachic objections, realizing that the whole problem was created primarily, or at least aggravated, by lack of trust between rabbis and physicians with neither side appreciating the concerns of the other.

The only exception to my disinclination to agitate for religious advances by legislation was on the appalling rate of abortions in Israel. This was a subject on which I was to turn public attention with increasing urgency from the mid-1960s on. But I did so only because of its much wider moral ramifications and above all its catastrophic effects on Israel's human resources and therefore security. This was a violation of Jewish law where agitation and legislation need not alienate religious sympathies.

Such critical comments as I made from time to time on Israeli affairs dealt in the main with the broader issues – the erosion of the Jewish purpose through secularization, the unholy alliance between religion and politics, and the growing radicalism within religious Zionism. But these persistent criticisms were more than outweighed by stressing the immense positive achievements of Israel and instilling pride in them. Throughout my enormously stimulating years in America, my commitment to Zionism was never challenged, either within me or by others.

# 3

# 'Chief' in Britain –
# Challenge of the Six Day War

When, late in 1965, it was announced that Jacob Herzog had been elected Britain's new Chief Rabbi in succession to Israel Brodie who had retired at the age of seventy, I noted the news with more than passing interest. Not that I had ever aspired to that position or had the slightest intention of crossing the Atlantic again on a one-way trip except eventually to Israel. But my affection for and interest in Anglo-Jewry, in whose midst I had studied and served for the most formative thirteen years of my life, had always remained extremely warm. I was therefore greatly cheered when Herzog, a friend of mine, and adviser to four prime ministers of Israel, for whose extraordinary intellect and reputation I had the highest esteem, agreed to accept this key post, especially at a time when Anglo-Jewry was still in turmoil over the 'Jacobs Affair' and many had written off the future of the British Chief Rabbinate altogether. The affair was sparked off by the refusal of Chief Rabbi Brodie to approve the appointment of Rabbi Dr Louis Jacobs as Principal of Jews' College, and subsequently as a minister within the United Synagogue, since his theological views on the Divine authority of the Torah, by then publicly expressed, were deemed too unorthodox and therefore unacceptable. Dr Jacobs's cause was vigorously taken up by the *Jewish Chronicle* in a bitter campaign against the Chief Rabbi and for the establishment of Conservative Judaism in Britain. After several years of communal commotion, nothing did more to break the back of the religious crisis in Anglo-Jewry, then still seething, than the mere announcement that a man of Jacob Herzog's eminence was to be the new incumbent of the beleaguered office. Alas, ill-health forced him to withdraw from it a few months later, and he died tragically young in 1973.

Not long after Herzog's withdrawal, a proposal that I should fill the void was made to me by Sir Isaac Wolfson, chairman of the Chief Rabbinate

Council in his capacity as President of the United Synagogue. I knew him well, especially as he frequently worshipped at the Fifth Avenue Synagogue whenever he stayed at a nearby hotel in New York. To say that the approach took me completely by surprise would be an exaggeration, since private suggestions and journalistic speculation had occasionally linked me with the prospect of this appointment. But to state that I expected, let alone wanted, the office would be equally untruthful. Nothing was further from my mind and ambition than to exchange my freedom and comparative comforts of the material as well as vocational rewards in America, for the headaches and constraints of an awesome office in which my manifold duties would be rigidly defined by constitution and tradition, which would allow me little time to pursue my favourite academic and literary interests, and which was still in the throes of embittered controversy and denigration. There was no false modesty at all in my first reaction of inadequacy to meet such a challenge.

But weeks of consultations with leading colleagues and other friends, and above all with my revered father-in-law, Rabbi Elie Munk, then the widely esteemed head of 'Independent Orthodoxy' in Paris, led to the conclusion that I had no moral right, whatever the risks and sacrifices involved, to turn down a call to serve a community to which I still felt so intimately bound, in a country which had once saved my life and the lives of my immediate family. The election was unanimous, though there was some prominent support, especially by the *Jewish Chronicle* which transferred its persistent agitation against Chief Rabbi Brodie to me, for the candidacy of Rabbi Dr Louis Rabinowitz, formerly the Chief Rabbi of Johannesburg, then retired in Jerusalem. He wrote to me following my election: 'I always knew the better man would lose.'

Succeeding an illustrious Herzog for the second time, I was installed in office by Chief Rabbi Brodie, also for the second time – he had inducted me as Chief Rabbi of Ireland eighteen years earlier – at a resplendent service in London's St John's Wood Synagogue on 11 April 1967. As the first British Chief Rabbi to make a Zionist reference in his Installation Address, I pledged to bring the influence of my office to bear 'on cementing the bonds of our common heritage between Israel and the Diaspora' and 'consolidating our part in the upbuilding of the Land of Israel, by encouraging Aliyah and by freely aiding the spiritual and material growth of Israel as a land flowing with the milk of Torah and the honey of prosperity'; adding: 'It is our assignment, blessed as we are with peace and prosperity, to complete the re-birth of Israel. As they restored the *soil* of Israel we must restore the *soul* of Israel.'

Little was I, or the thousands who watched the ceremony inside the synagogue and elsewhere by closed-circuit television, to know that within a few weeks this pledge would put us all to our severest test. My new office soon thrust me into the heart of Israel's worst crisis and then its greatest triumph; Jewish life and my Zionism were never to be the same after that. By henceforth placing Israel at the centre of my concerns, rivalled only by my commitment to Jewish education within Anglo-Jewry, I assured that the functions of my office were also to undergo a radical and permanent change.

After weeks of mounting gloom and despondency in the face of the growing odds against the Jewish State and its abandonment by the United Nations, the outbreak of the Six Day War on Monday, 5 June 1967, found the community in a state of deepest anxiety – and there was an almost panic-stricken search for means to match Israel's valour with expressions of support and solidarity. In this oppressive atmosphere, a mass rally at the Royal Albert Hall was convened for that Monday night. I was to be the principal Jewish speaker. It proved to be the most moving and challenging public experience of my life, as I addressed an audience of some 10,000 massed inside the hall and overflowing outside, filled equally to overflowing with emotion. We had not yet received the news that by then Nasser's air force had already been wiped out and that one of the most spectacular victories of all times was assured; the meeting was still heavily laden with fears for Israel's future. I opened my address with these words:

Nearly thirty years ago my illustrious predecessor, Chief Rabbi Dr Hertz, addressed a massed assembly in this very hall to arouse the conscience of the world on the catastrophe that lay ahead for European Jewry. Alas, the cry was too weak and too late to avert disaster. Today we have reached another turning-point in Jewish history, perhaps more fateful than any in our long and checkered past. . . . We are here this evening to make quite sure that we will not be too weak and not be too late this time. We are not going to have another Holocaust in the martyred history of our people. The hope of two millennia, the toil and sacrifice of two decades, is not now going to be wiped out in two weeks or two months.

Thunderous applause greeted my angry reply to a bitter and widely publicized attack on me by a well-known Jewish columnist, Bernard Levin, in the *Daily Mail* a week earlier:

I make no apology for having called last week, before the Board of Deputies of British Jews, upon the Anglo-Jewish community to mobilize all its resources in the defence of Israel. Nor will I ever be deterred from doing my religious and my moral duty in this moment of our people's anguish by anyone coming forth with the dangerous nonsense of dual loyalties. Let me try, as plainly as I can, to clear up this diabolical confusion. As a British citizen, England is my country. As a Jew, Israel is my people. When my father and my mother, my brothers and my sisters, are in danger of being murdered, I will defend them whatever their nationality, and if I were not to do so, my fellow-citizens would have nothing but contempt for me. I am, therefore, overcome with grief, I am sickened to the depth of my heart, by the spectacle of some Jews who, having previously betrayed their God and betrayed their religion, are now publicly calling upon their fellow-Jews to betray their people.

I then announced several emergency measures, including an appeal for the curtailment of all personal parties and functions, and for the suspension of all communal projects, with the sole exception of the Jewish education of our own children; the convening of a conference of rabbis and ministers from all over the country for the following day 'to consult together on the help we can render in directing and co-ordinating efforts to mobilize our community'; and the opening under the aegis of my own office of an Israel Emergency Office 'to receive enquiries and to direct offers of help'. But besides calling on Jews to rally to Israel's defence, on the British nation 'summoned by Providence and destiny to complete the Balfour Declaration', and on the nations of the world to take up our cause, the main burden of my address was still our own spiritual mobilization:

You may ask, 'What can I do in this emergency?' The industrialist who gives a million or the little Jewish child who pours out his heart in prayer to God to have mercy upon our people, the volunteer who gives his service in order to prop up Israel's economy, or our communal leaders who now fight for Jewish survival against the scourge of assimilation with redoubled vigour – they all stand in the front line of the battle against Jewish extinction.... For, let us make no mistake, the battle of Jewish survival is being fought in our own midst just as grimly as in Israel. How can we survive, and what kind of a people are we going to be, if our children will be aliens to our heritage; and if we are going to suffer more casualties than our troubled and martyred people has already sustained through massacre, through repression and through assimilation in the past thirty years?

Before continuing with the long-term effects of this electrifying event, and anticipating later events, I must relate an extraordinary experience. As I emerged from the packed Albert Hall into the milling crowds outside, an Israeli girl, perhaps in her late teens, stopped me. Her face contorted with grief, she sobbed in Hebrew: 'Are you the rabbi who spoke inside?' 'Yes, I am.' 'I am from Israel. My country is in mortal danger. Please, Rabbi, pray for my country also on my behalf, for I cannot pray.' Moved to the core of my heart, I promised to honour her request with all the fervour I could muster. By a coincidence stranger than fiction, six years later during the Yom Kippur War, when we set up blood-donation units in two of our synagogues, during one of my periodic visits to greet the queues of volunteers, a young woman came up to me, again to tell me of her distress in Hebrew: 'Do you remember me when I asked you in the Six Day War outside the Albert Hall to pray for my country? You prayed, and my country was saved. It is in danger again. Please, Rabbi, pray for me again so that Israel will prevail!' Evidently in the intervening years she still had not felt the urge or summoned the will to learn how to pray by herself. For me, this experience had epitomized the real challenge to Israel as well as to me and to all religious leaders – how to turn our people from what Chief Rabbi Hertz once called 'Hebrew-speaking heathens' into Jews who would find in their religious heritage not only an emergency prop, but their national and spiritual self-fulfilment!

The practical after-effects of the Albert Hall rally followed in quick succession, soon to leave their permanent mark on my role in the community and the conduct of my office as well as on my Zionist thinking. At the conference of rabbis and ministers I broke the historic news I had just received by telex that Israeli soldiers had broken into Jerusalem's Old City and had liberated the Western Wall. The conference included Reform and Liberal spiritual leaders, and this set the pattern of working with all sections of the community on such general causes which did not impinge on our religious differences. These included Jewish defence, Jewish–Christian relations and Soviet Jewry, as well as Israel, but excluded joint religious services and other forms of religious and educational co-operation, despite some demands for such 'communal unity', and especially for combined Israel Independence Day services, in the early years of my incumbency. Gradually, the line of demarcation I had already drawn in my Installation Address became more generally accepted, with just occasional attacks on this policy from both the Right and the Left.

The Israel Emergency Office was soon closed and turned into a regular Israel Department within my office. It was ably directed by my friend Rabbi Maurice Unterman, minister of the prestigious Marble Arch Synagogue. A few months later, other departments were added to deal with youth, students, welfare, Soviet Jewry and Jewish–Christian relations. The ministers I had chosen to head these departments constituted the Chief Rabbi's Cabinet, which functions with much success to the present day.

On the initiative of the first member of my Cabinet and under his leadership, thirteen rabbis and ministers of the United Synagogue left their congregations for a week's pilgrimage to Israel, where they avidly imbibed the inspiration and religious fervour so ebulliently in evidence. Never before had so many rabbis from this country undertaken such a mission, and never before had the stimulating atmosphere of Zionist aspirations breathed for months afterwards from so many pulpits.

All these and many other activities, including my participation in the Albert Hall rally, were still sparsely reported in the *Jewish Chronicle* which,

for long smarting from the collapse of its campaign against the Chief
Rabbinate, was not to come fully to terms with my appointment for several
years. In fact, during the first few months of my incumbency, in its efforts to
promote a rival Chief Rabbinate, it referred to me invariably as 'the Chief
Rabbi of the United Hebrew Congregations' – naturally without completing
the full official title 'of the British Commonwealth of Nations'.

Another immediate consequence of the Six Day War was my official visit
to Israel on the first resumed El Al flight on the Sunday following the
conclusion of hostilities. A little of the excitement which had stirred all Jews
was conveyed to me when the pilot, advised that I was on board, invited me
to come to the cockpit and to take the co-pilot's seat. While still over 100
miles from our destination, he showed me on his radar screen the coastline
all the way down along the Sinai peninsula, exclaiming with undisguised
excitement: 'All this is ours now.' As we started our descent, he told me that
regulations insisted that no passenger should be in the cockpit for the land-
ing, but since this was his first arrival in 'the new Israel', he wanted me to
remain seated beside him and to give him a special blessing for this
momentous experience.

From then on, the visit was an uninterrupted story of sheer ecstasy. That
Sunday, on my arrival, I was taken with the first group of civilian visitors to
the 'Kotel' on which the entire Jewish world's joy and thankfulness for
Israel's deliverance was fixed in a reunion of infinite emotion. The demolition of the surrounding area was already well under way, in preparation for
the vast crowds expected three days later for the festival of Shavuot – the first
time this hallowed site would be open to the general public. There I met and
congratulated General Narkiss, commander of the forces which had
reconquered and reunited Jerusalem. There was a sequel to that meeting a
few months later, when he and I spoke at a fund-raising function in London.
In his address, reflecting on the war, the General said that there had been no
miracles; the victory was won simply because Israel had a better army, with
superior ingenuity and resources. In my speech I quoted the Talmudic
maxim: 'The one to whom a miracle happens recognizes not his miracle',
and he was the man of the miracle! At our subsequent meetings, he never
forgot this retort. For me this little encounter was again symptomatic of the
yawning spiritual gap in Israel's society, underscoring the challenge facing
our religious leadership. I later wrote about the General that 'he was like the
first Russian cosmonaut who could not see God in outer space'.

The next day I was taken to Rachel's Tomb and the Cave of Machpela
amid indescribable scenes of spiritual rapture. In the Arab areas every house
flew a white flag, but underneath the veneer of demonstrative friendliness
with which some greeted the Israelis, the population appeared sullen and
demoralized. But these Arab reactions were hardly noticed at the time, and

seemed of no consequence in the wave of boundless exhilaration which swept Israel and the Jewish world, to the acclaim of most nations, certainly in the West.

The climax of my visit was to come on Shavuot. By 5 o'clock in the morning Jerusalem's streets were packed with jubilant Jews, most of them clad in festive white, all converging on the 'Kotel' in endless streams, ecstatically shaking hands with the equally jubilant soldiers guarding the route. As we pressed through the already assembled throngs crowding the newly cleared plaza in front of the Wall, the human mass was so dense that Chief Rabbi Isaac Cohen, my successor in Ireland, who had walked with me, was unable to take off his shoes as traditionally required for the Priestly Benediction in the Festival service we had joined. It was estimated that some quarter of a million Jews visited this sacred site on that one day, to be followed by millions of others in the next few days and weeks.

There was a distinctly religious dimension to the aftermath of the victory. Militarily incredible as had been the rapid defeat of Egypt's, Jordan's and Syria's armies, leading to the occupation of Sinai, the West Bank and the Golan Heights, the whole fervour was concentrated on the reunification of Jerusalem and the restored Jewish access to the Western Wall. Everyone told of miracles he had witnessed or of which he had heard. Even battle-hardened soldiers wept like children as they saw the Wall, and unashamedly hugged and kissed its ancient stones. The whole nation seemed to be gripped by an irresistible spiritual uplift, restoring the centrality of Israel's holiness in the national conscience. To the religious element, this widespread rediscovery of the Jewish soul was immensely heartening, even if for some this reawakening of the Jewish spirit was only superficial or altogether lacking, as General Narkiss was to affirm publicly. For my part, I described the rabbinic reactions in my 'Review of Recent Halachic Periodical Literature' which I had until then regularly contributed to *Tradition* (New York) in the following passage:

Most of the numerous responsa on questions resulting from the victory dealt, not unnaturally, with the most significant *religious* aspect of the War: the conquest of Jerusalem's holiest sites, not only enabling Jews to have access to them for the first time in twenty years, but placing them under Jewish control for the first time in nearly 1,900 years. Though only an incidental by-product of what was essentially a struggle against the threat of sheer physical annihilation, the liberation of the Jewish Holy Places – historically comparable to what the Crusades were meant to achieve for Christendom – gave Israel's victory celebrations their peculiarly devout, almost unworldly, character, with the only parades to mark one of history's most spectacular triumphs being the endless streams of pilgrims wending their way to the Western Wall in reverent exhilaration. But the return of the Holy Places also produced its crop of religious problems – and a few bitter inter-religious controversies.

Obviously, such a unique spiritual upsurge did not leave me untouched, either. I too was caught up in the confident belief that, having witnessed miracles of Biblical magnitude, Israel's spiritual advance towards its national purpose as envisaged by the Hebrew Prophets was at hand. And when a few months later, I again visited Israel to include the first Tisha B'Av at the Wall – floodlit that night for the first time – I also wandered among the milling crowds of fasters wondering whether to mourn or to rejoice.

Yet I could not altogether repress some still vague doubts and fears. The reliance on military might as the solution to our problems had always worried me, and this uneasy feeling was not assuaged by the scale of the victory, or even the rather muted martial response it evoked. Least of all could I accept that the enforced dissipation of Arab dreams and aspirations would last for ever with the fear of Israel's military prowess. I often referred to these hesitations in my speeches and writings during the ensuing years of only gradually fading Jewish euphoria.

Looking back in retrospect at my feelings at the time, scarcely articulated as they were, I now find them presented with almost uncanny likeness by Amos Oz in his masterly *In the Land of Israel*, published in 1983. The book reflects much of my thinking, though I could not be further from the author's secularist–socialist–humanist Zionism. In his debate with the Gush Emunim settlers of Ofra (whose founders I visited in its earliest days in 1975), he challenges their reaction to the Six Day War:

What was most painful was not the strange and alien language of the yeshiva students, but the total lack of sensitivity or receptiveness toward our moral distress. After the victory there was some agonizing among us. Values, ideals, conscience, world view – all these made it impossible for us to ignore the implications of having become an occupying power. . . . The people of Israel entered the war on the basis of a national consensus that it was fighting to defend its very existence, and nothing more than that. . . .

That consensus was trampled immediately after the war, and the country was filled with new hymns and new hungers and the blowing of rams' horns. All of this was, for us, a shock and a source of agonizing moral dilemma, but not one of the men from Rabbi Kook's yeshiva understood the pain, the moral problem, or that there was any moral problem at all. . . . The insensitivity of the yeshiva students appeared to us – and in the interests of honesty I will use sharp words – to be crude, smug and arrogant, power drunk, bursting with Messianic rhetoric, ethnocentric, 'redemptionist', apocalyptic – quite simply inhuman. And un-Jewish. The Arab human beings under our domination might never have been. It was not an affair of, as it were, human distress, but of signs and oracles of tidings of 'the end of days', and of 'the beginning of the Redemption'.

Indeed, these Messianic stirrings troubled me most, as they began to surface among religious Zionists and beyond. The reconquest of virtually the whole Biblical Land of Israel fuelled these expectations, soon to be crystallized by movements advocating 'Greater Israel' as a religious imperative rather than as a political or military necessity for Israel's security. Pseudo-Messianic movements had wrought enough havoc in Jewish history to make me frightened by any indication, however promising the signs, of practical policies being based on irreversible strides towards imminent Messianic fulfilment. For this reason I could not share the determination of some of my leading colleagues to amend our traditional liturgy and observances relating to our mourning for Zion. Pending our ultimate and final salvation, I felt that, just as we had preserved the celebration of our national triumphs even in times of suffering, we should preserve our expressions of mourning and longing even in times of partial, and possibly reversible, fulfilment.

These impressions and reservations governed my Zionist thinking and activities throughout the ensuing years. There were now of course many new opportunities to participate, sometimes at high levels, in the ongoing Israel–Diaspora dialogue. In Britain as elsewhere in the Diaspora, the Six Day War had permanently reclaimed countless Jews for the Zionist cause, including the conversion to Zionism of the Reform movement and the emergence of an entire new generation of dynamic workers, mainly fund-raisers, for Israel. In time, the latter were to become my principal partners in the Jewish Educational Development Trust I established to fund an ambitious programme of educational expansion and intensification. After some years of argument and persuasion, I succeeded in convincing these energetic new leaders to extend to Jewish education their commitment to Israel, on the grounds that without intensive Jewish education there would in future be no Jews, no Zionists, and no supporters of Israel.

Other opportunities, too, came my way, especially in my new official capacity. I was invited to join the governing boards of the Hebrew and Bar Ilan Universities, and of the Shaare Zedek Hospital in Jerusalem. I rejoined, following my participation in its inaugural meeting, in Amsterdam in 1957, the Conference of European Rabbis, and on the death of its founder, Chief Rabbi Brodie, early in 1979, assumed its presidency with Israel always high on the agenda. Since then two one-week meetings of its Standing Committee have been held in Israel. Incidentally, the Conference is the only international Jewish body to conduct all its proceedings in Hebrew only.

I particularly welcomed the invitations to take part in the President's Seminar on Israel and World Jewry at his residence in Jerusalem, first under President Katzir, then under President Navon, and now under President Herzog – always highly stimulating events at which problems besetting Jewry could be discussed in depth among prominent academics and Jewish leaders drawn from Israel and many parts of the world. I also pursued my specialized interest in medical ethics in Israel as President of the Institute for Medicine and Judaism associated with the Yad Harav Herzog, which published the first Hebrew *Medical Guide According to the Jewish Tradition* in 1977. I often joined the Prime Minister's, later the President's, JIA missions to Israel, always obtaining some fascinating new insight into Israel's political, social, educational and even military establishments, their leaders and their problems.

Despite my greatly increased involvement in Zionist affairs, including my unreserved advocacy of Aliyah and of teaching Jewish subjects in *Ivrit* at our schools, I remained studiously aloof from the political arena. Unlike my predecessors, I refused to accept the presidency of the British Mizrachi. Apart from my objections to attaching political labels to rabbis, I was increasingly disenchanted with the movement's inactivity in Britain, notably in Jewish education where I had hoped it would pioneer new yeshiva-high-school-type schools, and with its policies in Israel where too great a priority was given to religious legislation rather than to religious influence. I had my opinions on Israeli policies and was startled by their manifest ambivalence – subscribing to UN Resolution 242 but opposing the Rogers Plan to implement it; constantly offering the Arabs negotiations without any pre-conditions – on condition that Israel kept what it had; denouncing the incipient menace of PLO terrorism – whilst asking, in Golda Meir's fateful words, 'Who are the Palestinians?'; and bitterly decrying the world's growing isolation of Israel – whilst telling the nations with disdain it could not care less about world opinion. But I kept my views to myself, apart from some incidental references to peace as Judaism's highest ideal or to the plight of the Arab refugees to which Jews ought to be particularly sensitive. If there were controversies on which I began to take a public stand, they were strictly confined to religious issues. They included the abortion scandal, the 'Who is a Jew?' debate, and the role of the rabbinate and of religious parties in Israel. But all these were as yet minor interventions which caused few ripples in the complacent waters of the establishment, whether national or religious.

The Jewish State had now been established for some twenty years, and there was little need for me to introduce any religious innovations to reflect its place in Jewish life, in our prayers and our calendar. The special Prayer for the State of Israel, more beautifully worded than that used in Israel and some other countries, had been placed in the regular Sabbath and Festival services by my predecessor long ago, and its text adorned the eastern wall of most of our synagogues alongside the Prayer for the Royal Family. The religious celebration of Israel Independence Day, with its special Order of Service, had also been an accepted feature for many years. To avoid the annual argument over the single communal Yom Ha'atzmaut service which would unacceptably include non-Orthodox as well as Orthodox officiants – ostensibly designed to demonstrate communal unity, but actually a constant cause of disunity – I encouraged special separate services to be held in each synagogue. Not only would such local services enable far more congregants to participate; but such a 'normalization' of Yom Ha'atzmaut in our religious calendar, I felt, would also bring its celebration more naturally in line with our other festivals. After all, we did not organize communal Pesach or Tisha B'Av services to proclaim Jewish national unity!

What I did innovate after the Six Day War and its reunification of Jerusalem was a special Order of Service, circulated to all our congregations, for Jerusalem Day on 28 Iyar. As in Israel, it included the full recitation of *Hallel*. But in the wider community, Yom Yerushalayim caught on even less than Yom Ha'atzmaut, and after the first few years the special insertions were recited only by the regular daily worshippers, though I did attend some well-attended services organized annually by Herut.

The only real challenge facing me in the liturgical sphere was the constant agitation for the authorization of the change of the accustomed Ashkenazi pronunciation to the Israeli Sephardi accent in our synagogue usage. The popular argument was once again that such unification would promote Jewish unity and demonstrate our solidarity with Israel. To me, this argument appeared absolutely nonsensical. I could not see why variations of accents compromised the unity of the Jewish people any more than the diversity of accents in different parts of Britain, or of any other country, undermined the common loyalties in those nations. Moreover, the agitation came often from people who would not know the difference between Ashkenazi and Sephardi Hebrew, as they neither knew Hebrew nor were to be seen in our synagogues for most of the year. Even if we introduced the change, they would not notice it! It seemed to me an altogether perverse notion that we were to be united as a people, not by common ideals, by common observances, by common traditions practised by all Jews, but by a common pronunciation unfamiliar to most Jews! The ultimate irony was that all the Chief Rabbis of Israel, from Rabbi Kook onwards, had without exception used the Ashkenazi pronunciation in their own prayers, clearly without offending the Jewish national spirit centred in Israel.

But what concerned me even more was the halachic aspect. Most past and contemporary rabbinic authorities, emphatically including Rabbi Kook, were strongly opposed to any change in the ancestral and accustomed pronunciation of Hebrew used in the prayers. Their ruling was based on precedents already found in the Talmud and the codes of Jewish law. In interpreting this ruling, I was particularly concerned to preserve the natural manner of rendering traditional prayers, both individually and in public.

The artificiality of using a pronunciation with which one is not completely at home would destroy its purpose as 'a service to the heart'.

However, I increasingly faced a purely practical problem. On 12 July 1962, my predecessor had issued a directive, notwithstanding his earlier opposition, permitting the Sephardi accent to be adopted at Jewish day-schools and Hebrew classes, provided that 'the teachers will have had adequate guidance beforehand'. Within a few years, this became the accepted practice in most of our educational institutions, with the result that most of our children and young people became proficient in the Sephardi pronunciation only. Soon, most Barmitzvah boys recited their portion in that accent, and it gradually became the norm with the younger generation. In the light of these changed circumstances, I issued in 1968 'not a ruling or an edict', but the following 'Guidelines of Policy' to my colleagues:

The question of how to render our prayers at synagogue services is obviously a religious matter. It can be determined only by competent religious authorities in the community; under no circumstances should it be referred to a meeting of the synagogue members for decision by voting.

No general ruling can be laid down for indiscriminate application to the whole community, since there may be some crucial local variations. Consequently, there should be some flexibility within the framework of a general policy. But the Office of the Chief Rabbi should be advised if any change is contemplated in a congregation.

In principle, there should be no change from one customary pronunciation to another unless the majority of regular worshippers are familiar with the new pronuciation to be adopted. It would then be a matter for a rabbinical decision actually to determine the change-over.

Even where the Ashkenazi pronunciation is currently in use, there is no objection to worshippers normally using the Sephardi or Israeli pronunciation being called up to the Torah, or even reciting the Maftir and Haftarah, if that pronunciation is the more familiar one with them. Under similar circumstances, prayers may also be occasionally conducted in the Sephardi pronunciation. But any regular Reader or Baal Koreh should, of course, be fluent in, and publicly use, the pronunciation traditionally accepted by his congregation.

Every encouragement should be given to use the Hebrew language, naturally with the Sephardi pronunciation, as a vehicle of instruction in our day-schools and Hebrew classes, wherever possible. But where the hours of instruction are so minimal as to render it impossible to train the children to have any competence whatever in the language, and it is taught solely for synagogue purposes, the Ashkenazi pronunciation should be retained or, at least, should preferably be retained. In any event, a switch-over at the Hebrew classes should never occur unless the teacher is fully at ease in the use of the new pronunciation.

To these instructions, I added an explanation of the reasoning behind them, which included the following paragraphs:

The use of the accent is entirely irrelevant to the commitment to, or identification with, Israel – in the same way as the use of a Scottish or a Cockney accent has nothing whatever to do with a Briton's loyalty to his country.

What should, above all, be emphasized is the need to understand Hebrew, whatever the accent. Today, when the vast majority of our worshippers are no more familiar with Ashkenazi than with Sephardi Hebrew ... the question of how to pronounce the unknown language is surely a matter of purely academic interest. Hence the stress must be on greatly expanding the facilities among youth and even adults for mastering Hebrew as a language so that the synagogue service will be familiar to them. Once that is achieved, then by all means let the Israeli accent gradually prevail and by sheer common usage become the accepted pronunciation of our public worship as well.

It might also be mentioned that the common preference in favour of the Sephardi pronunciation has no scientific or historical foundation. There is sound scholarly support for the view that the Ashkenazi pronunciation is at least as ancient as the present-day Sephardi accent, as proved, for instance, by the fact that the Yemenite Jews – for thousands of years separated from the rest of our people – pronounce Hebrew in a manner much closer to the Ashkenazi than the Sephardi form. There are also other indications to warrant the opinion that the division between the Ashkenazi and Sephardi pronunciations probably already existed in Talmudic times when the Babylonian Jewry became the origin of the communities that later found their homes in the Mediterranean lands and became the Sephardi segment of our people, whilst the Palestinians populated the more central and northern regions of Europe and became the original forebears of the Ashkenazi communities, each retaining the peculiarities of their pronunciation of Hebrew that they had brought from Babylonia and Palestine respectively during the Talmudic period.

Into a category similar to the agitation for changing the pronunciation of Hebrew as an expression of solidarity with Israel came two other popular demands for religious innovations which often challenged me, though they were outside my jurisdiction. Both resulted directly from the emergence of Israel, and both were widely articulated to stress its supremacy over Jewish life in the Diaspora. First, there was the clamour for setting up a Sanhedrin which, it was argued, would be able to modify Jewish law in the light of modern circumstances, whilst at the same time unifying its administration under the more authentic direction of a rabbinic legislature based in Israel. Second, there was a constant plea for the abolition of the second days of the Festivals to bring their observance in line with Israeli practice. Quite apart from purely halachic obstacles, both demands seemed to me unreasonable and impracticable, and I frequently argued against them.

The Sanhedrin suggestion had of course enjoyed powerful advocacy by a few outstanding rabbinical scholars, led in particular by the late Rabbi J.L. Maimon, Israel's first Minister of Religious Affairs, against the opposition of most of the leading rabbinical authorities. I could not see how such a body could be set up under existing conditions, nor was it likely either to fulfil the expectations or to enjoy the respect of those most vociferous in their contention. In an address on 'Halachah in Modern Jewish Life' at the Conference of the Memorial Foundation for Jewish Culture in Geneva on 10 July 1973, I presented my reasoning in this way:

True, historically we had the Sanhedrin which legislated for the Jewish people at large, though (contrary to popular misconception) its principal function was not to ease but to strengthen the observance of the law. However, its operation required two indispensable conditions, among others: its unquestioned recognition by the majority of our people, and the availability of seventy universally acknowledged sages able and willing to serve on it. Today, neither of these conditions can even remotely be fulfilled. In their absence, the premature convocation of a Sanhedrin would only add the insult of mocking a venerated historical institution through popular indifference to the injury of further aggravating the religious strife within the Torah community.

On the subject of the Festivals in the Diaspora, I always suspected that most of those advocating the abolition of the second days did not properly observe the first days either. Far from enhancing the special distinction of Israel, the proposed change would compromise it. In a series on 'The Excellence of the Holy Land' in the classic commentaries on each Portion of the Week, originally featured in the Fifth Avenue Synagogue bulletin and later published as a booklet by the Education Department of the JNF in London, my piece on 'Emor' included the following:

In regard to no religious observance is the distinction of the Land of Israel more manifest to this day than the celebration of the Festivals. Even while temporarily living in the Diaspora, a resident of the Holy Land is marked out by his observance of one Festival day only, just as visitors from abroad to the Land must demonstrate their exilic status by keeping an extra day after their Israeli brethren have already completed their festive holiday. There could be no greater tribute to the Land than this requirement of Jews outside to observe two Festival days. Whatever the original reason for the enactment and its retention, the duplication of the Holy Days in the Diaspora no doubt serves to compensate the Jew who lives in a non-Jewish environment for the wholly Jewish atmosphere inside the Land he misses. For those constantly living on the territory and in the society of Israel, one Festival day is sufficient to infuse the ordinary days of the year with the spirit of Judaism, whilst those outside need at least double the dosage of the Festivals – when the Jewish soul is regenerated – to withstand and become immune to the diseases of assimilation and indifference to Jewish values.

Before we pass from this relatively peaceful era to the turbulence of the Yom Kippur War and the bitter controversies it was to spark, perhaps this respite provides an opportunity for some reflections on the travels and conferences which became such a regular feature of my life on assuming my new office in 1967.

From the frequent references to conference addresses and other appearances in many parts of the world, the reader may obtain the impression that I henceforth spent most of my time in non-stop journeying. Unfortunately, such journeys have become an occupational hazard for leading rabbis no less than for other national, communal and even professional leaders and officials. They have all become 'missionaries', constantly asked to go on one mission or another. In my case, these travels were fairly extensive, though my aggregate absences from London on such missions would rarely exceed 10 per cent of my time in any one year and often total much less. In most cases, I have to attend various conferences *ex officio*, as occupant of the most prestigious Chief Rabbinate in the Diaspora, often doing so merely in succession to my predecessor, Sir Israel Brodie, who in fact had travelled more widely and would sometimes be away on an overseas tour for six months, whereas I had to content myself with a maximum of six weeks for a round-the-world tour which took me to ten Commonwealth communities and demanded sixty speeches! And Chief Rabbi J.H.Hertz's 'First Pastoral Tour to the Jewish Communities of the British Overseas Dominions' lasted from October 1920 to August 1921, but of course he travelled by sea and train – there never was a second tour.

The international conferences, most of them in Israel, fell into several distinct categories. There were the annual governors' meetings of the Hebrew and Bar Ilan Universities as well as of the Shaare Zedek Hospital. They lasted usually for three days, and I attended them with gradually decreasing frequency, though they often proved stimulating, if only because of the interesting personalities I would meet and the friendships made. Such annual meetings are obviously essential for running these institutions, but their effect on the direction of policies is more questionable. I certainly found it difficult to turn the expression of my views into anything more than an opening for constructive and friendly debate; for example, I frequently urged Bar Ilan to seek a more distinct role in bridging Israel's religious–secularist polarization and in providing some original synthesis rather than a mere combination of Jewish with general scholarship, on the lines on which New York's Yeshiva University had succeeded in creating America's

'Modern Orthodoxy'; and I often asked for a greater emphasis on Jewish values in the instruction at the Hebrew University, especially in its medical school.

Then there were the annual Prime Minister's, later President's, missions, with their gruelling programmes of briefings by political and military leaders, rushed visits to social institutions and army installations, mini-seminars on endless statistics, all interspersed with hours of coach travel and running commentaries, and of course a daily fare of receptions, luncheons and dinners with their spate of speeches, in between inspecting the latest 'secret' product of Israel's armament industry or the most recent sports amenities added to Project Renewal. These 'fact-finding' expeditions do sometimes yield some worthwhile facts and occasionally even some intriguing opinions which sustain the momentum of fund-raising – Israel's biggest industry. But the real Israel is no doubt more clearly visible to visitors spending a week with Israeli relatives in their homes than to VIPs inside American-style hotels or walking on red carpets outside. In more recent years, pressed by ever-growing communal commitments, I have usually forgone these rather expensive opportunities for discovering facts just as readily available at a fraction of the cost and time by a little discriminating reading.

Usually the most rewarding of these junketings were the travels for rabbinic conferences and academic seminars. These experiences invariably included opportunities to pass a few days in the company of some unusual brains, to hear several really instructive or challenging papers, and to contribute to the thinking of others for longer than the duration of one's address or interjection. In fact, few intellectual experiences can be more gratifying than to hear or read opinions expressed at these conferences quoted years later, even without any attribution. Moreover, most of these conference and seminar contributions are subsequently published in books or magazines, so that the more permanent record of these proceedings makes them more valuable than the rather ephemeral effects of most other visits.

Yet, the cumulative value of regular sojourns in Israel, however brief, is considerable. They provide a living bridge with Israel, its leaders and its people. Among many other benefits, these visits demonstrate to Israel and the Diaspora alike how dependent each is on the other. Only by attending these conferences do the visitors discover how urgently Israel needs the financial, political and moral support of Jews outside, and the hosts find out how indispensable Israel has become in sustaining the dynamics of Jewish life in the Diaspora. Moreover, from a personal point of view, these visits have rewarded me with many invaluable friendships, with the continual joys of a homecoming one can only experience in Israel, and – following the caricatures in which I was occasionally portrayed – with the opportunities to present myself to Israelis as I really was, without horns!

# 4

# The Yom Kippur War –
# From Ecstasy to Agony

By the turn of the decade, the euphoria of the Six Day War had evaporated. So had the short spell of spiritual reawakening, to be replaced by a creeping growth of crass materialism, ethnic strife between the privileged and the under-privileged, and political complacency under the imaginary shelter of invincibility. This was shaken neither by the enervating War of Attrition, nor by the ascendancy of the PLO in spectacular acts of terrorism and obscene receptions accorded by the United Nations.

Then the Yom Kippur War burst upon us. Only ten months earlier, I had heard Defence Minister Moshe Dayan in a 'briefing' to a British JPA (it was then still the Joint Palestine Appeal) mission. He assured us, citing comparative statistics on planes and tanks, that Israel was now militarily so superior that the Arabs would no longer dare to attack. Alas, the 'impregnable' fortifications on the Golan Heights and of the Bar Lev Line along the Suez Canal collapsed almost overnight. For the first time in thirty years, fears of an imminent holocaust were openly expressed as the Syrian armies, having stormed through the defences of the Galilee, threatened the whole north of Israel. The 'ideal borders' of 'Greater Israel' had proved far more vulnerable than the 'indefensible borders' of little Israel in 1967 – a lesson which I never forgot in my subsequent thinking.

The heavy pall of gloom cast over the Jewish community was further aggravated by the growing bias against Israel almost everywhere in the world, no doubt not unconnected with the oil embargo now imposed by the Arabs, leading to the catastrophic rise in oil prices which was to signal the near-strangulation of the world's economy. Even the eventual triumph of the Israeli army in pushing back the Egyptians and Syrians far into their own territory and threatening both their capitals could not relieve the despondency among Jews everywhere as news of the fearful loss of life and limb sank in. The contrast in Jewish as well as world reaction to the heady days following the Six Day War could not have been greater in every respect. I hopefully described this contrast at President Katzir's seminar on World Jewry and the State of Israel on 6 July 1975, in the following terms:

Such are the unfathomable mysteries of Providence and Jewish history that the 1967 and the 1973 wars may yet reverse the hitherto-accepted roles in their effect on the consummation of the Jewish purpose. In retrospect, one wonders whether the Six Day War, with all its ecstasy, may not have induced one of the most calamitous recessions of the Jewish spirit in our annals. Political and military attitudes apart, it bred an inflated sense of over-confidence, an immobility of mind, a feeling of complacency, a disdain for the outside world, and an extravagant taste for high living which spilled over into a moral pollution of the national character once distinguished by faith, integrity, selflessness, idealism and frugality. The Yom Kippur War, on the other hand, its heartbreak notwithstanding, may well yet release invaluable spiritual energies and in a mighty burst of power redirect our destiny to its historic orbit.

Anglo-Jewry again sprang into feverish activity. An emergency appeal once more yielded an unprecedented response, and blood-donation centres were set up at two of our leading London synagogues – I was asked to sanction their operation during the Festival of Succot into which the war had dragged. Requesting a directive from the Israel Chief Rabbinate to support my sanction, I received only confused messages in return, but finally obtained an affirmative ruling from the Israel Army Rabbinate. Only months later was I to find out in Israel that most of the blood supplies, immediately flown there by El Al in a remarkably efficient operation, were in fact not needed as there had been ample volunteers donating blood in Israel itself.

That fateful Yom Kippur proved a radical turning-point in the Jewish mood as well as in Jewish fortunes. The bitter criticism within Israel itself of the government's failure to prevent the disaster was later to be officially backed in the damning report of the Agranat Commission. The novel stance of open and unrestrained self-criticism soon spilt over into the Diaspora, shaken as it was by the rude discovery that Israel, far from being the unassailable guarantor of Jewish security everywhere, was now itself contributing to an ominous feeling of increasing Jewish insecurity, fanned subsequently by the infamous United Nations Resolution which equated Zionism with racism, and a corresponding Jewish reaction which equated anti-Zionism with anti-Semitism.

Of course, the commitment to Israel was undiminished, and the efforts in its support and defence were greatly intensified. During the war I had joined a Board of Deputies delegation to the Foreign Secretary to plead for greater sympathy by Britain and in particular for the release of urgently needed tank spare-parts. Lord Janner, leading the delegation, literally wept as he presented the agony of Israel's predicament; his tears were scantily rewarded.

Later, when I approached a leading Church dignitary to ask why he and others had not spoken up to denounce the aggression committed against Israel on Judaism's holiest day, he simply told me: 'We were so absolutely convinced that Israel would win over its enemies in a few days that it just didn't occur to us to raise our voice on behalf of Israel.' I understood from his reply how far we had become victims of our own over-confidence.

The new mood of self-questioning and reappraisal emboldened me, too, to search aloud for the causes of Israel's ailments and the prescription to heal them. I gave two lectures critically analysing our predicament, one in Hebrew to a prestigious Tel Aviv forum during a visit in November which had taken me to the newly occupied positions in Syria far beyond the Golan Heights and within sight of Damascus, the other before an audience of rabbis and communal leaders in London at the end of January. I expressed my conviction that the convulsive changes in Jewish fortunes and prospects precipitated by the Yom Kippur War represented above all a profound spiritual crisis of momentous proportions, stressing that among the salutary effects of the war were a greater unity between Israel and the Diaspora than ever before, and the intense soul-searching which had replaced the past inclination to self-righteousness and sole reliance on military power.

For the first time I expressed views explicitly which I had previously only hinted at. I spelt out the fallacy of secular Zionism in fostering the illusion that Jewish Statehood would solve the Jewish problem and eliminate anti-Semitism; I expressed the realization that Israel had neither a claim nor the ability to prevail if it surrendered its unique spiritual purpose; I stressed the need to separate religion from politics if Judaism and the Jewish State were to be united; I underlined the challenge to religious leaders to promote our people's moral regeneration, to interpret current events in the light of Jewish teachings, and to be ready to make territorial concessions if true peace could thereby be secured; and I stated the need to fight for Jewish survival by resisting the evils of ignorance and assimilation with the same grim determination as the attacks of Israel's enemies in battle. My plea with all its criticisms was well received, though it contained all the opinions which were later to cause such a furore. Indeed, on re-reading my speeches in the wake of the Yom Kippur War – and I delivered many in a similar vein in Britain and Israel as well as in America – I find that I added or changed nothing of substance on fundamentals in the years to come, as the exposition of these opinions in the following chapters will show.

# 5

# Soviet Jewry and Israel – First Taste of International Controversy

At this point I must turn to a drama which, although acted out far from both Israel and Britain, had considerable bearing on Israel, its policies and my assessment of them. I had always taken a deep interest in the plight of Soviet Jewry, having already pledged in my Installation Address that I would seek to concentrate among my priorities 'on alleviating the religious attrition and communal isolation of our Russian brethren – the most painful Jewish problem of our day'. I had taken a prominent part in numerous rallies, protests, marches, statements to the press, and interventions with government and Church leaders. I had participated in the first Brussels Conference on Soviet Jewry in February 1971, intended to draw international attention to this agonizing story which had really been brought on to the Jewish agenda with the wondrous reawakening among Soviet Jews themselves in the wake of the Six Day War.

In January 1972 I was invited by the Jewish Agency on a three-day visit to Schönau Castle, the transit centre near Vienna, to greet some of the then mounting flow of Soviet Jews on their way to Israel. It was still a hush-hush operation, and I was cautioned not to reveal in public what I had seen, particularly the considerable numbers involved who spent only a couple of days at the transit centre before proceeding to Israel. The experience was overwhelming as I for the first time in my life encountered living Jewish martyrs – Jews who cheerfully exposed themselves to harassment and other grave risks inside Russia simply because they were determined to live as Jews. I was both humbled and exalted as many of them told me the story of how they had rediscovered their Jewish identity and persevered in their resolve to be reunited with their people in Israel.

Taken out early one morning to the main railway station in Vienna to witness the arrival of some of them in the separate railway carriage assigned to them, I was embraced by a Jew from Georgia who presented me, as the first rabbi he had ever met, with a beautiful copperplate of Moses and the Tablets which he had made at home and which I treasure among my most prized possessions to the present day. Another identified himself on the platform in fluent Yiddish as a young Jew from Vilna and introduced me to his little daughter Dakara. Asked about the significance of this unusual name, he explained that he decided on it when he heard of the sinking of the Israeli submarine *Dakar* so that he and his family would never forget what they owed to the sacrifice of Israelis to enable them one day to live in Israel. In utter humility I could only comment that it had not occurred to any of us Jews living in freedom to immortalize the gallant Israeli sailors in this way.

On returning to Britain from this profoundly stirring visit, I organized a more substantial campaign to initiate and support Soviet Jewry projects, particularly those directed towards their spiritual rehabilitation. I continue to sponsor or support some of these projects to the present time. Realizing that these early pioneers in the exodus from Russia were motivated primarily by their desire to live as Jews, I also for the first time pleaded for a revision of the slogan that inspired the Soviet Jewry campaign, by completing the plea of Moses 'Let My people go' with 'so that they shall serve Me'. While the call was later echoed, notably in numerous resolutions of the Conference of European Rabbis, its message never sank in among those responsible for policies on Soviet Jewry, with progressively ever more baneful results.

This leads me on to my principal encounter with Russian Jewry – a ten-day visit to the Soviet Union in December 1975. Having related some of my experiences on numerous platforms in five continents and in several newspaper articles, including two extensive features in *The Times* and the *Observer*, I confine myself here to aspects of relevance to Israel and my relations with the Zionist leadership.

The original suggestion of an official visit – the first by any Chief Rabbi from the West – was made to me early that year through a prominent representative of the Soviet authorities then visiting London. At that time the Helsinki Conference, which was to lead to the Accord on European Security, was being prepared. I was told that the hoped-for détente between East and West would have to include a détente with the Jewish people, and it was in this context that a visit by me as part of a cultural exchange programme would be welcomed. I insisted at once that I could only contemplate accepting the invitation if I could freely determine my programme and I would require several months before I could give a definite reply. I then engaged in prolonged consultations with quite a few well-informed individuals and official bodies in Israel and America as well as Britain. I was generally encouraged to proceed with the plans, provided that I went in response to invitations not only by the official 'Jewish community' but also by the 'Refusniks' then organized mainly around the 'Scientific Seminars' meeting regularly in Moscow and some other cities. In due course, these invitations reached me – one more formal from the President and Rabbi of the Moscow Synagogue, and two others more enthusiastic from the leaders of the 'Scientific Seminars', Professors Lerner and Azbel respectively. In finally accepting the invitations, I also stipulated that I would want to have an opportunity not only to meet whatever groups identified as Jewish in the three cities of Moscow, Leningrad and Kiev, but also some leaders of the Russian Orthodox Church so that I could gain some comparative insight on the possibilities of religious life within the citadels of communism. The visits I was to pay to the Theological Seminaries in Leningrad and Zagorsk, where (together with another in Odessa) 800 students were being trained for the Russian Orthodox priesthood in intensive eight-year programmes, proved most illuminating in pointing up the stark contrast between the relative freedoms enjoyed by the Church and the utter desolation of Jewish life in the Soviet Union. In fact, it was at the Leningrad Centre that I met the only Israeli citizen I saw in Russia – a Greek student who had attended theological courses in Jerusalem for several years and was sent to complete his studies in Leningrad before returning to serve the Orthodox Church in Jerusalem!

Already at the first meeting in London, in connection with the proposed 'détente with the Jewish people', reference was made to the restoration of diplomatic relations with Israel. However, as a superpower, Russia could not be expected to take the first initiative, I was told. That summer the Soviets were going to commemorate the Thirtieth Anniversary of the Red Army's victory over the German Fascists. Might this not be a fitting occasion for Israel's Prime Minister to send a congratulatory message to the Kremlin on a victory which had, after all, also helped to save hundreds of thousands of Jewish lives? And, who knows, once a diplomatic ball is made to roll, the likely acknowledgement of the message might lead to further developments. There was never any response from Israel to the signal, as was later to be confirmed to me. Nothing was published about this incident until March 1980.

From the moment I arrived in Russia, accompanied by Moshe Davis, the Executive Director of my office, Israel was never far beneath the surface in our private and official discussions and statements. In my formal statement of greetings on arrival at the airport, I told our hosts, reading from a prepared text:

We want Soviet Jews to know how close they are to the hearts of all of us and the rest of the world. If we care for them so deeply it is not only because Soviet Jewry

constitutes about one-fifth of our people and is the third largest Jewish community in
the world, with twice as many Jews as Western Europe has. Even more important is
the leading role which Jews from these lands have played in recent centuries as the
mainstay of Jewish spiritual and cultural life. . . .

I hope I may have the historical privilege of making some humble contribution
towards the fostering of good relations between peoples in the spirit of the Helsinki
Accord, towards opening up unhindered and direct and personal and communal
contacts with the Soviet Jewish community, similar to those we enjoy with Jewish
communities elsewhere, in the spirit of our age-old Covenant. . . .

We became rather more explicit in our long meetings with senior Soviet
officials. Immigration to Israel actually featured as the principal subject in
the session with the Deputy-Director of OVIR, the agency responsible for the
issuance of exit visas – and, what concerned us even more, for refusals. We
were given exact figures of the considerable number who had left Russia by
then, including several well-known artists and scientists who had been
allowed to go after years of agitation in the West, without any corresponding
expression of gratitude for their release! When we countered the claim that
emigration permits were denied only for limited periods strictly for security
reasons, by showing that this was patently incompatible with the facts as we
knew them, we were asked to submit a list and were assured that those cases
would be reviewed by OVIR in due course. We were invited to take similar
steps regarding prisoners of conscience for whose release we had pleaded.

On meeting with the Deputy Minister of Cults, we were likewise advised
to present in writing the demands for relief from the religious, cultural and
communal disabilities suffered by Soviet Jews, including specifically the
right to teach Hebrew and to publish a religious magazine, among numerous
other matters we raised. Following our return, these submissions were made
in considerable detail, with but meagre results except in one limited sphere:
exit permits, which were eventually granted in the years ahead.

The visit was both heart-rending and heart-warming – harrowing because
I had witnessed the anguish of so many Jews and the utter devastation of
Jewish life, and exhilarating because I had seen examples of Jewish
regeneration and spiritual heroism for which there were no parallels in
modern Jewish history.

Returning safely to London after this extraordinary experience, I was
never quite the same again; the scars and the inspiration have been with me
ever since. I presented my first impressions at a packed public meeting in
London's largest synagogue, starting with the words: 'I feel I have been to
another planet and found a vast scene of utter desolation, which Jewishly
speaking looks like the scorched surface of the moon.' Echoing this theme, a
newspaper reported: 'The gathering that greeted the Chief Rabbi Immanuel

Jakobovits at St John's Wood Synagogue on his return from the Soviet Union was not unlike the excitement that greeted the astronauts on their return from the first trip to the moon.' I began to analyse some of my findings, only a few of which I felt I could then share openly with the public in the numerous reports, interviews and articles in which I was invited to communicate my impressions and assessments. I agonized over my reactions to the trip no less than I had done over agreeing to it. In part, my accounts were purely factual, such as the opening of my *Observer* article:

My stipulations about meetings with Jewish activists were never expressly approved or disapproved. Yet they were indispensable. . . .

There were nagging pressures to do more sight-seeing and pay more theatre visits, and efforts to shunt me off to Leningrad or Kiev for the weekend to prevent me from addressing the six-hundred-strong congregation in Moscow on the Sabbath and the seminars on the following two days. With some persistence, the 'unavailable' time, the 'unattainable' train reservations, or the 'lost tickets' to bring me back from Leningrad, turned up. In the end, the official car at my disposal brought me to the very homes of the activists I wished to visit!

But I also included some early, though still cautious appraisals, as I continued further down in the article:

There are, of course, subtle changes in Russian attitudes and responses to world opinion. One need only contrast the earlier success in securing the emigration of 120,000 Jews with the failure of the Jackson Amendment to maintain, let alone to increase (as had been agreed with the American Administration before the deal was leaked) the rate of emigration, now reduced to a bare trickle. Notwithstanding détente, the 'spirit of Helsinki' and all that, the Russians were prepared to face severe hardships by cancelling massive credit and trade agreements rather than to be seen to surrender to Western pressures in a glare of publicity.

Hence my insistent plea on my return from the visit that we constantly reappraise our policies. These certainly require greater flexibility, as well as more sophistication and diversification, if they are to be effective in countering the present worsening condition of Soviet Jewry.

I also wrote in my article for *The Times*:

The picture emerging from wide-ranging travels, meetings and discussions was far more complex than fairly extensive, though fragmentary, information of conditions in the Soviet Union had previously led me to expect. The shadows turned out to be darker, the gleams of light brighter, and the grey areas in between much larger. . . .

The stark contrast between hope and despair arises from the ambivalence of the official attitude which leaves the wide grey area between *approved* legality and forbidden illegality largely undefined. It is not illegal to demand exit visas, yet applicants may find themselves intolerably harassed. It is not against the law to receive phone-calls or letters from abroad, but the phones may be disconnected and the mail stopped. It is not unlawful to perform circumcisions or religious marriage ceremonies; to teach Hebrew as a language in schools or provide private religious instruction in homes; or even to publish a religious journal and other literature for those interested. Yet most Jews shrink from any such activities for fear of being branded, with consequences ranging from job dismissal to incarceration....

I included a direct reference to the key role of Israel:

And if the Soviet authorities would recognize, as I repeatedly told them, that the desire to live a fuller Jewish life in Israel, after praying for the return to Zion for two thousand years, is not a betrayal, détente may eventually include some accommodation with the Jewish people which has shared with the Soviet peoples so much suffering and sacrifice in the struggle against fascism, and which now sees in Soviet policy such a grim threat to its very existence, and to human rights in general.

All I could state on the visit's long-term aims was:

Only time will tell whether some success also attended the wider objectives of exploring and securing ways to remove the grievances which have caused such worldwide concern and agitation, among Jews and non-Jews alike.

Meanwhile, public reactions to the visit, while warmly supportive in some quarters, were acutely critical in others, notably in Israel. Under the headline 'Jakobovits "duped" by Soviets, say those who have lived there' the *Jerusalem Post* quoted several prominent Soviet immigrants, denouncing the visit as 'a public relations exercise by the USSR against Aliyah and against the forthcoming Conference on Soviet Jewry', and my published conclusions as 'another instance of how many Western people are simply naïve, get taken in by clever Soviet propaganda, without thoroughly checking the facts'.

The real source of the irritation was expressed more boldly in another newspaper report from Britain where the President of Herut 'took strong exception to the Chief Rabbi's suggestion that the "Let My people live" theme should be as prominent as the "Let My people go" slogan. He said that it was unrealistic and might harm the campaign.' Like others in Israel, the National Executive of the British Zionist Federation also 'unanimously reaffirmed' its opposition to the 'Let My people live' call.

Here was the crux of the controversy I had sparked off. My plea that without intensifying efforts to press for Jewish revival inside the Soviet Union, Aliyah would gradually dry up for lack of Jews determined to live a full Jewish life in Israel was simply unacceptable to the seasoned Soviet

Jewry campaigners. They could not be dislodged from their stale assumption that if we only shouted 'Let My people go' loud and long enough, Soviet Jews would reach Israel by the hundreds of thousands. Alas, the events of the years to come were to prove otherwise: emigration fell to negligible figures and, out of those few, the vast majority increasingly dropped out on their way to Israel in favour of America and elsewhere, where many virtually opted out as Jews altogether. For those left behind in Russia, the repression through harassment, exile and imprisonment became ever more grim, the worldwide agitation notwithstanding. But the campaigners still wear their blinkers and rehash their slogans with undiminished fervour in an endless succession of routine rallies, demonstrations and conferences. The campaign has collapsed, but the show goes on.

I was not then, or ever later, opposed to all public protests: in fact, I participated in many of them. They were necessary not only to keep the desperate plight of Soviet Jewry on the Jewish and world agenda, but also to lift the spirits of Soviet Jews themselves. Every action on their behalf soon became known to them, and the knowledge that Jews outside cared served as an invaluable boost to their morale – and indeed to their quest for Jewish identification. What I questioned was the reliance on these demonstrations as the principal means of influencing Soviet policies. To this end, more discreet methods might have proved far more effective. Moreover, the concentration on public agitation, often bound to be counter-productive, diverted attention from the at least equally urgent need to enrich the Jewish experience of Soviet Jews, both before and after they left Russia.

Refuting the barrage of criticism prior to and following my visit, I told my St John's Wood Synagogue audience on my return:

I cannot accept that by stressing the religious and communal needs of Soviet Jews – expressed in the slogan 'Let My people live' – I have somehow undermined the campaign for Aliyah under the slogan 'Let My people go'. There is no dichotomy between these two slogans. Any debate on such lines is completely unrealistic and irrelevant to the real condition of Soviet Jewry.

Even if the doors of the Soviet Union were freely opened to emigration, the most optimistic estimate is that only about half a million Jews would avail themselves of the opportunity, while some believe that the figure would not be much above 100,000. In either case, the bulk of Soviet Jewry would still remain.

As a leading Jewish activist has put it to me in Moscow, 'Never in Jewish history have we discarded or written off more than a million of our own people.' Moreover, far from being mutually exclusive, the two slogans are complementary and intertwined. For without the strengthening of Jewish consciousness and of Jewish communal life, there would be few Jews left sufficiently committed even to desire Aliyah. On the other hand, the resolve of Soviet Jews to remain Jewish and the recent miracle of Jewish revival, however limited, would be gravely weakened without the galvanizing force and the colossal impact of the struggle for Aliyah that has been going on for the past few years.

It was the first time I was embroiled in an international controversy that I had caused. Alas, it was not to be the last. The need to redouble efforts to promote religious and cultural activities inside Russia was not the only conclusion I drew from my visit. In official contacts with the Soviet authorities before and during my visit I had also discovered that in their eyes the attitude towards Soviet Jewry was largely bound up with the much wider issues of East–West relations and particularly Soviet policies relating to Israel. But the acceptance of this premise was again strenuously resisted in Israel, to the point that the Soviet Jewry department, responsible for directing the global campaign, was attached as a separate unit to the Prime Minister's office and completely divorced from the Foreign Ministry. It was argued that the two aspects of Russian policies affecting Jews were considered to be unrelated. My impressions belied this assumption, and I felt that better co-ordination between these two aspects by Israel might conceivably benefit both Soviet Jewry and Israel. On the positive side, however, the visit convinced me that Israel alone was the source of inspiration for Soviet Jews, first through the reawakening of their Jewish consciousness in the Six Day War, then by galvanizing whatever traces of active Jewish life were to be found in Russia, and finally by offering the only lasting hope for their full spiritual rehabilitation – a hope sadly often neglected on their arrival in Israel itself.

Challenged by these concerns, I made a special trip to Israel within a month of my Russian visit to report on it to Prime Minister Rabin and to discuss these concerns with him. In an emotion-packed meeting lasting for over an hour, I poured out my heart and pleaded for a fresh appraisal of Soviet Jewry policies, with special emphasis on the critical need to recognize that only those encouraged and given the facilities to live as Jews in Russia would eventually seek their destiny in Israel, or at least preserve their Jewish identity there. The Prime Minister acknowledged the validity of my stress on 'Let My people live', though he seemed less inclined to pay much attention to the other major issues I had raised. He also confirmed that the signal on the Red Army anniversary had been received, but his experts had advised him that acting on it would be a futile exercise. In practice, the officialdom conducting the campaign was already so deeply entrenched that the policies remained substantially unchanged. The principal thrust for most religiously motivated activities among Soviet Jews in Russia as well as in Israel and even in America – activities which gathered growing momentum and yielded increasing results in the years to come – came from unofficial quarters, sponsored mainly by religious groups, including my office. I returned from my brief visit to Israel with my aversion to the inertia of establishments hardly dented and with a renewed experience of the Israeli aversion to welcoming the opinions of 'outsiders'. There were of course notable exceptions to the establishment attitudes directed from Israel. The most realistic policies on Soviet Jewry, it appeared increasingly to me, were being quietly pursued by the Aguda and Lubavitch, with ever more significant results over the years, both inside and outside Russia.

As a postscript to my Russian visit I must relate a conversation which I have since passed on to hundreds of audiences in all parts of the world. Befriending an old Jew whom I had met regularly at the daily morning service in the Moscow Synagogue, I was approached by him on the last morning of my stay. 'Rebbe,' he said, 'I must ask you something. We hear from time to time of the agitation in the West demonstrating for the right of Soviet Jews to go to Israel. For us these reports sometimes cause us considerable discomfort. Unfortunately we live in a communist Medinah; leaving this country is regarded almost as treason, and we cannot easily go. But you live in a free Medinah; you need no exit permits and are not exposed to any risks if you want to leave your countries. Why don't your Jews go on Aliyah when you can, whilst clamouring for us to go when we can't?' I had no answer, especially when I realized that by then a greater proportion of Soviet Jews had in fact gone to Israel than Jews from England or America.

'We also hear much', he continued, 'about the commotion you make on the rights denied to us to raise our children as Jews, to learn Hebrew, to get religious instruction and to have Jewish schools. Alas, in this atheist Medinah such things are forbidden, and we cannot give our children a Jewish education. But we have visitors from America, from England and other Western countries. On Shabbat they come to our synagogue, and when we honour them by calling them up to the Law, they often cannot even read the benediction for the Torah properly. In your countries, Jewish education is not illegal and you face no penalties for passing on Judaism to the next generation. Why don't you raise your children as Jews?' Again, I was shamed into silence, for I had no answer. To my mind, these two questions constitute the biggest challenge of Soviet Jews to their brothers and sisters outside!

Following my visit, intermittent contact with the Russian authorities was maintained, and suggestions for another visit were received from time to time. I was unwilling to contemplate this until I had concrete responses to the representations I had made. As the spirit of détente progressively evaporated, the Jewish situation in Russia worsened correspondingly. My main efforts continued on the cultural and religious front in Israel as well as in the Soviet Union itself, where Jewish learning and observance were significantly intensified to embrace hundreds eager to deepen their Jewish roots.

On the public level, my next major involvement occurred in December 1980, when I was asked at short notice to lead a delegation of European Chief Rabbis to plead the cause of Soviet Jewry at the European Security Conference in Madrid. We found the heads of the American and British delegations exceedingly sympathetic and helpful. Thanks to the latter, I was introduced to the Deputy-Head of the Soviet delegation. In a ten-minute conversation, I had the opportunity to present our anguished pleas for the release of prisoners, exit visas and the alleviation of the religious and cultural repression suffered by Soviet Jews. Mentioning specifically the ban on Jewish literature and the teaching of Hebrew, although 150 languages were officially recognized, I was told that there were only eighty classical languages so recognized, excluding Hebrew, and I left with the rather vague assurance that the situation was constantly under review but that he was not authorized to give me any definite commitments. The detailed report I subsequently circulated among leaders and agencies dealing with Soviet Jewry in several countries again emphasized my reservations on the direction of the campaign, although its albeit limited effectiveness was fully recognized. It was largely with Israel in mind that I included the following 'Assessment and Conclusions' in the report:

It is evident that the Soviet Jewry campaign has aroused the intense concern of Western governments as the principal item on the Human Rights agenda. It is also clear to me that Jewish campaigners throughout the world have been far more successful in highlighting the plight of Soviet Jewry than Christian or other ethnic communities have been in mobilizing world opinion on behalf of other oppressed minorities.

I also have a distinct impression that the mounting world pressure on Human Rights is not a matter of indifference to the Soviet Union which is acutely embarrassed and irritated by the agitation.

What I am not sure is whether – however successful the campaign in the West, and however much supported by Western governments, and however anxious the Russians may be to avoid irritations – the Russians are likely to be forced into any realistic concessions on the Human Rights front.

Past experience is hardly encouraging. The intensified campaign for Soviet Jews has not succeeded in easing their plight which is, if anything, more grim today than at any time since Stalin. Nor have far more powerful Western pressures, including trade and other boycotts threatening détente itself, made the slightest impact on Soviet policies in Africa and Asia, especially lately in Afghanistan.

It seems unlikely, therefore, that Russian attitudes to Soviet Jewry will be materially affected by outside agitation. The Soviets are exceedingly sensitive to not being seen to 'capitulate' to Western pressures, as already shown by the drastic emigration decline following the Jackson Amendment at the time.

It is far more likely that the fate of Soviet Jews will primarily be determined by global calculations, such as Russia's strategic and economic interests, East–West relations generally, and Soviet attitudes towards Israel and the Middle East.

In the end, efforts to secure any significant advance on Human Rights, including relief for Soviet Jewry, may have to contemplate some form of linkage with other Soviet concerns, much as the present Western opposition to such a notion is appreciated.

My main concern in the report was, of course, the Jewish response to the challenge of Soviet Jewry:

On the other hand, Jewish Soviet Jewry Campaign policies, which have hardly changed over the years, may also not be entirely blameless for the present pitiful situation, particularly regarding the appalling drop-out rate which deals such a devastating blow to the whole campaign.

We are now paying a heavy price for neglecting the demand to 'Let My people live' almost exclusively in favour of the slogan 'Let My people go'. They go, or went, but of late mostly not to Israel. The only motivation for Aliyah, whatever the hardships and uncertainties, in preference to settlement elsewhere, is the overriding desire to live a fully Jewish life, inculcated by an appreciation of Jewish values. Had efforts over the years at spiritual rehabilitation been intensified inside the Soviet Union as well as during the often-prolonged transit of migrants in Rome, far more Soviet Jews might have opted for Israel because they want to live as Jews, rather than for other countries because they want to escape as Jews.

Moreover, the Soviet authorities are more likely to make some internal concessions to relieve repression of religious and cultural activities than visibly to relax policies on imprisonment and emigration. Regarding the former, we should not forget, Jews are far worse off than other religious or national groups, whilst in respect of the latter, Jews are treated no differently from other discontented minorities who also seek to emigrate and whose leaders also suffer cruel incarceration and exile.

The conclusion seems inescapable that the 'Pros' of the establishment guiding world Jewish policies on Soviet Jewry are still often governed by assumptions and slogans which are now long dated. What is needed is bold fresh thinking in a constant reassessment of the ever-changing conditions determining Soviet attitudes.

In a confidential note on the grossly inadequate arrangements made for this mission of some ten European Chief Rabbis, I included the following observation which sums up the relationship with officialdom generally:

One cannot help but feel that the Chief Rabbis, like other communal leaders, are simply given their orders as pawns expected to go through the conventional motions, without the slightest concern to consult before or after the exercise, or indeed to give such a Mission any meaningful effect, either by the required press-reportage or by reviewing policies in the light of the information and assessments gained from the enterprise.

Together with others sharing some of my views, notably Rabbi J.B.Soloveitchik and Dr Nahum Goldmann, I may have been entirely wrong, and even more moderate Jewish policies might have proved equally unsuccessful in ameliorating the fate of Soviet Jewry in the face of Russian hostility. But that existing policies had failed disastrously could hardly be disputed, and to me it appeared that this failure stemmed primarily from political rigidity, combined with the refusal to recognize the primacy of spiritual factors in the reclamation of Jews from the threat of extinction. Moreover, these two deficiences seemed to me to reflect and to characterize the missing essentials in Israeli policies and attitudes generally, judging by the progressive deterioration of Israel's internal and external relations, its morale and its image, its fragmentation within and its isolation from without.

# 6

# Prime Ministers –
# And More Controversies

Until 1975 I had never had an exchange of views, in person or by correspondence, with any of Israel's prime ministers. I had met them all, but only at social or formal occasions. I had a few words with Ben-Gurion while he was on a visit to America, and in a tribute at a memorial service in London on his death late in 1973, I commented on the paradoxes and contradictions of this remarkable leader who, like Churchill, had 'roused his people to their "finest hour" when they stood alone':

He was at once dreamer and realist, rebel and authority, revolutionary and traditionalist, thinker and man of action, partisan and conciliator, leader of the dominant party and founder of a splinter group within it, agnostic and venerator of the Bible, lone iconoclast and man of the people. He may not have been religious in the strictly traditional conventional sense, yet he was possessed of profoundly spiritual qualities and insights, drawing from the Bible with almost prophetic fervour and messianic commitment the inspiration for his passion for social justice . . . and for his aspiration to turn Israel into a beacon of light unto the nations. . . . Alas, it was granted to him no more than to Moses to witness the realization of his most cherished ambition, and he had to depart from his people before they reached the Promised Land of Peace.

My rapport with Golda Meir was somewhat closer, but our stances were still poles apart. When she came to London shortly after the Yom Kippur War to address a group of Anglo-Jewish leaders, and I expressed our admiration for her fortitude, our solidarity with Israel and our faith in its future, she acknowledged that she had been 'moved beyond words'. I was similarly moved when, on a JIA Prime Minister's Mission, after I sat next to her at a festive banquet in the Knesset talking with her about the importance of Jewish education, she included in her address to our British campaign leaders a passionate plea to work for Jewish education, even religious

49

education, arguing 'Let our children at least know what they reject!'
Following her death I spoke at a memorial meeting in January 1979 attended
by over 800 people, including the then Leader of the Opposition, Mrs Margaret Thatcher, and numerous other notables. While still critical, albeit in
very subdued tones, of her extreme secularism and her inflexible policies, I
hailed Mrs Meir as the personification of 'a mother in Israel' whose leadership as a woman recalled that of Deborah. However, she and her predecessors, all of them stalwarts of the Labour establishment, belonged to a
generation of Zionist pioneers whose vision of the Jewish people, restored
to normality by Jewish nationalism, even if distinguished by 'Hebrew culture', had little in common with my understanding of Israel's purpose in the
struggle for Jewish survival. I found too few points of contact between the
circles encompassing political and religious leadership – distanced as they
were by the great divide on Israel's essentially spiritual traditions and
destiny – to render any meaningful dialogue possible.

But, oppressed by the dramatically worsening Jewish condition in the aftermath of the Yom Kippur War, which affected Israel and the Diaspora alike,
and being constantly reminded that all criticisms and challenges must be confined to private and direct contacts, I increasingly felt the urge to communicate in person some of my frustrations with existing policies to Israel's
leadership. I persisted in these discreet efforts for several years, though they
only added to my exasperation. Until 1978, the only occasion on which I took a
public stand in a political matter was in June 1975 when I protested to Prime
Minister Rabin about the honours conferred on the murderers of Lord Moyne
(assassinated by members of the Stern Gang in 1944) on their re-burial in
Israel; I was responding, I believed, both to the call of the Jewish conscience and to the sentiments of the overwhelming majority of British Jews.
My letter, dated 27 June, was released to the press, and read in part:

... I cannot conceal the anguish and perplexity felt by many members of our
community – and which I share – regarding the construction placed upon the honours
accorded by Israel's national and religious leaders to those responsible for the killing
of the late Lord Moyne. ...

The conscience of Jews is deeply troubled. Although history does sometimes
reverse a previous judgement, it would be morally unjustified to do so merely
because of a change in the political situation. There are today no grounds for
reversing the moral verdict on the murderers of Lord Moyne. The assassination was
unequivocally condemned by the responsible leaders of the Zionist movement inside
and outside Eretz Yisrael, notably by Chaim Weizmann and David Ben-Gurion; by
the leaders of the Jewish community in this country, Chief Rabbi Dr J.H. Hertz and
Professor Brodetsky, President of the Board of Deputies, indeed by Jewish leaders
throughout the world.

The world should know that the honours shown at the funeral were in no way intended to condone the deed or to impugn the memory of the late Lord Moyne, but simply as an act of traditional Jewish reverence for the dead. . . .

It is essential to reinforce confidence in the moral stature of Israel; to reiterate our total abhorrence of violence, and to reaffirm the fundamental Jewish commitment to the sanctity of life.

Even after this, I never directly criticized any decisions by the government of Israel in public, though I did challenge religious support for them and advocate alternative policies.

My first direct attempt to counter the spiritual malaise afflicting Israel after the Yom Kippur War as I saw it was in June 1974 when I addressed a personal letter to twenty-six Israeli and seven American leaders and intellectuals, including some government ministers, university presidents and newspaper editors, almost all of them outside the religious camp. The letter, I hoped perhaps rather over-optimistically, would set in motion some fresh thinking on the direction of Jewish life in Israel. After detailing my anxieties over the dangerous divisions and the spiritual crisis in Israeli society, it summarized two practical proposals:

I have urged, both publicly and in private discussions – at any rate during the present emergency when religious faith and national unity are such indispensable assets to Jewish survival – that we shift the emphasis in our spiritual confrontations and challenges *from legislation to education*. More specifically, I suggest that

1. secularists be persuaded to admit some regular religious education and religious experience in all schools in Israel, and
2. a moratorium be called on all new legislation of religious significance, such as conversions, civil marriage, public Sabbath observance and autopsies.

I then explained my main concern:

We are now paying a fearful price for the lack of a spiritual faith among so many of Israel's children. The rigid demarcation in the State system between religious schools for only a minority and non-religious schools for the rest, has raised a generation which put its entire faith solely in the invincibility and infallibility of its military establishments. Moreover it produced a generation which recognized as the only *raison d'être* for the Jewish State the security it had to offer, vainly believing that fulfilment of the Zionist dream would normalize the Jewish condition and eliminate anti-Semitism. . . . Both this faith of self-confidence and this secularist dream have now been shattered and, in the absence of any other faith, numerous people nurtured in an atmosphere of spiritual nihilism are now on the brink of despair. Desolate and disillusioned, many ask what are we fighting for? . . . Insufficiently exposed to the magnetic spell of the Land's sanctity and the fascination of living in a society suffused by the uniquely Jewish values, they are bound to question their attachment to the

Land and the sacrifices it calls for, once they believe that they can find at least equal
security elsewhere with lesser risks and privations.

Next I had to try and dispose of the deeply ingrained prejudice against any
religious influences:

> Profound as are the heart-searching and the quest for enduring Jewish values in
> Israeli society today, the religious establishment is all but impotent in reaching out to
> the masses and in relieving their spiritual starvation. I believe there are two principal
> impediments to making religious influences more widely effective: (a) the fear of
> religious coercion (which feeds the suspicion that religious power is being used to
> oppress the non-religious majority, infringing their freedom by laws which,
> estranged from the religious tradition, they cannot appreciate or value); and (b) the
> politicization of religion (whereby the growth of religious influence represents
> a potential threat to the voting strength of other political parties and their
> interests)....
> New thinking must devise a formula aimed at achieving three vital objectives: to
> replace the present internal strife; resurgence of religious faith to overcome the
> existing despondency, and to restore the historic identity of the Jews; and the
> disengagement of spiritual causes from partisanship and political bargaining....

After setting out further particulars on the suggested moratorium and the
religious education programme, the letter ended:

> ... I am led to believe that such a scheme could win acceptance if it were endorsed
> by leading intellectuals and 'opinion-makers', including especially some who are not
> specifically identified as belonging to the religious establishment or indeed to the
> 'religious camp' in general. I am inviting your views on these proposals, and more
> particularly your agreement, if you so see fit, eventually to associate yourself publicly
> with the call for their adoption.

At a conference in February 1974 convened by the Chief Rabbinate of
Israel and attended by some twenty leading rabbis from Israel, Europe,
America and South Africa, I had already suggested a moratorium on new
religious legislation in return for some religious instruction at all Israeli
schools. But the suggestion was received with little enthusiasm by my
colleagues, and it was bitterly opposed in public statements by the Mizrachi
as well as the Aguda, the religious parties which had an interest in maintaining the *status quo*, whilst yet pressing for further religious legislation.
Stifled by the religious establishment, I then decided to turn for help outside
its ranks. This time the immediate response was gratifying. Most of my
respondents replied in warm and supportive terms, some of them with reservations. Encouraged by this response, I then invited the personalities to
whom I had written to meet with me during my next visit to Israel planned

for October. By then, however, the enthusiasm had waned; even among the few I did ultimately meet, consensus eluded us on practical steps to be taken, or even on a joint declaration. I later summarized the experience, and the arguments it had sparked with some of my correspondents, in a paper delivered on 6 July 1975 at the Continuing Seminar on World Jewry and the State of Israel convened by President Ephraim Katzir at his residence in Jerusalem (my counter-arguments are given in brackets):

The responses were highly interesting and yet disappointing. They all more or less agreed with the need and its urgency, even to the extent of endorsing the plea for religious education in principle as an antidote to the existing spiritual starvation. But none were really prepared for the crunch – the leap of faith, as it were, over the gulf between recognizing the malaise and administering the cure in practice. Several respondents feared that any inclusion of religious instruction in the regular school syllabus might create resentment (in Diaspora Jewish day-schools, the exclusion of religious instruction would be unthinkable!). A renowned scholar-general wrote: 'If Orthodox teaching were introduced as the sole expression of Judaism, it would present no less a danger to Jewish unity than the politicization of religion. Should not the courses and prayers therefore be conducted by the various religious trends?' (As if school-children in Israel should be entangled in the arguments and divisions from which even their comrades abroad are still happily protected.) A professor of Hebrew Law doubted if formal instruction in spiritual values would altogether appeal to Israel youth and if enough teachers could be found combining a religious commitment with a Zionist orientation (perhaps we should send *shlichim* [emissaries] in reverse!). While he largely agreed with my contention that the key lay in education rather than legislation, he still regarded the legislative process as an essential tool to promote the religious character of Israel. He wanted rabbinic attitudes to become more flexible; yet he urged that school courses should concentrate on the application of Jewish law and ethics to modern conditions (but this can hardly wait until the dynamic process in the evolution of Jewish law has run its course).

Although I had assembled a fascinating collection of correspondence with some of Jewry's leading intellects and public leaders, extracts of which I later circulated with their permission, I sadly had to abandon the effort. I was clearly unequal to the self-imposed task of dislodging the religious and secularist establishments from their entrenched positions, or of building bridges between them.

Yet I tried again, mindful of the injunction in the Ethics of the Fathers, 'It is not your duty to finish the work, but neither are you free to desist from it', and prodded on by the ever more depressing state of Israeli and Jewish affairs. In the most universal blow ever aimed at the Jewish people, the United Nations had passed the Arab-Soviet-Third-World-sponsored resolution condemning Zionism as racism, thus in effect demanding the dismantlement of both Israel and Judaism. UN resolutions hostile to Israel had been commonplace, but none could compare in virulence to this one. Its impact on Jews everywhere was devastating, and a worldwide Jewish campaign to counter it sprang into frantic activity. To galvanize the Jewish response to this infamous threat, Prime Minister Rabin convened a three-day Leadership Conference in Jerusalem for early December and I was among the few rabbis invited to participate. This, I thought, presented me with a renewed opportunity. Surely a conference convened under such august auspices and under the unprecedented pressure of such a global onslaught should come up with some radical effort to rethink time-worn formulas of Jewish salvation in a world vastly different from what it had been when the Zionist programme was first formulated and then cast into a rigid mould!

Realizing that I stood little chance to present and argue my views at the conference, I wrote a lengthy letter to the Prime Minister beforehand. To reinforce it, I indicated that I would distribute copies to participants at the conference. Since this letter really encapsulated my philosophy and critique of Zionism as expanded in the rest of this book, I reproduce a great part of it here. After some introductory paragraphs on the significance of the conference and my hopes for it, I began with a little piece of forgotten history to justify my plea:

I recall ... that Chaim Weizmann at his inauguration in 1949 as Israel's first President turned to Chief Rabbi Herzog [and said]: 'My installation restores Jewish political sovereignty in succession to the kings of Judah and Israel; your task is to resume the heritage of the Hebrew Prophets and to provide the moral opposition and spiritual challenges to the political establishment.'

In our consultations on one of the gravest crises in our history, I deem it my role, as one of the few rabbis summoned, to heed Weizmann's call, unworthy though I am and inadequate as my attempt may be.

We have been convened to deliberate on the Jewish response to the most concerted worldwide attack ever mounted on our people. We are well aware that the infamous UN resolution, by proscribing Zionism as 'racism', in effect asks us to liquidate the State of Israel and to undermine Jewish existence everywhere....
Zionism clearly cannot be expunged from Judaism without amputating the heart of the Hebrew Prophets and the Psalms, mutilating our liturgy and law-codes, and completely truncating the faith which has sustained us in our millennial tribulations....

It is comparatively easy to refute the scurrilous charges made against us and to present the justice of our cause to non-Jews. We can point to the fearful price we have paid as history's first and principal victim of racism at the cost of six million lives; to Zionism as the forerunner of the national liberation movements to which the newly emerged nations – mainly responsible for the resolution – owe their own independence ; . . . and to the pioneering role of Jews in promoting human rights and social justice, from the Prophets to Jewish civil rights fighters in America and elsewhere. . . .

I thought a purely practical suggestion might prove helpful, or at least make my real challenge more acceptable :

The Israel Government might also consider arraigning before the International Court of Justice the governments which voted for the resolution on a charge of racial discrimination against the Jewish people by virtue of their vote, or at least to convene an assembly of eminent jurists to prepare and document such a charge.

But, having gone through the motions of self-justification, protest and indictment, we might as well realize that denunciation and argument are largely an exercise in futility, as was proved at the UN. We live in a brutal world which is hardly interested in the refinements of truth and justice. And since when has anti-Semitism ever been amenable to logic or reason ? . . .

Alas, even if our propaganda were better, and we would persuade a few more politicians, and church leaders, and scientists, and other voices of conscience to cry out a little louder against the injustices inflicted on us, we would still not be saved. . . .

To my mind, a key to our predicament was precisely our tendency always to blame others for our travails, and never to seek the remedy in our own response :

However, the more urgent, more difficult, and also more rewarding question is, how do we interpret our reverses to our own people ? What is the *Jewish* response to the crisis of survival which now besets us all, and how do we steel ourselves to persevere in our grim ordeal ? . . .

For those conditioned by decades of secular Zionist teaching to limit their vision of Israel's purpose as merely a haven of Jewish security, the shock-waves caused by the collapse of this ideology may be devastating. Their impact is already felt in declining Aliyah and increasing Yeridah-rates, and in the blighting disillusionment which has driven some of our youth, estranged from our traditions long ago, to ask 'What are we fighting for ?', others to challenge the justice of Israel's cause, and yet others to question the purpose of Jewish survival altogether. In the Diaspora, too, the danger is real that disenchantment and perplexity may alienate countless Jews from Zionism and Judaism alike. Only those fortified by our faith and familiar with the peculiar dynamics of Jewish history will be among the fittest to survive as Jews, both corporately and individually. . . .

Our conference, if it is to have any enduring value, cannot escape from the task of re-examining yesterday's visions and illusions in the light of today's realities. . . . Why has Zionism, meant to eradicate anti-Semitism and to 'solve the Jewish problem' by making us equals among the nations, now become the principal 'Jewish problem', a main generator of anti-Semitism and Jewish loneliness among the nations? Only the semantics have changed. Anti-Semitism has become anti-Zionism, and instead of sporadic pogroms we have periodic wars and continual terrorism. How can one explain our subjection by the world community to the very double standards Jewish independence was intended to eliminate? The inescapable answer is that our premises were false and we have built our expectations on an illusion.

The myth of gaining national equality through statehood has now been exploded, just as the early German-Jewish Reform philosophy – that Jews could gain individual equality through religious assimilation – has been reduced to ashes in the Holocaust. . . .

And so back again to my principal charge:

Our spiritual starvation is now nothing short of a national disaster. At a time when the assets of deep faith, idealism, self-discipline and pride in being Jewish are absolutely vital in the armoury of Jewish self-preservation, it is an invitation to national despair, if not suicide, to tolerate the spiritual alienation of two-thirds of Israel's children, and the totally inadequate Jewish education for most Jewish children elsewhere, to the point that many never even see Jews at prayer and remain complete strangers to traditional Jewish thought, values and observance.

Withal, I gladly acknowledge that there is today much soul-searching and a growing quest for spiritual values. This is indeed the most hopeful portent to emerge from the agony of the immediate past. Only, what most are searching for simply does not exist: A Judaism without religion, a faith without belief, a Torah without *mitzvot*.

I wanted him to be quite sure that I was equally critical of my own camp:

I realize, with much pain, that our religious establishment is at least as responsible for this blight as our secularist leadership. Torn by strife and preoccupied with political battles over legislation rather than with persuasion, religious leaders all too often abdicated their Prophetic role as moral mentors and spiritual guides to the perplexed, thereby estranging the masses of our people instead of attracting, enlightening and uplifting them. Between the extremes of the introvert traditionalists and the rabid secularists we have produced the great divide of polarization and fragmentation which now threatens to add to our external peril the bane of internal dissension, so ominously reminiscent of the 'causeless hatred' which sealed the fate of the Second Jewish commonwealth. Only a national return to our common spiritual commitment can repair this potentially catastrophic breach in the unity of our people.

Additionally, and more specifically, I would set out several propositions which events force us to acknowledge as the key to survival through regeneration. . . .

1. It is significant that three novel questions, never previously asked or debated in our long annals, have been raised simultaneously: 'Who is a Jew?', what is 'Jewish identity', and how do we ensure Jewish survival? The moment

we are no longer certain and agreed on who and what we are, Jewish survival becomes problematical.

Alluding again to UN resolutions, I wished our predicament to be seen in a wider perspective:

2. The question 'Why Jewish survival?' troubles not only some spiritually impoverished Jews; it bedevils the world at large. Why indeed, if we are widely regarded as being at the heart of so many of its gravest crises and perils; if, in the public image, we create problems rather than solve them?

3. Having long exceeded the life-span of other nations, and in a callous world insensitive to the death of millions by starvation or violence, we can hardly expect support and sympathy for our claim to national survival, possibly at the risk of the world's economic stability if not its peace, unless we make an indispensable contribution to mankind's enrichment as a model society dedicated to moral excellence, ethical integrity and a passion for social justice as its national purpose. Without such purpose the Jewish people becomes redundant and expendable by history.

Image-repairing by better public relations, as so often urged, seemed utterly futile and misguided to me:

4. Were we to be the one people on earth striving as our supreme objective to eradicate crime, vice, selfishness, social inequality, the breakdown of marriages and the generation gap – through self-discipline trained by religious idealism – our image in the world, among Jews and non-Jews, would be vastly different and we would not be exercised by the problem of Jewish survival.

5. The claim, to which we now increasingly resort (in the absence of any other which cannot be invalidated), that 'the Bible is our mandate' to legitimize our title to the Land and our Zionist aspirations is a sham if used by Jews who do not accept the dictates of this mandate in their own lives whilst expecting non-Jews to subscribe to it at their cost.

6. The quest for equality, together with its corollary, the abrupt disengagement from our spiritual commitments, has already deleteriously affected the ethos of our national existence and even our security. Whilst the benefits of equality have eluded us, as the nations still do not treat us as equals, the liabilities of equality afflict us, as we now sadly experience many social and moral aberrations which used to be unknown in Jewish society.

And here's the rub:

7. As any objective observer knows, only Jews intensely committed to Jewish learning and living are now completely immune to the erosion of faith, as they are to the inroads of assimilation and inter-marriage on the wider front in the global struggle for Jewish survival.

8. They now also constitute the bulk of Western Aliyah, since what attracts them to Israel is its holiness rather than the security it may offer.

9. Moreover, this is now the only element of our people, because they live in strict accord with the precepts of Jewish ethics on birth-control and abortion, which is numerically prolific and immune to physical attrition, both inside and outside Israel. Had Israel's Jewish population at large been prepared to face similar hardships in upholding Jewish law, it would now number over five million, including at least two million more Sabras who would have been raised without the colossal costs and problems involved in the transportation and absorption of immigrants amounting to but a small fraction of this number.

I could not omit my constant, perhaps obsessive, preoccupation with the Arab refugees:

10. Finally, and in a special category, the abandonment of Jewish spiritual values has political ramifications bearing on Jewish security, too. As an example I would refer (after much anguished thought) to the vexed problem of Arab refugees. Whoever and whatever caused their plight, had we as Jews – faithful to our heritage of special sensitivity to the sufferings of the stranger and the homeless – cried out in protest against the intolerable degradation of hundreds of thousands inhumanly condemned (albeit not by us) to rot in wretched camps for over a generation; had we aroused the world's conscience over a tragedy of such magnitude (even if we could *do* little about it), and not left it to terrorist gangsters to draw the world's attention to this stain on humanity – who knows? – we might have prevented the growth of a monster-organization which has already destroyed so many precious lives and now threatens, with the blessings of the world community, the existence of Israel more acutely than the Arab armies ever did, not to mention their worldwide dissemination of anti-Semitic venom.

Summing it all up, the appeal was direct and unequivocal:

May I therefore urge, Mr Prime Minister, in the spirit of the timeless ideals which have preserved us through all our vicissitudes to this day, and for the sake of the millions of our fellow-Jews who are no longer bearers of our heritage through apathy, defection or repression, that we call for a massive mobilization of all our spiritual resources, so as to assure the unity, faith, courage and vision of our people in the resumption of our historic assignment.

These supremely anxious times demand not only the reappraisal and sublimation of the Zionist purpose, but the revision of our national priorities. The moral and spiritual training of Israeli youth is just as vital as their military training, and Jewish schools in the Diaspora, too, are in the front line of our national defences. . . .

While decrying the double standards to which we are wickedly subjected by the international community, let us also rally our people to bear with pride this abnormal treatment as a tribute to the superior moral standards expected from us, and as a Providential reminder that, like Jonah, we cannot escape from our historic mission as moral path-finders among the human family in which we are destined to play a unique role to vindicate our equally unique record as an eternal people.  . . .

Letter or no letter, the conference went through the well-tried motions of indignation, denunciation and defiance, as speaker after speaker arraigned the nations for their wickedness and called on Jews to redouble their solidarity with Israel and their unflinching commitment to Zionism. The converted were duly re-converted, but I cannot recall a single fresh idea or new insight having been probed at this emergency meeting of top 'Jewish leaders' called together from all parts of the world in the unprecedented shadow cast over Israel's, and therefore Jewry's, fortunes. My taste for the expression of critical views by purely personal contacts and communications outside the public arena was not exactly whetted. I left the conference in a downcast mood little different from the depressing atmosphere in the world outside. I was only partly deflected from my disillusionment by my visit to Russia later that month and my private discussion with Mr Rabin shortly thereafter, as already recorded.

Staggering from crisis to crisis, the Rabin government eventually came to grief, bringing thirty years of uninterrupted Labour rule to an abrupt end in the break-up of its coalition with the National Religious Party – over a delivery of American fighter-planes too late on Friday afternoon to prevent a desecration of the Sabbath by the welcoming party. The fighter-planes may later have defended Israel, but on arrival they successfully torpedoed a whole era of Labour dominance. The general election in May 1977 brought the perennial Leader of the Opposition, Mr Menachem Begin, to power, faithfully kept there for the next six years by the indispensable support of the decimated Mizrachi and especially the ascendant Aguda.

My distaste for Begin's policies then, as thirty years earlier, did not diminish my respect for him personally and my admiration for him as a true leader, indeed as a Jewish leader, who speaks as a Jew with a deep reverence for the Jewish tradition and its spokesmen. Politically, I could not see much difference between him and his predecessors in their intransigence on matters of substance, whatever the variations in tone and tactics. Golda Meir had been just as determined to push the Palestinian problem under the carpet, to resist initiating any serious peace negotiations at the cost of territorial concessions, and to rely on might alone as the long-term answer to Israel's predicament. Moreover, it was the Labour government which started the settlement policy on the West Bank in response to the ever-louder clamour of the religious radicals and their increasing supporters.

I summed up my reaction to the change of government in my Rosh Hashanah message of 1977:

The election results ... were greeted with stunned surprise and lingering resentment in many circles, both Jewish and non-Jewish. The first shock after twenty-nine years of changeless dominance only gradually gave way to grudging recognition, later followed by hesitant and sometimes qualified congratulations to the new Prime Minister and his government. For some Jewish establishment organizations, the concessions made to religious demands in the formation of the new government were as galling as the feared radical changes in its political orientation.

Whilst the verdict of Israel's voters was reluctantly accepted as the price to be paid for maintaining Israel's democratic way of life, the ascendancy of religious influences continues to be viewed with undisguised horror, sometimes even amounting to a declared threat of withdrawing support from Israel should these influences prevail. Some die-hards evidently wanted to pursue the secularization and national assimilation of the Jewish State, and hence resist enhancing its Jewish character, at all costs. ...

This reaction is simply unacceptable historically; it is morally indefensible and potentially dangerous, as it imperils Jewish solidarity with Israel and threatens further to fragment Jewish cohesion in the Diaspora.

But I stated my reservations quite openly:

I neither share the Likud's political ideology, nor advocate the uncritical endorsement of government policies in Israel by Diaspora Jews. I am even on record as dissociating myself, for a variety of reasons, from the stand of Israel's religious parties on the 'Who is a Jew?' issue. But none of these reservations can shake my identification with Israel, my unqualified recognition of its government, and my wholehearted support for the nation's security and prosperity.

Indeed, however deep our differences on his long-past record and present policies, I proudly salute the first Prime Minister of Israel to be guided primarily by Jewish imperatives in all his pronouncements, whether public or private; a visionary leader cast in the heroic mould of Zionism's early pioneers and idealists; a charismatic personality who knows and reveres the Jewish tradition, and who has already done so much to uplift Israel's sagging morale and confidence.

Finally a reference to an appointment for which I waited nearly thirty years:

I warmly greet the first government of the Jewish State to include a religious Minister of Education, promising to put an end to the spiritual desolation of its youth and their frightening alienation from Jewish values. This appointment will, I hope, unite the Yishuv presently divided into two peoples who no longer speak a common language nor share with us common commitment to the Jewish heritage and destiny.

Traditional Jewish education will restore our role as bearers of a unique civilization vindicating the Jewish claim to survival. . . .

On sending a copy of this widely publicized message to Mr Begin, I received an acknowledgement from him: 'I wish to express my tribute to you for the inspirational words of Jewish unity, faith and solidarity you so beautifully articulate.'

My judgement was perhaps a little coloured, and certainly confirmed, by my experience in visiting the two countries which had greeted Mr Begin only a few weeks earlier on his first trips abroad as Prime Minister. I followed his still fresh footsteps in America as well as in Romania, where my wife and I paid the first of three unforgettable visits. The Romanian experience proved even more moving than the Russian visit. It was the only country in the world where we could still see living vestiges of nineteenth-century 'shtetl' life, where the pitifully few survivors of the Holocaust had rebuilt some semblance of Jewish life in the very communities in which they were born, where the Aliyah rate was over 90 per cent, and where highly organized forms of communal life and superb social services functioned efficiently under the dynamic leadership of Chief Rabbi Moses Rosen. The community was still under the spell of Mr Begin's visit, his insistence on staying at a second-rate hotel to enable him to walk to the synagogue in Bucharest on the Sabbath, guarded by a large contingent of the Romanian army, and his *Kiddush Hashem* in demanding strict kashrut observance at all functions in his honour. The impact on uplifting the respect for Jewish religious conduct was quite dramatic and had long-lasting effects. Little did I know then that, during Mr Begin's visit to Bucharest, the first historic steps had been taken which led President Sadat of Egypt to Jerusalem three months later.

Obviously still ignorant of these momentous developments, the elusive search for peace agitated my conscience with ever-increasing intensity, aggravated as it was by Israel's growing unpopularity even in previously friendly countries, and by the spread of terrorism to Jewish targets in many parts of the world, including the attempted assassination of the veteran Zionist, Mr Edward Sieff, in London. Mr Moshe Dayan, now Israel's Foreign Minister, had visited London in the summer of 1977 and given the usual 'briefing' to Jewish communal leaders. Disheartened by the performance, I wrote to him privately later on the same day. For the first time, I set out my own long-germinating ideas on the attainment of peace, generated in numerous discussions with friends whose acumen I respected and whose judgement I valued.

In my letter, dated 23 August 1977, I explained that, if time had allowed, 'I would not have concealed from you that many Jews – not to mention most non-Jews around us – feel puzzled and utterly bewildered by Israel's policies as currently pursued, or at least seem to be pursued, and as demonstrated by your presentation this morning.' I continued:

I am not a politician, and I do not pretend to know the political answers to Israel's present predicament. . . . But as an ordinary and passionately concerned onlooker, granting the strategy, I cannot comprehend the tactics. Surely, to maintain essential Israeli interests, it is not necessary to make provocative proclamations legalizing existing or new settlements on the West Bank, publicly to vary the status of Arabs in the Administered Territories in a manner bound to cause widespread irritations, or flatly to refuse to contemplate any form of Palestinian sovereignty, when clearly this is the nub of the whole problem. . . .

To my mind, we should say, by all means, let the Palestinians have their homeland; we desperately want peace, and we shall gladly meet all legitimate Arab demands, including major territorial concessions even on the West Bank; *provided* we *first* have *convincing evidence* that this will mean real peace and unchallenged security for Israel. For this we would require as a *sine qua non* the PLO completely changing its Charter, demilitarizing all evacuated territories, international guarantees, normal diplomatic and trade relations with all Arab countries, etc.

Since the Arabs are likely to reject these conditions, let their intransigence, instead of Israel's, be seen to be the impediment to peace. The result would be the same as you seek to achieve, but in the eyes of world opinion, or even Jews in the Diaspora, Jews rather than the Arabs would appear to pursue policies of moderation and reasonableness. . . .

Mr Dayan courteously but curtly acknowledged my letter, and that was the last I heard of it.

Meanwhile, the Sadat visit to Jerusalem set history into motion, culminating in the Camp David Accord and the signing of the Peace Treaty between Israel and Egypt in Washington. Although I was stirred by this extraordinary drama and its immense significance, I could never summon any real enthusiasm for it. Sadat, I feared, would gain all he wanted and, in return, while Israel would win a possibly precarious peace with its strongest Arab neighbour, the root of the problem – the Palestinians – would still be by-passed and continue to be a festering sore constantly holding real peace at bay. Of course, as a convinced 'moderate', I could hardly come out publicly or even privately against the peace with Egypt. But the doubts continued to gnaw within me on a strategy which evidently relied on the accommodation with Egypt to enforce a comprehensive peace which would shield Israel on a more permanent basis from terror and the threat of war. Sadat had made it quite clear in his Jerusalem address that the return of Sinai to his sovereignty would not lessen his demand for Israel's surrender of 'all Arab lands'. Even the promised Palestinian 'autonomy' seemed to me only a semantic device to befudge the issue and to lay the seeds for future conflict.

As for Mr Begin's role at Camp David, I could never disabuse my mind of the impression that he agreed to the total surrender of Sinai not on his initiative, but only under intense pressure from President Carter, just as Ben-Gurion did in 1956 under similar pressure from President Eisenhower.

On the other hand, I was well aware that Jewish public opinion overwhelmingly supported Mr Begin, soon to be at the peak of his popularity culminating in the award of the Nobel Peace Prize to him as well as to Mr Sadat. Even by the middle of 1978, the proposed autonomy talks were still far from turning completely sour. Moreover, I was acutely aware that politics was remote from my specialist knowledge or experience, and any involvement in it might not be understood or acceptable, rendering my rabbinical position correspondingly less effective.

# 7

# 'Another Way' –
# The First Open Challenge

What eventually tipped the balance in favour of public intervention by me was the religious aspect of Israel's new direction. This became increasingly decisive in the formulation and execution of Israeli policies as well as in their image throughout the world. The religious parties held the balance of power, maintaining a right-wing government and uncritically supporting every political decision in return for the promise of a few crumbs of religious legislation and considerable financial support for their institutions. This in itself seemed to me grossly damaging to religious interests. Much more ominous, to my mind, were the pressures for more extremist policies which were virtually all generated from religious quarters. Government policies appeared almost controlled by the religious fervour of these diverse groups – the Gush Emunim movement of pioneers transferring their idealism to the speedy settlement of Jews in Judea and Samaria; Chief Rabbi Goren heading the rabbinical establishment; Lubavitch turning its worldwide publicity machine into an uncompromising campaign against 'yielding an inch'; the fringe element of Rabbi Meir Kahane's 'Kach' fanatics advocating the driving out of the Arabs from 'Greater Israel', by force if necessary; and the hardline attitudes of nearly the entire Orthodox leadership, especially in America, at least to the extent to which they were vociferous in their public statements.

The suggestion that Orthodox Judaism was monolithic in its insistence, on purely religious grounds, on the preference for the occupation of the Biblical Land of Israel to peace – and to the Land's quality of Jewish life – appalled and frightened me, as a menace both to Judaism and to Israel. I never disputed the legitimacy of these extremist views, and I was aware that support for them was to be found in Jewish literature and history; but I did feel challenged to show that more moderate views enjoyed equal validity.

Without questioning the authenticity of the religious 'hawks', I was anxious to prove that some 'doves' were at least equally kosher.

And so the stage was set for the ignition in the next two years of three fierce controversies which raged in Jewish communities throughout the world. The first was sparked off deliberately; the other two quite accidentally.

I discussed my predicament with Mr Geoffrey Paul, editor of the *Jewish Chronicle*, whose friendship and judicious judgement I had learned to value. We soon discovered that in our basic thinking we were on the same wave-length. He decided to publish an editorial more or less along the lines of the proposal I had submitted to Mr Dayan nearly a year earlier. And, having exhausted the publicly favoured method of discreet intervention long ago, I agreed to consider submitting in due course a letter in support of the editorial, based largely on religious arguments.

The editorial appeared in the *Jewish Chronicle* on 23 June 1978 under the heading 'Another Way'. It asserted the case rather more boldly than I had done:

What is difficult for Israel's friends to say without being accused of treachery – but which must be said – is that, being at the heart of the conflict, no solution can be effective without doing justice to the strivings for some sovereign Palestinian entity. Anything short of this recognition is bound to keep feeding the frustrations of the Palestinians and their supporters everywhere, erupting in continual terrorism and threats, and acts, of aggression.

It then continued:

What Israel has to seek and espouse is a long-term peace strategy combining her maximalists' primary concern for territorial safeguards with the minimalists' overriding yearning for an accommodation. There is such a way, but it needs boldness. It must offer the Palestinian Arabs sovereignty and self-determination in exchange for peace. But the onus is upon them to prove *in advance* that such a peace would be genuine and lasting and this proof would have to be adduced before Israel vacated one inch of the territory presently under occupation. What is required of Israel is an undertaking to withdraw from occupied territory, with negotiated adjustments, *following and subject to* an agreed period of normal diplomatic trade and tourist relations with all the Arab States at present in a state of war with her, starting with immediate revocation of the Arab boycott; the cessation of all and every act of terrorism by States or organizations; Palestinian renunciation of force or any designs against Israel's territorial integrity; and the firm agreement, internationally underwritten, that all territories vacated by Israel will remain completely demilitarized, except for a police force for internal security.

It might be naïve to assume the Arabs would accept; but, in the event that they did, an extended period of completely normal relations with all Arabs inside and surrounding Israel would be bound to transform the psychological climate with dramatic effect. Hatred would be transformed into tolerance, fear into confidence, and the prospect of a true and lasting peace brought nearer than anyone had dared to hope in these past thirty years. True, the more likely outcome is that one, or even all, of the Arab States will reject the Israeli initiative. But, at the very least, Israel would have reversed the present image of Israeli 'intransigence' and Arab 'moderation' and the pressure would be on the Arabs instead of Israel, to make concessions. After all, what more could be asked of Israel? Her enemies would be challenged to expose their true intentions, her friends regained and encouraged, her supporters reassured, and the Jewish people firmly united at her side. . . .

The editorial evoked some debate, but it was civilized compared with the hysteria which erupted on the publication of my letter two weeks later. While endorsing the editorial's proposals, I simply shifted the main accent in the argument from the purely political to the religious aspect. With only two very minor omissions, the text of my letter read:

Your bold editorial 'Another Way' raises issues even transcending peace with the Arabs. It might also affect peace among Jews, now threatened by more perilous divisions than any other controversy in the history of the Jewish State. Your proposals seem to offer an alternative to, and a compromise between, the two sides in the present debate for and against territorial concessions. Whilst stipulating a period of genuine peace with *all* Arab States *before* ceding any territory, the proposals would yet break the current deadlock by a firm commitment *now* to meet Arab claims in exchange for convincing proof of peace, supported by other safeguards spelt out by you (border adjustments, demilitarization and international guarantees). Apart from turning the tables on the Arabs by challenging their sincerity in the quest for peace, your formula would thus also narrow the gap between our internal factions, taking account of some major demands and fears on both sides of the big divide, in seeking peace with security.

In an effort to pre-empt the critics, the letter continued:

Of course, your proposals are still liable to arouse opposition, mainly from three groups (partly in combination): 1. those who reject them for reasons of security; 2. those who insist on retaining 'the historic Land of Israel' at all costs on religious grounds; and 3. those who object to Jews outside Israel expressing any views, other than in support of official Israeli policies.

1. I claim no competence on the security aspect. But one need not be a political or military expert to ask whether the existing *status quo* will prove tenable, and whether the likely alternative to an *eventual* withdrawal *on Israeli terms*, holding out some prospects of true peace, will not be a *speedier* withdrawal *without any returns*, enforced by America, as happened in 1956. . . . Nor is much sophistication required

to appreciate the tremendous diplomatic gain which would accrue to Israel from seizing the initiative instead of merely reacting to events or to the initiatives of others (Dulles, Rogers, Kissinger, Sadat – and soon no doubt Carter–Vance). Again, in the event of Arab acceptance (unlikely though that may be), would not the security risks after a period of peace be infinitely smaller than the present situation with its constant threat of continual terror and renewed warfare?

Then I came to the gist of my argument:

2. Here as a rabbi I am on safer ground, and need not ask questions or speculate. Paradoxically, the most intransigent stance today is generated by religious elements. But vociferous as their 'rejectionist' clamour is, it should not drown out the 'small still voice' of 'moderates' like Rabbi J.B.Soloveitchik and many others.

No religious Jew disputes our claim to a Divine mandate (and we have no other which cannot be invalidated) extending over the entire Holy Land. What is arguable is whether we must, or indeed may, at this time assert it at the risk of thousands of lives, if not the life of the State itself. To be sure, there are authentic sources and valid precedents for both views. . . . But the preponderant opinion in Jewish history and literature seems to favour conciliation and peace notwithstanding the cost of territorial sacrifices. Even Joshua and Ezra did not complete the occupation of the entire Land.

Obviously, for religious Jews, settlement in Israel has a special dimension as a religious ideal – hence their quite disproportionate share in the Aliyah rate. But by the same token their conscience must be particularly sensible to other, perhaps overriding religious imperatives, too, such as to the pursuit of peace as Judaism's highest ideal; to the preservation of life which suspends all other laws; to the inhuman condition of thousands of Palestinians in wretched refugee camps, whatever and whoever the cause; to the justice of some Arab claims even when they conflict with ours; and, above all, to the Jewish character of Israel which would be vitiated by retaining a large Arab population within her borders, especially when on present demographic trends Jews would be in a minority within the next fifteen years.

The haunting fear of a new pseudo-Messianism also had to feature:

Even more alarming are the avowedly Messianic components in the policies of some religious groups. The pages of Jewish history are littered with the lethal shrapnel flung out by the explosion of pseudo-Messianic movements. As high expectations of imminent deliverance were cruelly shattered, they left behind them a trail of devastating disillusionment, stretching from the collapse of the Bar Kochba rebellion to the fearful aftermath of the Shabbetai Zvi débâcle. Messianic *hopes* are the essence of faith and indispensable to our survival. But to base national policies on the certainty of such expectations can invite catastrophic consequences.

Altogether, the battle-cry 'not an inch', with its 'all-or-nothing' overtones, evokes ominous echoes of Masada – an episode without parallel in Jewish history and entirely out of tune with Jewish teachings. Never before or after this epic has a Jewish religious sect declared its preference for collective death with dignity over life under foreign subjection. If such a philosophy had ever been embraced by our people, Jewish history would have ended long ago with national euthanasia.

I could not conclude without vindicating the principle of speaking out:

3. Here simply as a Jew I find myself least vulnerable. The cry to stifle participation in the great debate on Israel's future comes strangely *from* those who constantly remind us of the partnership between Israel and the Diaspora. It comes just as strangely *to* those who are committed to the centrality of Israel in their lives and who express their views only because of their supreme concern for Israel, realizing that on her security now depends their own security. The attempt to silence dissent and constructive criticism also sits particularly ill with a people which cannot forget the awesome price paid for silence in the face of suffering and injustice not so long ago. Are we, of all people, again to become the 'Generation of Silence', responsible for aberrations or missed opportunities by default? Rather should we heed the Prophet's cry: 'For the sake of Zion I will not remain mute, and for the sake of Jerusalem I will not be silent.'

The reaction was immediate and furious. But it soon became clear that what caused the furore was not so much the contents of the letter as the status of its author and, to some extent, its garbled reportage elsewhere. It appears that a pre-release of my letter had been distributed to news agencies, causing the *New York Times* to feature a two-column despatch, on the day of the letter's appearance in the *Jewish Chronicle*, under the banner headline 'British Chief Rabbi Assails Israel for Hard Line on Mid-East Peace'. Similar reports appeared in Israel and elsewhere, releasing an instant bombardment of protests descending on me by frantic transatlantic telephone calls and cables, and soon by a flood of letters. But I must add that not all the mail was hostile – at least an equal volume of supportive correspondence reached me. Of the many letters subsequently published over a period of several weeks in the *Jewish Chronicle*, the ratio against me and my views was about sixty to forty (presumably protesters write more readily to newspapers than supporters); but of the numerous letters addressed to me personally, especially from Israel, some 60 per cent supported my stand. To me, far more significant than the relative proportion of opposition to support was the difference in tone and authorship.

Before briefly analysing this difference, I must return to the *New York Times*'s report. The heading was misleading enough, but much worse were the distortions and downright falsifications contained in the report. For instance, it attributed to me speaking out 'strongly against "the intransigent stance" of Israeli political leaders', when in fact I had been very careful not to go beyond stating the patent fact that 'the most intransigent stance today is generated by religious elements', without referring to the Israeli government and its policies. I immediately submitted a letter of protest and correction to the London correspondent who had transmitted the report. He agreed to telex my rejoinder to New York for publication without delay; but newspapers do not readily open their columns to proofs of misleading reportage, and despite promises – followed by excuses – and several transatlantic calls, it was not until three weeks later that the following letter finally appeared:

I was deeply disturbed on learning of your 7 July news article 'British Chief Rabbi Assails Israel', purporting to report on a letter of mine published on the same date in the London *Jewish Chronicle*, Anglo-Jewry's communal weekly.

My letter contained no word of criticism of the Israeli government. It referred to the 'intransigent stance' by some 'religious elements' (not by 'Israeli political leaders', as your report states), contrasting this with the stance of 'moderation' of many other Jewish religious leaders.

I wrote as one of those 'committed to the centrality of Israel in their lives and who express their views only because of their supreme concern for Israel, realizing that on her security now depends their security'.

Several weeks having elapsed, a reminder of what the actual proposals had been became even more necessary than when I wrote the letter:

My letter expressed general support for proposals previously put forward in a *Jewish Chronicle* editorial. These had suggested that Israel should break the present deadlock and seize the initiative by offering a firm commitment *now* to cede territory (with several safeguards) only *after* a period of completely normal relations with *all* Arab States, including the Palestinians.

I argued that this seemed 'to offer an alternative to, and a compromise between, the two [Jewish] sides in the present debate for and against territorial concessions' and that 'apart from turning the tables on the Arabs by challenging their sincerity in the quest for peace [the formula] would thus also narrow the gap between our internal factions, taking account of some major demands and fears on both sides of the big divide, in seeking peace with security.' Urging consideration of alternative peace plans is surely not the same thing as criticizing the Israeli government, as your report alleges.

The bulk of my letter dealt with purely religious arguments and teachings bearing on the debate. While I acknowledged that there were 'authentic sources and valid precedents' for both the maximalist and the minimalist views, I believed 'the preponderant opinion in Jewish history and literature to favour conciliation and peace, notwithstanding the cost of territorial sacrifices,' adding, 'Even Joshua and Ezra did not complete the occupation of the entire Land.'

And a special word for my enraged American friends:

> However inadvertently, the article turned what was an attempt on my part to express support for certain peace proposals into an attack on Israel's government. By thus attributing words and views to me which I did not express, you caused a grievous injustice to me, potential damage to Israel and unnecessary distress to American Jewry, in whose midst I was privileged to serve for eight years and whose valiant support of Israel I cherish and applaud.

Virtually all the attacks came from Orthodox quarters. Some simply hurled abuse and even obscenities at me. One accused me of 'treachery'; another asked me to resign. A New York doctor wrote to me that I was 'the new Neville Chamberlain of 1978'. Four presidents of national Orthodox organizations in America were not content to communicate their disapproval to me, but rushed into print with public statements without even bothering to ascertain what I had actually written, basing their protest simply on the mischievous *New York Times* version. The Rabbinical Council of America 'regretted' my statement and 'explicitly rejected its implications'. The Canadian Mizrachi called it 'unwise, untimely and inappropriate'. Having generally succeeded in silencing Orthodox dissenters – and there were still a few of prominence, but their voices were muted – the Orthodox establishment was clearly irked most by my having dissociated myself from what they wanted to appear as unanimous religious endorsement of the extremist policies they wished Israel to pursue.

The only non-Orthodox organizational protest came from Mr Theodore Mann, Chairman of the Conference of Presidents of Major American Jewish Organizations. His broadside was of special interest, both for its content and for its sequel. First, he issued a sharp public statement denouncing me. This was promptly disowned by several of the organizations comprising his Conference, whose leaders wrote to me expressing their dismay with him and their support for me. Dr Arthur Hertzberg, a leading American Zionist explained the procedure in a personal letter to me:

> I simply want you to know how letters of the kind that Ted Mann wrote you are conceived. They are not created in any deliberate process. In my own experience at the Presidents' Conference, decisions are made elsewhere than in New York, generally by having some bureaucrat suggest what he thinks would be pleasing to the incumbent Prime Minister of Israel. I have no doubt that some comparable process was at work here.

The explanation was almost prophetic. As soon as Mr Mann retired from his leadership of the Presidents' Conference, he himself publicly proceeded to criticize Israeli policies far more sharply than I had done! But while in office, he added to his angry public statement a personal letter which attributed to me infinitely more influence among the world's leading statesmen than I even enjoyed in my own community:

You undoubtedly knew the certain consequences which would ensue from your public criticism: that Jews and non-Jews alike would conclude that if even the Chief Rabbi of Great Britain thinks the Prime Minister is inflexible, then it must be so; that President Carter, whose public criticism of the Prime Minister is so similar to yours, would be encouraged to engage in more of the same; that President Sadat would wait longer before returning to the negotiating table, on the sensible assumption that such criticism will weaken the Prime Minister.

The letters of support, many from very well-known national and communal leaders, usually applauded my courage (of which I was genuinely not conscious) and thanked me for 'stating openly what many of us think'. I was particularly touched by the enthusiastic endorsement from several new immigrants in Israel, and by a letter from a Zionist veteran who wrote:

I feel sure that the vast majority of Israelis who want their sons and grandchildren to work and live for Israel and not to die for it would like to be identified with the point of view which you have expressed.

Within my own community the debate was animated but civilized. Even the Joint Chairman of the British Herut Movement, after I had received him and his colleague to explain my stand, wrote to me:

We particularly appreciate the opportunity which you took to listen to our views and to the discussion over our differences. We understand now completely the reasons which motivated you to write as you did, although to be frank, we are still of the view that it would have been better if the letter had not appeared.

We were, however, particularly heartened by your readiness to accept our suggestions to consider the sending of a message to Prime Minister Begin, prior to the peace talks.

Very willingly, I did send this message to Prime Minister Begin. Dated 24 August 1978, it read, translated from the original Hebrew:

On the eve of the Camp David deliberations, at a time when all eyes are turned to you, we pray to the Guardian of Israel that His messengers will protect you in all your ways. May we merit to see the good of Jerusalem, and the fulfilment of the Biblical prophecy: 'And you shall dwell in your Land safely; and I will give peace in the Land.'

In fact, my personal relations with Mr Begin remained unaffected by this controversy as by their much more violent sequels during the following two years. He always greeted and received me with great respect, and for my part I had no reason to allow our wide differences to modify my high regard for his great leadership qualities and deep Jewish commitment. When he made his first official visit to London soon after Sadat's journey to Jerusalem in November 1977, I was present at a memorable dinner in his honour given by the British Prime Minister, James Callaghan, at 10 Downing Street in an atmosphere of warm cordiality. Mr Begin was to have attended the Sabbath service at the Marble Arch Synagogue, but at the last moment was kept at his nearby hotel by an injury to his foot. I none the less preached my sermon on 'Jewish leadership' in his honour as if he were present, and the text was later handed to him. It was the eve of Chanukah and, referring to the recent Sabbath reading on the Dream of Jacob, I told the packed congregation:

A truly Jewish statesman looks beyond the purely physical needs of his people and lifts his vision above the ground to encompass the soul as much as the soil of his nation.

We are honoured today to salute a leader ... who always proclaims his visions in distinctly Jewish terms, who is as much at home with us in the synagogue – 'And this is the gate of Heaven' – as he is 'with the rulers and counsellors on earth'; a statesman who has won the acclaim of his people and the respect of the world precisely because he sees Israel's national rebirth as *'Mutzav artzah'*, firmly based on the land, and yet *'Verosho magi'ah hashamaymah'*, as the foundation for the Jewish genius in linking Heaven with earth, in relating the contemporary to the eternal.

I could not let the occasion pass without a challenge:

A Jewish leader, summoned to interpret the age-old dreams of our people, knows that we did not dream, yearn and pray for thousands of years to be restored to Zion merely to have a State like any other. He knows that as Jews we could have had equality for the asking long ago, had we been prepared to give up our non-conformity and our distinctly Jewish commitment. He knows that our Prophets envisaged more than a state which exports oranges or scientific know-how, and imports the depravities we assimilated in our Dispersion; just as he knows that the slogan 'The Bible is our mandate' is a mockery if the Bible is used to push claims against others but ignored as the mandate to claim obedience from its own people....

But I also felt a special tribute was due:

No one in this congregation may be in a better position personally to testify to the Prime Minister's extraordinary achievements towards these objectives than I, being probably the only one here who has followed him within weeks to the only two other countries he has visited as Prime Minister, the United States and Romania.... Over and over again I heard rousing tributes to his thoroughly Jewish vocation and dignity, summed up with the supreme accolade a Jew can gain, hailing him for his *Kiddush Hashem* – the very ideal, I am told, which once moved young Menachem to become what he is, when aged seven in Brisk, startled on seeing his father retaliating against a

Polish soldier who had beaten a rabbi, he was told: 'A people that is prepared to die for *Kiddush Hashem* will live for *Kiddush Hashem*.'

I ended with a reminder that national liberation was not enough for the Jewish people:

Today he leads that people through its most critical test. And tomorrow is Chanukah – an anniversary older than observed by any other monotheistic faith or civilized nation; a festival which entered the Jewish calendar and law codes not simply because it recalls a great and fateful military triumph, but because the liberation of our Land was but a means for the reconsecration of the Temple – a battle which saved not only Jews and the Jewish people but Judaism ... [and through it] made possible 165 years later the birth of one great monotheistic faith, and 600 years after that of another. Thus many hundreds of millions now owe their faith and moral values to the miracle of Chanukah.

Likewise with peace today. 2,500 years ago, Jeremiah enjoined the Jewish exiles: 'Seek the peace of the city to which I have exiled you and pray for it to the Lord, for in its peace will you have peace.' And we prayed for the peace of the nations, knowing that on their peace and security depended ours and that we were the first to suffer under conditions of instability.

Now the roles are reversed. Let the nations now join us in praying and working for Israel's peace and security, for on Israel's peace depends the peace of the world; just as Israel's return to its Prophetic assignment as a model society would advance the moral order of all mankind. ...

A year and a half later Mr Begin was again in London, addressing a packed peace rally on 22 May 1979. In my vote of thanks to him I was a little less reticent on the differences between us, as I briefly referred to the controversy I had sparked off the previous July on religious support for extremist policies:

As you know, I do not share the view of some of my more vociferous and militant colleagues and their followers that Jewish national policies can or should be determined by Biblical promises or Messianic expectations, and my intervention a little less than a year ago to disengage religion from politics, though perhaps irritating at the time, may now, I hope, be welcome as strengthening the religious voice of conciliation against the clamour of religious enthusiasts whose ardent support has turned into bitter opposition.

By then, of course, his agreement to evacuate the whole of the Sinai, as stipulated in the Peace Accord with Egypt signed in Washington on 26 March 1979, was fiercely opposed by the religious radicals and later led to an anguished confrontation on the enforced demolition of Yamit, the model settlement town in Sinai where Mr Begin himself once resolved to live on his retirement. The opposition to Mr Begin and his policies did not come only from Gush Emunim, the religious pioneer settlers. Lubavitch placed full-page advertisements in the Hebrew and American press denouncing Mr Begin and his peace treaty as an unforgivable surrender of Israel's vital interests. Yet, even more startling was the religious censure of the peace treaty from another quarter.

# 8

# Chief Rabbis –
# Friendships and Collisions

I was in Jerusalem on the day the treaty was signed. Whatever my reservations on the wisdom of the whole strategy – I always preferred not to give up any territory in order to retain the maximum leverage for a comprehensive accommodation with all Arab countries – I still felt that, leaving aside its contemporary significance, the first peace agreement to be signed on behalf of the Jewish people in two thousand years was a notable event which called for some religious expression of thanksgiving. I telephoned Chief Rabbi Goren to ask whether he had issued any instructions for special prayers, perhaps *Hallel*, to be recited in the synagogues on that day or the following Sabbath, and I would act likewise in Britain. He answered me quite abruptly that, far from celebrating, he rather felt like proclaiming a fast!

He had not always been so intransigent. When he was still Chief Rabbi of the Israel Defence Forces, he once took me on a tour of some army installations. At that time, Israel was under strong American pressure to accept the Rogers Plan, which called for far-reaching territorial concessions on Sinai and the West Bank, and he told me: 'My heart tells me we will not accept: my mind tells me we will accept.' Over the years, our relations were always cordial, certainly until he came to London as my guest for the launch of our Kol Nidre Appeal in September 1979. At a rabbinical conference I invited him to address, he asked me to sign with him and other leading rabbis a halachic ruling forbidding the ceding of any territory as a violation of Jewish law. I could not agree with such an absolutist interpretation of what I believed were very diverse opinions in halachic sources, and I presented my reasoning accordingly. He was less than thrilled with my dissent, especially since it seemed to be shared by the majority of my colleagues.

As I recall, my relationship with the Chief Rabbinate of Israel had always been very personal as well as official. My own jurisdiction in Britain, as before in Ireland, was of course entirely independent. All rabbis traditionally exercise rabbinical authority only over the communities appointing them. In fact, the Chief Rabbinate of Britain, as it evolved from the rabbinate of the Great Synagogue in London, pre-dated that of Israel by several centuries. Nevertheless, I recognized the pre-eminence in Jewish learning and position of Israel's Chief Rabbis, and I freely consulted them on particular rabbinic problems facing me.

Perhaps it was only a coincidence that all the Ashkenazi Chief Rabbis of Israel until Chief Rabbi Goren's accession had previously served in Britain. The first, Chief Rabbi A.I.Kook, had been Rabbi of London's Machzike Hadass congregation during the First World War. His successor, Chief Rabbi Dr Isaac Herzog, had held rabbinical posts in Leeds and Belfast before he became Chief Rabbi of Ireland, a position he held for seventeen years until 1936; I succeeded him thirteen years later. And his successor in Israel was Rabbi I.J.Unterman, who had served for over twenty years as Communal Rabbi of Liverpool.

My ties with the last two were particularly close. Not only had we lived for ten years in the Dublin home previously occupied by the Herzogs, but they had attended our wedding celebrations in Paris in 1949. On the passing of the saintly Rabbi Herzog, our affectionate relationship was maintained with his equally illustrious wife and their two distinguished children, Chaim and Jacob. My friendship with Rabbi Unterman dated back to my student days and his friendship with my late father; it continued throughout his distinguished Chief Rabbinate of Tel Aviv and later of Israel. I was told that in 1966 a conclave of Anglo-Jewish leaders called upon him in Jerusalem, and he enthusiastically endorsed my candidature for the office of Chief Rabbi of Britain. Whenever I subsequently visited him, he most warmly offered me his counsel and gave me his blessings, and I felt his passing at the age of ninety, the revered doyen of Israel's rabbis, as the personal loss of a friend.

My own name had also twice been mentioned in connection with that high rabbinic office – once in May 1971 when an Israeli journal reported that the Dayanim of the Supreme Beth Din of Israel planned to put my name forward for election as Ashkenazi Chief Rabbi two months later, and then again in October 1976 when the *Ma'ariv* newspaper featured a similar report, publishing my denial at the same time. To live one day in Israel had always been my cherished ambition – but not as a rabbi, let alone as Chief Rabbi, and certainly not as long as these offices were highly politicized and administered under state control. The power to enforce the authority of the office is of course far superior in Israel; so has been the rabbinic scholarship of all its incumbents. But in influence and the exercise of spiritual leadership in the wider sense, the opportunities in Britain, as in several other countries, seemed much greater.

Unhappily, Chief Rabbi Goren departed not only from the British ante-cedents of his office, but also from other traditions, including the friendship I cherished with him as well as his predecessors. We found ourselves on opposite sides in two further controversies which were shortly to follow each other.

The first uproar started quite innocently with an invitation to some dozen Israeli correspondents posted in London for a luncheon at my home on 12 February 1980. From time to time, I had such informal get-togethers with various groups of journalists, particularly when I wanted to discuss some issue in greater depth than could be covered in a mere press statement. This time, my sole concern was to urge Israeli correspondents to include more substantial reportage on Jewish life in Britain in their despatches to Israel.

I had for long been troubled by the abysmal ignorance of Jewish affairs in the Diaspora on the part of the ordinary Israeli. Periodically, groups of Israeli army invalids would be invited for a holiday in Anglo-Jewish homes; their programme usually included a reception in our home as well. Most of these visitors had never been outside Israel before, and when asked about their impressions, they invariably answered that they never imagined to find such an intensely active and highly organized community. They had pre-viously known next to nothing about our Jewish schools, our well-attended synagogues, our Zionist activities, our concern and support for Israel. It was all an eye-opening revelation to them. I always felt convinced that Israelis should be as well informed about Diaspora affairs as they expected Dia-spora Jewry to be about theirs. This mutual identification would also encourage Aliyah by strengthening the sense of fellowship among new immigrants. For these reasons, I had often urged the need for regular in-struction on Jewish life in the Diaspora at Israeli schools. I raised this with the Israeli Ministry of Education and at governors' meetings of the Hebrew and Bar Ilan Universities which I attended. I had also put my plea to several Israeli editors to ask for more space to be allotted to Jewish affairs abroad in their newspapers. My representations were well received, but never acted upon. So I decided I would have another try by pressing my case with the agents of communication between Britain and Israel directly.

I presented the case to my luncheon guests with all the persuasive powers I could muster. They listened courteously; but when I was finished and invited questions and discussion in the informal setting around the table, they showed scant interest in the subject I had raised. What did interest them was to probe further into my stand on Israeli policies which was well known to them. Never afraid to state and explain my convictions, I readily answered their questions.

Asked about my attitude to the territories, I reiterated my belief that the Palestinian issue lay at the heart of the Arab–Israeli conflict, continuing:

'There are many who believe that an accommodation with the Arabs will never be found. I do not and cannot share this despair. If I did not have absolute faith that some time in the future – in ten, fifteen or even twenty years – an understanding with the Arabs would eventually be reached, I would rather salvage what can be salvaged and we might as well liquidate the State, for it could not for ever prevail against a hundred million Arabs in a hostile world.' I added that I would give up nothing until the Arabs had proved that Israel could live with them in peace. Following ten years of normal relations with them, all options should be open for negotiation, including a demilitarized Palestinian State with adjustments to the 1967 borders. In reply to a question on the future of Jerusalem, I said that I was strongly opposed to any re-division. Among the options to be contemplated after ten years might be sovereign enclaves encompassing the Moslem Holy Places, not dissimilar from suggestions already mooted by Mayor Kollek of Jerusalem. Further pressed by my now eager interlocutors, I stated that I could not see why such enclaves could not serve as the 'capital' of whatever future Palestinian entity might emerge on the pattern of the Vatican in Rome. Above all, as recorded in the notes written soon after the meeting, I expressed my fear that fundamentalist religious attitudes against ceding any part of the Biblical Land of Israel might be seen as the principal obstacle to peace. Such 'Jewish Khomeiniism' would be a catastrophe not only for the survival of Israel but for Judaism itself; hence my concern, as a religious leader, not to remain silent. After the luncheon, both my Executive Director and I felt that, given my known attitude, nothing very explosive had been added to the by then long-protracted debate. But we deeply regretted that the object of our exercise in calling the journalists had apparently been overshadowed by the subsequent informal discussion on issues I never intended to raise, though on which I did not mind commenting.

Within hours, the storm broke. Furious telephone calls reached me from Israel on the 'shocking and astonishing' reports of my 'statement' just transmitted by Israel Radio. By the following morning, the Israeli press featured despatches under the headline 'Liquidate Israel Now!', reporting that I had 'advocated' a Palestinian State, expressed 'support for the PLO', agreed to 'Jerusalem becoming an Arab capital', and similar entirely unqualified attributions. None of the published reports, incidentally, made a single reference to the plea on information about the Diaspora which had been the sole subject of my 'statement'.

Over the next few days, the storm increased in violence and swept over Jewish communities everywhere. Fed by the garbled and selective reportage of what I had said, the Israeli press fulminated. The *Jerusalem Post* alone published three feature articles attacking me – two by staff-writers and one by Rabbi Louis Rabinowitz who, for full measure, included the allegation that at a recent rabbinical conference in England I had declared 'not only a refusal to have *Hallel* recited on Independence Day, but actually a suggestion that Independence Day be abolished as a religious festival'. In fact he knew – for I had invited him to the conference – that I issued Orders of Service for Independence Day, including *Hallel*, with instructions to all synagogues to follow it at festive services! When subsequently challenged, he withdrew the charge with apologies in a personal communication. Other defamatory articles appeared in *Hatzofe*, *Ma'ariv* and elsewhere. All kinds of charges were invented, such as the plainly outrageous claim that I 'do not believe the Holocaust should be remembered or used to teach any lessons'!

State and government leaders reacted with restraint. President Navon, who knew me and my views well from our seminars at his residence, was reported to have expressed 'surprise'. Mr Begin did not make any public utterance or personal representations. Mr Zevulun Hammer, the Minister of Education, mildly commented, 'If he said it, it typifies a Diaspora outlook.' Alone among religious leaders, my old friend Dr Burg, the Minister of the Interior, refused to make any comment until he had seen the full text, saying merely, 'I hope he was misquoted.' Indeed, he soon convinced himself in a telephone conversation with me that this was so.

The fiercest denunciation came from the religious 'hawks' and their rabbinical mentors. Chief Rabbi Goren, having 'taken evidence' in what was almost a monologue on his part by telephone, duly convened the Chief Rabbinate Council, which he chaired, to castigate me publicly and officially for 'undermining the eternal right of the Jewish people to Eretz Yisrael, the land of its fathers'. To argue, to present facts, or even to withdraw words which might cause offence, proved of no avail. Taking the opportunity to present my views correctly once again, I transmitted the following message to him, here translated from the original Hebrew:

In reply to your call – any suggestion of liquidating the State – Heaven forfend! If there is the remotest possibility that my words will be misunderstood, I completely withdraw them. My intention was and remains to strengthen our firm belief that ultimately we will achieve a true peace which will ensure the existence of the State and prevent its liquidation. In my opinion, if it seems that the obstacles to emerging from our present distress arise from religious extremism, I tremble for the heartbreak in the future this will cause to Israel and Judaism. Rabbis have the responsibility for the ethical standards of our people internally and externally, which includes 'seek peace and pursue it', whether amongst ourselves or in our relations with the outside world. Only as a nation faithful to the Torah and the teachings of the Prophets can we rely on the promise of the Creator: 'And you shall dwell securely on your Land.' You are welcome to publish this statement in its entirety – it falls within the terms of 'There is salvation in the multitude of counsel.'

My detractors were not to have the last word. This time even Orthodox voices were raised in my defence. Chief Rabbi Ovadia Yosef, who had long been a good friend and an outspoken moderate, immediately announced that 'he dissociated himself completely from the strong unseemly words' used by the Chief Rabbinate Council. Heartening, too, was the public comment by Rabbi Menachem HaCohen, the Labour Knesset member who had always been a thorn in the flesh of the religious establishment: 'Good for him; let's hope he will not be frightened by his own boldness.' But above all this time, articles supporting me appeared in the Israeli press – one long feature in *Hatzofe*, and another in the *Jerusalem Post*, both written by well-known Orthodox contributors. In addition *Hatzofe* and *Ma'ariv* published a long letter explaining my stand, from my son, Rabbi Shmuel Jakobovits, of Jerusalem, who had lived in Israel for over twelve years and, like my wife and the rest of my children, shared my views. People told me later how impressed they were by the content and style of his presentation, even if they did not agree with its conclusions.

Above all, the *Jerusalem Post* readily agreed to accept my own rejoinder, which was published in a long feature article on 24 February under the title 'The Rabbi's Role in Israel's Predicament'. It included the following passages:

I recognize that I am a rabbi and not a politician. But while I have for long advocated the separation of religion from party politics, all political decisions affecting the fate and faith of our people must inescapably have a religious and moral dimension. . . .

Religious or quasi-religious fervour is, after all, today the most vociferous dynamic of Zionist militancy at one end of the political spectrum, just as it is of militant anti-Zionism at the other end. Whether I live in Jerusalem or London, I cannot help being alarmed at the prospect of Jewish religious fundamentalism being seen (rightly or wrongly) as an impediment to peace, with incalculable damage to Judaism itself, especially in a world now threatened with reversal to the Middle Ages by religious fanaticism elsewhere. Hence, I want Jewish religious voices of moderation to be heard.

I do not deny that contrary opinions may be equally authentic, nor do I denounce those who hold them. Differences of opinion can be healthy and constructive. . . .

Turning to the right of Diaspora Jews to let their voices be heard, I stated:

Jews in the Diaspora, though not entitled to participate in Israel's decision-making process, should contribute to it freely by expressing their views, even in public and even if they are sometimes critical. I grant that some factors in our grim predicament can be understood and evaluated only by those living in Israel (and I suspect I would also be more 'militant' were I already living there), but there are other factors that are bound to be more clearly visible abroad, and more objectively assessed with the perspective of distance, particularly when they relate to the attitudes of a generally hostile world far beyond Israel's embattled borders. . . .

Rabbis faced special responsibilities and challenges:

Perhaps it does require spiritual leaders to remind us that human life is threatened not by bombs but by the hatred of people using them; that the goodwill of nations is purchased by the efforts made to understand them; that justice is rarely one-sided; that peace is more enduring if attained by the Torah ideal that 'No man shall covet your borders', and that our gravest peril lies in internal hatred and intolerance, bred not by divided opinions but by a refusal to respect them. . . .

The threat of the existing policies generating ever more embittered polarization between 'hawks' and 'doves' inside Israel is grave indeed. Perhaps it needs an outsider to advance a formula which provides some middle ground which may lead to a consensus – neither to give up any territory until tangible experience of peace is at hand, nor to foreclose any future options by the word 'never'.

If such a formula fails to bring peace with the Arabs, it might at least promote peace among Jews, and save them from the threat of civil unrest. That, again, is the business of rabbis. . . .

Many Israelis think and proclaim that there will never be an accommodation with the Arabs. This is the counsel of despair which in fact sadly drives 30,000 Israelis a year to Yeridah. I cannot see how Israel can be viable in the long run unless we remove this despair and promote confidence. To promote realism tempered by hope, too, is the task of spiritual leaders. . . .

I closed on a very personal note:

I care desperately for the security of Israel, not simply because I have a son and three Sabra grandchildren in Jerusalem and a brother among the pioneers of Kibbutz Lavi; because I am convinced that the security of Jews in England as elsewhere now depends on Israel's security and decisions taken in Jerusalem; or even because the centrality of Israel is the cardinal fact of Jewish life today.

I care above all because in Israel converge all my people's hopes and national aspirations accumulated over the millennia and from Israel I seek the fulfilment of our national destiny as a light unto the nations.

In America, I was rather surprised to find that the hysteria aroused by my remarks, or rather by the way they were reported, was even more violent than in Israel – and more orchestrated. The organizations again thundered with dismay and denunciation; this time even the President of the Central Conference of American Rabbis (Reform) added his protest. The American-Jewish newspapers were full of vilification. One carried a large display advertisement over two names unknown to me, headed 'Open letter to all the Rabbanim of the Diaspora and of Eretz Yisrael', stating:

We ... cannot and will no longer be silent in view of that outrageous and infamous statement made by Dr Jakobovits, Chief Rabbi of London, to the Jewish press at a luncheon in his home concerning his views of the Palestinian State in Yehuda and Shomron with Jerusalem as its capital. ...

There is very little room in this narrow frame of advertisement to express the extent of outrage this disgraceful statement of the Chief Rabbi caused among the Jewish people. We ... turn to you, our great leaders, for guidance, indeed for help, for a Psak Din. ...

Another widely read paper featured a lengthy article under the title 'Orthodox Groups Blast Jakobovits', 'quoting' the revered Rabbis Moshe Feinstein and J.B. Soloveitchik as having assailed me with 'shock and disbelief'.

In March, I visited America for my annual round of lectures whilst the furore was still at its height. My eldest son, Dr Yoel Jakobovits, who lives on the Yeshiva Ner Israel campus in Baltimore, and is close to Rabbi Feinstein as a medical consultant, gave me a message from the renowned Rabbi assuring me that he had made no statement of any kind. I had not doubted this, as his own moderate views were well known to me. I had the same experience with Rabbi Soloveitchik, whom I visited, as I occasionally did when in New York. Again, he told me at once that he had neither seen my statement nor made any comment on it. When I mentioned the furore which was raging around me, he told me to act as my conscience dictated without caring and without bothering about my critics. I knew of course that some years earlier he had been on record as having expressed even more conciliatory views on Jerusalem and the territories than I had ever uttered. In fact, when I was still the regular contributor of the 'Review of Recent Halachic Periodical Literature' in the Orthodox American journal *Tradition*, I included in my abstract of rabbinic writings on the occupied territories the following passage:

The moderates' principal flag-bearer was Rabbi J.B. Soloveitchik. In a widely publicized address for which even the usually unfriendly *Ha-Pardes* (January 1968) gave him effusive editorial praise, he berated the exaggerated importance attached to the Jewish 'Holy Places', including the Western Wall, when compared to the deliverance of over two million Jews, and he ridiculed rabbinical interference with what were essentially security problems which could only be determined by Israel's government and army authorities. Any religious precepts not to surrender the Holy Land to non-Jewish control were suspended, as was any other religious law, in the face of any threat to life, in this case possibly the lives of millions (*Amudim*, Cheshvan 5728).

With the frenzy whipped up by a highly misleading press campaign, the going in America was indeed rough. Two of my scheduled lectures were cancelled – one in Omaha where the sponsors had been forced to withdraw the invitation, and the other in New York where posters had threatened that the function would be disrupted by busloads of pickets. Presumably the threats came from the cohorts of Rabbi Meir Kahane's Jewish Defense League. His regular column in the *Jewish Press*, headed 'But they are all Jakobovits', flayed me and my critics alike:

Poor Immanuel, G-d is not with him. From Jewish atheist to Torah Council of Sages, they leap upon his words and raise high the banner of Israel over his prostrate body.

But when all the sound of fury passes, and they are prepared to look honestly at what was said and what they say, the truth remains that they are all Jakobovits.

Anxious to be understood at least by my closest friends and colleagues, I asked to meet with the Executive of the Rabbinical Council of America with whom I had been so intimately associated for the past twenty years. It proved the most sterile meeting I can remember, as one by one they recited their litany on breaking the united front of the Orthodox rabbinate, on undermining the current peace talks, on caring about 'What will the "goyim" say?', and on weakening the Jewish lobby in Washington (the contradiction in the last two charges did not strike them!). My attempts to counter their anger and to mollify their opposition by arguing that reason, or Jewish teachings, or Israel's interests, might justify, if not call for, alternative views, proved about as effective as trying to empty the ocean.

The only agreeable experience in New York – apart from the strong support privately expressed by several personalities, including a few leading Orthodox rabbis, who were well-known but preferred not to be quoted – was a meeting with a group of intellectuals convened and chaired by Rabbi Shlomo Riskin, the charismatic builder of the Lincoln Jewish Center. Though himself already enthusiastically pioneering a new settlement in Judea, he was open-minded enough to greet me most warmly, to welcome the presentation of my views, and to allow most of the audience to express their support, including their fears shared with me over the alienation of countless young Jews whose critical or dissenting views were not tolerated by the official leadership and therefore suppressed.

It was only when I left New York for engagements in various parts of the States that the oppressive atmosphere of virtual persecution really began to lift. I usually lectured on Jewish medical ethics or some other relatively non-controversial subject, but the first question invariably addressed to me was on 'the controversy' I had stirred up. At the beginning, I sensed the atmosphere was tense, if not even hostile. But as soon as I gave my ten-minute reply explaining what I had said in London and why, the atmosphere was completely transformed. For instance, after addressing two crowded meetings in New Haven, the *Connecticut Jewish Ledger* reported at great length on the presentation of my views, adding: 'All who had the privilege of hearing him both at Yale Medical School and at B'nai Jacob, were first and foremost impressed by his warmth, his humanity and his great brilliance and devotion to basic Jewish life and law.' Even where I had not spoken, some Jewish papers outside New York went much further in their sympathetic comments. Under the heading 'Courage of Rabbi Jakobovits', the *Boston Jewish Advocate* wrote an editorial detailing my views and proposals, adding:

Our main concern with the suggestion of Rabbi Dr Jakobovits is not to agree or to disagree with it in its present form, but to praise this honourable man for epitomizing spiritual leadership. ... He has made us think and re-think, in moral terms, the Jewish imperative as it confronts the territorial imperative. Agree with him or not, we are thankful for the genuine, outspoken and thoughtful spiritual leadership he offers to his peers and to his people.

Even among colleagues outside New York, I found it possible to establish a reasoned rapport. In Baltimore, I was invited to meet and address that large community's Board of Rabbis. Some thirty attended, covering the entire spectrum from rabbis of the Yeshiva Ner Israel to Reform. Many expressed agreement with my views, and even those who did not argued rationally and with understanding.

On my return to London, New York's tempest still pursued me. I received in the post an impressive-looking, gold-sealed summons from the Beth Din of the Rabbinical Alliance of America to answer charges of 'Speaking against the interests of the Jewish people and Israel as Chief Rabbi'. I replied at once, indicating my willing acceptance provided 1. I received proper documentation on what I had allegedly said; 2. the judges hearing the case were impartial, not having previously expressed any opinion on the charges, and 3. I was free to bring a counter-action for defamation of character. I never even received an acknowledgement of my acceptance. But a few days later I heard on Israel Radio that I had been summoned to appear before that Beth Din – an announcement which was presumably the whole purpose of the exercise!

Apart from Israel and America, the storm raged fiercest in South Africa. Notwithstanding our long friendship, and without checking what I had actually said, Chief Rabbi Bernard Casper bitterly condemned me from his Johannesburg pulpit, and then promptly repeated his charges in the local and Israeli press that I was guilty of 'a stab in the back to Israel' and that 'Faith is the very thing that the Chief Rabbi never seems to mention' – convincing proof that he had not seen my statement. His predecessor, Rabbi Louis Rabinowitz, writing from Israel in his regular *South African Jewish*

*Herald* column under the title 'Rabbi Jakobovits' New Friends', bundled me together with 'Neturei Karta, Mapam, the Communists, the Black Panthers, Uri Avneri and Me'ir Pa'il'. Such was the antagonism aroused, that the local Board of Deputies abandoned a plan to invite me to be the principal speaker at its forthcoming biennial congress – an action described by a leader of the Board, whose more balanced views often agreed with mine, as 'a disservice to the individuals concerned and the people of Israel'. Only after the damage was done did Chief Rabbi Casper write to me, 'I cannot help wondering if I did not perhaps over-react to what certainly seemed to me, at the time, an outrageous stand on your part. . . . I am frankly sorry and I hope you will excuse my lapse.' He then continued: 'In mitigation, I have to say that I was provoked by what was presented as such a deliberate and calculated pronouncement on your part, designed to stir up a "doveish" public opinion whom you urge "to be no longer silent".'

In Australia, the Sydney Beth Din – still under my jurisdiction as Chief Rabbi of the Commonwealth – published a denunciation which included this pearl of rabbinic wisdom:

To express views on future relationships between Israel and the Arabs, to appear to approve a Palestinian State, and to accept that Palestinians are a separate ethnic group [*sic*], one must have in-depth knowledge and skill in political judgements which are not usually possessed by rabbis.

Once again, it was left to a prominent lay leader, Mr Isi Leibler, now President of the Executive Council of Australian Jewry, not only to withhold comment until he had verified my views with my own words, but having seen them in my *Jerusalem Post* article, to write to me:

I am sure that all but a handful of people, including those that may not share your views, will recognize your statement as a thoughtful and dignified expression of a responsible viewpoint.

I can well visualize the personal aggravation you have undergone over these last few weeks. Yet I am confident that in the long run, particularly now that you were provided with the opportunity of expressing your viewpoint without sentences or even phrases being quoted out of context, most of those critics who rushed so quickly into print to denounce you, will recognize that you were unjustifiably slandered and that your concern for Israel and the Jewish people and mantle of responsible spiritual leadership is something that many of them could well strive to emulate.

I will conclude this condensed round-up of reactions abroad in Holland, because its principal spokesman had a bearing on the European rabbinate as a whole. Amsterdam's Rabbi Meir Just, always known for his religious zeal strongly veering towards the political 'right wing', was reported as accusing me 'of having made his remarks to gain popularity among certain groups . . . [and] given support to Christianity and Islam [*sic*] at a time when they were trying to take Jerusalem away from the Jewish people'. He reportedly also 'stated that the members of the Conference of European Rabbis were ashamed of what Dr Jakobovits had said and dissociated themselves from it'. He later told me that he had been misquoted, and we remained good friends.

This particular reference was to the biennial conference over which I had just presided in Switzerland. In my Presidential Opening Address I had included a dispassionate presentation of my views, with special emphasis on the need for mutual understanding and tolerance among rabbis. Of the hundred rabbis who attended the three-day session, only Rabbi Just took violent exception to what I had said, often misrepresenting or misinterpreting me completely in his remarks. Others, too, disagreed with me, but in rational and friendly terms, and they never challenged my right to express my convictions. Quite a few, however, supported my stand, with or without reservations, including notably Chief Rabbi Moses Rosen of Romania, Chief Rabbi David Rosen of Ireland, Rabbi Mordecai Piron of Zurich, formerly the Chief Rabbi of the Israel Defence Forces, and Grand Rabbin Max Warschawski of Strasbourg who was the Chairman of the Conference's Standing Committee or executive. Far from any expression of 'shame' or 'dissociation', the conference reflected a much broader diversity of opinion than could be found in the Orthodox rabbinate anywhere else.

The sanest place of all was Britain. The first reactions were predictably opposed to my views, but not to my right to express them. This time not only Herut and Mizrachi came out against me, but even Mr Greville Janner, President of the Board of Deputies, pressed to make some public comment, issued a statement. It was cautiously worded, and I told him I had no objection to it, since I never claimed I had spoken on behalf of the Jewish community, any more than I did in publicizing my views on Sabbath observance or any other teachings of Judaism as I understood them. Mr Janner's statement quite properly asserted:

The Chief Rabbi is, of course, fully free to express his own personal views. That is what he did. I understand that he made it plain at the meeting [with the Israeli journalists] that he was speaking for himself.

Whether or not it was wise or helpful for him to express his views as he did . . . was a matter for his own judgement. We regret certain of his comments and reiterate our firm support, and that of our community, for this [peace-making and normalization] process. . . .

We express again our solidarity with Israel and its people in their determination to remain strong, secure, free and independent and we, like the Chief Rabbi himself, have total confidence in the developing vigour, vitality and mission of the Jewish State.

Some criticisms were less restrained. But, on the whole, my community treated me with considerable sympathy, whether out of loyalty or genuine support. Alone among leading Jewish newspapers, the *Jewish Chronicle* had reported my remarks accurately from the beginning, as recorded at the opening of this chapter. It had not editorialized on the controversy at all; but its principal columnist, Chaim Bermant, wrote several incisive pieces strongly applauding my stand. The correspondence columns were again filled for weeks with letters for and against me. The debate there as elsewhere in Britain was conducted without rancour, in sharp contrast to the torrents of abuse abroad. Only one provincial Anglo-Jewish weekly carried a critical editorial, as far as I knew – the Manchester *Jewish Telegraph*, which commented: 'Politics and Rabbis Don't Mix'.

My own personal mail-bag from virtually all over the world was even heavier than last time, with my file of 'Letters for' considerably bulkier than the file of 'Letters against'. I again answered each of the scores of communications individually, conveying my appreciation to those who had written to support and encourage me, with special warmth for the many outstanding personalities among them whose opinions or positions in Jewish life I valued highly. I provided my critics with a rebuttal of their arguments as well as a correct version of my original remarks. In some cases I succeeded, for example when a judge of the New York State Supreme Court, on receiving my reply, withdrew and apologized for the vehement letter of protest in which he had written that 'the statement attributed to you has stunned me more than any trial or case I ever had before me in my more than twenty years on the Bench . . .' Perhaps the most apt epilogue to the uproar in the Israeli media, where it all started, appeared in the British Aguda's *Jewish Tribune* – in a column which more often than not was sharply critical of me:

. . . So why all this violent opposition from the Israeli press against Chief Rabbi Jakobovits' views? Their main contention is that the remarks should never have been made in public as they are liable to aid and abet Israel's enemies.

I am suggesting that this is a dishonest contention, for it was exclusively the Israeli press which was given the 'scoop' and they published it. If they are really so convinced that Dr Jakobovits' views are damaging to the cause of Israel, they should have forgone the temptation of the banner-headed news item and no one in the outside world would have known of the interview in the first instance.

Israel's journalists want to have their cake and eat it. They manufacture a scoop, publish it, and then adopt a holier-than-thou attitude by postulating that the remarks are injurious to the State of Israel and should never have been made or published.

If this story has been related here in some detail, it is not because it describes the stormiest chapter of my life. Happily, my disposition has always helped me to ride out any public criticism with relative resilience, so long as I am at peace with my conscience. To my mind, the whole story epitomized my travails less than the travails of the Jewish people – the intolerance of Jewish leaders, especially rabbis; the unwillingness to countenance criticism, and the tendency to distort it where it cannot be suppressed; the refusal to break the mould of conventional thinking in the search for fresh approaches to overcome the Jewish predicament; and the irresponsibility, to the point of recklessness, of much of the Jewish press.

The hurricane had hardly abated when another was in the making, though this time the irresponsibility originated in Cairo and only finished in Jerusalem.

Towards the middle of May 1980, my office received a request through the Egyptian Embassy in London that I receive Mr Makram Mohammed Ahmad, managing editor of Egypt's leading paper, *Al Ahram*. He had met other Jewish leaders in various countries, and he was anxious to have an entirely informal chat with me. I declined, suggesting that he turn to our lay leaders instead; but on further persistent representations, I was advised it would be unwise and discourteous to refuse to talk to a distinguished visitor from Egypt in the then existing climate of 'normalization' when Jews and Jewish organizations sought every opportunity for a dialogue with prominent Egyptians.

And so I reluctantly agreed to the meeting, especially when it was made clear to me that it was not intended to be an interview. I stipulated that should Mr Ahmad wish to publish anything about our conversation afterwards, he would first check the full text of any report with me to make sure I considered it balanced and accurate. He readily agreed, and visited me on 20 May. Before we started our two-hour conversation, I again repeated my stipulation, and he confirmed the understanding without any reservation. On that basis, I had no objection to the conversation being taped, especially since Moshe Davis, my Executive Director, was present throughout, whilst my visitor was unaccompanied.

The following are extracts from the chief points made at the meeting, as drawn up by me with the help of Moshe Davis:

Asked about my attitude to the current autonomy talks, I explained at some length the supreme anxiety felt by the Jewish people for Israel's security, bearing in mind our long history of suffering and martyrdom culminating in the Holocaust and accentuated by the continued commitment of several Arab States and organizations to Israel's destruction. While reaffirming my own stance in favour of peace and moderation, on moral and religious grounds, *I stressed that Israel could not be expected to make any further concessions until the Arabs demonstrated that Israel would live in peace and security with them.* Since genuine peace could only be built on mutual trust and understanding, I repeatedly urged Mr Ahmad to appreciate that in the absence of Arab voices of moderation, such voices from the Jewish side were bound to be muted. Hence, influence should be brought to bear on Arab leaders outside Egypt to moderate their present intransigence. Only thus would a mood of conciliation prevail in Israel, too. . . .

On a Palestinian State, I said that *this would be suicidal for Israel so long as present attitudes prevailed* and the PLO charter was not repudiated. Nor would such a State be in the interests of Egypt or any other Arab nation. Much as I sympathized with the plight of the Palestinians in wretched refugee camps, it would be immoral to satisfy their national aspirations at the cost of a member-state of the United Nations whose very existence they openly challenged. Moreover, Palestinian terrorism was of a particularly hideous kind, having introduced into the history of human brutality deliberate attacks on children, sportsmen, air passengers and other innocent civilians for political ends – a form of terror now rampant throughout the world which must not be tolerated or encouraged.

Naturally, I wanted to explore my visitor's reaction to the peace proposals I had supported:

I reminded Mr Ahmad that Jordan already occupied three-quarters of the original Palestine, and that 60 per cent of its population were Palestinians – an argument he dismissed completely. But regarding the proposal I had supported, he did see merit and even feasibility in the suggestion to reconcile Palestinian aspirations with Israel's security by a prolonged period of completely normal relations between Israel and the Arabs in exchange for a pledge to negotiate the emergence of some Palestinian entity *after* convincing evidence of real peace was at hand and a new climate of mutual acceptance had been created to reassure both Israelis and Arabs that they had nothing to fear from each other.

On Jerusalem, I acknowledged that the City was holy to three faiths – though to Christians and Moslems only because Jews had sanctified it in the first place 3,000 years ago. Any re-division of Israel's capital would not only be offensive to Jewish sensibilities, but desecrate the character of the City meant to unite rather than to divide people of different creeds. However, I could envisage Vatican-type enclaves, and I also mentioned Teddy Kollek's suggestion for municipal devolution to provide autonomous borough government for Jewish and Moslem areas under Israel's sovereignty.

Obviously I said nothing of any substance which I had not publicly stated before. I heard nothing further for nearly six weeks, and by then had no reason to anticipate hearing anything further on what was agreed had been a 'strictly private conversation'.

Then a bombshell burst outside my home early on the morning of 24 June, as a BBC reporter, complete with recording-machine, impatiently knocked at the door just before I was about to rise for the daily synagogue service at 7.30 a.m. He showed me a lengthy Associated Press despatch just received on the *Al Ahram* 'interview' which had appeared that morning, and which had already caused much commotion in Israel. The report in that despatch had altered my words in the conversation beyond recognition, stressing especially my alleged condemnation of Mr Begin's settlement policies and introducing many other quite baseless attributions in quotes. Asked for my comments, I gave the BBC reporter a brief statement, challenging the veracity of the main attributions. On receiving my denial, the BBC 'dropped the story' completely, and it never featured in any news broadcast.

However, in Israel the press and my critics again went through their furious motions, this time armed with the damning evidence from Cairo, of all places, long before my denial could catch up with it. Meanwhile, the following cable was sent to the editor of *Al Ahram* in Cairo on 25 June:

> STRONGLY PROTEST YOUR REPORT MEETING WITH CHIEF RABBI STOP REMARKS
> ATTRIBUTED SUBSTANTIALLY INCORRECT AND MISREPRESENT VIEWS
> EXPRESSED STOP AGREEMENT BY YOUR REPRESENTATIVE TO SUBMIT FULL
> TEXT TO US FOR PRIOR APPROVAL WAS NOT HONOURED
>                    MOSHE DAVIS
>              EXECUTIVE DIRECTOR
>              OFFICE OF THE CHIEF RABBI

We received no reply from Cairo. But on 1 July the Press Counsellor of the Egyptian Embassy in London wrote to me:

> In view of the controversy which has been touched off by the publication in *Al Ahram* of an article by Mr Makram Mohammed Ahmad, I would like to provide you hereunder with a translation of that part of the text of Mr Ahmad's article which concerns you.

The letter then cited three fairly long paragraphs from the article. In it the author states that the Chief Rabbi 'had started a severe storm of challenge to Begin when he had declared that silence *vis-à-vis* Begin's behaviour could no longer be justified because it blows up the possibility of co-existence between the Arabs and the Israelis'. The article, as transmitted by the Embassy, closes with a reference to my 'suffering from the effects of the severe campaign organized by Begin's supporters because he had said that the Jewish Promise as mentioned in the Old Testament justifies neither the usurpation of territories, nor the building of settlements nor the imposition of our occupation on three million Palestinians'. Following the 'translation' of the article, the Press Counsellor's letter concluded:

> It is clear from the above that Mr Ahmad did not quote you directly anywhere in his article. What he actually did was to describe a storm which he was told by many

people, both in this country as well as in France, had been raging before his arrival in England. I hope that this puts what Mr Ahmad has written in its proper perspective.

It would have done, had this been the true contents of the article, with allowances made for whatever comparatively mild misrepresentations it contained due to Mr Ahmad's informants 'in this country as well as in France'. However, the real article bore little resemblance to its alleged translation in the Embassy letter. Through the good offices of the *Jewish Chronicle*, I obtained my own full translation of it; in direct contradiction to the Egyptian Press Counsellor's assurance, the article appeared not as a report of my views from second-hand sources, but as an 'interview' given with 'initial reluctance', and freely *quoting* what Mr Ahmad purported I had told him. The article put words into my mouth I had never uttered and projected views, by exaggeration or embellishment, I never held, whilst skirting the major points I had made in our conversation on the need for Arab moderation if any progress towards real peace was to be made.

There were, then, three contradictory versions of what had transpired in my home on 20 May: the actual account, as I knew it and as was attested by two of the three people present and by the tapes of the conversation; the article itself, as rendered from the Arabic into English; and the conflicting account of it, as communicated in the letter from the Egyptian Embassy. To vindicate myself, I could simply have published the three mutually exclusive versions, exposing not only Mr Ahmad's breach of faith, but more importantly the contradictions between the Cairo and London Embassy versions, thus revealing the untruthfulness of both. But such an exposure of Egyptian double-talk might have done damage to the delicate state of Israel–Egypt relations, for which I did not wish to assume responsibility. I therefore just sent all the material to the proper quarters in Israel, to let them decide on whether and how to use it, at the same time clearing myself at least in their eyes of the wild charges which by then were being hurled at me. I had evidently satisfied those whose understanding mattered to me most; no representations of any kind were made to me by or on behalf of the government of Israel.

Astonishingly, on the very day after the publication of the *Al Ahram* article, I found *The Times* carrying a front-page report from Tel Aviv under the bold heading: 'Britain's Chief Rabbi vilified in Israel.' It began: 'The Rev. Shlomo Goren, the Chief Rabbi of Israel, today ferociously attacked Dr Immanuel Jakobovits, the Chief Rabbi of Britain, and called upon British Jews to cast him out.' It continued by quoting Goren: 'I call upon the rabbis in the world and the Jews of Gt Britain who hold the holy city of Jerusalem and the land of Israel sacred to spew this dangerous man from our midst.' *The Times* item also included my comments on the *Al Ahram* article in which I stated that my views as reported represented 'wishful thinking' on the Egyptian newspaper's part.

Rabbi Goren's call on Anglo-Jewry to 'spew me out' had the effect of rallying the community behind me. The *Jewish Chronicle*, in its News and Feature Service dated 26 June, reported:

> Reaction to Chief Rabbi Goren's attack was strong and immediate, ranging from a cable to him from Lord Mishcon calling his statement a 'Hillul Hashem', to a statement from the President of the Board of Deputies, Mr Greville Janner, QC, MP, calling Rabbi Goren's words 'deplorable'. He added: 'It is surprising that apparently he did not trouble to check his facts with his distinguished colleague, with whom the lay-leadership of the British Jewish community has a close, affectionate and respectful relationship.' Mr Ab Kramer, the Deputy Chairman of the British Zionist Federation, reacted even more strongly. He said, 'Rabbi Goren's advice to us is unacceptable and I reject totally what he has said about Chief Rabbi Jakobovits. Rabbi Goren should look to his own affairs and put them in order. He should not meddle in matters that do not concern him.'

The Anglo-Jewish Association expressed 'every confidence in his good sense, integrity and loyalty to the State of Israel', and its President, in a message of support, added: 'We are very happy to extend the platform to him on the occasion of our Annual General Meeting on 16 July.' Through Rabbi Goren's unseemly intervention, the flames ignited in Cairo were effectively put out, and the renewed debate it had generated soon faded. It gave me little joy when less than three years later, the fate he wished upon me was imposed upon him by his own community. For my part, I strictly abstained from responding to attacks by him or any other rabbi. When a Dutch Jewish newspaper editor interviewed me in writing, and asked 'What is your reaction?' to Chief Rabbi Goren's attack, I simply replied: 'Out of respect for the honour of the Torah, I have not reacted and will not react to Chief Rabbi Goren's attack.' To the many similar questions put to me at public meetings in Britain and Israel I likewise replied invariably: 'The honour of the Torah is more precious to me than my own honour.'

On the dust raised abroad by the *Al Ahram* affair, I will only cite one not untypical instance. A popular New York Orthodox weekly, with a wider circulation than any other Jewish paper in English, under the heading 'World Jewry in uproar over *Al Ahram*', knew rather more about the background to the story than I did, when it reported: 'Jakobovitz [*sic*] had been visiting Cairo last week upon an invitation from President Sadat and was interviewed by the Egyptian newspaper.' I had never been to Cairo and never closer to Egypt than when Rabbi Goren, then still serving in the army, invited me to join some twenty army chaplains on a trip to Mount Sinai, and we returned via Abu Rodes. There we looked across the Red Sea to the

Egyptian bank on the other side! The capacity of some elements of the press to invent facts and statements is matched only by their addiction to making mischief.

When I once showed some of the defamatory press cuttings I had collected to a prominent Queen's Counsel friend, he told me they could be worth a million dollars to me in libel damages. However, I preferred to earn my living by teaching and disseminating the truths as I knew them rather than by profiting from other people's untruths. Moreover, my slanderers knew very well that I would hardly purchase my good name at the cost of shaming the Jewish name by court proceedings or rabbinical squabbles.

But there was a limit. It was exceeded when the *South African Jewish Herald* of 14 October 1980 purported to report on an article of mine in *L'Eylah* (the magazine published twice a year by my office) under the libellous heading 'UK Chief Rabbi again speaks for PLO'. The article had actually stated the opposite in accordance with my oft-repeated and unqualified public denunciation of the PLO. This time, on legal advice, I wrote to the paper's editor, demanding both 'an unreserved apology in terms acceptable to me' and a reprint of my *L'Eylah* article in full, failing which I would take appropriate steps to obtain proper redress. I added:

> Irrespective of any amends you may make, voluntarily or by Court Order, I am shocked and grieved that a Jewish newspaper, ostensibly serving the cause of Judaism and Israel, should stoop to such a blatant falsehood as your heading contains, and by it provide support for Israel's mortal enemies.

On 23 December the paper duly published a grudging apology and correction in a long editorial, together with a somewhat mangled though complete reprint of my *L'Eylah* article, under the correct banner headline 'UK Chief Rabbi rejects "Peace Now" views', followed by the equally correct sub-heading, quoting me: 'Palestinian State now would be suicidal for Israel.'

Sadly, this was still not the end of the matter. Less than a year later, a knighthood was conferred on me in the Queen's Birthday Honours of June 1981. This prompted Rabbi Rabinowitz to devote his *Jewish Herald* column of 14 July to a scurrilous attack under the quarter-page heading, 'Arise, Sir Immanuel', suitably embellished in colour by a photo-montage of the Queen standing over me in semi-kneeling posture. His article suggested that I was 'somewhat disappointed' with the knighthood, as I must have expected a peerage for services rendered to the British government; for it was only after I had allegedly stated 'that the Palestinians were justified in claiming that East Jerusalem should be their capital' that Lord Carrington, the British Foreign Minister, 'came out with a similar anti-Israel suggestion which was more or less identical with that put forward by the official spiritual head of Anglo-Jewry', and that 'since then England has gone even further in espousing the Arab cause, to the extent of the Queen taking the unprecedented step of going to meet the King of Saudi Arabia at the airfield when he arrived on an official visit to England recently'. Therefore, 'there might be some collusion in this coincidence'. Granted, the writer could not have known that, following the EEC Venice Declaration, I had in fact written to Lord Carrington, a year before I received my knighthood, strongly attacking British policies which urged the association of the PLO with the peace process, and that I had received a lengthy and rather sharp reply from Lord Carrington to my three-page letter. On competent advice, I did not publish that correspondence until nearly two years later, so as to keep my personal lines of communications open. But Rabbi Rabinowitz should have known not only that his allegations were preposterous, but that I was on record as having publicly opposed British and EEC Middle-East policies. Only a renewed threat of legal action elicited from the editor a printed apology which included the following statement:

> Indeed, we are aware that the Chief Rabbi called and led last July's anti-PLO Trafalgar Square rally specifically as a protest against Lord Carrington's policies – the largest demonstration ever held by Anglo-Jewry.
>
> Rabbi Rabinowitz has apologized for his imputations and we are happy to say that if there was some suggestion by Rabbi Rabinowitz of some collusion between the Chief Rabbi and Lord Carrington – the basis for the suggestion being that Rabbi Jakobovits hoped that he might thereby acquire a peerage – it is wholly without foundation.

Subsequently Rabbi Rabinowitz himself wrote to me, explaining that in his Kol Nidre sermon that year he specifically referred to sins committed by speech and in writing, adding 'and since I always try to apply my preachments not only to my congregants but to myself also, I humbly beg your forgiveness, as I did that of the Almighty, for any such sins I have been guilty of with regard to you'.

By contrast with the precipitate rabbinic flagellations, the Vice-President of Israel's Hitachdut Olei Britannia (British Immigrants' Association) wrote to me asking for a clarification of my views following a meeting at which these were raised and debated. I replied to him at length in a letter which was afterwards widely circulated. It began:

> Since you are the first to seek my views before attacking them, as so many others have done, often based on misinformation, it is only right that you should be the first to receive a restatement of my thinking in the light of the recent controversies sparked by conflicting and inaccurate reports.
>
> Another reason, too, makes the Hitachdut Olei Britannia – representing the 'home'-based extension of my 'constituency' – most appropriate in this context.

Having pioneered the response to our constant encouragement of Aliyah, you are entitled to know what we think and do about Israel's future, and I feel more accountable to you than to anyone else.

This reply led to an invitation to deliver a lecture to the Association in Tel Aviv. The subject was 'The Jewish Purpose – A Reassessment', and the date was set for 20 November 1980. It was to be my first visit to Israel since the two great controversies during 1980 which had generated so much antagonism against me. I had been told it might be wiser not to attend the summer meeting of the Bar Ilan University governors. The fear that tempers might still be inflamed by November caused the organizers of the lecture to take elaborate precautions against pickets, hecklers and other anticipated disturbances. In the event, I was well received, the audience was receptive and friendly, and I encountered no problems of any kind. Thereafter I resumed my fairly regular visits to Israel, and when leading the large delegation of European rabbis on a week's visit a few months later, the reception accorded to me at all our numerous meetings and visits, including several new settlements in Judea and Samaria, could not have been more cordial.

The sarcastic reference to my 'New Friends' made in my controversial statements did, of course, have some truth in it, though – like the best lies – it was only a half-truth. Would-be allies came forward not only to support me, but also to seek my support. Some neither received nor presumably expected any acknowledgement, for example a letter from the Neturei Karta in Jerusalem hailing my conversion to anti-Zionism. Other overtures were more serious, and led to some interesting correspondence and discussions, but never to any identity of views or expression of public endorsement on my part. During one or another of the controversies, I had received letters of encouragement from several political notables, including a former Israeli Ambassador in London and several leaders of Israel's Labour establishment. More persistent efforts to find common ground came from the former Mapam Cabinet Minister, Victor Shemtov. Whilst we saw eye to eye on some aspects in the pursuit of moderate policies and their moral dimension, including the need to cultivate better relations with Israel's Arabs, many gaps between our respective convictions obviously remained unbridgeable.

The 'Peace Now' movement also approached me. Their leadership invited me to meet them during one of my visits to Israel, and a delegation of the movement also called on me in London. They were particularly keen to obtain religious, preferably rabbinical, support for their programme. Much as I welcomed the remarkable phenomenon of constructive dissent they represented, later to become such a significant feature in salvaging Israel's honour at the height of the worldwide campaign of denigration caused by the high toll of life in the Lebanon war, I declined to identify myself with them for two principal reasons. Even if this was not strictly a political movement, any such identification would still violate my principle as a rabbi not to join any partisan groups. More important still, my ideas on the attainment of peace fell considerably short of theirs. I was opposed to peace *now* in the sense of offering an immediate accommodation by territorial concessions, without first allowing a prolonged intermediate period to create a new climate of mutual understanding and co-existence which would ultimately put the risks to Israel at a minimum and the prospects of real peace with its Arab neighbours at a maximum. I believed the 'Peace Now' campaign – its activities in any case a little too addicted to popular slogans for my liking – concentrated on opposition to existing policies rather than on long-term and well-thought-out alternative objectives.

Naturally, I felt very much more drawn to 'Oz VeShalom', the religious counterpart to 'Peace Now'. Apart from the religious outlook uniting us, its leaders were very much more on my wave-length; I could obviously relate more easily to religious academics than to retired army officers. Moreover, some of these leaders were well known to me personally, Professor Uri Simon even being a distant relative. I maintained contact with them, and they republished some of my writings in their literature. But again, my reluctance to wear any partisan label, combined with some substantive differences, kept me from joining their ranks or giving them any formal support.

My reaction was somewhat different and more positive when I heard of the formation of another group, calling themselves 'Netivot Shalom', sparked off originally by the trauma of the Yamit evacuation, and not long thereafter strengthened by the moral impact of the war in Lebanon. I had always felt a special affinity of outlook with the group's original mentor, Rabbi Aaron Lichtenstein, of the Har Etzion Yeshiva, and son-in-law of Rabbi J.B. Soloveitchik. But while he never actively pursued his commitment to religio-political moderation, the group became a national force, albeit of limited impact, only when Rabbi Yehuda Amital, also Dean of Har Etzion Yeshiva, was 'converted' to it and boldy campaigned for its aims. Here was a development for which I had long waited: the emergence from within the Gush Emunim-Yeshivot Hesder heartland of a purely religious challenge to the whole 'Greater Israel' concept which had hitherto been its main plank. As Rabbi Amital himself explained in a two-page feature article published in the *Jewish Chronicle* on 5 April 1983:

I have witnessed the danger of certain ideological formulations which have found expression among the religious public who remain steadfast in their belief in Eretz Yisrael.

This ideology took on a unique shape during the last days of Yamit. As a result, an ever-widening rift has developed within the Yishuv and Diaspora communities, causing a desecration of God's name and real harm to the battle being fought over Eretz Yisrael....

He then saw several other warning lights, culminating in the Israeli army entering Beirut, and religious support being unreservedly given to these actions:

Within this political camp, there is absolutely no discussion as to the necessity of peace; one dare not even mention it. Talk of peace as a fundamental aspect of Torah and morality, even without giving it precedence above various fundamentals of our faith, is considered heresy. It seems that every problem between Arab and Jew – be it in Galilee, in Judea, in Samaria, in Lebanon – contains only one possible solution: that of a strong and militant stance.

A further warning light 'came when some elements, especially the religious Zionists, expressed satisfaction at the clear and open display of anti-Semitism which took shape during and after "Operation Peace for Galilee"'. In terms so familiar to me, he asked:

Can we really believe that anti-Semitism will be the motivating factor behind the ingathering of the Exiles, and not rather hope that education geared to instilling a love and desire for the good ... land will cause the exiled of our people to return home?

It was music to my ears when he then proceeded to attack the whole philosophy which had assigned religious priority to the retention of territory over the pursuit of Judaism's moral imperatives:

Often during the past few months we have heard the statement being made by those who express a desire for the immediate physical conquest of Eretz Yisrael: 'The views and attitudes mentioned above are the authentic and true explanations of the Torah.' *Woe to the ears that hear such a statement!* ...

The hawkish and militant attitude among many elements of the Religious Zionist community defies the very path of Torah and the spirit of Judaism, as well as the course the religious community has taken since the establishment of the modern Yishuv in Eretz Yisrael. Yet even greater damage has been caused to the strength of the Jewish heritage and tradition among our people....

The article had a considerable impact on its readers, as did the expression of the author's views in Israel. Here was not just some foreign rabbi, remote from the realities of Israel, meddling in its affairs; or a critic with allegedly questionable Zionist credentials seeking to challenge official rabbinic rulings and authentic religious doctrines, a heretic who could be formally denounced for 'undermining the eternal right of the Jewish people to Eretz Yisrael'. Nor was this a mere academic cloistered in his university away from the realities of the true aspirations of the faithful. Here was a widely respected Israeli rabbinical leader nurtured in the philosophy he now rejected – for the very reasons which had agitated me over the years and caused such obloquy to be heaped on me. It was a refreshing and reassuring experience. Immediately after the publication of Rabbi Amital's article, I wrote to him to express my admiration, and soon thereafter our thinking converged again when we met and appeared together in a symposium featuring two Israeli and two European rabbis during our conference meeting in Israel in May 1983.

Returning to my own controversies, they had one quite unexpected spin-off. In the 'Restatement of my Views', as published in *L'Eylah*, I had included the following sentence: 'Recognizing that Zionist militancy is today generated mainly from religious quarters – for instance, Meir Kahane, Gush Emunim and Lubavitch – I am most anxious to ensure that Orthodox voices of moderation be also heard.' The association with militancy, let alone with Meir Kahane, outraged the leading supporters of Lubavitch in London, all of them personal friends and close partners in my Jewish educational endeavours, and they sent me a letter of protest. My friends might have been unaware that writers close to Lubavitch had spearheaded the damaging press campaign against me in America, and that the summons against me had been issued by a Lubavitch-related Beth Din. But they could have known about the extremist political stance of Lubavitch as widely publicized in Israel and America; they evidently preferred this to remain unknown in Britain. It might not agree too well with Anglo-Jewry's basically moderate outlook to compromise the image of Lubavitch as a purely educational force. As a consistent supporter of Lubavitch institutions, I had no interest in damaging that image. But I was concerned to expose and challenge any political extremism in religious circles. I was also puzzled by the growing contradictions I detected between the movement's super-nationalism of uncompromising militancy and its anti-Zionism in withholding any religious recognition from the Jewish State. I pursued these concerns in my reply, asserting that

... my article neither attacked Lubavitch (though the most vicious and defamatory public attacks on me, especially in America, were Lubavitch-inspired), nor did it 'equate' Lubavitch with Meir Kahane. It simply stated the incontestable fact that Lubavitch, together with others I named, is today among the major Orthodox forces pressing for political militancy. If in this respect Lubavitch has something in common with Meir Kahane (whose *Ahavat Yisroel* is also beyond question), the fault is surely not mine.

It is evident to me that you (like so many others) are simply unaware of Chabad's political stance and agitation. Did you know, for instance that Lubavitch promoted full-page advertisements in the Israeli and American (non-Jewish) press attacking the Israel government (which I have never done) and denouncing the Camp David Accord;

that Lubavitch asserts a 'halachic ruling' against yielding an inch, based on the 'unanimous opinion of *all* military experts', despite contrary views by Generals Dayan, Rabin, Peres, Weizman and others, and following an interpretation of a Sabbath law which is disputed by many leading sages, including Chief Rabbi Ovadia Yosef;

that Lubavitch has publicly charged the Israel government with complicity in sheltering the PLO murderers in Hebron and deliberately failing to arrest them; and

that a Lubavitch rabbi in London refuses to recite the Prayer for the State of Israel because he does not recognize the State?

This led to an exchange of several letters, especially with Rabbi F.S. Vogel, the head of the British Lubavitch Foundation. He explained that the Rebbe's pronouncements against the peace treaty with Egypt, against the surrender of a single inch of occupied territory, etc., were governed purely by halachic considerations. I could not accept either the halachic reasoning or the political implications of this stand and, when the arguments between us were exhausted, I was told, why not write to the Rebbe directly? I did so, and a lengthy correspondence ensued, consisting of some half-a-dozen long letters to each other, written in Hebrew on the halachic arguments and in English on other ramifications.

I had known Rabbi Menachem Schneerson, the illustrious Rebbe of Lubavitch, fairly well, visiting him from time to time while I lived in America and occasionally afterwards. His acquaintance with my wife's family went back to the early post-war years, when as a student in Paris he frequented their home. I have always held him in the highest esteem, both as an outstanding scholar and as the phenomenal builder of the Lubavitch movement from a little-known sect into the most dynamic force of Jewish religious regeneration of our times, now controlling an empire of hundreds of institutions on which the sun never sets. I had visited, or spoken at functions in support of, many of these institutions in five continents. Our friendship was warm, despite my immunity to Chasidism and differences between us on several Israeli issues, including the 'Who is a Jew?' agitation led by Lubavitch.

In our correspondence, which remained cordial throughout, the Rebbe reaffirmed that he was 'completely and unequivocally opposed to the surrender of any of the liberated areas currently under negotiation, such as Yehuda and Shomron, the Golan, etc., for the simple, and only, reason that surrendering any part of them would contravene a clear *psak-din* (ruling) in the code of Jewish law, and that this had 'nothing to do with the sanctity of Eretz Yisroel' or with any expectation of Messianic redemption. The ruling referred to requires Jews to defend a border town in violation of the usual Sabbath laws even if the attackers come merely for the sake of plundering 'stubble and straw', lest the attack leads to a threat to Jewish lives. Such a threat, he maintained, could be determined *only* by military experts, and since *all* of them agreed that any ceding of territory would put at risk Jewish lives, the Sabbath rule had to be invoked to prohibit any territorial concessions. In further letters the Rebbe categorically dismissed my arguments that there were no Jewish towns on the border inside the territories; that military opinion in Israel was by no means unanimous; that political and economic considerations might equally affect Israel's security; that a peaceful accommodation might in the end save more Jewish lives; and that several leading halachic authorities altogether disputed his interpretation of the Sabbath ruling and its relevance to the current situation.

What particularly interested me was that his insistence on retaining the territories had 'nothing to do' with the holiness of the Land, or by implication with the Jewish claim to it; the principle would apply equally, he argued, to the defence of Jewish settlements outside Israel, being solely a matter of protecting lives in potential danger. Later he wrote to me that he agreed, in answer to a question he had received, that the Land's sanctity was a separate and additional factor in his opposition to any territorial compromise.

Less academic in our written debate was his explanation why he had urged during the Yom Kippur War that the Israeli army should pursue its counter-offensive in Syria to Damascus. This had a bearing on the ill-fated Israeli incursion into Southern Lebanon then under way. He had also urged the Israelis 'to finish the job' by advancing all the way to Beirut, and he was to make this plea later from the moment the invasion of Lebanon started in June 1982. What, then, moved the Rebbe to support this Sharon-like bellicosity so vociferously? He had urged the taking of Damascus, he wrote, on the basis of the halachic injunction to pursue the enemy 'until it fall' (Deut. 20:20):

... *not* for occupation, but to ensure that it 'never' again will pose a threat. It was *then* also common knowledge that Soviet advisers were present there, with headquarters, etc. Only a few hours of occupation would have been sufficient to accomplish the task [presumably as did the months-long occupation of Beirut in 1982! *I.J.*]. But for 'strange' reasons, it was not done. The results of the failure are evident, and have been particularly underscored recently by the moving of the Soviet SAMs, and the military actions that were necessary to counter Soviet penetration, including the bombing of the nuclear reactor in Iraq (though the latter action shows a salutary departure from the policy of appeasement and subservience).

I reproduce all these arguments in some detail to explain why I developed such an often-articulated aversion to modern political and military calculations being determined by religious imperatives in the Torah or the *Shulchan Aruch*, enjoined as they were under such vastly different security conditions from those predominant today. The lesson of Beirut should have put paid to such halachic strategy once and for all! If there are Torah principles to be applied in all circumstances, especially in Israel's contemporary predicament, they should be focused, in my view, on such imperatives as the pursuit of peace, the sanctity of human life, whether Jewish or not, the duty to sanctify the Divine Name by efforts to win the acclaim of the nations, and other such injunctions. Above all, as I wrote in one of my letters:

> Surely, any G-d-fearing Jew, let alone a rabbi, must affirm that the ultimate security of Jews in the Land of Israel lies neither in armies nor in borders but in our spiritual worthiness through 'the study of Torah and the practice of Mitzvot', and that this must be our overriding and most urgent aim as well as the principal teaching of all rabbis, as confirmed by the whole of our sources and our history.

In our correspondence, the Rebbe also repeatedly denied any personal involvement in the agitation against me in America, though the denial stopped short of disavowal or condemnation. The denial was unnecessary. I never suspected or alleged such involvement, and I assured him that 'throughout my correspondence with my friends here I affirmed my conviction that the Rebbe had no prior knowledge of this campaign of vilification against me, and had certainly not instigated it'. What I did charge was that the campaign was conducted by men 'inspired by Lubavitch and influenced by [the Rebbe's] thinking'. As happens so often, particularly in the many violent inter-Chasidic rivalries, it was just a matter of zealots 'out-zealing' their mentor – in this case, even if they were not actual members of the Lubavitch movement, but merely sympathizers with its political philosophy.

# 9

# The War in Lebanon –
# Fall-Out on the Diaspora

The War in Lebanon, precipitating an unprecedented trauma for Israel and Jews everywhere, dramatically changed the whole Zionist scene. It also thrust me into more intensive and prolonged Israel-oriented activities than ever before. In a sense, the war may be said to have opened in London on 3 June 1982, with the tragic bullet which struck the widely respected Israeli Ambassador, Shlomo Argov, passing through his brain and inflicting an injury from which he began only after months to make a slow mental and even slower physical partial recovery.

The assassination attempt had three immediate personal effects on me. It required me to observe a far stricter security regime than before. For years, especially since the attack on the life of Edward Sieff, the Jewish community had been very security-conscious, and I had become accustomed to some security people accompanying me to, at and from all major public engagements. After the Argov shooting, the restrictions on my freedom of movement were tightened considerably, and I could not leave my home even for the daily morning service without a security escort. As I reminded various lecture and radio audiences later in Israel, it could certainly no longer be argued that decisions made in Israel affected the security of Israelis only; I was freer in the streets of Jerusalem than in those of London.

Secondly, the shooting deprived Israel and Anglo-Jewry of an outstanding spokesman at a time when he was most needed. In the absence of an Israeli Ambassador – and a successor was not appointed until over a year later – the media as well as the community frequently turned to me to fill some of the void with comments and guidance, especially on the moral perplexities which were to face us under the mounting pressure of events and their biased portrayal in the press.

But above all, that bullet had cruelly hit an exceedingly precious personal

friend. Over the fifteen years since I had assumed my office, there had been
five Israeli Ambassadors in London, all men of considerable calibre. Differences of outlook never interfered with the affectionate relations I had with
each of them. We often met not only at numerous public functions but also
privately at our homes. Yet, the ties between myself and my wife and
Shlomo and Chava Argov had some extra dimension of intimacy and mutual
trust. Strictly correct as Shlomo always was in his loyalty to the government
he represented, he nevertheless showed great understanding as well as
respect for my views, especially when these were under such bitter attack
in other quarters. Whenever I consulted him – and this was not rare – he
advised me wisely. From time to time we would spend several hours
secluded together, and were able to compare very frankly the perplexities
which beset us over Israeli politics and actions. I was not therefore surprised
when, in his first public statement a year after his shooting, he so critically
censured as senseless the war it had sparked off.

I had visited Israel twice during the first month of the war. The first was
very briefly for the Barmitzvah of my brother's son in Kibbutz Lavi, just as
the first cease-fire in Lebanon was being greeted with immense relief. The
second was two weeks later to attend the governors' meeting of Bar Ilan
University. Hostilities had started again, as the Israeli army pushed farther
into Lebanon; but I could then only describe the mood I found in Israel as
resigned, almost to the point of indifference – quite unlike that in previous
wars.

On two occasions meetings scheduled with Prime Minister Begin had to
be put off due to his indisposition. I was particularly anxious to discuss with
him an initiative on Soviet Jewry suggested by the Conference of European
Rabbis to be undertaken by some of us. I was therefore delighted to hear
from his adviser on Diaspora Relations, Mr Yehuda Avner, a friend since
the 1940s who was to become Mr Argov's successor in London a year later,
that the Prime Minister would be happy to receive me during my visit. I duly
met him for an hour or so, finding him relaxed and completely at ease,
affected no more by past differences between us than by the anxieties about
the war on which he was to give a major Knesset speech later that evening. In
fact, when I told him I wanted to relate a short homily on the current Portion
of the Law, he said, why make it short? Before entering his office, Mr Avner
urged me not to raise the Soviet Jewry issue with the Prime Minister, since
he was personally committed to the Brussels III Conference on Soviet Jewry
then planned for Paris in the autumn, and he knew that the European rabbis
were distinctly unenthusiastic about yet another conference. So we talked
about other matters, perhaps of even graver consequence, in a conversation
I found fascinating and revealing as well as extremely friendly. Since my
meeting with Prime Minister Rabin five and a half years earlier, where we

talked in English, my Hebrew had evidently improved sufficiently to conduct the conversation this time exclusively in Hebrew.

Without the slightest reference from either side to the war in Lebanon or to the recent controversies I had stirred up, our discussion ranged widely. I mentioned that, in contrast to politicians who had to deal with day-to-day affairs, spiritual leaders, as successors to the Prophets, were expected to have broader visions extending over years and decades ahead. I illustrated this with my homily on the forty-nine day, seven-week count of the *Omer* incumbent on every Jew, whilst only the Beth Din were required to count the seven years and forty-nine years of the Sabbatical and Jubilee Year cycles. Accordingly, I put three long-term questions to him in the course of our talk, and he answered each quite categorically, and to me significantly. By present population trends, the Arabs will outnumber the Jews inside the present borders of Israel within the next ten to fifteen years; what would then become of the Jewish State? His reply was simple. Even the figures published by the Government's Statistical Bureau were misleading, since they did not take into account the even higher rate of Arabs leaving Judea and Samaria than Jews emigrating from Israel, so there would still be a net Jewish gain in fifteen years' time. I did not argue either on the calculations or the implications of this reply.

Next, I enquired about the future of the Palestinians. Whether we liked it or not, whether historically with or without any justification, the Palestinians recognized themselves as a national entity and so did the rest of the world. They were hated as aliens in the Arab countries into which they were dispersed. How could this festering problem one day be resolved? The answer was equally straightforward and absolute. He asked for a copy of the PLO Covenant to be brought in, and showed me its reference to the Palestinians calling themselves 'a part of the Arab nation'; as such they had plenty of Arab countries in which to find a home. Finally, I enquired: If some day in the future he were to feel assured that the Palestinians no longer harboured any aggressive intentions against Israel, and were prepared to live in peaceful co-existence, would he then agree to some Palestinian entity being established? In his vocabulary, was the short answer, the word 'if' does not exist. It was replaced, I thought rather sadly, by his constantly recurring use of the word 'never'. We touched on several other interesting points and then parted, without either having convinced the other, but perhaps both understanding each other a little better – and my admiration for his stamina even further enhanced.

On my return from Israel the fall-out from the war in Lebanon on Diaspora Jewry became daily more poisonous. The media were full of shocking stories on the many thousands of civilian casualties and tens of thousands of refugees caused by Israel's 'brutally ruthless' advance into Lebanon. Anti-Jewish feelings became so inflamed that there were already two major terrorist outrages with loss of life against Jewish targets in Paris and Rome. In Britain, Jews felt highly uncomfortable, even if not in physical danger. Whilst some were morally increasingly uneasy about Israel's actions, all were incensed by the double standards so blatantly applied to Jews. We were as yet far from the climax of the war in Beirut, and Israeli objectives were still limited. I appeared in several television and radio interviews, explaining and putting into perspective Israel's actions as far as I could. Initially I could see no greater moral objection to military action for 'Peace in Galilee' to protect the lives of tens of thousands of citizens than to such action by Britain to secure the freedom of 1,800 islanders 8,000 miles away. But I did not conceal my fears, either. *The Times* of 6 July devoted its first leader to an interview I had given, heading it 'The Two Cities of Zion':

The Chief Rabbi went to the BBC yesterday to meet the criticisms of Israel which have been vigorously put by the World Council of Churches. He spoke of his fears for Israel: two fears. The first was in his belief that the Palestine Liberation Organization had the power to carry out the extermination of Israel, and also to threaten the security of Jews anywhere and everywhere else in the world. The second was his fear of what war is doing to the character of Israel, and to the religious ideals upon which the State was founded. . . .

Neither Israel's security as a State, nor her legitimacy, is now threatened by Palestinians. . . . Why therefore this chronic sense of insecurity so eloquently expressed yesterday by the Chief Rabbi, when he coupled his fear for the safety of all Jews with profound misgivings about the fact that the Zionist dream had become distorted into a boast of militarists? It is important for the West, cradled in its Judeo-Christian cultural tradition, to recognize the overwhelming symbolic influence that Israel has to the Jews of the Diaspora. . . .

As the Chief Rabbi illustrated yesterday, it is the fusion of spiritual Judaism with Israeli militarism which must trouble many Jews in the Diaspora, who are no less devoted in their faith for being citizens of other countries. Israel is a bastion of democracy surrounded by States which neither recognize the word nor practise the deed. In that sense it is the repository of many of the hopes and ambitions of Western civilization and thus suffers from the expectations of higher standards in its behaviour than do its neighbours.

Quite independently of this thoughtful and by no means unfair editorial, I had submitted an article to *The Times* which was published as its main feature on the following day under the title 'The Questions I Cannot Answer'. Once again I had to strike a careful balance between explaining and challenging. At the start I referred to my recent two visits to Israel, and then continued:

All Israelis are embittered by the callousness, complete insensitivity and double standards with which they believe the world treats them. . . .

They are appalled by the patently verifiable misinformation spread in the Western media, with PLO-inspired reports on more people rendered homeless than there are inhabitants in the region. They point out that far more (perhaps ten times as many) Palestinians and Lebanese have been killed by fellow-Arabs than by Israelis – in Jordan's bloody action against the PLO in 1970, in Lebanon's brutal civil war, and in constant inter-group murders.

Israelis, all of them, are shocked beyond belief by the present outcry against them compared with the silence of the Christian world when the PLO terrorized and massacred tens of thousands of fellow-Christians.

And Israelis are outraged, having sacrificed many of their own sons in an effort to reduce casualties among civilians (where the PLO had placed their lethal weapons and vast ammunition stores), by being compared with Nazi Germany or charged with genocide.

They asked me over and over again why, and I had no answers. Jews the world over ask the same questions, indeed, many find no explanation for this irrational hostility other than an ominous recrudescence of anti-Semitism.

I had no compunction in drawing a line between popular Jewish opinion and my own:

I do not share such a view, nor do I surrender faith in human progress. But I do find it cynical in the extreme for the Jewish people to be lectured on concern for civilian casualties by those who resorted to saturation bombing and atomic devastation, wiping out whole cities, when that terror threatened the freedom of the Western world.

For Israel, after all, the alternative to self-defence is not defeat but extermination, and the terror organizations and armies still committed to her destruction command more weapons than the Nazis ever had! . . .

The Arabs and notably the Palestinians must accept Israel as a fact of life, renouncing war and terror to obliterate the Jewish State. And the Israelis must recognize that the root of the problem lies with the Palestinians and their homelessness.

But I also mentioned my doubts and fears:

Greater than the fear that the present action in Lebanon may not achieve these objectives or that the human cost may be too high is the deep concern for the cumulative effect on the Zionist dream.

Our people did not persevere through martyrdom, nor yearn for the restoration of independence in order to boast the finest army in the world, or export ingenious weapons. . . .

The Jewish national purpose seeks its glory in the conquest of crime and vice, striving for moral excellence, and exporting renewed contributions to the brotherhood of man from the cradle of civilization. To help rid the world of the scourge of international terrorism would not be the least of these contributions, but only provided it is not the last.

As the war progressed with growing ferocity, and the hysteria against Israel increased correspondingly, the morale of Jews was severely put to the test. The following are extracts from a full-page 'Message to Anglo-Jewry' I published in the *Jewish Chronicle* on 16 July:

For British Jews, the war in Lebanon is a triple agony: the critical injury inflicted on Israel's beloved Ambassador, Shlomo Argov, as the war's first victim; the grievous loss of life on both sides as the war proceeded; and the hostility of Britain's government, media and people as the poisonous fall-out from the war. How can – how should – we react as Jews, as lovers of Zion, as British citizens? . . .

The moral, political and local defence problems raised by this war are too complex for a monolithic response. The first prerequisite for any reaction must therefore be to cultivate greater tolerance for diversity of views, preserving our solidarity with Israel and the cohesion of the community by uniting on basic essentials, while still respecting inevitable differences on attitudes.

Not everyone who blindly supports every action of Israel serves her best interests, and not everyone who criticizes her policies is a traitor. . . .

It is cold comfort for Anglo-Jewry to know that elsewhere in Europe attitudes are even more hostile than here, as I can testify from recent conversations with the Chief Rabbi of France and several other friends in some European countries.

I then turned to the subject which exercised, and exasperated, the community most:

I do not doubt that Israel is being judged and condemned by standards not applied to any other nation. But I think it is neither true nor wise to attribute this discrimination simply to anti-Semitism.

Not true – because I know any number of prominent non-Jews who have for long been strongly slanted against Israel and yet have a genuinely friendly disposition towards Jews, highly respecting them as fellow-citizens, denouncing any manifestation of anti-Semitic discrimination, staunchly supporting the cause of Soviet Jewry, and similarly identifying with Jewish concerns. And not wise – because I fear that such attribution can only tend to be self-fulfilling.

By charging people with anti-Semitism, you help to breed anti-Semitism. You give aid and comfort to the real anti-Semites and their movements, and you alienate true friends.

You also undermine Jewish confidence in the basic decency and tolerance of the society around us, and thus contribute to Jewish insecurity, whether subjective or objective. I believe that, generally, the unqualified equation of anti-Zionism with anti-Semitism holds true only in the Communist and Third Worlds.

Included among the causes I listed was a gentle hint:

The causes for the antagonism towards Israel are many and complex. Among other factors, there are vested interests in relations with Arab countries; there is a residue of Christian hesitation to come fully to terms with the restoration of Jewish sovereignty in Zion; there is the genuine sympathy with the sufferings of the Palestinian refugees; and there is estrangement caused by a certain abrasiveness not uncommon with some Israeli leaders and spokesmen, not to mention their policies.

For my part, I accept that we are being subjected to double standards. If this means that a higher morality is expected from us than from others, I take this as a compliment, nurtured through the Biblical heritage by respect for Israel's role in moral pioneering.

Above all, what must unite us all without dissent at a trying time like this is our common commitment to Judaism as well as to Israel, and our resolve to strengthen both. . . .

Having only recently been among so many Israelis in their ordeal, I had to be their emissary:

Israel needs, and is entitled to, more than enormous financial help from us. In their loneliness, they want to see us, and we should make extra efforts to plan visits there. They want to hear from us. Write or phone to your relatives or friends there. Inquire about their well-being. Tell them about the activities for Israel in your congregation. Reassure them that you share their bitterness over the distortion of the facts in our media. . . .

No less important is the strengthening of our spiritual defences, the mainstay in all our tribulation over the ages. If you really believe the Almighty is our ultimate salvation, go to the synagogue and pray harder and more frequently.

And so to the perennial call for intensified Jewish education:

Our children are not asked to defend the Jewish people by giving up the best years of their life for army service, and sometimes to make the supreme sacrifice. But surely we can demand of parents that they raise their children as creditable Jews, proud of their faith and familiar with their heritage, so that we do not face the appalling catastrophe of losing more by assimilation than by war, terror and persecution. . . .

Surely our grim predicament should unite us all in seeking to redress our distorted image not as a people of the sword, so sadly imposed on us in a cruel world, but as a people meriting Divine favour and human respect by striving to live up to the Torah injunction: 'And all the peoples of the earth shall see that the Name of the Lord is called upon you, and they shall have reverence for you.'

Whilst constantly urging my community not to allow wide differences of opinion to affect our resolute support of Israel, I was upset with Israeli ignorance of, and indifference to, the tribulations of Diaspora Jews who this time bore the brunt of world hostility more acutely than the average Israeli. The absence of any spiritual guidance in and from Israel also distressed me. Haifa's Chief Rabbi, Shear Yashuv Cohen, a good personal friend, had written to me complaining about the bitter world press campaign against Israel, and implying that Diaspora leaders ought to do more to counter this campaign by presenting the 'simple and basic facts' to the public. It was evident from his letter that, enlightened as he was and numerous as were his contacts with Jewish personalities and organizations abroad, the writer had little idea of the anguish experienced by Jews in this country as well as in Europe generally and elsewhere. I replied:

I need hardly tell you how deeply we have shared the agony of recent events with you. Indeed, we have probably felt the hostility aroused by these events even more intensely than you, and correspondingly the onus of defending Israel's honour has weighed more heavily on us.

While I appreciate the gravity of your challenge to me 'to explain the simple and basic facts of the situation' to the wider world, I am surprised by your apparent assumptions that this is 'simple' and that I have not so far done so. In fact, I have done little else these past few months, before both Jewish and non-Jewish audiences. . . .

Then I turned from defence to challenge:

Although I am surprised that you are evidently not aware of our predicament here generated by the war in Lebanon and of my reaction to it, I do not blame you but rather your press and other media for not reporting what goes on here or elsewhere in Europe (unless some anti-Israel outrage claims fatal victims). I find Israeli ignorance on Jewish concerns in the Diaspora, whether created by or in support of Israel, quite appalling. I can only construe this as part of the syndrome of disdain for the outside world, including its Jews, which is such a worrying feature of the Israeli mentality, and especially its Orthodox segment.

There is a peculiar contradiction here, not to mention the abandonment of the whole concept of *Kiddush Hashem* among the nations. On the one hand, the world is told we could not care less about your opinions or our image. And on the other hand, Jewish leaders abroad are blamed if 'simple and basic facts' are not properly understood by the world. . . .

My friend knew me well enough for me to add:

My greatest anguish in this crisis, frankly, is the bankruptcy of our own spiritual leadership, notably in Israel itself, in addressing ourselves to our own people. Blaming everything on others whilst maintaining a stance of complacent self-righteousness, we seem to have departed completely from the Prophetic tradition. Indeed, it is mainly the religious element which supports and keeps in power a

government which has set Israel and the Jewish people on the present course, leaving
it to the secularists to articulate the Jewish conscience and salvage the Jewish honour.
What a perverse reversal of our roles! . . .

Another experience further aggravated my sense of frustration with the
abdication and irrelevance of spiritual leadership in Israel in a crisis which
had, after all, profound moral ramifications. This war, like the others before
it, produced a flurry of rabbinic pronouncements and halachic writings.
Since this was the first war to be planned and started by Israel as a preventive
action, the question of its religious status as an 'obligatory' or an 'optional'
war had to be resolved, affecting many different rules in the codes of
Jewish law. In a formal ruling given by the Chief Rabbinate of Israel, and
endorsed by many other rabbis, the 'obligatory' character was affirmed
without reservation, since the campaign was designed to protect Jewish lives
potentially at risk not only from terrorist action across Israel's northern
border, but – as the vast stores of heavy weapons captured proved – possibly
from the threat of a major PLO attack endangering the whole of Israel. Long
dissertations also appeared in rabbinic journals on the Biblical status of
Southern Lebanon, on the right to start such a war on the Sabbath and other
kindred halachic issues – all of them, to my mind, ignoring the most
agonizing halachic perplexity posed by the war: its enormous toll of life,
both Jewish and non-Jewish, especially among Lebanese civilians unwit-
tingly caught in the bloody conflict.

   In an halachic discourse delivered to a London congregation of cogno-
scenti, I had examined in a purely academic exercise the principal sources
and codes of Jewish law on the limits, if any, to which innocent lives could be
sacrificed even for self-defence. I came to no definite conclusion, as different
sources seemed to indicate conflicting verdicts. I subsequently wrote this up
as a rabbinic responsum and submitted it to several rabbinic journals in
Israel for publication. But the editors – all eminent rabbis – urged me not to
publish it, as the subject was too explosive and would raise controversies
even more violent than those I had previously provoked. Evidently not only
did rabbinic scholars hesitate to provide any guidance in the light of Jewish
teachings on the legitimacy of inflicting civilian casualties on such an enormous scale, and indeed Israeli army losses by the hundreds, but they did not
even want the question raised and discussed. And this attitude was shared by
rabbis who were far from being fanatical nationalists or even avowed Zionists. I could not fathom their timidity in failing to grasp such an obvious
moral nettle which so painfully exercised Jews everywhere, not to mention
the world around them.

   By Rosh Hashanah, the Israeli forces had bombed and battled their way
into Beirut, and the first news of the Christian slaughter of Palestinians in the

refugee camps under Israeli protection was reported in the media, it seemed almost gleefully, with shattering effect. The world was enraged, focusing the blame exclusively on Israel instead of the murderers, and the Jewish mood reached an all-time low of despondency. At this stage, protests against the war had assumed massive proportions in Israel itself, with 400,000 citizens – well over 10 per cent of the total population – participating in a Tel Aviv peace demonstration. It was clearly no longer unpatriotic to question the wisdom or justice of pursuing the war beyond the twenty-five-mile limit originally announced as Israel's goal. Voices demanding a judicial enquiry into the massacre also began to be raised, though the government still firmly resisted this demand. I issued a statement, which *The Times* published in full, expressing my horror at the massacre and adding:

It is hard to believe that any Israeli authority bore responsibility for the crime, but Israel can only be completely exonerated if it is openly shown that its personnel took every possible step to prevent the carnage.

As Jews so deeply committed to the sanctity of life, our anguish is not lessened by the memory that the slaughter of nearly 100,000 Christians and Muslims in the Lebanese civil war, triggered by the incursion of the PLO, failed to evoke comparable world condemnation and reaction.

I ended with a veiled reference to the new Reagan Middle East peace initiative:

Sadly, in pursuing the war to Beirut, it is apparent that the Israeli objectives to stabilize the region and enhance the prospects of peace have not been achieved, especially after the assassination of Bashir Gemayel. Jews continue to be determined in their commitment to Israel and its security, and I profoundly hope they will support all efforts legitimately and genuinely undertaken to achieve those ends, wherever they are initiated.

On the day this was published, President Navon himself boldly called for a judicial enquiry. Eventually, Israel's government grudgingly agreed under the enormous pressure for such a vindication of justice by Jews inside and outside Israel, let alone by world opinion. But this decision came only after Yom Kippur, when it helped immensely to restore respect for Israel as well as to uplift Jewish morale. Meanwhile, the despair within the community was exemplified by the following cable I received, as did some other friends, from a respected communal leader, always a staunch supporter of Israel and its fund-raising campaign:

WE CAN NO LONGER BE APATHETIC AND SILENT WHILST BEGIN'S POLICIES ARE DES-
TROYING ISRAEL AND ENDANGERING FUTURE OF ENTIRE JEWISH PEOPLE. ARGUMENT THAT
EXPRESSION OF OPPOSITION STRENGTHENS OUR ENEMIES NO LONGER APPLIES AS ISRAELI

ELECTORATE OPENLY SPLIT. ISRAEL HAS BECOME AN OCCUPYING POWER. ISRAELI LIVES
LOST DAILY. WE CANNOT WIN BEIRUT SITUATION. WE CANNOT OCCUPY LEBANON FOR EVER.
WE HAVE NO COMPREHENSIBLE POLICY. AMERICA'S GROWING HOSTILITY THREATENS
REMOVE ISRAEL'S ULTIMATE GUARANTEE SECURITY. MORAL, POLITICAL AND ECONOMIC
CONSEQUENCES ARE HORRENDOUS. . . . IF WE DO NOT SPEAK UP NOW TO EXPRESS OUR
VIEWS WE WILL CONDEMN ISRAEL TO A THIRD DESTRUCTION.

My greatest immediate challenge, then, was how to guide my colleagues
in relating to these events when the synagogues were at their fullest and
congregants would thirst for a message both relevant to their uppermost
concerns and in the spirit of the Days of Awe. No one was more agitated
than the organizers of the annual JIA Kol Nidre Appeal, and they relied on
me, as its chief sponsor, to prevent its feared collapse under the weight of
such widespread disenchantment. They pleaded for the community to be
rallied by the rabbis traditionally making the appeal in our synagogues. I had
already urged unstinting support for Israel at the pre-Yamim Noraim conference of ministers which usually 'launched' the Kol Nidre Appeal; but as
the public mood became grimmer with the subsequent massacre and the
debate on setting up an enquiry commission, the alarmed JIA leaders wanted
me to send out a further message for the guidance of ministers, which I had
in any case planned to circulate before Yom Kippur. This 'Letter to my
Colleagues', as many told me later, helped them considerably and, defying
all expectations, the Appeal proved more successful than ever before. The
letter stated:

This year we are clearly facing a greater difficulty – and more awesome challenge –
in addressing our congregants on Yom Kippur than ever before. In their travail and
perplexity, they look to us for guidance, comfort and reassurance to sustain their
faith. But they also have a right to expect from us a profoundly spiritual message –
suffused by the inspiration of our religious teachings and providing a wider vision to
understand our current predicament than they can find through their own efforts in
reading the daily newspapers or even the pronouncements of our own political and
communal spokesmen. . . .

I cannot and would not tell you what to say. I am myself woefully short of answers
and inspiration, and seek Divine guidance as much as you do. But I know that the
responsibility resting on spiritual leaders at a time like this is enormous, perhaps even
greater than on those in charge of our people's and our communities' more mundane
concerns.

And so I simply want to share with you some thoughts evoked in my mind and
conscience by our present tribulations, hoping that these shared thoughts may prove
of some help to you.

I started with a principle which invariably guided my own use of the pulpit:

First and foremost, we have to remember that in the pulpit, especially on Yom Kippur, we address ourselves solely to our own people, not to our enemies, detractors or critics. This is neither the time nor the place to deal with and denounce the injustices of others or to affirm our own righteousness. If after the sermon worshippers will say, 'That was exactly what I am thinking', then it need not have been delivered; for they knew its message before it was given.

Without pretending to be news commentators or political analysts, we must obviously address ourselves to the agonizing problems confronting Israel and world Jewry, so long as we speak in terms and thoughts which could not just as well be used by any layman. Points which require urgent emphasis, both in the Kol Nidre Appeal and the sermons, include:

Whatever reservations some or many may have on Israeli policies and actions cannot and must not affect our unshakeable support for Israel and its people – our people. On the contrary, such reservations make it all the more vital to demonstrate to ourselves, to Israel and to the world that we are absolutely united in our stand by Israel and our determination to support its people and institutions, especially at this time of enormous need to maintain Israel's essential social and educational services under the crushing burden of the war and its damage to the economy.

To withhold this support on the grounds of disagreement with the Israel government's policies is to punish a brother by starving him. Moreover, such destruction of Jewish solidarity with the people of Israel is a betrayal of our faith. This year, more than ever before, abstentions amount to, and will be interpreted as, a vote of no confidence in the future of Israel and the basic unity of the Jewish people.

With opinions among ministers themselves being sharply divided, I knew the following plea had little chance of success with them all, but I made it nevertheless:

Divisions of opinion on Israel's policies must now be accepted as an inescapable fact of life. There can be no monolithic response to the perplexities facing us, particularly when they involve such profound issues of conscience. No attempt should therefore be made to impose our personal views on those who disagree with us, least of all from the pulpit. This can only accentuate divisiveness and bitterness among ourselves. Rather should we strongly encourage tolerance and mutual understanding transcending our differences.

The judicial enquiry commission on the massacres had not yet been set up, of course:

On the trauma of the Lebanese massacres and their catastrophic aftermath, we should tread with the utmost caution along the narrow path between the banalities of generalities in expressing our horror and the specifics of judgement, whether exoneration or culpability. Rather should we plead for collective remorse and atonement for any part, however indirect or unintended, fellow-Jews *may* have had in this horrendous pogrom, and for the *Chillul Hashem* caused by the dishonour done to the Jewish name. These consequences are indisputable. They call for humility as a first step in the long haul to regaining Jewish self-confidence and respect among the nations.

On the other hand, the danger of fuelling anti-Jewish feelings is as great as generating a spirit of despondency and lack of faith among ourselves. As in tending to the sick we visit, we must promote confidence in our national recovery, certain that wisdom and justice will eventually heal the wounds of the past and assure Divine protection for Israel's cause and safety. In one form or another, we must proclaim 'Zion will be redeemed through justice' even more than through the might of armies and the location of borders.

If there is any long-term lesson to be learned from the events culminating in the Beirut tragedy, it is that 'Not by might nor by power but by My spirit', teaching the futility of might alone, is a pragmatic truism for the Jewish people no less than a religious and moral imperative. . . .

My correspondence file again became very bulky, both on the Lebanon war generally and on the public statements I had made. This time, the numerous unsolicited letters from leaders and members of the community were overwhelmingly supportive, mostly simply congratulating me on my articles, interviews or other public addresses. I again replied to each communication. My post-bag from non-Jews, also considerable, was far more diverse. Some letters, several written anonymously, simply spewed hatred against Israel and Jews. Of the professional Arabists, Mr John Reddaway, formerly of the Foreign Office, founder and leading member of CAABU (the British pro-Arab lobby), engaged me in protracted correspondence following my *Times* article in July. He sought to dispute my contention that the casualty and refugee figures had been wildly exaggerated, but his venom lessened as the exchange of letters proceeded. However, there were also very heartening letters. For instance, Canon Paul Oestreicher, Secretary of the British Council of Churches which could at times be far from friendly, wrote to me on 21 September:

> May I in these brief words express to you my deep sympathy at the agony of the last months, but especially in the last few days. Spiritually it has been a great testing-time for Jews everywhere. May I assure you of my prayers and good wishes.

Another much-appreciated personal letter came from Canon Douglas Webster, Chairman of the Executive of the Council of Christians and Jews. It was dated 'Yom Kippur – 27 September':

> On this of all days I feel I must write to you, for you have been so much in my thoughts and prayers during the last few weeks of anguish. I think I realize a little how much suffering this must have brought to you and I greatly long for a time of

happiness, peace and reconciliation. Your own wise and steadying words have been an enormous help and must have brought relief to many as well as comfort. . . .

As the war dragged on to an uneasy and still costly stalemate, nerves gradually steadied and near-normality of Jewish life was restored, punctuated only when the Kahan Commission's Report on the Judicial Enquiry, with its severe censure of leading political and military figures, was finally published – on 8 February, my birthday, forcing me to abandon a television breakfast programme in my honour for which I had already been all-set at the studio. I greeted the report as 'a moral triumph without parallel in the history of justice'.

Although I would not usually take sides in political controversies inside Israel, least of all by writing to the protagonists themselves, I believed the moral stakes involved in the Judicial Enquiry debate were such that together with Mr George Gee, President of the United Synagogue, I had cabled President Navon our acclaim and support for his courageous stand in demanding the enquiry. I had also written to Mr Yitzchak Berman, the veteran Liberal leader, commending him on his resignation from the Cabinet in protest against its refusal at the time to set up such an enquiry. I enclosed a copy of my Yom Kippur 'Letter to my Colleagues'. He replied on 8 November:

It was very kind of you to have written to me about my resignation. Your gracious comments on this subject are most encouraging.

The original decision of the Cabinet refusing to request the President of the Supreme Court to appoint a Commission of Enquiry . . . was, of course, a colossal mistake. . . .

I was in Europe recently and had occasion to come across most disturbing tendencies in the public opinion regarding Israel which are shared, as you point out in your letter, by a considerable section of the Jewish community.

One can only hope that, with the passing of time, this wave of anti-Israel and anti-Jewish feelings will gradually subside – to some extent at least.

I read with great interest your warm and brilliant circular letter to the rabbis.

Official Orthodox opinion, for the most part, once again did not share my views on the enquiry and its report – or indeed on my definition of *Kiddush Hashem*. On 20 September, Mr Julius Berman, the Orthodox Chairman of the Conference of Presidents of Major American Jewish Organizations, issued a public statement supporting the Israel government's refusal to have a judicial enquiry and declaring: 'We reject the idea of any participation or involvement by the Israeli Defence Forces in this terrible event. . . . Any suggestion that Israel took part in it or permitted it to occur must be categorically rejected.' By 28 September, when the Commission was set up, a new statement said: 'In Israel, Prime Minister Begin has now called for a full-fledged investigation and examination of the catastrophe in the camps. We welcome that call. And we are confident that the investigation will probe deeply and that justice will be done.' As I wrote early in October to my brother-in-law, Rabbi Fabian Schonfeld of New York, a former President of the Rabbinical Council of America, whose staunch support of Mr Begin and Gush Emunim never interfered with our relationship and mutual understanding:

> I am bemused by the erratic course of 'American Jewry's' reactions. A couple of weeks ago, Julius Berman issued a statement 'rejecting any idea of Israeli involvement' and supporting the government's stand against any investigation. Last night I heard him on Kol Yisrael warmly endorsing the setting up of the judicial enquiry! With such leadership of the world's largest Jewish community. . . .

Other Orthodox leaders were less 'warm'. Although Mizrachi Cabinet ministers had eventually pressed their colleagues for an enquiry, the Aguda coalition partners, who were of course outside the government though they kept it in power, not only opposed the setting up of the enquiry but rejected its findings when they were announced, regarding the whole exercise as a disservice to the Jewish people whose good name was impugned because of the indirect responsibility attributed to Israel's leaders. I was flabbergasted by this betrayal of the Jewish commitment to justice. I was also deeply disturbed by the unseemly manner in which they traded their continued political support for the coalition, irrespective of its policies, for financial and legislative favours. I later pursued this, personally and in correspondence, with leaders of the Aguda in Israel and in America, urging them to weigh the short-term gains against the likely immense damage to wider Orthodox interests by further alienating less religious Jews in Israel and throughout the world from traditional Jewish values and their adherents. In their replies they indicated that the more moderate elements of the Aguda, such as the leading Yeshiva Dean Rabbi Eliezer Shach who had denounced the war in the Lebanon from the beginning, were unable to resist the enormous pressures exerted by the more hard-line leaders, notably the Gerer Rebbe, in what had become a fierce internal conflict.

Meanwhile, the Lebanese venture was turning into more and more of a nightmare. Each of Israel's principal war aims collapsed as casualties continued to mount. The PLO had not been eliminated, Lebanon had not been united as the second Arab State to sign a peace treaty with Israel, and attention had not been diverted from the Palestinian problem which festered on the West Bank with increasing unrest and violence.

During the controversies in which I had been involved, I had often said I wished my fears would prove wrong and my critics be proven right. I, too, would have liked Israeli victories to be final, Jewish rule over the entire Biblical Land to be peacefully accepted, and a show of strength to deter any future threats of war and terror, so that Israel could live in quietude and concentrate on building a model society of spiritual excellence and social justice. Alas, the fears remained more realistic than the hopes, and I had yet to find reasons for changing my basic attitudes to Zionist policies which I began to form on my first visit to the Land of Israel thirty-six years earlier – my abhorrence of violence and scepticism of the sole reliance on might as a solution to our problems, my concern not to underrate the Palestinian Arabs nor to ignore their aspirations, and above all my conviction that the Jewish return to Zion and its consolidation are contingent on the national return to Jewish aspirations and values. Their relevance to Zionism will engage us in the second part of this book.

Before concluding the narrative section of this book with a chapter on some experiences with the Churches on Zionism, I must here refer to a further instance of Israeli attitudes to wider Jewish interests when these do not directly affect Israel itself. I have already recounted how the fiercest of all the public controversies I encountered began with an invitation I extended to Israeli correspondents in London in order to urge them to give greater coverage to Anglo-Jewish affairs on which Israelis were so abysmally ignorant (as they were on Jewish life in the Diaspora generally). These journalists, as I related, did not overly care about my concerns, and instead needled me on Israeli affairs until they drew blood. During the Lebanon war, this attitude of relative indifference became even more pronounced. I mentioned this very plainly in the letter addressed to my colleague in Haifa quoted on p 109. Not long after another quite unrelated episode in which I became involved dramatically demonstrated the same phenomenon to me.

In April 1983, in what looked like the biggest scoop of the century, the German *Stern* magazine announced that, after years of painstaking detective and research work, it had authenticated the discovery of the 'Hitler Diaries', salvaged from some plane wreck towards the end of the war. The hoard contained several volumes of 'original' entries covering over three decades. In Britain, serialization rights had been bought by the London *Times* and *Sunday Times*, following the definite verification of the find's authenticity by no less an expert than Lord Dacre who, as Hugh Trevor-Roper, was the leading historian of the period, and who published an article explaining and confirming his absolute certainty that the claim was true. Extracts from these 'diaries' were soon to be serialized in these newspapers, followed by the rest of the world's press and media which anticipated the impending revelations with bated breath.

I viewed with the utmost alarm and horror the prospect of worldwide saturation publicity being given, for weeks on end, to some doctored version of Nazi propaganda. When the announcement was made, it sounded to me ominously reminiscent of the 'discovery' and publication of *The Protocols of the Elders of Zion*, and the damage likely to be done in providing grist to the mills of anti-Semitism could well exceed the still-festering poison planted by the infamous forgery spread all over the world some sixty years earlier. From the hints already given to the press, I had little doubt that this was a gigantic hoax, a multi-million-pound Nazi conspiracy to launder the Hitler record and thereby to rehabilitate Nazism and all the evils it stood for. Richard Verrall's *Did Six Million Really Die?*, denying that the Holocaust ever took place, looked puny to me by comparison to a propaganda on-slaught which would fill the press of the whole world in the weeks and months to come.

Haunted by this prospect, and still unable to prove my assumption that the 'diaries' were a forgery (before Lord Dacre himself threw doubt on and finally recanted his preposterous authentication), I felt that Jewish and indeed wider moral interests demanded that the dissemination of this mass poison be suppressed even if it were genuine, as was then widely assumed. My fears and suspicions prompted me to submit the following letter, which *The Times* published on 26 April under the heading 'Hitler Diaries: Resurrection of Evil?':

Not as a religious leader, but as a human being – victim and survivor of history's most monstrous tyranny – I protest vehemently against the publication of the so-called Hitler diaries. Whether they are authentic or not is quite immaterial to the outrage of resurrecting the incarnation of evil and his propaganda, rehabilitating him for a generation which knew not this master-gangster. His crime was against the whole of mankind, and against so many in this country who made the supreme sacrifice fighting in the cause of freedom and justice. Publicizing his case is an unpardonable threat to our most elementary moral values.

From the hints already published it is clear that the diaries, even if they are genuine, are calculated to whitewash the blackest chapter in the annals of man. The involvement in the Hess mission, the feigned contempt for his henchmen, the admiration for Chamberlain, the implied attempt to save the British at Dunkirk and above all the 'pains to distance himself' from the mass-extermination of the Jews which he ordered – all this must distort the gruesome record of history.

Hailing this find 'as the biggest literary discovery since the Dead Sea Scrolls' is a sacrilege which only compounds the insult to the millions who perished and suffered under this tyranny. That such a brutal dictator, who was convinced that his Reich would last for a thousand years, should care to rewrite his history as 'a testimony to posterity' seems implausible and preposterous.

It would be the cruellest irony if mercenary exploitation were to afford more tangibility to Hitler's principal murder weapon – his brainwashing propaganda – than to the obliterated human remains of his death factories.

In the name of decency, morality and truth, I call upon men of good will everywhere to prevent this proposed affront to the past and depraving threat to the future.

The letter attracted a blaze of publicity on the day of publication and for days after, including several television and radio interviews, some beamed across the oceans. The pros and cons of my stand against 'the freedom of the press' were widely debated. The argument abated only as the evidence of a forgery mounted, to be eventually admitted by the principal culprits. It was only more than a year later that 'counter-investigative journalism' finally revealed that there had indeed been a Nazi conspiracy with enormous financial resources responsible for this colossal hoax.

All this apparently has little to do with the relations between Israel and world Jewry, the context in which I mention this episode. But however marginal, there was a link, and it disturbed me deeply. Given the millions invested in the hoax, and the many millions more to be made out of it, one could perhaps understand the gullibility of the press and its sensation-hungry readers in so uncritically swallowing the scoop – hook, line and sinker. Suspecting the involvement of 'reputable' people not publicly known as Nazi sympathizers, one could perhaps also understand, though never condone, the reluctance of the governments concerned to investigate the political motives behind this conspiracy and to prosecute those implicated on the gravest charges of conspiring by fraud to promote the revival of Nazism.

But how does one explain the apparent indifference of Israel to the menace of an infinitely more publicized version of *The Protocols of the Elders of Zion*, as the diaries threatened to become at the time? The fall-out from such a propaganda pollution could have infected the atmosphere for Jews everywhere, and possibly, like radiation, only showing its lethal effects over the years – except, of course, in Israel where Jews would have been immune. The still-lurking assumption that anti-Semitism is good for Israel because it promotes Aliyah is as untenable as the illusion that Zionism is the antidote to anti-Semitism. Both propositions, I believe, are historically untrue, morally indefensible, and politically dangerous.

# 10

# The Pope and the Churches – Pleas for Understanding

My encounters with Christian religious leaders bearing on Israel began, as already related, early during my Irish sojourn with the challenge of Dublin's Archbishop over the Holy Places. These encounters culminated in my meeting with Pope John Paul II on 31 May 1982 in Manchester during his historic visit to Britain. I had never met a pope before, and indeed had declined occasional suggestions to join any of the various Jewish delegations on their increasingly frequent pilgrimages to Rome following the thaw in Jewish–Catholic relations under John XXIII.

This time the organizers of the visit had invited representatives of the Jewish community to greet the Pope, and I was to lead the delegation. As his stay in London coincided with the Shavuot festival, I explained that we had an engagement already fixed some 3,500 years earlier, and so the venue was moved to Manchester, after considerable difficulties in accommodating us in an already heavily overcrowded programme had been overcome. Nevertheless, the ten minutes allocated to us eventually extended to over twenty, largely because I took rather longer to read my address to him than the organizers had anticipated. He greeted us cordially with 'Shalom', and in my prepared statement, later published in full in *The Times*, I told him, *inter alia*:

The visit's ecumenical aspirations, while primarily of inter-Christian concern, are of course of profound interest to Jews as well, all the more so since the Papacy had often been a cause of conflict and suffering in the long history of the Jewish people. Happily, past tragic relations have lately been reversed, notably by the enlightened policies of Catholic–Jewish reconciliation pioneered by Pope John XXIII; a momentous turning-point to which the late Cardinal Heenan gave such powerful momentum.

As Pope John Paul II, you have maintained and further promoted this inter-faith understanding. Yourself hailing from a country in which you witnessed and shared the supreme agony of the Nazi Holocaust, including the massacre of three million Polish Jews, your election aroused special interest among the Jewish people. Also of particular relevance to Jews are the as yet unpredictable consequences of the religious stirrings within the Communist world, sparked by the Catholic revival in Poland under your spell. These consequences may well eventually alleviate the plight of some two or three million Soviet Jews among other repressed religious communities in the USSR and her satellites. . . .

Whilst enormous strides have been made in advancing Jewish–Christian harmony, some items on our common agenda still remain to be resolved. They include the elimination of the last vestiges of religious prejudices against Jews and some residual Christian hesitations in accepting the State of Israel as the fulfilment of millennial Jewish dreams. We seek understanding for our love of Jerusalem – a city holy to three faiths because Jews first sanctified it as their capital three thousand years ago. . . .

The Pope seemed somewhat taken aback by my having gone beyond formal greetings to some matters of substance. He acknowledged my remarks, saying that he could not then answer the 'arguments' I had presented, before proceeding to read his warm message of greetings to me, our delegation and our community.

In my address, I had two – unfortunately somewhat conflicting – objectives in mind. I wished to preserve the happy state of Jewish–Christian relations in Britain, whilst at the same time seeking understanding for our utmost concern for Israel and Jerusalem, hopefully helping to bring these on to the Catholic–Jewish agenda.

Israel had always been the one subject to which I found it difficult to extend my very close personal relations with British Church leaders. Since I had assumed office in 1967, I had enjoyed the friendship of each of the three Archbishops of Canterbury and two Cardinal Archbishops of Westminster, as well as, in particular that of Dr Stuart Blanch, the Archbishop of York who retired in 1983. We visited each other in our homes, and we consulted together on moral issues facing the nation or scheduled for parliamentary legislation. No help I requested on Jewish concerns – whether anti-Semitism or Soviet Jewry – was ever refused. The bonds between us were such that, when Cardinal Heenan died, *The Times* mentioned our friendship in its obituary. Perhaps British Jews were more fortunate than many others, living in a country where tolerance and respect for tradition were still deeply rooted virtues. The relationship was also significantly advanced by the Council of Christians and Jews. Founded by Archbishop Temple and Chief Rabbi Hertz during the war to fight anti-Semitism, it has been active ever since under the joint presidency of the Chief Rabbi as well as of the heads of the Anglican, Catholic, Scottish and Free Churches, with the Queen as its patron – an instrument of Jewish–Christian amity at a higher level than anywhere else. But Israel never featured on its agenda, though I often used its annual meetings, when the five presidents usually sat together on the platform, to plead its cause.

Soon after the Pope's visit to Britain, he met PLO-leader Yasser Arafat in Rome – to the consternation of Jews everywhere, and indeed of many Catholics, too. Prior to the meeting, I cabled him:

IN SPIRIT OF OUR MANCHESTER MEETING I EARNESTLY PLEAD RECONSIDER ARAFAT RECEPTION STOP UNTIL PLO COVENANT CHANGED TO EXCLUDE AVOWAL OF ARMED STRUGGLE AND DESTRUCTION OF JEWISH STATE SUCH RECEPTION IS LIABLE TO CAUSE GRAVE DAMAGE TO MIDDLE EAST PEACE PROSPECTS AND TO JEWISH–CHRISTIAN RELATIONS AS WELL AS ENCOURAGE INTERNATIONAL TERRORISM STOP I RESPECTFULLY INVOKE THE INJUNCTION AND BLESSING OF PSALM 122 VERSES 6 TO 9

Several weeks later, I received a lengthy letter from Cardinal Willebrands, the President of the Commission of Religious Relations at the Vatican, explaining that the Pope 'is prepared to receive all ... who ask for it ...'; that this 'is in no way a sign of approval of all the ideas and actions attributed to that person'; and that he had expressed his opposition to terrorism and his hope for a peaceful solution which 'should involve the recognition of the rights of all peoples, particularly those of the Palestinian people for a homeland of its own and of Israel for its own security'. These words meant 'to affirm that the recognition of Israel by the Arabs is a basic condition for the construction of peace'. The letter also stated 'that the attitude of the Holy See towards the Jewish people and its strong opposal to all forms of anti-Semitism have in no way been changed by this audience'.

I had meanwhile attended the meeting of the Standing Committee of the Conference of European Rabbis on 1 November in Paris, and, reinforced by the declaration we issued there, I replied to Cardinal Willebrands:

... I delayed reacting to [your letter] pending an opportunity to consult with some of my leading colleagues in Europe on what is now clearly a major setback to the progress in Jewish–Christian relations initiated with such high hopes and substantial success at Vatican Council II.

The opportunity for such consultations presented itself on 1 November at a meeting of the Standing Committee of the Conference of European Rabbis. This Committee comprises Europe's Chief Rabbis and other leading rabbis. From this meeting emerged a Declaration in which we stated, *inter alia*:

To Church leaders we urge that the great advance made towards Jewish–Christian understanding should not be compromised or reversed; hence we seek the elimination of the residual Christian hesitations in accepting the State of Israel as the fulfilment of millennial Jewish dreams; and the recognition of the special bond of

Jews with Jerusalem as a city holy to three faiths because it was first sanctified by Jews as their capital 3,000 years ago. While still under the shock of the meeting between the Pope and Arafat, we appeal in particular to the Vatican to update its historic Guidelines on Jews by similar guidelines on Israel and Zionism, bearing in mind that anti-Zionism is now the principal ferment of anti-Semitism, and that the Vatican cannot promote peace in the Middle East – based as it must be on the mutual recognition of all states in the region – so long as the Vatican itself withholds recognition from the Jewish State.

We earnestly hope that these collective sentiments of the Spiritual Leaders of Europe's Jewish communities will receive due consideration, thus contributing both to the advancement of harmony between Jews and Christians and to the promotion of peace in the Middle East. The friendly reception the Pope accorded to me in Manchester, as indeed to other Jewish delegations elsewhere, encourages my confidence that all causes for friction between our two great faiths will be progressively removed in order to secure the stability of the civilization nurtured by our religious traditions.

Later, participating in the 'International Hearing on Anti-Semitism' held in Oslo in June 1983, I was to refer more fully to the role of the Churches in the rising tide of anti-Jewish prejudice generated by the war in Lebanon:

The Christian role [in contrast to the anti-Zionist agitation emanating from the Soviet and Arab countries] is less specific and more intangible. Despite enormous strides in Jewish–Christian relations, pioneered by the enlightened policies of Pope John xxiii and the subsequent Guidelines of Vatican ii (no doubt partly as indirect after-effects of the Holocaust), the improvement of these relations has always stopped short of coming fully to terms with the restoration of Jewish Statehood. As Israel is now central to Jewish life and aspirations, it is inevitably the key to attitudes towards Jews in general.

Presumably for theological reasons more than any other, the Vatican is joined only by Islamic countries in having withheld formal recognition of the State of Israel from the beginning, and by Communist and Third World countries which withdrew this recognition after the Six Day War. The World Council of Churches has likewise been distinctly unfriendly towards Israel with almost unvaried consistency over the past three-and-a-half decades.

As Israel progressively loomed larger in Jewish as well as world affairs, this unfriendliness was bound to spill over into Jewish–Christian relations generally. Due to the largely negative attitude of the Churches towards Zionism, these relations are now more strained than they were two or three decades ago. The Guidelines on relations with Jews urgently await similar guidelines to revise relations with Israel and Zionism, if the forward thrust in Jewish–Christian understanding is to be maintained and not reversed.

I expanded on the theme in the course of my Lambeth Interfaith Lecture, which I delivered at Lambeth Palace on 25 October 1983 under the chairmanship of the Archbishop of Canterbury. Dealing with unfinished business on the agenda of Jewish–Christian dialogues, I said:

Pride of place on the Jewish side would doubtless be accorded to the rising centrality of Israel in Jewish life, and the ramifications of this fact in Jewish–Christian relations. Basic to the ground-rules governing any interfaith parleys must be the right of self-definition by each partner.... In the self-definition of Judaism a major impact is bound to be made by the restoration of Jewish sovereignty in response to Jewish religious visions and prayers over nineteen centuries of national homelessness, as inspired by the Jewish reading of the Hebrew Prophets and their promise. Corresponding to the emergence of Zionism, and the concern for Israel's security, as a principal dynamic of Jewish self-expression, is the equal and opposite shift from anti-Semitism to anti-Zionism as the principal expression of anti-Jewish prejudice. Any re-definition of Church attitudes to the Jewish people which leaves this fundamental change out of account is therefore dated and incomplete.

It seemed relevant here to relate our internal religious divisions to the concept of peoplehood which made Judaism so distinct from Christianity:

I am often asked whether and how our internal divisions between traditional and progressive Jews, or between Orthodox and Reform Judaism, compare with the denominational factions within Christianity. The answer is, there is no comparison. And in this answer lies the key to understanding Judaism.

Theologically and doctrinally, our divisions are much more far-reaching and fundamental than the corresponding differences between various Christian denominations. We differ on matters affecting the very foundations of Judaism, on what we define as our most cardinal principles of faith, such as the Divine authenticity of the Written and Oral Laws, the binding character of Biblical and Talmudic legislation, and the role of this law in private and public Jewish life. All this obviously touches the very heart of Judaism.

Yet, these divisions, profound as they are, did not lead to schisms even remotely comparable to the denominational divides within Christianity. For transcending our theological divisions are the cohesive factors uniting us as one people, with a common history, with a common fate and a common destiny, expressed in a commitment of corporate responsibility in which all Jews, irrespective of their beliefs or heresies, look upon this common peoplehood as a supreme expression of their Jewishness. Jewish peoplehood is itself an integral and indispensable part of Jewish religious identity, and any rapport with Judaism and the Jewish people must appreciate this unique combination of religion and peoplehood. Hence the crucial importance of Zionism and Israel in this rapport, and hence the large grey area on Jewish–Christian understanding in this respect which still calls for definition on the Christian side, unencumbered by any political calculations.

It was perhaps idle to expect 2,000 years of antagonism and prejudice, based in essence on conflicting definitions of post-Biblical 'Israel', to be suddenly removed by Israel's re-emergence as the modern Jewish State. But it is to this reconciliation that Jewish as well as Christian efforts must be directed if Israel's place among the nations, certainly in the Western world, is to be consolidated.

# Part Two:

# Zionism in Thought

# 11

# Religious Zionism –
# Conditional Covenant

Years before the State of Israel was established in 1948, when Jews were so exasperated with Britain's White Paper restrictions on immigration and the British resistance to Jewish statehood generally, it was said that there was only one thing wrong with the Balfour Declaration: the full-stop had been put in the wrong place. It reads: 'His Majesty's Government views with favour the establishment in Palestine of a national home for the Jewish people . . . it being clearly understood that nothing shall be done which may prejudice the . . . rights of the existing non-Jewish communities, etc.' It was made to read: '. . . it being clearly understood that nothing shall be done.' Full-stop. I once commented in a sermon at the time that this misplacement of the full-stop merely reflected our own misplacement of a full-stop in our demand for the Land. In seeking our independence, we had constantly echoed the cry of Moses before Pharaoh at the beginning of our history: 'Let My people go.' Full-stop. By placing the full-stop there instead of completing what Moses actually pleaded, 'so that they shall serve Me', we had distorted the quotation and missed the whole object of our demand for independence. Small wonder that the nations in their response likewise stopped short of completing their part in securing our freedom.

A similar misplacement of a full-stop had already occurred in the nineteenth century, when the early movement of pioneer settlers, forerunners of modern Zionism, called themselves BILU, made up of the Hebrew initials of the verse from Isaiah which means: 'O House of Jacob, go and let us go.' Full-stop. This, too, was a perversion of Isaiah's call, for it omitted the climax of the verse: 'in the light of the Lord.'

For me, Zionism is as unthinkable and as meaningless without Judaism as without Jews. If Zionism were to become just a Jewish national liberation movement, seeking a state for Jews like any other, it would destroy rather than fulfil the uniqueness of the Jewish people, robbing us of our claim to eternal existence and making us subject to the whims of history like all other nations which come and go, some in the fullness of time and others long before. As a mere liberation movement, with its territorial title-deeds buried deep in antiquity, Zionism might provide little more justification for Jewish independence in Zion than the Red Indian claim to sovereignty in America or that of the Romans in England.

Of course, the modern State of Israel is the cumulative product of the dreams, prayers, visions and labours of all sections of the Jewish people throughout the ages. I even acknowledge that in the more recent past secular Jews must claim pride of place over the religious community in their efforts to regain and rebuild the Land. But their Zionism could never have gathered the momentum needed for its realization without the combination of numerous forces within which the religious elements were and remain absolutely indispensable and indeed paramount.

In my address at the twenty-fifth Israel Independence Day Service in London on 6 May 1973, which I entitled 'From Tears to Joy', I summed up the diversity of Israel's mainsprings thus:

The reborn Jewish State is like a tree, deriving its nourishment from a mighty network of roots embedded in every layer of past Jewish experience. These roots stretch back to the Torah, which provided the original Divine mandate for the Jewish title to the Land and its sanctification, and which records the summons of Aliyah to the Land as the first commandment given to the first Jew. These roots extend to the Hebrew Prophets, who constantly affirmed the Divine promise of the Jewish people's eventual return to Zion following their dispersion among the nations. They spring from the Talmudic era which, having guided the transformation of our people from a life of national independence to an exilic existence, instilled the faith in our return to Zion and the rebuilding of Jerusalem in every daily prayer; in every Grace-after-Meals; in every greeting, whether of joy when founding a Jewish home or of sorrow when comforting mourners. These roots reach out to the Golden Age of the Spanish period, which sublimated the love of Zion in the passionate poetry of Yehuda Halevi and the arduous Aliyah to the Holy Land of Nachmanides and others; and to the mystic school of Luria and Karo, which flourished in Safed in the sixteenth century as a direct forerunner of the modern Yishuv.

Following these roots closer to our own time, I continued:

The more immediate antecedents of the Zionist movement and its evolution to the present day have likewise drawn their inspiration from the interplay and partnership of virtually every strand in the fabric of Jewish thought and ideology within the past century and a half. In the ever-growing momentum of the Zionist idea, there were fused together the religious fervour of spiritual pioneers like Rabbis Zvi Hirsch

Kalischer and Judah Alkalai, in the second quarter of the nineteenth century, with the secular nationalism of social revolutionaries and humanists like Moses Hess and Leon Pinsker, in the second half of that century. Among the vital forces that had produced the Jewish State are blended the rudimentary Zionism of Nathan Birnbaum, who coined the word 'Zionism' in 1890; the political Zionism of Theodor Herzl, who created the Zionist Organization in 1897; the cultural Zionism of Achad Ha'am, who fixed his gaze upon Zion as our spiritual centre; and the fusion of these trends called 'synthetic Zionism' by Chaim Weizmann whose sagacious leadership traversed the forty-year wilderness from the post-Herzl period to the presidency of the new-born State of Israel.

Transcending political and religious differences, I further added:

Towards the triumphant consummation of the Zionist ideal laboured militants like Nordau and Jabotinsky, as well as pacifists like Magnus and Buber, aristocrats like Brandeis and Herbert Samuel, as well as socialists like Ben-Gurion and Golda Meir; Orthodox rabbinical sages like Rabbis Kook and Maimon as well as Reform leaders like Stephen Wise and Abba Hillel Silver. Zion truly proved 'a city joining us all together', the cause through which Jews of every generation, of every persuasion and of every motivation, were drawn together in a common hope and a common triumph.

Zionism is, then, the common achievement, the common possession and the common pride of all Jews. Already Herzl declared at the First Zionist Congress in 1897 that 'Zionism is the return of the Jews to Judaism, before their return to the Jewish land', though he was as unfamiliar with Judaism as with Uganda which was equally acceptable to him, even if he never regarded Judaism as a mere '*Nachtasyl*'. Other secular Zionists also paid at least lip-service to the religious ethos which would have to suffuse the Jewish State, although in practice they, too, were either aliens or antagonists to the Jewish religious heritage. Somehow, their rebellion against any practical Jewish observance notwithstanding, they instinctively felt that the tree of the Zionist State could not endure and flourish if cut off from its religious roots. The religious party, sometimes parties, therefore served in every government of Israel since its inception; they were not only tolerated but welcome, despite the great majority of secularists among Israel's citizens and political leaders.

Within the religious community, which had made up the great bulk of world Jewry until the Holocaust wiped out its heartland, there have been, and continue to be, two diametrically opposed responses to the idea of Jewish statehood (examined in more detail in the study included at the end of this book). There are first the religious Zionists, who wholeheartedly subscribe to Jewish nationalism. Some of them indeed now spearhead its militant wing as well. They see in the Jewish return to Zion 'the beginning of the sprouting forth of the Redemption', as promised by our Prophets, yearned for in our prayers, and demanded by the religious imperatives of Jewish living. They see the Divine Hand of Providence unmistakably in the wondrous events before, during and since the establishment of Israel. Yom Ha'atzmaut is a religious festival for them, but for them alone. It is shared neither by the secularists, for whom the festival is not religious, nor by the religious non-Zionists, for whom the day is not a festival.

This second group of religious non-Zionists mainly comprises the fast-growing fortresses of Chasidism and the 'yeshiva-world', the B'nei Akivah yeshivot excepted. Together, these two elements now constitute the majority of strictly observant Jews, if one includes all who identify with them and their ideology. While the intensity of their opposition to political Zionism may differ, they are all united in their refusal to recognize the State as a religious phenomenon. They love and treasure Jewish life in the Holy Land no less passionately than others. They may even acknowledge the miracle of Israel as a providential haven for millions of Jews and as Jewry's principal Torah centre, and they encourage settlement of their followers there. With entire Chasidic communities being transplanted to Israel, and many of the thousands of foreign students at Israeli yeshivot remaining there, their Aliyah rate is indeed proportionately higher than that of any other group. But they cannot see any significance in Biblical terms of a secular state which they regard as the very denial of the historical ideals to which our people are committed. Hence, even those who accept the *de facto* existence of the State and co-operate with its government and parliament, such as the Aguda, limit that co-operation mainly to pressing for religious legislation and financial support.

While counting myself firmly in the camp of religious Zionism, I nevertheless have certain reservations which would place me somewhere off-centre between these two groups. I differ from both of them inasmuch as, unlike either in its attitude to the other, I can see legitimacy in each of them. My reading of Jewish sources and historical antecedents persuades me that similar divisions between religious nationalists and their opponents have always existed in the Jewish tradition, certainly since the conflict between Rabbi Yochanan ben Zakkai and the religious Zealots at the time of the destruction of the Temple on submission to Roman rule, and between Rabbi Akivah and his colleagues in the Bar Kochba rebellion against the Romans some sixty years later. Indeed, I deem the acceptance of both views as authentically Jewish to be an essential part of my Zionism, even if my personal preference in principle favours the more nationalist side.

Naturally, I share with both religious groups the belief in the inseparability of the Jewish State from Judaism and the hope, nay the faith, that Israel will eventually become a Torah state. But there is all the difference, in a Jewish context, between the separation of state and religion, which I totally oppose, and the separation of religion and politics, which I strongly advocate. While I recognize that religious parties may have contributed much to the Jewish character of Israel in the past, and certainly to the strength of its religious institutional life during the early formative period, I believe the disadvantages of the alliance between religion and politics now greatly outweigh the advantages. Indeed, I suspect that the majority of Israel's citizens would now be religious if this alliance had not estranged them. After all, the bulk of all immigrants, especially those from North Africa, arrived virtually without exception as Jews deeply steeped in our religious traditions. I believe they were lost not despite the religious parties, but rather because of them. In part, they alienated the population by their unseemly political manoeuvrings and by their coercive religious legislation, or attempts to impose it. But even more damaging was the effect of this politicization of religion on the other parties by practically forcing them into an anti-religious stance, for fear of being out-voted. In fact, the perpetuation of the religious parties, long after the rise of Israel made them obsolete and counter-productive, highlighted a strange paradox in Israeli life. I expressed my reflections on this in an interview featured in the *Jerusalem Post* on 9 April 1974:

On the one hand, Israel is enterprising, innovating and adaptable, but the moment it comes to anything that deals with personal commitment of any kind it is the most reactionary and most rigid country in the world where little has changed over the entire period of twenty-six years of statehood.

The political party system is precisely the same as it was before the State. The religious system, the organization of the rabbinate, the economic conflicts . . . are still the same. It is these areas where we have had no movement, partly because of the politicization of thought. Everything that goes on in Israel today is not only controlled, but I think strait-jacketed by political involvement.

Dealing specifically with the alliance between religion and politics, I commented:

The majority of the parties have to oppose the influence of religion, not because they are anti-religious or because they are dogmatically committed to atheism, but because by supporting the influence of religion they support the potential growth of an opposition party.

Putting on Tefillin in Israel today is a political act. It means that you show that you belong to a political party and that you are raising your child to become a potential member of a political party. Sending your child to a religious school today is a political act, and giving him religious instruction is a political act.

There is an even more fundamental difference which separates me from both major religious blocs. I cannot accept their disengagement from the universal dimension of Judaism, in thought and practice alike. For reasons which I understand but do not share, they both are indifferent to the outside world, looking upon it with disdain. They care little for Israel's image among the nations, and even less for any 'mission to the nations' whereby Israel is held responsible for advancing the moral order of mankind. Or, conversely, they see scant relevance in the telling phrase of the Talmud : 'No punishment comes to the world except because of Israel.'

Of course, to recognize that there can be legitimate differences of opinion does not mean that I do not hold and preach my own. Thus, with an eye especially on the non-Zionists, I have consistently urged the religious community to promote greater *religious* identification with Israel, such as when I told the First Conference of Ashkenazi and Sephardi Synagogues in Jerusalem on 9 January 1968 :

> Jews in the Diaspora will have to appreciate the radical impact of Israel's rebirth, an impact not so far sufficiently recognized in our religious and educational thinking. It is time that even synagogue services, and not only the Arab States, recognize Israel's existence. Diaspora Jews will also have to accept the fact that Israel's survival will henceforth depend on massive Aliyah even more than on financial support. It is up to our religious leadership and institutions to galvanize the response to the desperate appeal for Aliyah and not leave this or any other form of Jewish statesmanship only to Zionist organizations and secularist leaders. Only thus can religious Jewry regain its place of pre-eminence in guiding our people's destiny, and incidentally in assuring the growth of the religious component in Israel's population.

If Israel was largely irreligious, then the religious community and especially its leaders were not free from blame, at least in some measure, and I could not see a Zionist future without narrowing the gulf of polarization. In the same address I stated :

> The appalling rift between the religious and the irreligious elements of our people must be narrowed by calling a halt to the sterile *kulturkampf* of unreasoned mutual denigration in which neither side cares for the other and in which each glories in the other's disgrace. Instead of denouncing those who are perplexed through ignorance and rebellious through false teachings, we must grieve over their defection, befriend them and open their eyes to the splendours of our spiritual treasures. We must even acknowledge that we are not blameless for the tragedy of their irreligion, for we have failed to communicate our ideals in a language and through leaders they can understand. If Torah leaders do not encourage some of our best *benei Torah* to be trained for leadership, to become rabbis, doctors, lawyers, civil servants or social workers, but leave the strategic positions of government, administration and influence in the hands of the secularists, how can we then complain when the Jewish State, our institutions, our hospitals, and sometimes even our communities are not conducted

by the rule of the Torah? We must learn that in this democratic age our convictions can prevail only by persuasion, not by authority or legislation, only by winning the dissidents, not by coercing or ostracizing them.

At the same time, I never tired of appealing to those estranged from our heritage:

And the anti-traditionalists must learn that the Jewish people divorced from its traditions is a travesty of Jewish history and martyrdom; it is like a tree without roots, or a building on quicksand, doomed to destruction. They must realize that the days of Orthodox decline have passed. With far more Israeli and foreign students at Israeli yeshivot than at Israel's secular institutions of higher learning, with virtually all intensive Jewish day-schools throughout the world under Orthodox control, and with the birth-rate among the strictly Orthodox many times higher than among other Jews who perish because they produce too few and lose too many, combined with the superior tenacity of those steeled by the moral discipline of Jewish life, who can doubt the ultimate triumph of the Torah forces within our people? Our non-religious brothers, to appreciate the Orthodox mentality, must realize that our religious faith, as the *raison d'être* of our national existence, is no less precious to us than our land and our people. On our beliefs, they must understand, therefore, that we cannot compromise, nor can we legitimize religious forms alien to historic Judaism without making a mockery of our most sacred convictions.

In these sentiments, I was obviously not alone; I am sure most of my Orthodox colleagues shared them. But what they did not share if they were religious Zionists was my attempt to understand even those religious leaders to whom Zionism was anathema. The riddle was genuine enough. How could the greatest sages of our time, by whose words and rulings of Torah we lived and who directed the unquestioning thinking of their disciples, not acknowledge the religious significance of Israel's miraculous rebirth? What others, including the most secular of Jews, hailed as a happening of Biblical magnitude, as the providential fulfilment of religious dreams and prayers, evidently passed by these giants of Torah learning, in religious terms, simply as a non-event, unworthy even of the benediction recited over the acquisition of a new garment. Deeply bothered by this question, I could find only one explanation, which I based on a homiletical interpretation of a well-known Midrash.

On the exclamation by the Children of Israel in the Song of Moses after crossing the Red Sea '*This* is my God and I will glorify Him', our sages commented: 'Even the handmaid saw at the Sea what the Prophet Ezekiel did not see in his vision.' There are Divine manifestations which appear momentous to a simple handmaid and yet leave a prophet unmoved. The splitting of the Red Sea was a colossal physical event; it thrilled the handmaid with boundless excitement and stirred her to her depths with religious fervour. Not so the Prophetic Seer. His turn for spiritual ecstasy came a little later, when the roles were reversed. When God revealed Himself at Sinai in history's most momentous spiritual event, only Moses realized the full significance, whilst 'the people saw it, they trembled, but they stood afar' (Ex. 20 : 15). Maybe, I felt, even the ordinary kibbutznik could see something providential in the restoration of Jewish statehood which, however momentous, left the greatest men of the spirit still untouched, being as yet in their eyes of an essentially physical or material nature. But when a spiritual revolution sweeps the Land of Israel, returning the entire Jewish people to the assignment given at Sinai, then the reactions will be reversed.

For myself, however, no doubt lacking in such pure spirituality, the event already witnessed was spectacular enough to be regarded as a momentous turning-point in post-exilic Jewish history, warranting the annual recital of *Hallel* on its anniversary in thanksgiving for exceptional Divine favours bestowed on our generation. For me, the religious significance of Jewish statehood was always real and supreme.

Yet, in one crucial respect, I could never identify completely with the official line of most religious Zionists, veering towards the hesitations of those masters of Jewish teaching who regarded themselves as non-Zionists. It is the association of presently unfolding events with 'the Redemption' which I find questionable and potentially frightening, for both historical and more pragmatic reasons. Of course, one *hopes* that the State of Israel will prove the precursor of Messianic fulfilment. But there is all the difference between hopes and definite assumptions or certain expectations. The catastrophes of pseudo-Messianic disasters in Jewish history, from Bar Kochba to Shabbetai Zvi and even after, should serve as warning signals against conditioning our people to believe that the process of final Redemption is definitely at hand, with all the practical consequences that flow from such an assumption.

The Bar Kochba episode should teach a particularly instructive lesson. This courageous leader of the final desperate uprising against Rome had always been depicted in Jewish folklore as one of the greatest heroes in our history. Little wonder that there was fierce debate in Israel when Professor Yehoshafat Harkavi, former head of Israeli Military Intelligence, came out with a little book in Hebrew, later enlarged in English with the title *The Bar Kochba Syndrome*, showing that Bar Kochba led, in fact, to a greater calamity than even the Roman conquest of Jerusalem and the destruction of the Temple itself. After the Destruction, Harkavi argued, the Romans still tolerated a measure of Jewish self-government and religious freedom in Palestine. But once Bar Kochba made his futile attempt to rise against the Romans and this was crushed, the last vestiges of Jewish life and learning in

Judea were brutally wiped out by fearful persecution, and the Jewish fate of exilic suffering was sealed for the following 1,800 years.

Professor Harkavi sent me a copy of his book soon after it was published, and we entered into some correspondence. I pointed out to him that I, too, had often held up the Bar Kochba experience as a warning to us today, as indeed had Rabbi Samson Raphael Hirsch in his commentary on the Fourth Blessing in the Grace-after-Meals a century earlier. But where I differed from Harkavi was in seeing the warning not so much in the futility of Bar Kochba's provoking the Romans when there was no realistic hope of a permanent victory over them, but rather in the Messianic pretensions of Bar Kochba which proved an even greater catastrophe.

But while I was basically in agreement with Harkavi and his conclusions, I found myself on the opposite side in an argument I once had with Professor Yigael Yadin on the similarly controversial lessons to be drawn from the Masada epic. Whilst on a visit there with a JPA mission, and after listening to the famous archaeologist – by then also Deputy Prime Minister – describing his spectacular finds and his reconstruction of events at Masada, I asked him how he wished this episode to be taught to our children: as a supreme example of Jewish heroism to be emulated, or as a unique aberration of Jewish teachings for the preference of collective death with glory to the indignity of life under foreign domination. He seemed in little doubt about favouring the first alternative, a choice popular throughout Israel. I, on the other hand, was strongly opposed to the cultivation of such a 'Masada complex' as utterly un-Jewish.

There was of course a common theme running through all these arguments, with acute relevance to the interpretation of contemporary events. Redemption, Messianic expectations, or the alternative of a heroic death in preference to continued life in misery, these were clearly all interrelated, and I was haunted by the prospect of the Jewish future being built on these assumptions.

Closely allied to this line of thinking was the attitude to 'miracles' witnessed in the rise and defence of Israel. Naturally, I accepted and hailed the widespread acknowledgement that what had occurred could not be explained by the ordinary laws of logic and history, but manifested the guiding hand of Providence, so long as the attribution of such wondrous experiences to miracles served to strengthen religious faith and belief in God's 'special relationship' with Israel. But once miracles are invoked to formulate or justify practical policies, or to assume that the process of Redemption must be irreversible, miscalculations may invite disaster of irretrievable proportions. Hence, following the Talmudic injunction 'not to rely on miracles', I often warned against indiscriminate references to miracles. Thus, in my London address after the Yom Kippur War I made a careful distinction between the acclamation of miracles and the reliance on them:

The mere fact that a tiny people restored to a little land, with few natural resources, continues to be at or near the very heart of the major political, economic and strategic upheavals besetting the entire world, affecting the fortunes of super-powers and small nations alike, is itself the surest indication that the millennial drama of God's special relationship with Israel is far from played out. A numerically insignificant nation cannot bestride the front pages of the world's newspapers for twenty-five years without serving a special purpose in the evolution of man's history.

But let me caution against an over-emphasis of miracles, as is so common today in the quest for religious authenticity. Maimonides already warned against interpreting even Biblical miracles as serving to prove God or to legitimize His messengers (*Hil. Yesodei Ha-Torah* 8 : 1).

Rather more specifically, I added:

The quite extraordinary events of Israel's first twenty-five years have induced perhaps an undue tendency to look for a constant succession of miracles. There is something less than genuine faith and more than a trace of overbearing presumption in the widely current assertion: 'In Israel, he who does not believe in miracles is not a realist.'

True enough, if miracles are events which confound human calculations, wrought by a Higher Intelligence, some no doubt did occur in the latest war, too. With only 600 troops and under 100 tanks defending the fortifications in the South against overwhelmingly superior forces, and Israel having thrown back the Syrian invaders against similar odds after they had rolled across and down the Golan Heights to threaten Northern Israel with a deluge of blood and destruction, the outcome was nothing short of one of Jewish history's greatest wonders. Thanks to Divine help and the superhuman heroism of Israel's valiant youth, there was averted a catastrophe of near-holocaust proportions with potentially devastating effects on Jewish existence everywhere. Yet even these colossal military feats – which, in themselves, may well eclipse the achievements of the Six Day War – are now almost irrelevant to Israel's predicament.

What was so widely overlooked was that, sadly, miracles could also occur in reverse:

For alas, not all miracles were in Israel's favour. Equally against all rational anticipation were Israel's astounding unpreparedness, the unexpected strength and unity of the Arabs, and the stunning capitulation overnight, under oil-blackmail, of virtually all of Israel's friends, with but a few exceptions, notably the United States and Holland. There are circumstances, it seems, when we are not the sole beneficiaries of miracles. We may do well to analyse these circumstances if, as in the past, we are once again to merit the special solicitude of Israel's Guardian.

A somewhat similar distinction also qualified my comparison of Yom Ha'atzmaut with other festivals of deliverance fixed in the Jewish calendar long ago. I explained this in my twenty-fifth Israel Independence Day address:

Where all our other festivals celebrate events which occurred thousands of years ago, this newest festival in the Jewish calendar marks an event for which we have waited thousands of years and which many of us witnessed with our own eyes. Significantly, Yom Ha'atzmaut combines features of the other three festivals of national salvation in our calendar: the Passover deliverance from bondage to freedom, the Purim victory over anti-Semitic persecution and aggression, and the surrender of the 'many into the hands of the few' of Chanukah. In the rise of Israel, our generation has seen a combination of all three triumphs brought about by Divine help and human valour: millions of Jews have been liberated from humiliation and oppression, the counsel of those who hate us has been confounded, and vast armies bent on our destruction have been put to flight by but a fraction of their number.

But there is a crucial difference:

Yet, in one important respect, our latest festival seems to differ fundamentally from its notable predecessor, Passover, the original festival of our freedom. Pesach celebrates the beginning of our Exodus, not its conclusion; it records our departure from Egypt, not our entry into the Holy Land. In fact, neither Divine legislation nor Jewish tradition have ever fixed a date to commemorate Joshua's conquest of the land or any other conquest as a day worthy of special celebration. Passover feasts the start of the journey, not its end. The Jewish calendar immortalizes the opportunity for gaining and utilizing national independence, rather than its fulfilment; for in the Jewish scale of values we hail effort rather than success. . . .

Yom Ha'atzmaut will rank as a permanent and distinguished marker in our calendar, alongside our other traditional festivals, only if we regard it as opening rather than closing one of the great epochs of the Jewish experience; if we look upon the 5th Iyar 1948 as the beginning and not the end in our hard and long struggle for the realization of our ultimate Jewish destiny. The real challenges of Jewish independence are yet to be met. . . .

Perhaps Yom Ha'atzmaut was still but perfunctorily observed as a religious festival precisely because a major element was lacking in the parallel with Passover:

Passover was but the forerunner of Shavuot, our people's encounter with God at Sinai; it was the condition for our sanctification of the Land under Joshua forty years later; it was the curtain-raiser for the drama which led to the achievement of our spiritual glory with the building of the Temple under King Solomon 480 years later. So does the deliverance of Yom Ha'atzmaut in our times summon us to set our national sights on the essential ideals still unfulfilled: the striving for peace, the continued ingathering of our exiles, the promotion of righteousness in human and international relations, the search for Jewish identity and unity of purpose consonant with our historic traditions, and the resumption of our role as the People of the Book that, living 'not by might nor by power but by My spirit', will advance the moral order and spiritual commitment of mankind at large.

All these qualifications were part of a most fundamental divergence of opinion which separated my thinking from the generally accepted axioms of religious Zionists and which critically affected our very claim to the Land, leading me to other vital conclusions on the definition of Zionism. In my reading of all our sources, the Covenant mandating the Land to our people was never absolute and always conditional. The Land would be ours and we would dwell securely in it 'if you walk in My statutes and fulfil My commandments'. This proviso is reiterated over and over again in the Torah, the Prophets, the Psalms and throughout post-Biblical writings. As the Psalmist put it so dramatically, and with such a topical ring: 'If only My people would hearken unto Me, and Israel walk in My ways, I would soon subdue their enemies and turn My hand upon their oppressors.' The warning was clear and unequivocal. The Land could not tolerate a backsliding Jewish people, and would 'vomit it out' into exile, as twice confirmed in our history.

Indeed, the entire doctrine of reward and punishment, or Divine retribution – one of Judaism's cardinal principles of faith – as applied to the Jewish people collectively is invariably limited to the Land of Israel. For instance, the promise of rain, prosperity and peace for righteous conduct, just like the warning of drought and war leading to exile for violating God's law, whenever it occurs in the Bible, is specifically linked to Jewish conduct in the Land. The only reference to reward in the Ten Commandments assures length of days for honouring parents not anywhere except 'on the Land which the Lord your God gives you'.

This limitation is basic to the Jewish philosophy of history. When the Talmud attributes the destruction of both Temples to Jewish moral and religious failings, it is solely in relation to the national experience inside the Land, as expressed in the familiar liturgical phrase 'on account of our sins we were exiled from the Land'. It is only when the Jewish people controls its own national destiny on its own territory that such assertions are made. When collective Jewish suffering occurred elsewhere, such charges are never made. In none of the voluminous liturgical literature of the Middle Ages, such as the profusion of *Kinnot* (elegies) and *Selichot* (penitential compositions), is it ever suggested that the destruction of entire communities in the Crusades, for example, can be ascribed to the moral deficiencies of those communities. Similarly, it would be inconceivable that any authentic Jewish thinker would blame Jewish shortcomings for the Holocaust. Responsibility for national calamities is pinned on Israel only if they occur in its own land, and it would be as inconsistent with Jewish teaching to put the blame for such reverses on others as it would be to attribute Jewish tribulations experienced in exile to Jewish failures. Only in the Diaspora is the Jewish fate determined by factors entirely beyond our own control.

Nowhere is this causal relationship between crime and punishment, or national conduct and suffering restricted to the Land of Israel, spelt out more clearly than in the best-known affirmation of the Jewish faith, the *Shema* familiar to every Jew and posted on the entrance to every Jewish room. On observing the Divine commandments, it states quite unmistakably, all will be well and good, 'and you will eat and be satisfied'. But on defying God's law, Israel will lose its security, 'and you will perish quickly from off the good land which the Lord gives unto you'. Hence, I felt justified in writing in one of my widely publicized rejoinders on being lambasted for allowing the words 'Liquidation of Israel' even to pass my lips, albeit as an expression of faith that an eventual accommodation with the Arabs will not allow it to happen:

No one has yet complained that the *Shema* is demoralizing, giving aid and comfort to our enemies. On the contrary, it has sustained the will of our people to triumph over the threat of extinction, constantly renewing our efforts and our faith to merit redemption.

I could never see anything unrabbinical, un-Jewish or anti-Zionist in any such invocation of cardinal Jewish teachings. Quite the contrary, I regarded their suppression, especially by rabbis, as a heinous betrayal of Israel and Judaism alike, and as an unconscionable perversion of Zionism in its authentic formulation rooted to the Bible itself. Addressing the Annual Meeting of the Memorial Foundation for Jewish Culture in Geneva on 3 July 1979, I put the construction I placed on the Covenant between God and our people, and its negation, in these words:

Its basic terms were that if we would take care of the survival of His Torah, He would take care of our survival. For thousands of years, the agreement has worked, and we are here to prove it. But now the roles have been reversed: we worry about the survival of Jews, and let God worry about the survival of Judaism. This cannot work, as proved by the shrinkage of Jews today, especially under conditions of unprecedented freedom, affluence and opportunity. We had better bestir ourselves before the survival of the fittest has reduced our numbers, and correspondingly our security, by a higher toll than was inflicted by any holocaust, any massacre or any war.

Nor could a reversal of roles in the Covenant ensure the survival of Israel. I have never understood why rabbis should not be expected to say so, or indeed why our people should not be roused to recognize this fact of Jewish life as being at least as relevant to Israel's security as diplomatic skills, good public relations and ever-increasing arms' supplies. Even if it did not exactly endear me to the political and religious leadership, I stressed this essence of Jewish doctrine again and again. For me it represents the *sine qua non* of Zionism.

This outlook led to other practical ramifications, too. Each of the three assumptions which I considered mistaken – the belief in the establishment of Israel as *definitely* the beginning of the Redemption, the belief in miracles as Israeli realism, and the disbelief in the conditional character of our title to the Land – could lead to unwarranted and reckless decisions, based on the premise that the events we witnessed were irreversible.

Thus, even the Rebbe of Lubavitch, in the correspondence between us already mentioned, specifically referred to the 'patently visible miracles' as proof that 'the victory' gained in the Yom Kippur War, though achieved by non-believers, enjoyed Divine endorsement, arguing further that in respect of territories already under Jewish occupation, the usual halachic rule 'not to provoke the non-Jews' no longer operated, against what had been forcefully asserted by his chief antagonist, the leading sage, Rabbi Eliezer Shach, who was quite adamant in his advocacy of political moderation. Similar arguments induced the Rebbe to call persistently for the pursuit of the war in Lebanon 'to the finish'.

But the crux of the practical differences of opinion arising from the differing religious interpretations on the rebirth of Israel concerned territorial concessions for the sake of peace. These were of course unacceptable to those who believed that the process of Redemption was irreversible or that the Jewish mandate to the Land was absolute. They quite logically objected to any territorial compromise, not for security reasons but on purely religious grounds. Since I did not share the assumptions, I could not agree with the conclusions, either. I stated my views quite unequivocally in my London address on the Yom Kippur War early in 1974, that is, long before the re-statement of my views caused such a furore:

No rabbinical authority disputes that our claim to a Divine mandate . . . extends over the entire Holy Land within its historic borders and that halachically we have no right to surrender this claim. But what is questionable is whether we must, or indeed may, assert it at the risk of thousands of lives, if not the life of the State itself.

Any religious law is set aside, even fasting on Yom Kippur, if it involves a danger to life. Rabbis, in giving such rulings in respect of individuals, are required to rely on expert medical opinion to determine what constitutes such danger in particular cases. Similarly, it would seem, we are halachically compelled to leave the judgement on what provides the optimum security for Jewish life in Israel to the verdict of military and political experts, not rabbis. Included as a major factor in this difficult judgement must also be the overriding concern to preserve the Jewish character of Israel which may clearly depend on the proportion of Jews within the State. For in the suspension of religious laws for life-saving purposes, the threat to Jewish spiritual life and to physical life is considered alike.

Most importantly also to be borne in mind must be some more intangible factors of Jewish religious and moral concern. The present ceding of some territory, if necessary and consistent with security requirements, may conceivably be justified as a ringing act of faith to promote regional, and indeed international peace, and as a goodwill gesture of immense value to establish friendly relations with the neighbouring peoples, ideals of human fellowship to which Judaism is passionately dedicated.

But I did add one reservation which I never modified:

In an altogether unique category is Jerusalem. It enjoys a sanctity of its own and is the common possession of all Jews, wherever they may live, the gateway of all their prayers, the symbol of all their hopes, and now happily also the spiritual heart of Jewish learning, circulating inspiration to the most distant parts of our dispersion. To save life, one can amputate a limb or even excise parts of some internal organs. But not the heart!

It has always intrigued me how identical premises can sometimes lead to opposite conclusions. Among the profoundly perceptive spiritual responses to the Yom Kippur War which had particularly impressed me was an article at the time by Professor Harold Fisch of Bar Ilan University, and I had quoted from it in my own Tel Aviv lecture shortly thereafter. I therefore read with special interest his book *Zionist Revolution*, published in 1978. Beautifully written, brilliantly argued and full of well-documented erudition, it was a distinctly religious exposition of the case for 'Greater Israel'. He was one of the intellectual founding-fathers of the movement to promote Jewish settlement in the entire Biblical land through a specifically religious interpretation of history. His principal argument was that the abnormality of Jewish existence in exile now characterized Israel's own condition and therefore warranted Israel's reliance on 'abnormal' factors in securing its destiny. Knowing him well, I wrote to him soon after the appearance of his book:

What strikes me, of course, is how an analysis almost identical with my own can lead to opposite conclusions. . . . I too have diagnosed, for at least the past ten years, the principal Jewish malaise of our times as the bankruptcy of secular Zionism, its failure to 'normalize' the Jewish condition and its refusal to acknowledge the uniqueness of the Jewish myth (or mystique as I prefer to call it). Like yourself, I also see the anomaly of our exilic experience now transferred to Israel. Perhaps expressing it even more radically than you did, I have stated that Israel, far from having solved the Jewish problem, is now the Jewish problem, as highlighted by the equation of Zionism with racism, or its corollary, of anti-Zionism with anti-Semitism.

This leads you, as well as me, to the reaffirmation of the Covenant as the cornerstone of the Zionist faith. But what I miss in your book is any reference to the quintessence of this Covenant, instead of merely a reliance on its 'myth' as the operative dynamic of Jewish history. Your Covenant seems basically unilateral to me, whilst my understanding of it is mutual. . . .

This is where our conclusions begin to diverge. You argue that 'the "moderates" are fundamentally unwilling to contemplate the existential uniqueness of Jewish history' believing that 'since Zionism came to normalize the Jewish condition, it is intolerable that we should be involved now in a dispute of so abnormal a character that it is incapable of solution by ordinary diplomatic and political means'. Together with many other religious moderates, I personify, I suppose, the *non sequitur* of this argument. So did Rabbi Yochanan ben Zakkai and, I imagine, even a pacifist like Rabbi A. I. Kook.

The conditional nature of the Covenant was the point of divergence between us:

Accepting your premises, I arrive at the opposite conclusions. True, because of Israel's uniqueness, we cannot solve the Jewish problem as other nations solve theirs. But conversely, if we kept our part of the Covenant, we could rely on its transcendental character to ensure 'Israel dwelling securely in the Land' by 'abnormal means'. In the rabbinic parlance, if we were worthy, the end would be hastened. Indeed, the Covenant specifically invalidates the Jewish claim to the Land whenever its provisions are not fulfilled by us. Hence, to base national Jewish policies on the one-sided operation of the Covenant lacks all logic or justification, and we are bound to fall back on 'normal means', including especially the goodwill of the nations, to assert our claim to the Land as best we can.

In all my statements on the future of the territories, my concern was never so much to advocate their return to Arab rule as to remove the religious objection to an accommodation for the sake of peace, with security for Israel and justice for the Arabs.

Another anxiety, too, gnawed in my mind. More worrying than the diversion of Israel's scant material resources across the 'Green Line' was the depletion of Israel's equally scant spiritual resources. When, together with the delegation of European rabbis, I visited the newly established settlement of Elon Moreh overlooking Shechem in 1982, and the nearby Har Berachah within a few days of its establishment in 1983, I was full of admiration for the selfless idealism of the Gush Emunim pioneers. Their readiness to face incredible hardships and dangers for what they believed certainly exemplified the last vestiges of pristine 'Chalutzic' Zionism still left in Israel.

Yet, on witnessing their achievement, I felt a double heart-break. I feared for a possible repetition of the heart-rending agony which had occurred with the dismantlement of Yamit on its return to Egypt; but I was anguished even more by seeing Israel proper deprived of such valuable human assets. As I put it in an exchange of letters, following the 'Liquidation' uproar, with Mr S.Z.Shragai, the veteran Mizrachi thinker and writer; the letter is dated 19 June 1980:

Just as I believe Israel's precious economic resources would be more usefully invested in settling the Galil and the Negev rather than the West Bank (other than security posts), so do I believe that our even more precious spiritual resources, especially the wonderful idealism of Gush Emunim and the Yeshivot Hesder, would render a more constructive service to our people by concentrating on Israel's acute religious, moral, social and educational problems, helping to raise the whole level of Jewish life, than by frittering away their energies on political extremism which is today almost exclusively generated from religious quarters.

Apart from contemplating a Jewish return of some territories already occupied in the Biblical Land of Israel as perfectly compatible with religious imperatives, my concept of Zionism as the conditional fulfilment of a Divine promise led me to another conclusion, too. I always staunchly advocated Aliyah. Once, while on one of my two pastoral visits to New Zealand, I even told the small and isolated Jewish community in Wellington, in answer to a question on whether they should encourage their four most committed young people, all B'nei Akivah leaders, to go on Aliyah or to stay behind and continue with their invaluable work among the youth of Wellington, that they should definitely opt in favour of Aliyah, however irreplaceable their loss to that remote but resolute outpost of Jewish life on the fringes of the earth.

But that said, I have never believed in 'the liquidation of the *galut*' by anticipating, or actively working for, the eventual disappearance of the Diaspora in the foreseeable future. Nor do I believe that Jewish life in the Diaspora is doomed to disappear under the pressure of assimilation and demographic erosion. These factors will regrettably reduce the number of identifying Jews quite drastically, but all the indications I can see are that those who will survive as Jews will be much more intensely committed than the generation they replace, so that quality will make up for quantity in what has always been the process of Jewish regeneration.

More than that: much as I subscribe unreservedly to the centrality of Israel in Jewish life today and seek to translate this into the conduct of our religious and educational affairs, my understanding of the conditional Covenant does not allow me to regard Israel as indispensable to the future of Jewish existence. That Jewish life without Israel is unthinkable, yes; but impossible, no. Had the assumption of such impossibility prevailed at any time in the past, the Jewish people would no longer exist. Hence, I believe it is neither historically correct nor ideologically healthy to promote such an assumption by allowing Zionism to circumscribe the outer limits of the Jewish mystique and the capacity to survive. That capacity, I firmly hold, is unlimited and infinite. The belief in the eternal 'remnant' of the Jewish people is Jewish teaching no less authentic than Zionism, and I cannot sacrifice one for the sake of the other.

Clearly, I could not affirm without reservations Professor Emil Fackenheim's 'monumental religio-secular fact in modern Jewish history' that 'Galut Judaism, if most assuredly not Galut itself, has come to an end'.

To support his 'fact', writing on 'the Renewal of the Zionist Impulse' in *Forum*, Spring 1983, he quoted from Buber's famous letter of 1939 to Gandhi:

> Dispersion is bearable; it can even be purposeful, if there is somewhere an ingathering, a growing home center, a piece of earth where one is in the midst of an ingathering and not in dispersion, and whence the spirit of ingathering may work its way into all the places of the dispersion. When there is this, there is also a striving common life, the life of a community which dares to live today because it may hope to live tomorrow. But when this growing center, this ceaseless process of ingathering is lacking, dispersion becomes dismemberment. From this point of view, the question of our Jewish destiny is indissolubly bound up with the possibility of ingathering, and that is bound up with Palestine.

Fackenheim, recognizing that 1,900 years of exile had blatantly belied the assertion that 'dispersion becomes dismemberment', was forced to qualify Buber's categorical statement, but in doing so merely explained one half-truth by another:

> The pre-modern Diaspora, though lacking in a centre, was not 'dismembered', for it was in exile, accepted itself as being so, and believing the exile to be meaningful, waited patiently for its end. In contrast, the modern Diaspora, being modern, demands and fights for emancipation – and cannot do so while at the same time accepting exile as meaningful. . . .

Whether the 'pre-modern' Jews considered their exile 'meaningful' is open to question; so is the assumption that Jews cannot fight for emancipation 'while at the same time accepting exile as meaningful'. And both statements have no bearing on the inevitability of 'dispersion becoming dismemberment'. Such confused *non sequitur*s turn into dogmas when the proven teachings of fact and faith no longer operate to define the certainties of Jewish existence.

My reservations on Redemption, Messianic expectations, miracles and any unconditional title to the Land are all, in a sense, negative or limiting factors in my religious Zionism. But far outweighting these are the positive dimensions which I seek – and largely miss – in the vision of religious Zionists, and Jews generally. I have already briefly referred to my pain at the contemporary disengagement from Judaism's universal visions and to my acknowledgement that there may well be valid reasons accounting for this. I summed up my reflections on this phenomenon in a lecture on 'The Challenge to Jewish Spiritual Leaders' I delivered before the Institute for Judaism and Contemporary Thought at Bar Ilan University on 6 July 1979:

These trends [of disdain and total unconcern for the outside world, especially among religious leaders], albeit on a somewhat different level, are also widespread in Israeli society generally, thinking and acting as it still does in the spirit of Ben-Gurion's famous dictum: 'What matters is not what non-Jews think but what Jews do.' To my mind, this doctrine completely contradicts our basic understanding of *Kiddush Hashem* whereby traditionally we used to care very much about what non-Jews think about us and what impact our example and teachings have on them. There may be very good reasons for the current vogue of indifference to the non-Jewish world amongst spiritual leaders and secularist Israelis alike, partly as an indignant reaction to that world's callousness and partly under the enormous pressure of having to concentrate all available resources on rebuilding our battered faith and people out of the devastation of the Holocaust, with little energy and attention to spare for contributions to others. Nevertheless, the almost complete suppression of our universal commitment and aspirations is a grave defect of the contemporary Jewish scene, a shrinkage of the Jewish message and purpose which compromises both our assigned role as moral pioneers and our image among the nations.

The theme often recurred, though its formulation may have varied, sometimes adding a more specific nuance, such as when I told my Anglo-Jewish audience in Tel Aviv in November 1980:

Hunted and spurned though we were by the nations, we always saw their salvation through our impact on them as an essential in the scheme of our own Redemption. A Messianism limited to Jews was inconceivable to us. This vision informed our relationship with the non-Jewish world, our concern to be respected and to win acclaim for the Jewish name.

This concern is now out of fashion – and, I must add, particularly in religious circles. We have become introverts, all but disengaging ourselves completely from the moral commitment to the outside world which features so prominently in the Prophetic tradition. Today, this whole attitude is dubbed as a '*Golus*-mentality' and it has been replaced by a certain indifference, if not disdain. Reasons for this dramatic change are ample and natural. Western civilization's betrayal of the Jewish people, culminating in the Holocaust, followed by the cynical hostility of the United Nations and the world conspiracy against Zionism, could not but disillusion our faith in mankind and substitute self-reliance for solicitude *vis-à-vis* others, unless dictated by self-interest.

For me, the concept of *Kiddush Hashem*, the urge to make a salutary impression on the world, constitutes the heart of Zionism. The very word *Zion* means 'Signpost' or 'Showpiece'. When Abraham, the founder of Zionism, was originally commanded to go to the Land, the blessings defining the aims of the journey culminated in the assurance and the charge: 'And in you shall all the families of the earth be blessed.' Consistent with this assignment, the Prophets' vision of the Jewish return to Zion was invariably linked with Israel's universal purpose. Salvation was always deemed indivisible; there could be none for Israel without encompassing all mankind as well. When Isaiah summoned his stricken contemporaries to raise the banner of hope in Zion's eventual triumph, he saw its manifestation in the ringing words: 'And the nations shall see your righteousness, and all kings your glory . . . ; and they shall call them the holy people, the redeemed of the Lord.' The Psalmist, too, describes the jubilation on 'The Lord's restoring the captivity of Zion' as seen in the first instance in the non-Jewish reaction: 'Then they said among the nations, the Lord hath wrought great things for these'; only after that would the Jewish people themselves exclaim: 'The Lord has wrought great things with *us*.'

Not only is such sanctification of the Divine Name among the nations to be the result and purpose of the Return; it is also the cause of Israel's salvation. There is a remarkable chapter in the Book of Ezekiel (36) on the realization of the Zionist dream. It describes how the House of Israel, having lived in their land and defiled it by their evil ways, will incur the wrath of the Lord and be scattered among the nations. But their very exile would disgrace God's Name in the world: 'And they came among the nations where they went, and they desecrated My holy Name, as it will be said to them "These are the people of the Lord, and they have departed from this land." And I shall have pity over My holy Name which the House of Israel have profaned among the nations where they went. Therefore, say unto the House of Israel, Thus says the Lord God, not for your sake will I act, O House of Israel, but for My holy Name . . . and I shall sanctify My great Name . . . and the nations shall know that I am the Lord . . . by being sanctified through you in their eyes. And I shall take you from the nations and gather you from all the lands, and I shall bring you to your land.' In other words, God's own need to have His Name sanctified will force Him, as it were, to have compassion and to bring His people back to their land. God requires their Return, if only for the sake of ensuring the sanctification of His Name among the nations.

This Prophetic utterance is not just an isolated thought. The same reasoning was advanced at the beginning of our nation's history. Twice God had forgiven the Children of Israel – for the sin of the Golden Calf and for the sin of the Spies – and twice they were saved from extinction in response to the same argument by Moses in his pleas. He did not plead, as might be expected, that the people were sorry, had remorse and were determined never to repeat their backsliding – the usual requirement for Divine forgiveness and atonement. What Moses argued was that God Himself could not afford to destroy them; for what would the non-Jews say? 'Why should the Egyptians say, For evil did He bring them forth, to slay them in the mountains?...' And again, in the story of the Spies, Moses advances the same argument: 'And the Egyptians, hearing that You in Your might brought out this people from among them, will say to the inhabitants of this land, who have heard that You are in the midst of this people ...; now if You will kill this people as one man, then the nations which have heard the fame of You will say, Because the Lord was not able to bring this people into the land which He swore unto them, therefore He has slain them in the wilderness.' In both cases, the argument which prevailed to save Israel was the need to prevent the desecration of God's Name among the nations, and by the same argument Israel's future salvation will also be secured.

I expanded a little on this theme because I deem it absolutely crucial to an authentic understanding of Israel's purpose. Here lies the gravamen of my charge against those – and they include many religious leaders – who dismiss the nations' attitude to Israel with indifference and as of no consequence. They not only justify their unconcern, but belabour those who do care by contemptuously hurling at them the purported quotation, 'What will the *goyim* say?' There is no such phrase in the Bible. What it does say is the very opposite: '*Why* should the *goyim* say ...?' In plain words, we must not allow them to have a poor opinion of Israel and to denigrate our reputation, thus causing a *Chillul Hashem*; and therein lies our salvation!

*Kiddush Hashem* has therefore always been the paramount theme in my projection of the Zionist ideal. What was required in the first instance was to cultivate the conscious pursuit of *Kiddush Hashem* as Israel's collective ambition, for intrinsic reasons as well as for the sublimation of Israel's image in the eyes of the world. Thus, in my thirty-second Israel Independence Day address I suggested to the festive congregation:

> What a *Kiddush Hashem* it would be if the front pages of the world's newspapers would one day report that Israel is the first country in the world to have eliminated crime and vice, and solved the problem of broken homes and social inequality, to have found the key to creating a better, more honest, more idealistic and incorruptible society, in which people strive to make the times good rather than to have a good time.

This was not just a matter of image-building as a public relations exercise. We had to convince our people that through *Kiddush Hashem* the key to our national fortunes would be transferred from others to ourselves. The urgency of this message never left me; I even included a reference to it in the course of my address at the resplendent Centenary Service of the Great Synagogue in Sydney on 12 March 1978, televised nationwide throughout Australia:

> We know, and must prevail on our entire people to know, that in the final analysis the Jewish destiny will not be determined by shuttling diplomats or the whims of rulers who, preaching hate and practising cowardly aggression one day, appear as heroes of peace the next, just as in the past the fate of our people was not sealed by Egyptian Pharaohs, Roman Emperors, Spanish Inquisitors or frenzied oppressors of more recent times. Our fate rests ultimately in our own hands, determined by our worthiness, our resilience in the face of vicissitudes, and our powers of spiritual regeneration. . . . Our faith is unwavering that peace is assured if we turn Israel into a model society, cleansed of all crime, immorality, corruption, infidelity and other vices, as 'a light unto the nations'.

There was never any let-up in the urge to call for replacing the aspirations of other nations by specifically Jewish national ideals as the essence of Zionism. Even at the height of our agony, the massacre of Israel's Olympic athletes, I told our large London congregation of mourners in my address on 'The Infamy of Munich' on 11 September 1972:

> How would our Hebrew Prophets – the most perceptive and far-sighted commentators of all times on contemporary events, on the fortunes and misfortunes of our people – how would they have reacted to a calamity of such national poignancy and such universal ramifications? . . . They might even question some aspects of the Olympic ideal as quite alien to Judaism, much as we applaud the invaluable contribution of these competitions to the promotion of human fellowship and international goodwill. But whilst we participate in these Games under a torch lit on Mount Olympus idealizing the holiness of beauty and physical perfection, let us recall that this was the creed against which our Maccabean forebears once fought bitterly. . . .
> How wonderful it would be if one day we could initiate international competitions around a flame lit in Jerusalem which would exalt spiritual striving, which would bring together all moral pioneers who would compete for the alleviation of suffering, the eradication of poverty, the elimination of vice and crime, the conquest of disease, and the banishment of selfishness and materialism – a spectacle which would focus the eyes of the world on an arena dedicated to the beauty of holiness and the soul of man.

Of course, I was painfully aware that the principal blame for this Jewish national deficiency lay with the virtual abdication of spiritual leadership within my own ranks. No doubt there were good reasons for this, and I tried to analyse them in my Bar Ilan lecture:

With the secularization of Jewish life, initiated with the Emancipation in the last century and accelerated by the evolution and consummation of Jewish statehood, the role of rabbinic leadership underwent a dramatic change. This change was brought about not only by the progressive transfer of strategic key positions from spiritual to lay leaders, replacing rabbis by an assortment of politicians, communal organizers, efficient fund-raisers and public relations experts in the decision-making processes governing the fortunes of the Jewish people. To some extent this development was inevitable, as the external pressures of integration into a secular society combined with the internal exigencies of administering a modern state, and I suspect that rabbis, even if they were allowed to resume their traditional leadership role, would scarcely improve on the lay performance in the management of statecraft. Under modern conditions and pending the advent of the Messianic age, theocracy is certainly not for us, neither at the national nor at the communal level.

However, it was idle to ignore some more direct causes for the withdrawal of rabbis from the effective control of the national Jewish purpose:

But the displacement of rabbis as policy-makers, or even as pace-setters in the progress of Jewish life, is certainly not due only to their ousting or usurpation by their secular rivals. It must equally be traced to the deliberate withdrawal of rabbis from spheres of influence and activity which had traditionally been theirs. In large measure, they have simply abdicated their role in the governance of the Jewish destiny, the definition of the Jewish purpose and the mobilization of Jewish spiritual resources. Sadly, they represent neither the government nor even the opposition in the leadership of the Jewish people. Meat inspectors and catering supervisors, officials who marry and bury people, or who preach to the converted and denounce the rest, or even scholars who withdraw to secluded cloisters to instruct devoted disciples in the intricacies of the Talmud – all these are bound to be marginal in the direction of national or communal affairs.

Yes, I fully recognized their enormous contributions to Jewish life:

Of course, most rabbis *are* deeply involved in every aspect of Jewish life, ranging from Zionism to Soviet Jewry, and from the education of the young to the welfare of the old. But by and large, they merely amplify and embellish the acclaim for policies set by lay-leaders and endorsed by the *vox populi*. They conduct appeals, join protests, march in demonstrations and generally call on their communities to support accepted strategies and slogans. But they scarcely ever challenge national policies, let alone devise and propagate policies of their own.

Hence, my keenest challenges were always addressed to my own colleagues, especially when presiding at – or until 1979 participating in – the Conference of European Rabbis meeting in plenary assembly every two years, and the Conference of Anglo-Jewish Preachers in alternate years, as well as at more frequent rabbinical assemblies I convened in London. What concerned me most was the application of Torah ideals to the wider issues facing our people, and in terms meaningful and relevant even to those estranged from our religious heritage. To this end, I pleaded in an address on 'The Rabbinate as the Conscience of the Jewish People' at the Conference of European Rabbis held in Switzerland in December 1972 (here translated rather literally from the original Hebrew in rabbinic parlance):

Instead of limiting our activities and protests mainly to items regarding which our thoughts are not their thoughts and their ways not our ways, the demand of the hour calls for concentrating our attention on major problems which are not only as thorns in *our* eyes and as pricks in *our* sides, problems which agitate not only the faithful and which distinguish us from those who err, but rather also with the problems which are the cause of anxiety and perplexity to society at large, problems which unite all sections of our people and which cannot be solved except through the teachings and practice of Torah.

Referring to Joseph's assertion to his brothers that God had sent him 'to preserve you alive for a great deliverance', I continued:

How great would be the respect, or at least the recognition, for us if we came to 'preserve life', by efforts to enrich and improve the texture of life which has now become empty of all meaning and purpose, the life of masses among Jews, as among the nations, surrendered to the vanities of the world, and its amusements, a life without contents and without goals, without the joy of *mitzvot* or the satisfaction of work. We may not yet have a generation that thirsts for the word of the Lord, but there are many who genuinely search in the quest to raise the quality of life and the morals of society. It is up to us, if not in common endeavour with them, at least to relate to them with understanding, to find the formulae containing blessings and answers for the perplexed of our times, to guide them along the path they should walk.

And more specifically:

The emptiness of life leads to lawlessness and depravity. Whoever has eyes in his head will admit that the sanctification of life is a protective fence against the inroads of crime and vice which corrupt and erode the fabric of our society and its security. Why do we not hoist to the mast the fact that in observant Jewish circles there are scarcely any incidents of immoral conduct, violence and drugs among youth? The time has come to raise a worldwide alarm, 'warning the great over the small', that is, the leaders of the people concerning the youth, that other than a religious discipline forged in institutions of Torah and in homes illuminated by its light, we have no shield against the perils of certain doom through the rampant lawlessness, which has already claimed many thousands of victims to a life of emptiness and mischief.

Today, even many unsophisticated people recognize that this is a perverse generation. Sons despise fathers, daughters rise against mothers, as confusion stalks the
world.

Here is but one of several illustrations I gave:

As a direct consequence of neglecting Torah ethics, the Jewish birth-rate in Israel
and the Diaspora is now so low that for the first time in Jewish history we have to
worry about Jewish survival. Here, too, we have remained almost completely silent
and leave it to others to echo the anguished cry of our mother Rachel: 'Give me
children, or else I am as dead', or the claim of our father Abraham when he replied to
the assurance of his Creator, 'I will shield you, your reward will be very great' by
saying: 'Oh Lord God, what do You give me if I go childless' – cries which should be
today the motto of our people for the realization of our yearning to remain the living
people of Israel – *Am Yisrael Chai*.

I again returned to the spiritual challenge of the Munich massacre:

Following the terrible tragedy at Munich, for instance, maybe it was incumbent
upon the rabbinate of the world to articulate the religious and moral conscience of
the Jewish people, at least to the extent of raising the question whether it was
altogether right for a Jewish delegation to come to the accursed land from which the
voice of the blood of myriads of Jews still cries out to Heaven – especially to Munich,
a place destined for punishment, for shame and for betrayal, in order to participate in
the very cult of the body and of physical strength against which our Maccabean
ancestors fought with such heroism and mighty dedication. . . .

Naturally, the task of transforming the ethos of Israel and of revitalizing the
age-old visions of the Jewish people was too precious and too exacting to be
left to rabbis alone. It equally challenged our people's lay leaders. In
my Memorial Foundation address of 1979, I summed up the call for 'New
Priorities' in Jewish life as shifting the emphasis

from saving Jews to saving Judaism;

from the preoccupation with the Holocaust which has passed, to alarm over the
present erosion of Jewish life which threatens the future;

from Zionism as an instrument of Jewish normalization and self-defence to the
creation of a state exemplifying the noblest Jewish virtues in the Prophetic tradition;

from concentrating national and communal attention on external perils to the
imperatives of Jewish living and learning as the life-line to Jewish survival; and

from a negative image of Jews as protesters and demonstrators to a positive
projection of their role in the betterment of society.

In this presentation of religious Zionism and its challenges, I realized well enough, the targets were beyond any time-scale. Indeed, as I often emphasized, we lived in an impatient age, expecting instant answers to timeless problems. I could never see any justification for despair or despondency in our criticisms, however harsh and demanding. On the contrary, such historic processes were bound to take time, measured in decades and generations rather than in years. We could hardly expect Israel to become a religious state and a model society at this very early stage in its development. After all, had it not taken the better part of half a millennium from the conquest of the Land under Joshua to the consummation of Israel's spiritual glory with the building of the Temple under Solomon?

What mattered was not so much what we had already achieved or still failed to achieve; it was rather the goals we set ourselves as our national targets, the ideals we were *striving* to attain. And what mattered equally was to cultivate a sense of confidence, an invincible faith that these goals, so long as we aimed at them, would ultimately be reached.

If it were argued that setting our sights on such distant visions was irrelevant to the far more pressing problems we faced at the moment, I could only reply by pointing to 'the essentially irrelevant streak in Judaism' itself, as I did in my BBC Passover broadcast of 1971:

> Judaism refuses to allow relevance to be used as a yardstick to establish its value, or as a measure to determine what is important and what is worth preserving in our ancestral faith. It emphatically rejects the notion that religion serves primarily as an expedient to solve the problems of our day.
>
> On the contrary. In the past it was the peculiar distinction of the Jew that he saw the purpose of his life not in terms of the contemporary experience in which he suffered or prospered, but in terms of his place in the overall realization of the Jewish and human destiny. Just as classical Hebrew has no present tense for the verb, speaking of action only as belonging to the past or to the future, so did the Jew eliminate the present as an experience of intrinsic significance. It was regarded as a passing stage between past and future, whereby life assumed meaning only insofar as it perpetuated the traditions of the past and sustained the hope of a perfect future.

Examples of such 'irrelevance' covered our entire history as the characteristic of Jewish timelessness:

> Thus, when the medieval Jew yearned and prayed for the return of his people to the Holy Land and the rebuilding of the Temple in Jerusalem, the vision he had in mind had very little relevance to the prospects of a happier and freer life for himself or even his children. He projected his past heritage and future hopes to 'the end of Days', however many generations might have to pass before their realization. He would neither seek nor see any essential relationship between his own fortunes or

misfortunes and the ideal society for which his faith induced him to pray and strive. His Judaism was not so utilitarian as to provide promised short-term solutions to problems, however agonizing, which bedevilled his generation. Nor did he cherish his religious observances, imposing on himself far-reaching restrictions of diet, work, marriage and other freedoms, by asking himself: 'What benefit do I derive from this; how will such a discipline help to make my life easier and happier?' Much as his religion governed his outlook and most of his activities, outside no less than inside the synagogue, the one thing he did not expect from it was relevance in our sense of the word. It was meant simply to add a spiritual and moral dimension to his life. The resultant blessings of personal contentment, of domestic and social stability, of ethnic survival, while often taken for granted, were purely incidental; their attainment was neither demanded nor investigated.

Ours, as I often stressed, was the generation of Davids. King David, having shed blood in war, was disqualified from building the Temple, the symbol of peace and spiritual fulfilment. This had to be left to another generation, that of Solomon – 'The King of Peace'.

Meanwhile, what our hard-tried generation needed most, especially from our spiritual leaders, was the balm of comfort and the tonic of confidence. Referring to the striking comment of Nachmanides, the pioneer of Aliyah, on Jacob's tragic bereavement of his young and most beloved wife, Rachel, because, as he explains, on entering the Holy Land Jacob could not remain married to two sisters in violation of the Jewish laws on incest, I concluded my lecture to the British Immigrants' Association in Tel Aviv:

Perhaps that is why Rachel, and not any other Patriarch or Matriarch, became the immortal comforter of our people, giving the absolute assurance to our exiles that one day they would return to Zion. She who uttered the ageless cry ringing through the ages and especially in our own time 'Give me children or else I die', she who laid down her young life to demonstrate that the Holy Land cannot tolerate immoral desecration, she sustained our people throughout the long night of our tribulations to witness the realization of her promise in our own days. She remains the personification of our hope, the mother of our faith that, like the experience of Jacob her husband, the night will pass and we will prevail.

# 12

# Secular Zionism –
# The End of an Illusion

Secular Zionism starts with an historical error and culminates in a contemporary illusion. It projected the Jewish State as the direct successor to Jewish sovereignty in Biblical times, and it had little use for the intervening period of exile and dispersion which it regarded at best as a national irrelevancy and at worst as an aberration. In either case, secular Jewish nationalists – looking solely to the Bible for the legitimization of Zionism – would view or review Jewish history as if the past 2,000 years hardly existed and mattered even less.

The most noted Jewish social historian of our time, Salo W. Baron, linked this revision of Jewish history to 'the general secularization of modern life and the specific assimilation of non-Jewish patterns of thought by Jews which is characteristic of the Emancipation era'. Writing on 'Newer Emphases in Jewish History' in 1963 in an essay republished a year later in his *History and Jewish Historians*, he observes significantly:

In contrast to [Yehuda] Halevi's days, the Christian world now glorifies its statesmen, conquerors and men of wealth above its saints and martyrs. The Roman concept of the supreme sacrifice for patriotic and nationalistic causes has displaced the ideal of religious martyrdom among Christians and Jews alike. Historiography could only follow suit. The heroic fighter for Israel's independence in 1948 has taken the place of the great religious martyr of former ages in the consciousness not only of the Israeli population, but also of the majority of Jewish youth the world over. Not surprisingly, therefore, the Israeli historians have turned their main attention to the heroes of the First and Second Commonwealths at the expense of the previously much more intensively studied Jewish Middle Ages and early modern times. Historians in the countries of the dispersion have likewise taken up the Jewish role in their country's revolutionary armies, of their political struggles for civil rights, their endeavours to ameliorate the fate of the working man and other phases of political and economic Jewish life. Yet it is to be hoped that this newer emphasis on politics, economics and military affairs, however justifiable on objective as well as psychological grounds, will not totally displace the understanding for the *Leidens-und Gelehrten-geschichte* which had so completely dominated Jewish historical writing of the nineteenth and early twentieth centuries.

For a perceptive historian, even of Baron's unrivalled rank, such leap-frogging in the rewrite of Jewish history may be merely a matter of regret, calling for correction. For the Jewish people, this contrived break in Jewish continuity is of more fateful consequence, particularly when national claims are thereby invested with pseudo-religious validation.

'The Bible is our mandate' was, I believe, first used by Ben-Gurion in arguing the Zionist case before the Peel Commission in January 1937. One wonders how much weight this argument carried with the British decision-makers? Was the Bible to be the Jewish people's title-deed to Palestine as an *historical* document? In that case, one must presume, the Arabs could have produced rather more recent documents to show that the title-deed was changed or transferred long since Biblical times. Or did the Zionists invoke the Bible as a *religious* sanction to supersede any other legal or historical claims because it is Divinely ordained? In that event, the British could well have dismissed such a claim as sheer hypocrisy. For there would surely be something laughably inconsistent in using the Bible, because of its Divine authority, to impose demands on the British, or on the Arabs, whilst the very Jews to whom the Bible was given and whose lives it was to regulate refused to abide by its mandate, to meet its demands or even to believe in its Divine origin – at least as far as secular Zionists represented them and their religious beliefs and practices.

What makes this hypocrisy even more glaring is that the British them-selves probably respected the religious character of the Bible, and the Jewish claim to Palestine, more readily than the Zionist leaders making their plea in the name of the Bible. The Biblical tradition in Britain certainly had a good deal to do with the Balfour Declaration and, preceding it, with the long history of influential British advocates of a Jewish return to Zion. The Earl of Shaftesbury and George Eliot are but two examples of notable English forerunners of Zionism. When I once asked a long-retired senior British civil servant, who mentioned to me he was involved in the discussions on drafting the Balfour Declaration, what he thought was the most decisive factor in the British decision, he unhesitatingly told me it was the Bible-loving streak in the British tradition.

Another personal experience might be even more telling. While on my first lecture tour of America in 1957, still as Chief Rabbi of Ireland, I spent a

Shabbat in Kansas City with the late Rabbi Maurice Solomon, and he told me a remarkable story. He had known President Truman for many years from neighbouring Independence, Missouri. In the early 1950s, the Israeli Aguda leader, Rabbi Shlomo Lorincz, knowing of this relationship, engaged Rabbi Solomon's good offices in arranging an appointment at the White House, also insisting on his presence as an interpreter. The two rabbis were duly received by the President, and Rabbi Lorincz enquired: 'What prompted you, Mr President, to grant recognition to Israel on the day the new State was proclaimed?'

In his answer, Mr Truman, who by his recognition had really in effect conferred legitimacy and viability on the self-proclaimed State, did not refer to any political or strategic considerations which had weighed on him in making that fateful decision. He simply said: 'I felt Providence had summoned me to complete the Balfour Declaration.' I have since had this story confirmed by Rabbi Lorincz himself. Once again, then, it was Providence, and not any thought of expediency or material advantage, which by his own testimony motivated that great Gentile in a decisive contribution to the consolidation of the Jewish State. The Bible was certainly *his* mandate, as it had been that of the authors of the Balfour Declaration.

Alas, it was hardly the call of Providence which stirred the Jewish founders of political Zionism. As secularists, their vision was governed by altogether different promptings. They were led or driven to Zionism not by the Bible but by anti-Semitism. As I put it to my audience of Anglo-Jewish settlers in Tel Aviv in November 1980:

Political Zionism was born and sustained mainly out of negative factors: the intolerable conditions of Jewish homelessness. Pinsker's *Auto-Emancipation* (1882) was sparked by the Russian pogroms in 1881. The seeds for Herzl's *Judenstaat* were planted at the Dreyfus trial in Paris, and even Jabotinsky was only converted to Zionism at the age of twenty-three by the Kishinev pogrom in 1903.

There is no disgrace in that. They knew no better. They had been completely assimilated Jews until their Jewish conscience was aroused by their encounter with the hatred and persecution of Jews. Their immortal contribution to the Jewish people is not thereby diminished. To some extent, such a negative impetus to Zionism could perhaps even be rationalized. At least I saw some justice in arguing, as I did in my post-Yom Kippur War lecture in London in January 1974:

Just as the creation of all life is accompanied by the pangs of labour and the loss of blood, so did every major thrust leading to the rebirth and consolidation of our national independence result from the agony of suffering, persecution and slaughter. In 1840, it was the Ritual Murder charge against the Jewish community of Damascus that sparked Alkalai's conversion to Zionism. Forty years later, the Chovevei Zion movement led by Lilienblum and Pinsker was galvanized by the pogroms in Romania and Russia, especially after the assassination of Czar Alexander II in 1881. Some fifteen years later, the endemic scourge of Western anti-Semitism manifested in the Dreyfus Affair, precipitated Herzl's metamorphosis from his assimilationist beliefs into his Zionist zeal. In the growing turmoil of the past six decades, it was left to the cataclysmic events of the First World War to produce the Balfour Declaration and the ultimate disaster of the Second World War and the Nazi Holocaust to generate the superhuman energies of the final push towards the birth of the new State, a state itself born and defended in the martyrdom of three wars, at the cost of much precious blood.

The notion that Zionism was intended to, and would, 'solve the Jewish problem' remained as axiomatic with the secular builders of the Jewish State as it had been with the founders of the movement. When Ben-Gurion told the Peel Commission in 1937 'The Bible is our mandate', he immediately added:

The Palestine mandate is only a recognition of this right and does not establish anything new.... The international endorsement given to the Jewish National Home is an end in itself, with the object of solving the Jewish problem and for the purpose of removing the historic grievance that the Jews had against the world.

Golda Meir was no less certain that this was the *raison d'être* of Zionism, when she wrote in her autobiography, *My Life*:

Most people by now have at least some notion of what the word 'Zionism' means and that it has to do with the return of the Jewish people to the land of their forefathers.... But perhaps even today not everyone realizes that this remarkable movement sprang up spontaneously ... in various parts of Europe towards the end of the nineteenth century. It was like a drama that was being enacted in different ways on different stages in different languages but that dealt with the same theme everywhere: that the so-called Jewish problem (of course, it was really a Christian problem) was basically the result of Jewish homelessness and that it could not, and would not, be solved unless and until the Jews had a land of their own again.

But where these secular pioneers of Zionism, and their successors, can be severely faulted, with incalculably painful consequences to the Jewish people, is on their miscalculation which led to probably the greatest illusion, and the greatest disillusionment, in Jewish history. As they all emphatically affirmed, they firmly believed, and they seduced most of the Jewish people to believe, that Jewish statehood would 'solve the Jewish problem'.

Religious Jews, one assumes, never shared this fantasy, since their Zionism was bred by Judaism, not by anti-Semitism. They may not have accepted this belief in Zionism's cure of anti-Semitism, but I rarely heard them challenging it, either. The secular credo of Zionism as the antidote to anti-Semitism was too widely cherished to be openly disowned. I think I was still quite lonely, therefore, when, already in 1962, I asserted in my fourteenth Israel Independence Day address at the Fifth Avenue Synagogue in New York:

How far have the designs of history and the workings of Providence fulfilled the dreams of the early Zionist visionaries?... In many respects, the fulfilment has greatly exceeded expectations. In others, it has fallen short of them. One cannot but marvel at the almost uncanny precision with which Theodor Herzl forecast at the turn of the century that in fifty years' time there would be a sovereign Jewish State. This is perhaps one of the most spectacular prophecies in modern times. Yet how different is this Jewish State from Herzl's *Judenstaat* as he envisaged it.

The early Zionist dreamers sought to 'solve the Jewish problem'. Jewish statehood, they maintained, would eliminate the 'abnormalities' of Jewish existence. By having a country, a government, an economy like other nations, Jews would become like 'normal' peoples. They would no longer be looked upon as unusual, different people, exposed to all the hatreds and suspicions of the non-conformist.

In words sadly even more topical now than they were then, I continued:

Israel certainly has not 'solved the Jewish problem'. Jews today are as uniquely different as they had always been.... The dangers of anti-Semitism today are as great as they were before the establishment of Israel, as witness, for example, the fairly recent worldwide swastika epidemic. The Jewish problem has remained unsolved and will remain so in the foreseeable future. Jewish statehood has not 'normalized' Jewish life in the Diaspora. On the contrary, in some ways Israel has added for Jews many new problems which never existed before....

That was over twenty years ago, when Israel was still enjoying its heyday in the international community and world opinion. But the idea that Israel would remove the 'abnormalcy' of the Jewish condition and make the Jewish people equal among the nations always appeared to me not only absurd as a defiance of Jewish history but also dangerous as a national aspiration in assisting the process of de-Judaization by robbing the Jewish people of its sense of uniqueness. And ever since then the theme has constantly exercised me, nay haunted my mind. At that time it was still unpatriotic to question the principal objective of secular Zionism, and language to express such a heresy had to be guarded.

By 1974, events spoke louder than any speeches on 'the fallacy of secular Zionism'. I could afford to be much more explicit, as I was in several post-Yom Kippur War addresses:

The spiritual crisis may well trace its origin to the fallacious premises on which the earlier secular Jewish nationalists based their dreams, plans and policies....

Ignoring the perennial lessons of our history and faith, they sought to turn their backs on our past traditions and the spiritual ingredients in the mystique of Jewish survival, convinced that, if only we had a state like all other nations, we would 'normalize' the Jewish condition and lose the 'peculiarity' responsible for our sufferings and persecution. . . .

What an idle dream this was! The Yom Kippur War has shattered this illusion. Jews today are as different, as 'peculiar', and as lonely as they ever were. Far from having solved 'the Jewish problem', the Jewish State has highlighted it. . . .

To be sure, the successes of Zionism were immense:

Of course, Israel's achievements are immeasurable – its restoration of Jewish pride and self-respect; its ingathering of the exiles and provision of a haven for millions of hunted Jews; its immense contributions to Jewish learning and culture; its social and scientific pioneering; its intense enrichment of Jewish life everywhere; its revitalization of Jewish education and communal activity, stimulating the re-identification of countless Jews who would otherwise have been lost to our people. . . . But the one thing the Jewish State could not, and must not, and never will achieve is to turn us into a nation like all other nations, losing our historic identity as a unique people.

Zionism's failure to reach its original goals was more than an accident of history:

Did we really have to wait for the Yom Kippur War to expose the futility of the attempt to 'normalize' the Jewish experience by wresting it from its spiritual moorings? Where was our sense of logic, where were our historical and religious traditions? These should have forewarned us against such an enterprise. Without our national distinctiveness as religious pioneers and moral path-finders, committed to the destiny assigned to us at Sinai and by our Prophets, if we succumb to being like all other peoples, what purpose is there to be served by Jewish survival altogether? Surely our forebears did not endure so much cruel martyrdom 'for the Sanctification of the Divine Name', or offer thanks to God daily that 'He has not made us like the nations of other lands, and not placed us like other families of the earth and our lot like all their multitude', in order that in the end we should glory in being a people just like all others, or even boast the finest army in the world! Would it make sense to establish a Jewish State as a bulwark against individual assimilation only to find it turning into an instrument of national assimilation?

Eight years later, the worldwide recrudescence of crude, virulent anti-Semitism in the aftermath of the war in Lebanon made it clear that Israel, far from having solved the Jewish problem or even just highlighting it as in the past, was now the core of the Jewish problem, inasmuch as anti-Zionism became the principal feature and expression of anti-Semitism. As I plainly told the Oslo 'International Hearing on Anti-Semitism' in June 1983:

For Jews, the painful feeling of an up-turn in anti-Semitism, following its relative quiescence in the immediate post-war period, is compounded by cruel disillusionment on two counts. Jews had hoped that the two cataclysmic events in modern Jewish history – the Holocaust and the rebirth of the State of Israel – would have put, for entirely different reasons, a permanent end to the age-old scourge of anti-Jewish prejudice.

On the second disillusionment I added quite bluntly:

Perhaps even more devastating has been the shattering of the dream, nurtured by secular Zionism for over a century, that Jewish statehood would remove the 'abnormality' of the Jewish people, making them equals among the nations and thus eliminating the root cause of anti-Semitism.

But again I emphasized that religious Zionists were shielded from this disillusionment:

Religious Jews, I must hasten to add, never shared this illusion. For them, the restoration of Jewish sovereignty in the ancient Homeland was not primarily intended to provide a haven for persecuted Jews nor to 'solve the Jewish problem'. . . . It was simply to resume a fully Jewish life in fulfilment of millennial prayers and of the Prophetic vision for the realization of the Jewish destiny. If by living as Jews and being different from others, with or without an independent state, anti-Semitism was maintained or increased, then this is a price which Jews were and are prepared to pay for being Jewish.

It is not easy to disabuse a people of an illusion fostered as a national dream for a century or more. It is even harder to prevail on those who have proclaimed this dream as the inspiration of their philosophy and their colossal achievements to admit that their vision was only a mirage after all. To this day, the Reform movement, born in nineteenth-century Germany out of the conviction that Jewish emancipation and equality would be gained by making the Jew conduct himself more 'normally' like every Gentile citizen, has not really acknowledged that this original motivation for the reform of Judaism proved a gigantic error, suffering its diabolical *coup de grâce* in the gas-ovens of Auschwitz. Others had noted the parallel long before I repeatedly drew public attention to it, notably the Agudist leader Yitzchak Breuer. I quoted his analogy in my address to the Synagogue Council of America on 20 November 1974:

This is not the first time in the modern Jewish experience that the fallacy of seeking security through becoming like others has led to disastrous disillusionment and catastrophe. Let me quote from a remarkable book just published under the title *Concepts of Judaism*, by Yitzchak Breuer, German Orthodoxy's most profound and articulate thinker who died in Jerusalem in 1946. In a chapter on 'Judaism and the National Home', he compared the early classic Reform movement with secularist Zionism in what may now seem to reveal some truly Prophetic foresight and insight:

Both Reform and Zionism aspire to a solution of the Jewish problem. Viewed externally, the problem rests on the obvious incongruity between the Jews dispersed among the nations and their non-Jewish environment. The failure of social emancipation, inspired by Reform, led to the attempt at national emancipation, initiated by Zionism. If Reform attempted to normalize the Jewish individual, Zionism proclaimed as its ultimate aim the normalization of the Jewish community as a whole, i.e. of the Jewish nation. Normalization means in this context, assimilation. Zionism wished to assimilate the Jewish nation to all other nations. Reform took hold of religion and separated it from the nation.

Secular Zionism's promotion of promises it cannot deliver is not only limited to the solution of the Jewish problem. It has generally encouraged the notion that Jewish statehood is a *guarantee* for Jewish safety. Enormous as is Israel's contribution to the security of Jews, including its offer of a haven to all who are threatened by persecution, the Jewish State still cannot ensure that Jews will 'never' again face collective dangers.

We have it on the authority of such an eminent scholar in this field as Professor Yehuda Bauer of the Hebrew University that, if Israel had existed before the Second World War, it would have made no substantial difference to the Holocaust, although the number of victims might have been marginally reduced. He asserted this in a lecture, and personally confirmed it to me.

Under different circumstances, the same applies today to the helplessness of Soviet Jews who are completely at the mercy of the Russians, with or without Israel. To project Israel's purpose solely or mainly as the guardian of Jews who will 'never again' be defenceless, diminishes rather than enhances the real significance of the Jewish Return to Zion.

I altogether question the usage of the word 'never', so common in the contemporary Zionist vocabulary. Even a sober scientist like Professor Ephraim Katzir, the fourth President of Israel, declared in an article on 'The Second Century of Zionism', contributed to the Spring 1983 number of the Israeli quarterly *Forum*:

Israel and the Jewish people have learned the lesson of the Holocaust. We can rely upon nobody but ourselves when we are in mortal danger. While loving peace and hating war, ... contemporary Israel has chosen the path of active resistance and self-defence, for we will never again allow ourselves to be overcome by the forces of evil and hate and destruction.

'Never again'? Unthinkable, yes; impossible, tragically not. The former President, and countless others thinking and speaking in the same vein, evidently forgot that, since the Nazi Holocaust, the fear of another imminent holocaust was openly expressed not in relation to the Jews of Russia, or even of Khomeini's Iran, but of Israel – when the Syrians had briefly breached its northern defences early in the Yom Kippur War! Besides, does 'the lesson' now learned imply that had that lesson been learned earlier Europe's Jews could and would have resisted the Nazi onslaught against which all other European armies proved powerless?

The best illustration of Israel's immense contribution to the safety of Jews was the spectacular Entebbe rescue raid in July 1976. But this extraordinary story – often cited as proof that the long arm of Israel would 'never again' allow Jews to be 'selected' for slaughter – also showed the limitations of this claim. 'Never again' in this context is surely not only an exaggeration but patently irrelevant. There can be no absolute guarantee that an Entebbe-type mission will always be possible and succeed. And much more important, the whole argument is neutralized by remembering that the Jews at Entebbe were only threatened in the first place because of Israel and the Arabs' determination to combat and destroy it. Entebbe therefore dramatically demonstrates that the safety factor added by Israel works both ways.

The secularist diversion of Zionism to aims it could not fulfil led to further far-reaching failures. It helped to create a negative image of the Jewish people, both in its own eyes and in the eyes of the world. If the principal purpose of Zionism is to secure Jewish equality and security, then so long as these objectives remain elusive, all national efforts have to be bent on achieving them, however futile the exercise. The single-minded pursuit of these efforts turned us into a nation of protesters, demonstrators, into denouncers of the forces which frustrated these efforts. Our national energies were invested almost exclusively in fighting *against* manifest evils – the enmity of the Arabs, the betrayal of the United Nations including former friends, the double standards of the press, the monstrous propaganda of anti-Semitic agitators, etc., etc. Of course, these menaces had to be fought with every determination, but not so as to become the overriding Jewish purpose or the major dynamic of Jewish life into which these negative commitments turned at the cost of struggling *for* our Jewish ideals. Secular Zionism was a train on a single-track line, moving to a dead end of isolation, and with nearly all of Jewry aboard. Precious few were left to consider a journey to the spiritual uplands of true Jewish values. Few Jews, and even fewer non-Jews, saw the Jewish purpose, or the Zionist reality, in this light.

Even after the obvious collapse of secular Zionism's philosophy, which left Jewish equality and security as elusive as ever, the failure to reverse its thrust towards positive ends continued to be costly and damaging, if only because the negative Jewish image further alienated world opinion and international goodwill.

It was particularly the religious community which I persistently reminded of this charge, for example in my 1975 address at the Conference of Ashkenazi and Sephardi Synagogues in Jerusalem:

Preoccupied with the burning problems of our own survival, we have lost sight of our assignment as a light unto the nations. We need this return to our Prophetic ideals not only to restore the relevance of the Torah to the perplexities of our times and its spokesmen to their historic role as spiritual guides. At stake are not only the submission of Jews to authentic Judaism or the public stature of rabbis, but the survival of Jews and Judaism alike.

Countless people now associate Jews not with spiritual values or moral advances – with which we had always been identified in the past – but with international tensions and perils, with the threat to the world's energy supplies, to détente between the super-powers, to safety in civil aviation and to freedom from fear of a nuclear confrontation of universal dimensions. If we no longer have a unique and incomparable contribution to make to the enrichment of civilization, then by what right can we demand the world's support, with all the risks to international peace and prosperity involved, for the sake of preserving a small people which has already outlived the life-span of other nations, especially in these brutal times when millions die of starvation and violence unmourned and unmissed by the world community?

At least equally worrying was the second consequence arising from the fallacy of secular Zionism: the failure on the internal front. Zionism had always aimed not only at Jewish national rehabilitation but at the reclamation of all Jews, wherever they lived, by preventing their loss to the Jewish people through assimilation. To a very significant extent, Zionism succeeded in this objective. Without Israel, countless Jews would no longer identify with our people, and even if they did nominally, their lives would be empty of any Jewish content. For many Israel became the life-line which rescued them from Jewish oblivion. Fully recognizing this as a momentous achievement, there is nevertheless also a serious debit side to the picture. In my post-Yom Kippur War lecture in London, I put it this way:

Paradoxically, while the establishment of the Jewish State has greatly intensified Jewish consciousness and identification in communities everywhere, it has also weakened the main common denominator between them. In the Diaspora, many Jews have found vicarious refuge for the expression of their Jewish identity in the existence and support of Israel. For them, living as Jews by proxy has conveniently replaced the personal discipline of Jewish living. In Israel, again, large numbers of Jews have found in their national allegiance a substitute for traditional Jewish loyalties. For these Jews, the Diaspora became the vicarious haven of their residual Jewishness, as poignantly attested by the many Israelis who discovered their Jewish feeling and identity only when they visit the Diaspora and find communication with their faith and with fellow-Jews in the synagogue. Thus Jewish statehood helped to accelerate the secularization, or de-spiritualization, of Jewish life both at home and abroad, leading to an ever-widening gap between Jews and Judaism.

It may be difficult to draw up an accurate balance sheet of worldwide gains and losses of meaningful Jewish identification resulting from the existence of Israel. For instance, against the Russian Jews who have rediscovered their Jewishness through Israel must be set the many Jewish immigrants from North Africa who have largely become alienated from their traditional way of life after they arrived in Israel; wrested from their spiritual moorings, they have often drifted towards delinquency and other vices of a type and on a scale previously unknown in Jewish society, despite some recent advances towards social parity.

Another recent entry in this ledger must sadly record balancing the number of immigrants from Western countries attracted by Israel's Jewishness against the same or even greater number of emigrants seeking in Western lands the security and prosperity Israel could not offer them – most of the latter shunning any Jewish identification in their exile. Whatever the statistical conjectures, it is indisputable that had Zionists concentrated on cultivating the country's specifically Jewish ethos, by a collective return to traditional values, with at least as much zeal as on the promotion of more mundane needs, the balance sheet would show none of these losses. The North African Jews would not have been so widely deprived of the props on which their culture, their self-respect and their common denominator with other Jews rested; and the Yordim would not have left had they found meaning in the totality of the Zionist dream beyond the vacuous promise of security.

Conversely, Aliyah too was bound to be adversely affected by the secularist image of Israel as a haven for the homeless and a worthy beneficiary of charity to the poor. This off-putting image was further aggravated in the kind of needs projected by all the major Israel fund-raising campaigns. I drew attention to this at President Navon's seminar late in 1981, which prompted the *Jerusalem Post* to report me as having 'suggested that Israel abolish its fund-raising organizations'. I corrected this in a letter published on 19 January 1982, a letter which also explained the price exacted by Israel's secularism in terms of reduced Aliyah rates:

> What I did say was that the biggest disincentive to Aliyah was the present form of the magbit [the Israel fund-raising campaign], since it portrayed Israel ... mainly as a country of unfortunates, of refugees and disadvantaged people. Such an image was hardly likely to encourage Aliyah from the West.
>
> Recognizing that Western Jews were principally attracted by the superior quality and intensity of Jewish life in Israel, as shown by the disproportionately high religious Aliyah rate, I therefore suggested that the appeal should focus more on enterprises

(thinking of, e.g. Western-style community centres, specifically Jewish educational and social amenities) with which the donors themselves would identify – hopefully as potential Olim. Such a shift in emphasis would both highlight and enhance the very features of Israel's unique Jewishness which predisposed Jews from the free world to contemplate Aliyah, whatever the hardships, and which are the main *raison d'être* of the Jewish State.

Even greater than the combined number of Israelis who were alienated, of Yordim who left, and of Olim who did not come, was another loss: the additional Israelis, at least two million of them, who would have increased Israel's Jewish population and security if the religious discipline of life had governed the conduct of all Jewish citizens, as it determined the phenomenal growth of the strictly-observant element. At least since my lecture on Jewish medical ethics at the Eighth World Congress of the Israel Medical Association in Tel Aviv on 14 May 1970, when the Association gave me as their estimate of abortions in Israel the very high rate of 40,000 annually, and long before even the Aguda raised this in the Knesset in 1976, I had constantly stressed the immense threat to Israel's stability due to the catastrophic price paid for the neglect of Jewish ethics on abortion and birth-control. Though I naturally supported efforts to bring Israeli law on abortion more in line with Jewish teachings, I realized that this in itself was not the answer, as I told the 1972 Conference of European Rabbis in Switzerland:

Problems such as these cannot be solved by legislation, or even by appealing to patriotic feelings. No one produces children out of purely demographic motives. These are matters which are surrendered to the heart, regarding which it says 'And you shall fear the Lord your God.' For without a deep religious conscience no effective means has yet been found to control abortions and birth-prevention. Only through the Torah can we literally 'preserve in life a numerous people'.

Seven years later, I challenged a leading article on the subject in the *Jerusalem Post* in a letter the paper published on 1 December 1979:

News reports from Israel these days mostly make dismal reading. But as a national death-wish with catastrophic consequences, few items can rival your editorial (2 November) in support of the pro-abortion lobby, duly followed by success in the Knesset.

The editorial contained not a single reference to the national disaster of Israel's Jewish population having been reduced by 50 per cent or more through the neglect of Jewish ethics on abortion:

Instead, it advocates pity for 'the unwanted children' by strangling them. Unwanted, one might ask, by whom? Perhaps by you and the vociferous abortionists. But certainly not unwanted by the nation, or by most parents to whom every child, once it is born, is an infinitely precious blessing, whatever the sacrifice, and least of all by the children themselves who treasure life, whether they were 'wanted' or not before they were conceived.

Yet I knew that purely legislative pressure was not the answer, and I took issue with the Aguda when it threatened to leave the coalition over the refusal to tighten the law by new legislation. I continued in my letter:

> If I have nevertheless urged the Aguda, and its Council of Sages, not to abandon the coalition over this issue, it is not because I doubt its supreme importance from every point of view, religious and moral as well as national. Rather, scandalous as the present law legalizing rampant abortion is, I do not believe that legislation by itself will provide the answer. I agree with you that the amendment would, sadly, not make much practical difference. Even before the law was liberalized three years ago and abortions for social reasons were illegal, there were thousands of violations without any prosecutions.
>
> The ultimate solution to this as to so many other social problems afflicting our people lies in cultivating a religious conscience through nurture in the spiritual treasures of our faith. Where this prevails, parents cheerfully raise large and happy families, blessed with children who are generally immune to the scourges of crime and vice as to the erosion of assimilation, who preserve their dignity even in physical deprivation, and who assure Jewish survival by heeding Rachel's timeless cry, 'Give me children, or else I die!'

In sum, the secularization of Zionism had greatly aggravated the Jewish condition, both internally and externally. Our travails were partly inescapable, due to factors completely beyond our control. But partly, building the state on the firm foundations of our religious traditions might have reduced both the intensity and the extent of these travails. In a generalized appraisal of Zionism's impact to date on religion at large, I could not help but observe, as I did in my twenty-fifth Israel Independence Day address in 1973:

> Quite apart from the pressing problems of national security, economic stability and social and religious harmony, the restoration of independence, by a strange twist of fate, has in different ways precipitated a direct confrontation with all the three monotheistic faiths generated out of Israel's spiritual energies. There is the confrontation with Islam, now the world's principal breeding-ground for hostility against our people; the confrontation with Christianity, which has not yet come fully to terms with the Jewish return to Zion and its theological implications; and even the confrontation with Judaism itself which must still evolve a dynamic response to the modern experience of Jewish statehood, just as the Jewish people must yet rediscover the timeless values of its religious faith, to provide a national purpose transcending the quest for physical survival and material prosperity. This applies with special urgency in an age when the gulf between Jews and Judaism is constantly widening. There can

be no survival of Jews without Judaism, as our history has amply proved, any more than there can be Judaism without Jews. The State of Israel can clearly prosper on the strength of its age-old roots and vindicate the millennial tribulations of its nurture only if it is dedicated to both propositions.

In this passage it is frankly recognized that Israel's 'confrontation with Judaism', at any rate, is not confined to secularists. The religious response to Jewish statehood is as yet equally inadequate in many areas, on both practical and ideological issues. One might almost charge that the custodians and spokesmen of Judaism have themselves become secularized in many, if not most, of their attitudes to the wider concerns of Israel and the Jewish people. When they make pronouncements on security, or peace and war, or relations with the Arabs, or Israel in the international community, or even Zionist fund-raising, they usually speak in accents little different from their secular counterparts and scarcely distinguished by any specifically religious insights. I made this point when I referred to the uncommonly Jewish attributes of the late Yaacov Herzog inspiring his political philosophy, in my contribution to the Katzir seminar in the summer of 1975. Since his untimely passing, I said,

> I do not know of a single ranking personality in or near the seats of power in Israel or outside who views the convulsive events of our times through specifically Jewish eyes as he did, who interprets current happenings and trends in the light of the forces governing Jewish history and the dynamics of Jewish thought. This deficiency applies not only to secularist leaders who conduct Jewish affairs of state as would statesmen, politicians or diplomats of any other people facing our dilemma. I look vainly even to our religious and rabbinical establishments for an interpretation of our national fortunes and misfortunes which bears the unmistakable hallmark of distinctly Jewish perceptions. Men of piety and learning may have succeeded to the priestly functions of spiritual leadership in Biblical times. But the Hebrew Prophets are without heirs today; the whys and wherefores, the questions on how to put the jigsaw pieces of our jumbled world intelligently together, remain unanswered.

This deficiency strikes me particularly in regard to the charge of double-standards being applied to Jews and Israel. The charge itself is unhappily justified, and it probably ranks on top of the list of complaints against the non-Jewish world which so incense Jews. And yet one would expect religious Jews to view this charge differently from its trite treatment in purely secular Jewish propaganda. After all, religious Jews might be expected to see some connection between this charge and that of the Prophet Amos: 'Only you have I known among the families of the earth, therefore do I punish you for your sins.'

A revealing illustration came my way not many years ago at a dinner-party in our home, such as my wife and I give for special guests from time to time. The guests on this occasion included a British government minister and his wife, both among the proven 'righteous among the Gentiles' in their genuine friendship for Jews and Israel. Our other guests were a highly cultured and deeply religious Jewish couple who were quite prominent as active public figures in Israel as they had been in England before they went on Aliyah a few years earlier, the husband being a dear personal friend since our student days together at Jews' College. Not unnaturally, the conversation around the table soon moved to Israel and its vicissitudes. Our distinguished non-Jewish guests explained how their affection and respect for Israel stemmed from their Biblical upbringing. They took it for granted that the Judaeo-Christian tradition had conditioned the world, or at least the civilized part of it, to associate the very word Israel with superior moral standards. I knew the comment was sincere, and it flattered my Jewish pride.

Not so our Israeli guests. They retorted quite angrily: 'We resent being treated differently from anybody else.' It was one thing, they admitted, in the argument which ensued, for *us* to aim at higher standards and to demand them from ourselves as the people 'chosen' for spiritual excellence. But the world had no right to make such a demand, or to scrutinize our conduct more severely if it was not met. Clearly, very religious Israelis looked at Israel's image among the nations with very secular eyes, and moreover were greatly upset when well-meaning Gentiles viewed Israel's special assignment in the same light. To me, this sense of resentment always appeared strangely at odds with the most insistent traditional teaching on Israel's place among the nations – serving, as was expressly proclaimed on entering our Covenant at Sinai, as an incentive to becoming 'a kingdom of priests and a holy nation'.

More generally, a similar division of perspectives developed, not between religious and secular Jews but between Israel and the Diaspora, on the connection between anti-Zionism and anti-Semitism, particularly as anti-Jewish feeling became so virulent in the wake of the war in Lebanon. The nature of that connection became the subject of widespread Jewish debates, some very shallow at popular level and others quite profound at academic seminars and in sociological studies.

Conditioned to attribute every misfortune to the wickedness of others whilst themselves maintaining a stance of flawless self-righteousness, Israelis always found a simple reason for every manifestation of hostility: the anti-Semitism endemic in all non-Jews. Thus, Prime Minister Begin could count on much popular acclaim in charging even the American administration with anti-Semitism when it took decisions unfriendly to Israel. And the rabbis were often the loudest to concur with the assumption that all anti-Zionism was due to anti-Semitism, whether the antagonism to Israel emanated from Christians or from Arabs.

There is of course a grain of truth in this assertion as supported by authentic Jewish sources. Rabbis were certainly on solid traditional ground when they so often quoted the almost imperatively worded statement of the Talmud: 'By an accepted ruling (Halachah), it is well-known that Esau hates Jacob' – a statement no doubt intended to stress the irrational character of Jew-hatred and the futility of wishing it away, though I was always quick to add that this 'ruling' specifies Esau and not Ishmael. In discussing the theme at the Oslo 'International Hearing on Anti-Semitism', I also readily conceded to the participating panel of experts, both Jewish and non-Jewish, that the Jewish tradition itself acknowledged a causal relationship between Jews and anti-Semitism:

Jewish thinkers recognized this nearly 2,000 years ago when they remarked in the Talmud on the linguistic link between 'Sinai' the mountain and '*Sin'ah*' – the Hebrew word for 'hatred'. They explained that the heritage of Sinai was bound to generate some universal dislike for those marked off by its Covenant from the rest of the world.

I also added both a rationalization and a pragmatic explanation. On the one hand:

An anti-Semite, it has been said, is someone who hates Jews more than is necessary. There is, one must suppose, some inevitability in antipathy for the odd-man-out, the dislike of the unlike. The Jewish people are, after all, difficult to classify, mysterious in their determination to swim against the stream. They just do not neatly fit into any normal category where others find their secure and undisputed place. . . . Jews constitute the only people who all have a common faith and who do not share it with any other nation. From the beginning, Israel was destined to be, in the Biblical phrase, 'A people that dwelleth alone.' Jews have thus always been fated to be without any natural allies.

And on the other hand:

No doubt the exposure to this hostility has also proved a significant factor in maintaining the cohesion as well as the resilience of the Jewish people over the ages. The absence of all pressure from outside might well have spelt the extinction of Jewish life long ago, by succumbing to the opposite force of *attraction* to the environment through assimilation. Indeed, with the current anxieties on the threat of assimilation to Jewish survival, it has been said that Jews have learnt how to survive persecution, but have not yet learnt how to survive freedom and prosperity.

But all this is still quite irrelevant to the relationship between anti-Zionism and anti-Semitism. Already in my 'Message to Anglo-Jewry', at the height of the anti-Jewish 'fall-out' from the war in Lebanon, I cautioned my community that it was neither wise nor true to label every anti-Zionist an anti-Semite, and that such an attribution could only be self-fulfilling by breeding anti-Semites. Of course, where anti-Zionism altogether denies the right of Jews to an independent state, it may well be tantamount to anti-Semitism. But not so anti-Zionism in the more commonly accepted sense of being pro-Arab rather than pro-Israel in the ongoing conflict. Such anti-Zionism, I maintain, need by no means spring from sheer anti-Semitism. I did not doubt that:

Recent events have emboldened latent anti-Semites to express their bias more openly and more aggressively. It is also patently a fact that even in otherwise well-disposed non-Jewish circles the sheer virulence of the worldwide assault on Israel has aroused anti-Jewish feelings, and sometimes even actions against Jews or Jewish businesses.

But we must distinguish between cause and effect. That intense hostility to Israel spills over into antipathy against Jews is manifestly obvious. Anti-Zionism is certainly a cause of anti-Semitism. But the reverse is much more questionable, and often plainly untenable as a fact.

It was understandable, though not necessarily an objective reflection of the truth, that:

... clearly the perspectives look different from Israel. For many Israelis, embattled by implacable foes surrounding them and increasingly isolated within the world community, the attribution of their vicissitudes to plain anti-Semitism is both natural and expedient, though they forget that this alleged endemic anti-Semitism did not prevent virtually all civilized countries from extending a good deal of sympathy to the Jewish State, at least until the Six Day War. By such attribution, Israelis ward off accusations that their own actions and image contribute to widespread anti-Zionism. Consciously or unconsciously, they must also hope that, if there is any redeeming feature to the plague of anti-Semitism, it is its encouragement of Aliyah through the agency of fear among Jews in the Diaspora.

To my mind, both the assumption and the conclusion may be seriously flawed. As for the encouragement of Aliyah through anti-Semitism:

... this hope is, I believe, misplaced and misguided. Jews simply seeking safety are not likely to turn as their first option to Israel, where the defence of Jewish security demands an even higher cost in lives and economic sacrifice than elsewhere in the free world. Moreover, an Aliyah driven by persecution rather than by the attractions of Jewish life in Israel is worthless. Such immigrants are likely to be the first candidates for Yeridah when opportunity beckons elsewhere.

And as for the real causes of the antagonism towards Israel, these are many and complex, in my view:

Among other factors, there are vested interests in relations with Arab countries; there is a residue of Christian hesitation to come fully to terms with the restoration of Jewish sovereignty in Zion; there is the genuine sympathy with the sufferings of the Palestinian refugees; and there is estrangement caused by a certain abrasiveness not uncommon with some Israeli leaders and spokesmen, not to mention their policies.

I uncomfortably suspect that more secularist Jews in the Diaspora than religious Israelis agree with this analysis. Yet I cannot help feeling that this testifies less to the comparative objectivity of Diaspora Jews than to the inroads made by the secularization of Zionism even into religious thinking. National self-criticism, once such a prominent mark of the distinction between Israel and the nations, now serves to extol the glories of the Jewish past rather than to understand the present and to unlock the future. Out of this assessment emerged the subject for the next chapter.

# 13

# 'A Time to Speak and a Time to be Silent' – The Anatomy of a Dilemma

The very title of my office is indicative of an in-built dichotomy. As 'chief', I head a community; I must represent it and speak *for* it. As 'rabbi', I am a teacher; I must speak for Judaism *to* my community and to others. The two responsibilities are all too often, and quite inescapably, in irreconcilable conflict with each other. While accentuated in my own case, the problem obviously faces any rabbi and, for that matter, any lay leader, too. They must be guides and spokesmen at the same time, and to say what should be is not always synonymous with explaining, or justifying, what is.

The problem is not rendered much easier by consulting our sources. They also seem to reflect this unavoidable conflict, or perhaps even inconsistency. There are the numerous classic passages in the Bible and the Talmud warning against loose speech, cautioning the greatest care in every utterance, and hailing silence as the highest virtue. 'Wise men, be careful with your words!' warns the Sage Avtalyon in the *Ethics of the Fathers*. Our sages ranked slanderous speech, even when truthful, as the worst of all ethical offences. The most unforgiveable sin, rivalled only by the Golden Calf, committed by the people of Israel in the wilderness was the defeatist report on the Promised Land by ten of the Twelve Spies, which led to demoralization and rebellion. With such warnings, Simon the son of Rabban Gamliel did not hesitate to declare: 'All my days I have grown up among wise men, and I never found any virtue better than silence', as also recorded in the *Ethics of the Fathers*.

Yet, there are clearly circumstances when silence is damnable. Failing to give evidence on witnessing a crime is a serious offence; silence is the accomplice of crime. The very essence of man's supremacy among all living creatures is his capacity to speak. Where others see the supreme distinction of man as a *thinking* being – *homo sapiens* – the Jewish tradition, as expressed in the Targum on the Creation story, describes the progenitor of the human race as 'a *speaking* spirit'. For thought only exists by being expressed. Isaiah immortalized the duty to speak up in the ringing words: 'For the sake of Zion I will not be silent, and for the sake of Jerusalem I will not hold my peace.' All the books of the Prophets are filled with fierce denunciations censuring Israel, like Moses before them and our sages after them.

Normally, when in doubt on resolving this conflict, silence would seem to be the better part of valour. It is certainly easier, safer, and personally less risky. The wisest of men in the Book of Proverbs counsels: 'Even a fool, when he holds his peace, is counted wise.' The same advice is given in the Latin proverb: '*Si tacuisses philosophus mansisses*', and the French proverb 'Silence makes no mistakes'. Abraham Ibn Ezra reflected similar counsel when he scorned a Karaite heretic, alluding to Exodus 20:23: 'Seeking to ascend on the ladder of wisdom by his vanities, he revealed his nakedness on it.' Nevertheless, wise or not, the exercise of speech is sometimes inescapable, pursuant to the ruling in the Talmud that 'Silence is accounted as admission', or its fourteenth-century English equivalent 'Silence gives consent'. The dilemma is not so simply resolved, and the risks to personal standing may sometimes have to be ignored.

In regard to spiritual leaders, moreover, there is also a halachic directive which can hardly be ignored. The dictum in the Talmud that 'A Prophet who suppresses his prophecy is guilty of a mortal offence' was transferred in the Talmud itself, and subsequently in the Codes of Jewish Law, to rabbis: 'Any rabbinical scholar who has been duly ordained (Semichah) and refuses to teach (and issue rulings), such a scholar withholds Torah and puts snares before the public; to him applies the verse (Prov. 7:26): "And numerous are those slain" by his default.' Teachers who refrain from teaching must bear responsibility for the casualties of ignorance caused by their silence, and rabbis may be indicted before the bar of Heaven and of history for Jewish national aberrations compounded by their silence.

The problem in its contemporary context relating to Israel is real and perplexing, and there is none over which I agonized more often and with greater pangs of conscience. These pangs always tormented me particularly when terrorist outrages against Israelis or Jews elsewhere had claimed further victims. Whether visiting families bereaved by terrorist actions in Avivim in May 1970 and soon thereafter in Kiryat Shemona, or standing at the sickbeds of Edward Sieff and Shlomo Argov after they were shot in London, I was haunted by the oppressive feeling that perhaps if I and others had spoken out more forcefully in favour of peace, in the first instance through a recognition of the Palestinians' legitimate grievances and aspirations, the edge of their inevitable hatred bred by despair might have been blunted, and these terrible tragedies might have been avoided. Similarly, my qualms were particularly acute when men who themselves had a record of violence were elevated to positions of leadership in Israel. It would have eased my conscience had I felt free to state my innermost convictions as Jewish teachings in the manner I understood them.

Nevertheless, I was painfully aware that the battle between conscience and prudence could not so easily be resolved, especially in my position of public exposure and accountability. For I readily acknowledge that both sides of the argument on whether to criticize Israel publicly or not are genuinely compelling; both are fraught with grave consequences; and both are advocated with equal passion and conviction. The consideration in favour of the silence option is the more obvious, but this does not render it the more conclusive.

The arguments for silence hardly need listing, and it does not require any great perception or foresight to see their validity and be convinced by their logic. There is the unity of our people which can only suffer from displaying our differences in public. There is the fact that our enemies derive comfort if we oppose policies which they oppose and agree with demands they are making. There is the recklessness of gambling with lives other than one's own, of passing judgement in ignorance of all the facts at a distance in the armchair safety and comfort of our homes. Not least, among the many perfectly valid considerations, is the injunction to 'see the good of Jerusalem' and always to 'tip the scales for merit in judging your neighbour'.

The dilemma is, of course, not confined to criticism of Israel. On the other hand, it is more acute, though sometimes easier to resolve, for spiritual leaders than for politicians or communal spokesmen. I analysed the predicament in an article, 'Conviction or Consensus', featured in the *Jewish Chronicle* of 9 April 1982:

> Every rabbi is often caught between the conflicting pressures of conviction and consensus. In some respects, a spiritual leader can more easily ignore public opinion. When I make a statement on, say, Sabbath observance or abortion in Jewish law, I neither claim, nor am expected, to speak on behalf of the mass of the community, but solely as a spokesman for Judaism, responsible to my conscience, as dictated by my religious convictions and commitments.

There may be even purely communal issues which demand a careful judgement on whether it is wise to take a public stand:

> Happily, I have never had to compromise my principles, to speak or act *against* my convictions: I would rather lay down my office than do so. But I have been silent on some occasions when my conscience would have preferred speech.
>
> If some statement or action is particularly offensive to Orthodox beliefs and practices, conviction tells me that I should denounce it, regardless of other considerations. Often enough I do so. But what if my response, or any reaction thereto, is likely to

produce the very opposite of what I seek to achieve, causing confusion or hostility, alienating instead of consolidating support for traditional Judaism?

I have never feared public controversy. But what if, by joining in public verbal debate, I would serve only to give publicity to causes and opinions which are in conflict with our most sacred convictions? (Thus, I believe the 'Who is a Jew?' campaign has contributed to publicizing non-Orthodox Judaism and promoting its growth in Israel.)

The problem equally concerns public issues in general:

The decision on whether to follow the dictates of conviction (to voice my views) or of consensus (to contain them) is hard enough when it concerns sensitive public issues, such as the morality of strikes or nuclear disarmament, on which my views vary from passionately held opinions both inside and outside the Jewish community.

Here the distinction between political and religious leaders goes beyond purely pragmatic considerations:

What is at stake is not so much courage as honesty. For custodians of the moral law, there can be only one winner in the contest between truth and expediency, or between the effort to persuade and the temptation to win acclaim.

The difference between political statecraft and spiritual leadership is not unlike the difference between science and religion: the former deals with things as they are, the latter with things as they should be. The former pursues what is attainable in the light of immediate goals and realities, the latter is bound by absolutes in the quest of remote ideals, however elusive.

Politicians, accountable to their electorate, must seek a measure of popularity for themselves and their policies to prevail; otherwise they fail and their efforts are fruitless. Religious leaders can succeed without prevailing. They succeed if they only plant seeds eventually to produce fruits which others will garner.

They can succeed even in loneliness – by comforting a broken soul, by sparking some new idea, by challenging evil, by just proclaiming their faith in man's regeneration and contributing a few bricks to the edifice of future redemption.

These moral imperatives add immeasurably to the burdens of conscience. In the case of Israel, they can easily become unbearable when moral dictates combine with a profound belief that certain actions or policies may be seriously misguided or may even be heading perilously towards disaster. Yet, I acknowledge that these burdens must sometimes be borne in silence, occasionally even when, were I publicly to take a critical stance –

I realize that I have no mandate from the community to speak on its behalf. But then, nor did the Hebrew Prophets have any such mandate for their strictures, although they undoubtedly spoke as Jewish leaders.

In relation to criticism of Israel, passions are easily inflamed. In endeavouring to present my own thoughts on reactions to this dilemma, I will offer an illustration, not related to Israel, to show that I am by no means insensitive to the popular demand for silence even in circumstances which are contrary to the dictates of conscience. Following my second communal visit to South Africa, I wrote an article to rebut, or at least to soften, a bitter attack by Chaim Bermant made against South African Jews, and especially their rabbis, for not speaking out more forcefully against the evils of apartheid. It was published in the *Jewish Chronicle* on 4 February 1977, and contained the following passage:

[The] charge that they and their rabbis are morally bankrupt because they live in a racist society and do not publicly speak out against it is an indefensible slander. In numerous conversations with South African colleagues and communal leaders I have found them as affronted by the injustices and indignities of apartheid as rabbis throughout the world.

If they have not proclaimed the Jewish abhorrence of racial discrimination practised there as loudly as we and they would like, it is precisely because the only alternative to tacitly accepting the system without protest is to leave the country, voluntarily or involuntarily. . . .

I know of no precedent for Jewish communities being expected to choose collective martyrdom for such a cause. Were Jews morally in default when they lived in inquisitorial Spain (before 1492) or in fascist Italy (before Mussolini bowed to Hitler's anti-Semitism), or in Negro-baiting America (before the Civil Rights movement belatedly got under way and at a time when protests were not tolerated), and they refused to pay the price of persecution or expulsion for public protests against systems incompatible with Jewish values? Or have we ever denounced Jews under Czarist or Communist domination because they did not become dissidents and speak out against tyrannies morally offensive to Judaism?

It is easy enough to be an armchair critic from a safe distance. The realities in South Africa are too foreboding for Jews, and Whites generally, to justify outbursts of righteous indignation against a remote community trapped in the vice of an insoluble moral dilemma.

In the case of Israel, neither the dilemma nor its consequences were ever quite as black-and-white. Nevertheless, my sensitivity to the gravity of the stakes was at least as great, so that quite often I would suppress my conscience and keep silent, against my better judgement.

In weighing the pros and cons, there were certain principles which I regarded as imperative, inviolate and immutable. First and foremost, whatever the provocation and however violent the vilification, I would always eschew any word, in speech or in print, which might give personal offence. As I once wrote to a colleague, after he had subjected me to a vitriolic personal attack, 'I have never yet publicly denounced anyone personally, least of all a rabbi, however sharply I differed from his view which I believed to be reckless and a mortal danger to our people.' Another invariable principle was to recognize the legitimacy of other views, however much I disagreed with them. In a letter acknowledging a respected friend's enthusiastic acclaim for my stand in July 1978, I wrote:

I am the last person to claim that only my views are right and others are wrong. Our predicament is far too complex and fateful to warrant any such certainties. But I am convinced that 'salvation is in the multitude of counsel' and that only by widening the debate and the options, instead of relying on a monolithic approach, can we ultimately hope to prevail.

Often reassuring in considering a controversial or a critical statement was the historical fact that the most fundamental differences on national policies in times of crisis have always been argued out openly, forcefully and without undue rancour among Jewish leaders in the past. For instance, there is no record in the Talmud of any sanction, disowning or denouncing rabbis who went against the stream and believed in an accommodation with Rome at one time, or in a rebellion against it at another. As I wrote to Rabbi Bernard Rosenzweig, President of the Rabbinical Council of America, when he issued his statement attacking me in July 1978:

Such differences are tolerable and authenticated by numerous precedents in Jewish history. But the cardinal difference between us is that, while I respect and understand your views without sharing them, you and those following your line do not reciprocate these sentiments. It is in this intolerance, rather than in refusing to acknowledge a monolithic unity where none exists, that I find the major tragedy of our times.

Another categorical rule I unfailingly observed was never publicly to criticize the Israel government or any of its decisions – such as the annexation of East Jerusalem and the Golan Heights, or the settlements policy in Judea and Samaria. The nearest I ever came to an open disagreement with Mr Begin was when I told a large AJEX rally of Jewish ex-servicemen and women in London on 21 November 1982:

Israel's Prime Minister, as already recorded in his earliest books, is fond of using the famous dictum of Descartes '*Cogito ergo sum*' – 'I think, therefore I am', by adapting it, 'I fight, therefore I am.' I cannot subscribe to this motto. To live by the sword was the assignment given to Esau, and nothing could be more alien to Jacob, his brother. The Jewish version of Descartes' saying should rather be: 'I am, therefore I think.'

My expressions of dissent, then, were limited 1. to affirming the right to dissent; 2. to supporting and advocating alternatives to policies being pursued; and 3. to challenging the religious encouragement of political militancy as the sole interpretation of Jewish teachings.

Over the principle that Diaspora Jews had the right, and sometimes the duty, to express critical views, I had the least qualms. The arguments for counting in Diaspora Jews, so long as they were motivated by a deep commitment to Israel, seemed to me as overwhelming as the arguments for counting them out – because they did not live in Israel – appeared hollow. Quite apart from the vaunted partnership of all Jews constituting such a key affirmation in all Zionist propaganda, and even discounting the financial, political and moral support received from the Diaspora, the assumption that policy decisions made and pursued in Jerusalem affected Israelis only became patently untrue long ago. Events in Israel very directly determined the fate of Jews everywhere, including their physical security, and certainly their standing in the society within which they lived. Any disenfranchisement of Diaspora Jews from participation in the anguished debate on Israel's future was a denial of Israel's centrality in Jewish life – like treating the human heart without regard to the effects on other parts of the body.

Equally unconvincing, it seemed to me, was the argument that Diaspora Jews, being distant from the scene, could not make any worthwhile contribution to determine Israel's interests. Of course, in many respects this is true, and Israelis are in a far better position to know and assess the facts around them. But in other respects, Diaspora Jews see things from a superior vantage-point precisely because they are at a distance. Following the Talmudic dictum, 'A witness cannot be a judge', one can be too close, in space and in time, to a situation or an event to evaluate it properly, and objectivity increases with the perspective of distance. The argument is altogether untenable in regard to the impact of Israel's actions and statements on the nations whose friendship and support it seeks to win. Jews living among them are clearly in a far better position to assess Israel's interests in this respect and to determine what is best calculated to influence governments and public opinion. The decisions obviously must be Israel's only, and Jews outside do not and cannot claim any 'votes', whatever their contributions to Israel. But their opinions should be respected rather than spurned and valued rather than resented if these decisions are to enjoy the maximum benefits of objectivity, sound information and critical appraisal.

As for the unity argument, this was often entirely specious, if not altogether dishonest. It hardly required my say-so to tell the world that Jewish opinions were divided, inside and outside Israel. With the Israeli and Jewish press revelling in controversy, evidence of Jewish diversity of views could scarcely be concealed from the non-Jewish public and its leaders.

Any attempt to paper over these divisions by proclaiming Jewish unity where none existed, could only undermine the credibility of Jewish spokesmen, and therefore render them ineffective even when speaking on issues on which Jews were united. Moreover, if Diaspora leaders always merely echo or amplify official Israeli policies, seeming to act on Israel government instructions, their representations would automatically be dismissed as representing the thinking of Jerusalem rather than that of the communities in whose name they purported to speak.

The projection of such contrived unity was also liable seriously to promote Jewish disunity. So long as only 'approved' views were tolerated and dissent was suppressed, especially in public utterances on behalf of the community, many thousands of Jews felt that they were unrepresented, and this disposed them to dissociate themselves from any formal identification with Judaism and the Jewish people. This feeling of being unwanted, and thus excluded from the fellowship of Israel, became particularly acute among Jewish students and youth who were not prepared to sign on the dotted line or to have their criticisms brand them as renegades or traitors. I therefore often cautioned my critics not to push the demand for closed ranks at the top to the point where lower down this would inevitably lead to widespread disintegration of Jewish unity by alienation and disaffection. I made this point even when I was not directly under attack, for example in a personal letter to the Israeli Ambassador, Avraham Kidron, dated 12 July 1978, after he had written to the editor of the *Jewish Chronicle* protesting against its leader 'Another Way':

I fear there is a tendency in official Israeli circles to misjudge and underestimate the growing uneasiness, disenchantment and resultant estrangement of significant numbers of Jews in this country, even among those deeply committed to Israel. I find disturbing evidence of this at every level of our community – intellectuals, students, synagogue worshippers, and even JIA workers. The rift which you fear does already exist, even if it is officially ignored or suppressed. These important elements (whose thinking I neither share nor represent) cannot be reclaimed to the Zionist cause by cultivating a mood of complacency or resignation, by a pretence of unity where there is no unity, and indeed can be no unity. They require an encouragement to become articulate, or at least that they can be part of a House of Israel in which diversity of opinion is tolerated.

Much graver is the charge that by expressing criticism we help our enemies. Often enough, this argument certainly appeared plausible as it contained some factual substance. Many times my detractors sought to prove their point by telling me that my controversial statements had been quoted with relish, in or out of context, by Radio Jordan and generally by the Arab propaganda machine. Indeed, I myself had evidence of this when I saw a quotation from me following similar quotations from Pope John Paul II, President Ronald Reagan, and Prime Minister Mrs Margaret Thatcher, in a half-page advertisement placed by the Arab Women's Association in the *Guardian* in October 1982 under the banner heading 'More PLO Propaganda?'

This example is instructive and highlights the dilemma. The quotation came from a *Guardian* report of my statement on the Beirut massacres, and simply said, as correctly cited in the advertisement: 'No condemnation can be strong enough of those who perpetrated or connived in this outrage.' Identical words could have been used by any responsible Israeli or Zionist leader. Was I then not to denounce a heinous crime and those who perpetrated it, just because my words could be misused for pro-PLO propaganda? Granted the words quoted on other occasions could be construed as more critical or challenging than those included in this particular advertisement, was it really true that such critical expressions of opinion weakened our friends and strengthened our enemies? Did not Radio Jordan and the rest of the Arab propaganda machine find a far richer hunting-ground for anti-Israel, and sometimes plainly anti-Semitic, attitudes and policies in statements by Israeli leaders which dismayed Israel's friends and hardened the hostility of its foes? To avoid such provocation, would I ever be justified in telling Israeli leaders to change their view so as simply not to provide grist for the propaganda mills of our enemies? Surely not!

I included this argument in my response to the attacks on me by the various presidents of American Orthodox organizations when I wrote to each of them on 9 April 1980:

> As for bringing 'joy to our enemies', they do not have to wait for statements from me, however distorted. They find and use far better ammunition to support their hostility and intransigence in statements and actions emanating from political leaders in Israel and their supporters. Yet I would never argue that because such statements and actions provide aid and comfort to our enemies, the Israel government should change its policies to prevent such abuse.

Despite the comparison I had made to vindicate my action, I knew of course that there was a difference. My statements were intended to encourage moderates, whether among friends or among Arabs, or indeed among Jews. Official Israeli statements were intended to achieve the opposite: hardening Arab attitudes in order to justify a corresponding hardening in favour of maximalist positions by Jews and their supporters. But, clearly, whether conciliatory or militant attitudes were more likely to lead to peace and security was the nub of the argument itself, and this did nothing to encourage our enemies. Those foes who did not want peace were obviously supported in their intransigence by provocative rather than moderate Jewish statements.

If any proof were needed that it was not criticism as such which so angered my critics as a breach of Jewish unity, etc. etc., I found it in the fact that the criticism came under attack only when it was on the side of moderation. When official government policies were assailed more intemperately by groups and individuals who regarded these policies as far too soft and who called for greater extremism, they were never subjected to the charge of breaking Jewish unity or undermining the authority of Israel's government. If some American rabbi, for instance, publicly endorsed the more radical demands of Gush Emunim, or added his name to the signatories of a Lubavitch advertisement in the non-Jewish press denouncing Begin's peace treaty and his surrender of Sinai, such a rabbi would not be upbraided in outbursts of fury. Criticism of criticism was always highly selective.

However, my greatest difficulty in reaching a decision on whether to speak out or to remain silent was always how to live with my own conscience. I could never forget, as already stressed in my *Jewish Chronicle* letter of 7 July 1978 mentioned earlier, that our principal charge of complicity in the Holocaust was against the silence of the world, and that we of all people should not ever again allow history to point a finger at us as the 'Generation of Silence'. My friend Elie Wiesel once told me that when he spoke and wrote of 'The Jews of Silence' in connection with Soviet Jews, he meant not them but the Jews outside Russia. If I, or others, believed with every conviction that the pursuit of certain policies might lead Israel to disaster, or cause damage to Jewish interests for generations to come, what were we to do? Yes, in expressing my views, I laid myself open to the charge of 'irresponsibility'. Such a charge was publicly levelled at me by a cherished colleague, Rabbi Simon A. Dolgin, writing as Chairman of the Mizrachi-Hapoel Mizrachi World Organization. I could only reply to him as I did in my letter dated 24 June 1980:

I deem it equally 'irresponsible' to despair of ever reaching an accommodation with the Arabs, and thus to jeopardize the viability of Israel. I also think it 'irresponsible' to give religious sanction to policies which undermine the security of the State, if only by alienating the few remaining friends on whose goodwill and support Israel depends.

And I added:

Finally, it seems to me 'irresponsible' in the extreme to attack views by distorting them, such as the baseless allegation that I 'advocated a Palestinian State' or 'agreed to some redivision of Jerusalem'. I advocated leaving all options open after ten years of completely normal relations with the Arabs, provided Jerusalem remains the undivided capital of Israel.

In practice even these considerations did not usually prevail as I constantly wrestled with my conscience. More often than not, however passionately I felt on a particular issue and however weak the arguments against my speaking up appeared to me, I suppressed my criticism in deference to the case for silence. In fact, even with the self-imposed limitations on any expression of criticism featured earlier in this chapter, out of a total of hundreds of public statements on Israel, those with a stance even indirectly critical of Israeli policies could be counted on the fingers of my hands.

Occasionally I would escape the dilemma by a kind of compromise. When my conscience was particularly ill at ease, and yet I felt unable to react by an openly critical statement which might immediately attract attention with possibly harmful effects, I would express my views as part of a lecture or an article, likely to be noticed by more discriminating audiences or readers than would be aroused by provocative newspaper reports.

One telling example was Israel's involvement in the international arms trade. I had always regarded the export of conventional weapons as a far greater evil, and a more real threat to peace and human life, than nuclear armaments. The former had led since 1945 to over ten million people killed in some 145 wars – virtually all fought with weapons supplied by one country to another for commercial or political gain – whilst the latter had served as an effective deterrent, and there had not been a single nuclear casualty throughout this period. I therefore often denounced this immoral trade as one of the most heinous scourges afflicting mankind.

But I was well aware that Israel was amongst the worst offenders. Often my Jewish, not to mention rabbinical, commitment would have wished to register my sense of revulsion in some words of protest and condemnation, particularly at the absence of any religious scruples in Israel. But I knew I was entering here, literally and figuratively, a field full of high explosives. And so, in an address to the rally of Jewish ex-servicemen and women on 21 November 1982 in London, I 'sneaked in' the following passage, later recorded in the Spring 1983 issue of *L'Eylah*:

> It is sickening to read of leading ministers of great nations peddling their wares of death to all and sundry prepared to pay or borrow for them, often arming poor nations to the teeth – teeth which have no food and only bullets to bite. What a bitter irony that British servicemen were killed in the Falklands by weapons the British themselves had supplied to the Argentinians in a war which, like most others, would never have broken out without such supplies, and that France is already rushing to replace the Exocet missiles which have just sunk British ships. And how much sadder still that the people meant to export 'Torah from Zion, and the word of the Lord from Jerusalem' is now itself among the leading exporters of Esau's trade, competing for the blessing 'And you shall live by your sword' and even make money from it.

More recently the subject became acute again when it was suggested to me that I lead a delegation representing Anglo-Jewry to protest in Bonn against the planned German arms deal with Saudi Arabia. Much as I was affronted by Germany of all countries intending to supply arms to one of Israel's implacable enemies, I nevertheless refused to go, as it seemed an utter hypocrisy to preach on the immorality of arms sales on behalf of a country which itself was not innocent of this evil. But I went no further and made no statements of any kind, except to include the following in an article on 'The Holocaust – Forty Years Later' prepared for a WJC *Year Book 1984* to be published in America:

The Jewish people might as well face the brutal fact that nations do not acknowledge enduring moral debts to each other. If there is one people on earth which once acknowledged such a debt to others it is the Jewish people itself which, by assuming the assignment to become a light unto the nations, committed itself to a superior moral standard in relation to others. Yet when this claim is being pressed, it is rejected and resented by most Jews as 'double standards'.

A quite recent experience will illustrate this moral dilemma. West Germany contemplated supplying Saudi Arabia with arms. Israelis were outraged and summoned Jews the world over to join in denouncing the proposed sale of arms by the perpetrators of the Holocaust to hands which might well use them again for the destruction of Jews. The logic of the outrage was perfectly justified. Yet it lacked moral consistency, and therefore conviction, so long as Israel itself was among the leading arms exporters – to countries which include some of the worst offenders against human rights. It is idle to protest against the supply of arms which might be used for another Holocaust so long as the protestors themselves readily sell them to evil regimes for the suppression of human freedom and equality by violence.

But often enough I withheld or withdrew altogether even this form of literary criticism. By now I have a fair collection of articles which I carefully composed and yet never published, some on the advice of friends I consulted, and others because I myself eventually gave silence the benefit of the doubt. In this category, I already mentioned my halachic article on civilian casualties in the Lebanon war. Once this was refused by the editors of two journals who were well-disposed towards me, and although I did not agree with their judgement, I did not pursue the matter any further, as I could have done by finding other publications ready to feature it. But in most cases such unpublished articles never even reached any publisher, since I decided, or was prevailed upon to decide, that it would be wiser not to provoke renewed controversy. Sometimes I also feared that, strongly as I felt on the subject raised, my views might be misunderstood or misrepresented, as had happened with the critical statements I did make on very few occasions.

From one such article painstakingly put together and then withheld from publication, after obtaining conflicting advice from several knowledgeable friends I consulted, I will quote here as an illustration of my predicament. In my constant plea for greater tolerance to break the escalating cycle of polarization, I was anxious to show that two completely contradictory views of Israel could be equally valid as two sides of the same coin. I took my cue from the argument in the Talmud between the Schools of Shammai and Hillel on the manner of celebrating the Chanukah festival. Shammai's School held that the lights should be kindled in descending order, with eight lights on the first night and one on the last. According to the School of Hillel, the order is reversed, starting with one light and ending with eight. Under the title 'The Two Faces of Israel – A Plea for Mutual Understanding', I then elaborated the argument:

They clearly differed on the assessment of the event and its significance. For Bet Hillel, the miracle increased with each successive day. The excitement grew as the little cruse of pure oil the Maccabees had found, sufficient only for one day, wondrously burnt on, first for another day, and then yet another, until ever more miraculously it lasted for eight days. For Bet Shammai, the same phenomenon produced the opposite reaction. The sense of wonder decreased day by day, as the miracle gradually lost its novelty and was ever more taken for granted.

Presumably, they likewise differed on the reaction to Israel's national rebirth. For Hillel's School, each successive day gave cause for added joy and celebration, whilst in the view of Shammai's School the thrill of independence declined with the passage of time.

A similar difference of attitude and perspective marks the responses to the wondrous restoration of Jewish sovereignty in our time. For many, the excitement of 1948 has progressively faded, and the existence of the Jewish State evokes ever less awe and festive gratitude. For others, the wonder of Israel's continued existence, prevailing over ever-mounting odds, grows year by year, and the miracle is greater now than it was thirty-five years ago. . . .

Both views were authentic, I continued, 'these and those are the words of the living God', as the Talmud commented on all disputes between the Schools of Hillel and Shammai. On this basis, I then proceeded to juxtapose two columns indicating two conflicting, and yet complementary, assessments, both of which I believed to be true. The article, written during October and November 1982, ran into nearly six foolscap typescript pages, and I here reproduce only two fractional extracts – picked at random – on Herzl's vision, and on Israel's spiritual contrasts:

| | |
|---|---|
| Herzl's daring prophecy just before the turn of the nineteenth century that 'if you will it, it is not a legend' and that in fifty years' time there will be a Jewish state, has proved one of the most uncannily accurate and far-sighted political forecasts of all time. But even his vision | Herzl's confident promise that the Jewish state would 'solve the Jewish problem' has proved one of the greatest illusions of all time. Israel is now the core of the Jewish problem. Little did he foresee its aggravation of the Jewish condition, now more precarious than |

has been far exceeded by Israel's momentous achievements.

Most significant of them all is the Ingathering of the Exiles. Offering a haven to Jews wherever they suffer persecution, Israel has successfully absorbed a greater proportion of refugees than any other country, multiplying its original Jewish population by over five times. . . .

Spiritually, too, Israel has made enormous strides. Literacy has reached world-record levels. Israelis produce and read more books, magazines and newspapers *per capita* than any other country. They are in the top league in science, agriculture, medicine and the arts.

In this regeneration of the Jewish spirit, religion also flourishes as never before. The Bible, the Shabbat and festivals suffuse the whole of Israeli society. Kashrut is strictly observed in all official establishments, including the army. All matters of personal status among Jews – every marriage, divorce or conversion – is under Orthodox rabbinical control. The rabbinate is recognized and supported by the state, as are the rabbinical courts on a par with secular courts. Torah learning is at an all-time peak, far excelling the most intensive traditional communities of pre-war Eastern Europe, with tens of thousands of students at Israeli yeshivot and religious seminaries for girls. Religious Jews now even command their own university, their own hospitals and numerous other academic institutions. . . .

ever, and its many failings as well as successes.

Most significant among them all is the Exodus of its population. Disenchanted with their new home, one-quarter of all Israelis have emigrated, a greater proportion than have left any other developed country. This outflow has now even outstripped the inflow of new immigrants. . . .

Spiritually, too, there are many appalling defects. Scourges previously unknown among Jews – large-scale crime, vice, even prostitution – are now rampant in Israel, as are divorces, corruption and other evils we had hoped to leave behind us in our exilic experience.

In this moral decline, religious life also suffers grievously. The divisions between 'Dati' and 'non-Dati' – even to the point of separated neighbourhoods – are more pronounced in Israel than anywhere else. Two-thirds of Israel's children are raised without any religious instruction or experience, a percentage far higher than in most other Jewish communities. Synagogue services for state occasions are unknown. Rabbis are state-officials – functionaries who supervise foods, marriages, Sabbath observance in hotels and the like – rather than spiritual leaders or pastoral mentors, and their influence is often political more than spiritual, especially in the sphere of religious legislation – resented as coercive by most Israelis. Consequently, anti-religious sentiments are more bitter and widespread in Israel than in any Diaspora community. . . .

What eventually tipped the scales against publication was the obvious argument that only, or mainly, the right column would be used and quoted, whilst the positive assessments on the left would be overlooked, thus not only destroying the whole purpose of the exercise, but exposing myself once again to a negative projection of my Zionism, when in fact I seek to see the light and the shade equally. Intensely as I felt that such a graphic demonstration might contribute to greater realism as well as to better understanding, I nevertheless dropped the idea and preferred to remain silent.

The overwhelming majority of instances when I resisted the temptation to keep silent involved defending Israel and its actions. Here, too, the decision to speak out was not always easy. It is not only that you do not win friends by publicly pleading an unpopular cause, such as Israel often was. It is also a matter of carefully weighing the importance of an argument against the hostile retorts it is likely to evoke by way of published replies, against the risk of over-exposure in protesting too much and too often, and against drawing attention to an issue best left to die a natural death. Nevertheless, when I found major Israeli interests at stake or unfairly attacked, from whatever quarter, I would usually not hesitate to disregard these risks.

Thus, quite apart from countless addresses in support of Israel within the Jewish community and beyond, I frequently intervened to fend off criticisms of Israel or to press for some Israeli interest by direct representations to government or Church leaders as well as through the public media – in interviews, articles, and letters to the press. In the former category, I will quote from just two examples of letters hitherto unpublished. After the Yom Kippur War, the following plea went to the Ambassadors of Syria and Egypt in London in my name together with that of the Haham, Dr Solomon Gaon:

> We write concerning the Israeli soldiers who fell in battle during the recent war and whose bodies are still in Syrian/Egyptian hands.
>
> Great anguish is experienced by the families of these soldiers, who sorely wish the last burial rites to be performed in accordance with Jewish religious tradition. It would be a humanitarian gesture to assuage their grief by permitting burial of their fallen sons within a Jewish cemetery. Concern for due reverence and respect for the dead is shared by all religious beliefs and particularly by Islam and Judaism.
>
> We would, therefore, respectfully urge you to make strong representations to your government for facilities to be extended and arrangements made with the appropriate chaplaincy or International Red Cross authorities to effect the transfer of the bodies concerned. We would willingly intervene with the Israeli authorities to request that they make available any similar reciprocal facilities required by you. . . .

Again, after the release by France of the notorious PLO terrorist Abu Daoud, I wrote to the French Ambassador in London on 14 January 1977:

You have no doubt received numerous protests against the travesty of justice and international morality perpetrated last Monday in France by the abrupt release from detention of one of the world's most notorious terrorists.

If, as Spiritual Leader and spokesman of the Jewish communities in Britain and the Commonwealth, I add my voice to the chorus of dismay raised by civilized men everywhere, it is because of the special place of honour and affection in which France has for long been held by the Jewish people. ...

France was the first country to initiate the emancipation of Jewish citizens from the oppressive disabilities endured up to modern times. The friendship and help of France decisively contributed to the consolidation of the State of Israel in its formative years, just as France herself had to rely on the assistance of powerful allies for her liberation from Nazi terror.

The action of France, now harbouring the largest Jewish community in Western Europe, in beclouding this shining record is therefore a cause of special grief to Jews everywhere.

The damage done in freeing the suspected perpetrator of one of modern history's most dastardly crimes without due process of trial cannot immediately be undone. But may I at least plead with you to prevail upon your government to give some public expression of remorse instead of defending the indefensible. ...

*The Times* alone received and published some half-a-dozen letters from me in defence of Israel – such as those seeking to temper the Islamic frenzy raised by the Al Akhsa fire on 20 September 1969, asserting Jewish sensitivies in the accidental shooting-down of an Arab airliner over Israel on 28 September 1973, rejecting the 'An eye for an eye' charge applied to Israel's reponse to terrorism on 7 July 1976, and denouncing the comparison between the '*accidental* killing of civilians . . . with the Christians' massacres of Jews throughout the Middle Ages, or with the Nazis' deliberate extermination of six million . . .' on 27 November 1983 to rebut an article which made this comparison a few days earlier.

Whether in my direct representations or my published rejoinders, I was always careful to express myself in distinctly Jewish religious terms, and never to use expressions or arguments which would come more conventionally from Jewish lay individuals or organizations. I was also concerned, whenever possible, to strike some balance between accusation, or justification, and the acknowledgement of whatever credit I could find to the party addressed. I knew that in all these protests the cultivation of goodwill and understanding mattered more than simply going through the motions of denunciation. I was ever mindful of the advice my father often repeated: 'One hundred friends are too few; one enemy is too many.'

In this spirit, I was also convinced that it was no more important to protest against manifest evils than to acknowledge gratitude when due. I could never forget how the senior government officials in Moscow had complained to me that even when they did sometimes serve Jewish and Israeli interests, especially by having let well over 100,000 Soviet Jews – including many leading intellectuals and scientists and artists – leave the country, they never heard a single expression of acknowledgement, let alone of appreciation. Nor could I forget that we called ourselves not Abrahamites, Isaacites or Jacobites, but 'Jews' – after Judah, *Yehudah* in Hebrew, who was so named when his mother exclaimed 'This time I render thanks (*Odeh*) unto the Lord.' Gratitude was to be the hallmark of the Jew.

The need to express such sentiments struck me particularly at the height of our agony, when the slaughter of the Israeli athletes in Munich evoked such profound and worldwide sympathy. In my memorial address on 11 September 1972, I asked how our Hebrew Prophets would have reacted to a calamity of such national poignancy and such universal ramifications, and I included the following passage:

To the nations, I believe, their words would ring out clear with a double message: First, an expression of gratification that at last the peoples of the world have not left Israel to endure its tribulations alone, on its own.

In the past, we have all too often borne our ordeals in utter loneliness. When six million Jews were brutally done to death in a bloodbath unmatched in the annals of man, we had to weep by ourselves. The nations did not lower their flags to half-mast, there was no memorial meeting for the victims attended by leading representatives of the world's nations, great and small; the conscience of mankind was hardly stirred by that monstrous tragedy inflicted on our people.

How different this time, when the world has shared the trauma of our anguish, when we have received the most touching messages of sympathy from thousands of human brothers in positions high and low, from leaders of nations, and races, and creeds in all parts of the globe, and when at last we hear a universal outcry for concerted action to liberate the human race from the intolerable stain of wanton terror against the innocent.

In acknowledging this momentous advance towards the ideals of human brotherhood our Prophets were the first to preach, they might also have added a warning: the values of human life and dignity, no less than peace, are indivisible.

Likewise, when I received a touching letter of sympathy from Cardinal Heenan on that occasion, I was quick to reply to him in terms which I hoped would characterize the Jewish heart, including the following paragraph:

Having so often in our history suffered our tribulations in loneliness, we are on this sad occasion sustained in our grief by the worldwide outpouring of sorrow and sympathy, as exemplified by the noble sentiments expressed in your letter. It is our fervent prayer that the bonds of human fellowship thus cemented by a common sensitivity to human sacrifice and suffering will help to strengthen the resolve of all nations and governments to eliminate the scourge of violence and hatred from the human family.

Once I had made my decision – be it to remain silent, or to make my voice heard – I rarely regretted it afterwards. I can recall only one occasion when, having followed the advice of friends I consulted, I deleted a passage, I later experienced considerable pangs of conscience. In the draft of my Hebrew address given to the Conference of European Rabbis early in 1972, I had included a remarkable thirteenth-century rabbinical commentary I had come across on the symbolic remembrance in our New Year observance of Sisera's mother grieving for her son who had been killed in his battle against Israel under Deborah in the Bible. I used this passage to remind rabbis how Jews should feel about the sufferings of innocent Palestinian refugees; even the mothers of terrorists deserved our sympathy. But realizing that this was a 'touchy subject' I asked two leading participants at the conference – including our Israeli guest of honour, a revered 'old-style' Dayan – for their opinion, and they both strongly urged me to omit the reference, so I crossed out half a page in my paper. I was sorry afterwards, so much so that I included the reference half a year later in my address on the massacre of Israeli athletes at the Munich Olympics:

Our Prophets would have emphasized particularly the moral call to share in the ordeals of others, as we want others to share in ours.

It has always been the Jewish characteristic that our compassion extends to all who suffer, even our enemies. Our sages tell us that the hundred notes of the *Shofar* which we sound on the New Year are meant to echo the hundred sighs that rose from the bereaved mother of Sisera, when he was slain in his battle against the Jewish people in Biblical times.

As for the opinions I did publicly express in speech and writing over the years, I felt able to assert in my lecture: 'The Attitude to Zionism of Britain's Chief Rabbis in Their Writings' on 9 May 1979, delivered before the Jewish Historical Society of England (and reproduced in full at the end of this volume):

I cannot speak for my predecessors, and I do not know whether they would now reaffirm every word they have committed to print. But for myself, and with hindsight, I do not regret what I have written, nor would I wish to make any amendments or deletions.

Naturally, I deeply regretted some of the controversies which the *reports* of

my statements had caused. But these regrets concerned the misunderstand-
ings and misrepresentations to which I had given rise, not what I had actually
said or written. I still see no reason to change any of my views or my
expression of them.

# 14

# 'Who is a Jew?' – Case History of a Zionist Question

The previous chapter should have concluded my broad survey of Israeli statehood in the light of Jewish teachings, with its critique of secular as well as religious Zionism as reflected in my responses. If a further chapter is added on the endless 'Who is a Jew?' saga, a controversy almost conterminous with the existence of the State, it is for two reasons, both of which are central to the theme of this book. No single issue has epitomized the challenge to traditional Jewish norms created by the restoration of Jewish statehood more than this ongoing debate on the definition of Jewish personal status. And nothing has been more characteristic of the aims and limits of my own intervention in Israeli affairs than the various stages of my reaction to the different phases of this bitter and divisive controversy.

These phases unfolded in three distinct parts, and I either took a public stand or I resisted pressures to do so. The issue first erupted in a cabinet crisis in 1958 regarding the problem of the registration of *le'om* ('nationality' or 'nationhood') in the identity-card which every Israeli citizen had to carry. The secular political parties demanded that a simple affirmation of national identification with the Jewish people should suffice for such registration. This was vigorously opposed by the rabbinate of Israel and the religious community generally inside and outside Israel. The debate induced Prime Minister Ben-Gurion to consult some seventy leading rabbis and Jewish scholars in Israel and the Diaspora, and when their verdict overwhelmingly reaffirmed the traditional definition of Jewishness, the suggestion to legislate a secular definition of a Jew was dropped, though the debate itself continued to flare up from time to time.

The second phase began in 1968 when a naval lieutenant-commander, Benjamin Shalit, married to a non-Jewish woman, requested that their two children should be registered on their identity-cards as Jews, although they were born to a non-Jewish mother. The Ministry of the Interior refused this, and Shalit petitioned the Supreme Court for an injunction against the Ministry. On 23 January 1970, this was granted by a five to four majority decision of the Supreme Court judges. Although the judgement made it clear that it had no implication on personal status regarding marriages, which were under the jurisdiction of the rabbinical courts, the ruling that Israel would henceforth give legal recognition to self-declared 'Jews' of non-Jewish birth created an immediate outcry which was not confined to the religious camp only. Under the pressure of worldwide agitation, the Knesset passed a law which in effect overturned the Supreme Court ruling by specifying the definition of Jews as being only 'by birth to a Jewish mother or by conversion'. The controversy abated – but not for long.

The third phase shifted the ground completely from the religious– secular argument to the recognition in Israel's civil legislation of non-Orthodox conversions. For it was soon discovered that the new law did not stipulate that such 'conversions' had to be 'in accordance with the Halachah'. Once again, the 'Who is a Jew?' controversy erupted. A campaign led by Lubavitch, and increasingly supported by most leading rabbis, demanded an amendment to the law to rectify the omission. Under this mounting pressure, the National Religious Party sought a formal ruling from Chief Rabbi Goren on whether they could remain in the government unless the amendment was passed. The reply was in the negative. The NRP duly left the government and plunged the country into a political crisis which was not resolved until they rejoined, amid fierce protests from rabbinical leaders, without the amendment having been passed. The agitation continued to rage, as repeated efforts to amend the law failed. When, in 1977, the general election brought Mr Begin to power, the now ascendant Aguda insisted on a pledge by him to press for the amendment as the price for supporting the new coalition in a formal agreement which included this demand among some forty other conditions. Several renewed attempts were made to bring the amendment before the Knesset. Early in 1983 a vote was taken: the proposal was defeated. Despite great efforts by the Prime Minister in support of the amendment, the Liberals together with a few Herut defectors refused to vote for it, and the endeavours to amend the law had once again ended in failure.

In the first two phases of this interminable controversy I had identified myself totally with the religious opposition to the creation of a new category of Jews by purely secular definition or self-declaration. I set out my arguments in an article published in the *Jewish Review* (London) on 18 July 1958:

The crisis has exposed the most appalling danger facing the Jewish people through the emergence of Israel. By the very act of solving one problem which has bedevilled Jewish life in the past, the State may produce another, of even greater perplexity. If the secularists had their way, Israel might well disrupt that very unity of the Jewish people it was established to strengthen. On one side, Israel has removed for the first time in centuries the barriers between Jew and Jew; whether Europeans, Yemenites, Moroccans or Indians – Israel has made them conscious of the oneness that unites them all. On the other side, the same Israel would threaten to drive a wedge between different sections of our people.

There would be 'national Jews' (so declared by the State) and 'religious Jews' (so identified by history), and the ones would not recognize the others as brothers belonging to a common tribe. The worst disaster that could strike Jewry would become reality: there would be two unidentical Jewish peoples.

After explaining the long history of the traditional definition, from which religious Jews could never depart, I added:

Apart from purely religious considerations, it would be preposterous and utterly chaotic to transfer the prerogative of effecting admissions to Judaism (or Jewishness) from the jurisdiction of competent legal authorities to the arbitrary choice of private individuals. A person may freely choose to embrace another religion, but he cannot on his own render a conversion legally valid. No individual can be left to determine by himself his own (or his children's) religious status any more than his citizenship or nationality. Such matters of personal status are governed by strict laws in every civilized society, and their breach in Israel would be an intolerable affront to the Jewish conscience.

Again, in the second phase, following the Supreme Court verdict in 1970, I had no hesitation in pressing the religious demand for a parliamentary reversal of the court decision. In February 1970, I sent the following cable to Prime Minister Golda Meir:

ANGLO-JEWRY STANDS UNDIVIDED AND SOLIDLY BY ISRAEL IN PRESENT CRISIS AND QUEST FOR PEACE STOP HENCE SUPREME COURT DECISION IN DIRECT CONFLICT WITH JEWISH LAW AND HISTORY HAS EVOKED PARTICULAR ANGUISH STOP WE FEAR THAT THOUSANDS HESITATING ON BRINK OF INTERMARRIAGE WILL FEEL ENCOURAGED TO DEFECT FROM OUR COMMUNITY STOP BY SEPARATING JEWISH NATIONALISM FROM JUDAISM DECISION WILL GIVE COMFORT TO ENEMIES WHO DISTINGUISH BETWEEN ANTI-SEMITISM AND ANTI-ZIONISM STOP BY DEFINING JEW IN TERMS UNACCEPTABLE TO MAINSTREAM OF JEWRY A WEDGE WILL BE DRIVEN BETWEEN ISRAEL AND DIASPORA STOP KNOWING YOUR DEDICATION TO JEWISH UNITY AND YOUR CHERISHING OF JEWISH TRADITION I FERVENTLY APPEAL TO YOU TO REAFFIRM EXISTING REGULATION OF JEWISH
REGISTRATION

This intervention was publicized and aroused some opposition. Typical of the reaction of those aggrieved was an irate letter from Mr Leo Abse MP which appeared in *The Times* on 7 February 1970:

> The Chief Rabbi of a section of British Jewry, with extraordinary presumption, has sought to interfere with the ruling of the supreme court of a sovereign state. He is reported to have cabled the Prime Minister of Israel asking her to reverse the ruling of the Israeli Supreme Court that the children of a non-religious Jew and a Scotswoman may, at the choice of the parents, be registered as Jews.

He then denounced these 'racialist doctrines' and continued:

> Dr Jakobovits should be made to realize that Israel is not a colonial outpost of his group of synagogues. . . .
> As Ben-Gurion once remarked, a Jew is someone who calls himself one; and I shall call myself one as long – to quote another secular Jew Ilya Ehrenburg – as there is anti-Semitism.

He could not have put the case for the secular Jew more bluntly – or more honestly, quite frankly admitting that not Judaism but anti-Semitism made him declare himself a Jew, and would continue to determine his Jewish identity so long as it existed.

But for many Jews who saw some positive virtue in being Jewish, the issue was not quite so simple. The very fact that the oldest people on earth, bound by millennial ties of faith, race and history, should suddenly question its own identity and ask 'Who is a Jew?', dramatized the impact of Israel in radically changing, or at least questioning, the definition of Jewish peoplehood itself. Could it be, I asked, in an essay published in 1971, that the State intended to exemplify and cement the unity of the Jewish people should now serve to fragment it? I had little doubt about the answer:

> Such fragmentation would, of course, have been inevitable if the extreme secularists in Israel had won the day against the traditionalists over this question, and if the Israeli parliament had not overruled the Supreme Court's decision in favour of conferring Jewish identity on unconverted children born to a non-Jewish mother. There would have been two conflicting definitions of a Jew: one as defined by history and tradition, and the other as contrived by a secular state. Since one group would be unable to recognize the other as Jews, or marry its members, the seeds would be sown for a national disaster on a scale matched only by the division of Solomon's kingdom into Israel and Judah, two distinct and sometimes warring nations, a calamity which eventually led to the loss of ten of the twelve tribes of the Jewish people. Little wonder that the 'Who is a Jew?' controversy, touching such a raw nerve of the Jewish conscience, sparked off the gravest internal upheaval in the

history of the Jewish State, erupting into several cabinet crises and reverberating bitterly in Jewish communities throughout the world.

Perhaps the crisis of identity was unavoidable:

Underlying the conflict was the deeper crisis of Jewish identity which irritated modern Jewish life both *inside and outside Israel.* The incongruity of an essentially secular Jewish State emerging out of, and within, an essentially religious Jewish tradition and history was bound to produce tensions that could not fail to reach some breaking point. Added to these tensions were the secularist pressures on and among Jews in the Diaspora. For many of them, the most meaningful link with the Jewish people had long ceased to be of any religious significance: they identified themselves as Jews only in a purely secularist sense – through social, ethnic, cultural or national bonds.

So long as the forces of assimilation operated only on individual Jews, the crisis could be contained. However great and painful the losses caused by religious defection, they did not affect the corporate continuity of the religious element in Jewish existence. There *was* simply no recognized way to authenticate Jewish identity and to establish personal association with the Jewish people other than the criteria established by the religious community. No Jewish social club, ethnic fraternity, cultural society or political movement could challenge the exclusive right of religious authorities to determine and confer membership of the Jewish people. Officially, at any rate, Jewish identity remained a religious designation; even individually, while people could opt *out* of the religious community by defining their Jewishness in secular terms, they could not opt *in* to become members of the Jewish people except by entering through the portals of the Jewish religion.

But once assimilation to secular patterns found *national* expression in the State of Israel, all this changed radically:

Here emerged, for the first time in Jewish history, an official agency claiming the power, through its legislature and its judiciary, to enact and interpret laws affecting Jewish status by criteria other than religious allegiance.

The argument in favour of Jewish registration was always particularly pressed in respect of non-Jewish women married to Jews and their children who had been branded as Jews by the racist Nuremberg laws and experienced the horrors of Nazi persecution together with other Jews. If they now declared themselves as Jews, why should they be denied Jewish status? I found this argument especially repugnant:

By what logic or process shall suffering together with Jews, or even on account of Jews, turn one into a Jew? There were countless Christians, atheists and others in the concentration camps. Shall they all be entitled to be accepted as Jews on request, simply because they shared their ordeal with Jews?

The argument becomes even more unreasoned when used in conjunction with the resort to the Nuremberg laws defining anyone with even a single Jewish grandparent as a Jew. Shall the norms of Jewish law and tradition be revised to comply with the arbitrary whims of a diabolical tyrant? It would surely only add revolting insult to crushing injury to suggest that Hitler replace the sages of Israel in determining 'Who is a Jew?', and that his racist laws and persecution become a substitute for solemn acts of proselytization. Such an abject surrender by Judaism to the mad frenzy of its oppressor would forfeit the merit gained from all the martyred generations who defied tyranny and the evil ideologies behind it.

Subjectively, too, it was hard to see how joint suffering could ever be a guarantee for a common commitment:

People who survived the concentration camps are not likely to be any less diverse in outlook and allegiance than were those who entered them. Judaism may often be conducive to suffering, but suffering of itself can hardly be conducive to Judaism.

Other considerations, too, though often advanced, were hardly any more valid:

Nor can social integration among Jews, on its own, establish Jewish status any more than living among Britons can confer British citizenship. For the sake of mere legality, if nothing else, there must be some manifest act or ceremony to effect such a cardinal change as the transfer from one loyalty (or none) to another. One cannot just lose one's way into Judaism, as it were, dissolving one's identity and imperceptibly merging into another, without some pledge, some formal entry, some acceptance of the rules governing the group to be joined.

Service in the defence of Israel certainly merits the highest recognition and gratitude by Jews everywhere. The award of a prize, a title, the freedom of a city, or even honorary citizenship – by all means. But being a Jew cannot be a kind of medal, a distinction bestowed for meritorious service. A Jew *honoris causa* is at least as absurd as an honorary rabbi or even an honorary physician admitted to practise without any qualifications.

Even less plausible is the suggestion that a person should become Jewish by declaring himself to be so. Would a club or society admit members merely by virtue of a declaration that they regarded themselves as members? It is up to any simple organization, let alone an historic entity like the Jewish people, to determine its own rules for admission.

Above all, there was a much more basic objection:

Any entrance into the fellowship of Jewish peoplehood is a mutual covenant. *A convert joins the Jewish people no less than the Jewish people joins him.* They assume mutual obligations and commitments. Every Jew becomes a brother to him as he becomes a brother to every Jew. Such a covenant can never be unilateral, for it assumes the willingness of all Jews to regard the newcomer as one of them just as much as his agreement to consider himself so. And without a rabbinically sanctioned conversion a large segment of the Jewish people at least, to say nothing of Jewish law, would refuse, and could not be expected, to recognize him as a Jew, so rendering his or anyone else's claim that he is Jewish entirely meaningless.

Of course, what made the issue so crucial to Jews the world over was its effect on the already serious erosion of Jewish life through intermarriage:

By giving non-Jews (i.e. particularly the children of mixed marriages with a non-Jewish mother) the right to claim Jewish status without a conversion sanctioned by Jewish religious law, that is, according to the Halachah, Israel would deal a devastating blow to efforts to curb the inroads of assimilation and intermarriage already sorely afflicting Jewish communities in the Diaspora.

At present, the knowledge that such children will not be accepted as Jews – in their home communities or in Israel – without first fulfilling the conditions for conversion is often the only effective deterrent to young Jews contemplating marriage outside their faith. By removing this barrier in Israel, the flood-gates still stemming the tide of intermarriage elsewhere would be breached. Not only would rabbinical authorities in the Diaspora be subjected to intolerable pressures to be 'no holier' than Israel in policies on admissions to Judaism, but mixed couples and their children could always assure their recognition as Jews at the cost of a return ticket to Israel where the necessary papers could be legally obtained.

For these reasons, the arguments against the Supreme Court decision were not confined to religious spokesmen. They were also given eloquent expression by the Head of Government and the Leader of the Opposition in the memorable Knesset debate which reaffirmed the traditional definition. In a moving speech, Prime Minister Golda Meir declared:

I am not religiously observant, but had it not been for religion, we would have shared the fate of all those peoples who have disappeared. We are fortunate, indeed, that there are still synagogues in Moscow, Odessa and Leningrad serving as the only centre for Jews to come at least on Simchat Torah, as an outlet for their feelings of Jewish identity. I would like to tell you that in 1948 when I attended synagogue on Rosh Hashanah and Yom Kippur in Moscow, I did not stir from my place the whole day. I thought to myself that had I stayed longer at my post, I would have gone to synagogue not out of duty, as the representative of the Jewish State, but I, Golda Meir, my place is in the synagogue along with other Jews.

Above all else, in my view and that of the overwhelming majority of the Knesset, the survival of Israel comes first, before the State of Israel, before Zionism. . . . Any price is worth paying for the security of the State of Israel, so long as it is realized that its role is to preserve the Jewish people. Otherwise, it is pointless. The measure may not succeed in reducing the incidence of intermarriage, but at least it will grant no *Heter* [licence] for it.

And this was part of Mr Menachem Begin's historic utterance on the same occasion:

> Our people should have by now numbered 200 to 250 million souls. . . . Why have but thirteen million survived? There are only two reasons for that – slaughter and assimilation. And who knows if assimilation did not take what slaughter had spared – many millions in each generation. Were it not for the prohibition of intermarriage, we would have disappeared long ago. . . .
>
> What are your grievances against the Halachah which determines who is a Jew? . . . We interpret the laws of Israel for well over twenty years, in the light of English Common Law. If in the days of Queen Elizabeth I, a British judge passed a sentence, the Israeli judges are still bound by that precedent. . . . What is wrong, what is sinful, with the idea that in the fateful matter, Who is a Jew?, we should be bound by the interpretation of the Jewish Common Law – pardon my expression – the Jewish Halachah which is in force thousands of years? What free man can be insulted by that?
>
> I propose the following rule to the entire Knesset without distinction of party. Here it is: *That Judaism not be forced on any person, and no person be forced on Judaism.* Is that compulsion? . . . Suppose a person does not submit to traditional conversion and is still classified as a Jew; isn't that compulsion? Yes, that would be a compulsion imposed upon the entire Jewish people for generations without an end; upon millions no longer alive, upon those who are alive, and upon millions yet unborn.

The law was changed, and the danger that a new breed of Jew would legally emerge from Israel to split the Jewish people was averted. The battle was won, but the war was not over. Whether by the momentum created in over a decade of fierce agitation or by a miscalculation which sought to prevent the growth of non-Orthodox Judaism in Israel in the Chamber of the Knesset, the controversy carried on unabated, but this time about a different issue altogether.

Phase three concerned the recognition of conversions, or rather of those performing them, not so much in Israel as in America. By adding the amendment 'according to the Halachah', such recognition was to be denied. I was no less insistent on this denial than the most vociferous protagonists of the amendment. In fact, within my own jurisdiction in Britain and the Commonwealth, any recognition of a non-Orthodox conversion would be unthinkable. I nevertheless refused to support the renewed agitation and later strongly advised against it. In October 1971 I declined to sign a petition demanding the amendment. In my view, the battle was unwinnable, counter-productive and irrelevant to Israel's legislature. I set out the reasons for my rather solitary stand in the Orthodox camp in a letter to the Gerer Rebbe in Jerusalem written in August 1981 but not published until over a year later in the Hebrew journal *S'ridim*, issued twice a year in Jerusalem by the Conference of European Rabbis. The following is a translation of the letter:

You may know that, for some years, I have been numbered amongst the minority of Orthodox rabbis who oppose the worldwide propaganda regarding the 'Who is a Jew?' issue. Now that fortunately the excitement has died down for the moment, I should like to explain my reasons in the hope that you may approve the justification of the concerns troubling me.

In the first place, let me make it clear that I obviously accept that conversion according to Halachah is a basic necessity in maintaining the sanctity and unity of the Jewish people. Nobody knows better than I, as head of the London Beth Din, of the enormous damage done to numerous families and congregations through so-called conversions effected by those who defy the sanctities of Jewish law. But I see no connection between this and the 'Who is a Jew?' issue in Israel. In my opinion, any gain will be counter-balanced by serious disadvantages to the traditional community.

1. The whole question is irrelevant to the Land of Israel, where all matrimonial matters are controlled by the Orthodox rabbinate, so that there is no possibility that any convert received other than by Halachah can be married in Israel. Further, how many Reformers come on Aliyah, and how many of them are converts? So why stir up all this hostility on the part of large numbers of Jews over an irrelevancy? It is a problem in America and elsewhere, but thankfully not in Israel.

2. 'Who is a Jew?' is basically a question of Jewish religious law, which must be defined by halachic experts. How can this definition be left to the Knesset, which is a secular body and composed mostly of secularists? They may define 'Who is an Israeli?', and perhaps certain subordinate features of 'Who is a Jew?' determining national and secular rights, comprised in, say, the Law of Return, as I will explain.

3. So long as the majority of members of the Knesset and, sadly, of the whole Jewish people, are non-religious, I see no hope that even the greatest pressure will force them to yield to religious compulsion against their own 'consciences' and against the opinion of the majority, plus the prospect of great financial loss, caused by the probable withdrawal of Reform support.

There has been endless argument, ministries have fallen, and many efforts to change the law have failed, simply because the Knesset members persist in their refusal to accept the proposed amendment. Why should we persist in wasting our strength and efforts in an impossible conflict, leading only to further strife and futile battles?

4. Far from limiting the expansion and influence of the Reformers, the conflict has served to introduce them, as a sizeable segment of the Jewish people, to Israelis who otherwise would have known nothing of the Reformed religion and its leaders. Through all the media attention given to the 'Who is a Jew?' controversy, they were able to gain publicity and introduce the Reform aberration, attested by the growth of their institutions and influence in recent years. They have gained all the advantages from the dispute; nothing has been of such benefit to them as the 'Who is a Jew?' agitation.

5. Furthermore, I am disturbed by what will happen if we do succeed in amending the law one of these days and all Reform converts will have to be converted over again in accordance with Halachah to comply with Knesset legislation. The Rishon-le-Zion, at a meeting with representatives of the Reform and Conservative rabbinate (I have seen the official minutes), has stated: 'What difference does it make to you if we provide Orthodox conversion for your existing converts?' Does this not amount to dipping a person into a Mikvah 'with an impure object in his hand'? It is hardly likely that conversion of this type will involve any honest commitment to the observance of *mitzvot*.

At the moment, we are able to reject such converts who seek Orthodox marriage. But if secular law will require conversion in this superficial and inadequate way, we shall have to accept converts who, basically, have only been prepared according to Reform principles. Can there be a more flagrant perversion of the Halachah?

6. In the Diaspora, we already often experience great trouble from Batei Din in Israel (including ultra-Orthodox rabbis in Meah Shearim – need I say more?) who supposedly convert, according to proper Orthodox standards, tourists who come to Israel for a few weeks or months and then return with certificates of their Jewish status, though they observe nothing in the way of Sabbath, Family Purity, and so on. At present, we do not recognize such certificates. But what shall we do, both inside and outside Israel, if Israeli law will require the granting and recognition of conversions of this sort, and every Reform convert will be able to authenticate his Jewish status by an immersion 'according to the Halachah' like this?

On the other hand, if these converts are civilly not accepted because they are not prepared to observe the *mitzvot* in practice, what is to be done with the children of mixed marriages who come on Aliyah? Is the government to insist that they be sent to Arab schools?

To such and similar problems apply the two rabbinical dicta: 'Had the Torah been given entirely in the form of final rulings, there would never be room for a leg to hold firm', and 'Just as it is meritorious to say what will receive attention, so is it meritorious to refrain from saying what will not receive attention.'

Consistent with these considerations, when the renewed controversy escalated to a crisis early in 1974, I communicated my views privately to leading rabbis in Israel and America 'to prevent the humiliating predicament' of a defeat followed by a retreat. But this is exactly what happened, when the National Religious Party, acting under rabbinical instructions, carried out its threat to leave the government coalition unless the amendment was passed, and then soon returned with the amendment still not enacted. I wrote to Dr Burg, the Minister of the Interior, on 15 March 1974:

I know that you were subjected to intolerable pressures. . . . I had pleaded with Chief Rabbi Goren and Rabbi Soloveitchik not to press the 'Who is a Jew?' issue to the point of a major political crisis at this juncture. But evidently they capitulated one by one to the agitation generated by Lubavitch, although I recognize that the problem does present acute difficulties to the Orthodox rabbinate in America. . . .

In my letter to Rabbi Soloveitchik, I urged him to renew an initiative he had himself undertaken whilst I was still in America:

I believe the stage is now set for an all-out effort to renew the initiative you undertook quite some years ago, aimed at coming to some acceptable terms with non-Orthodox spiritual leaders – I presume with the Conservatives in the first instance – on securing halachic control over all marriages, divorces and conversions. As you know, lately such an idea has been mooted even in Reform circles.

If this were done on a global basis, it would solve agonizing problems bound to afflict future generations of far wider significance and ramifications than the present 'Who is a Jew?' issue. . . .

Alas, the intervention proved of no avail, and the National Religious Party came out with little glory from the abortive attempt to enforce the passage of the amendment. I issued a statement on 25 February 1974, before the National Religious Party rejoined the government:

Through its decision to withdraw from the government of Israel, the National Religious Party now has the worst of both worlds. The 'Law of Return' has not been amended, neither will religious influences continue to be exercised within the government. Moreover, the belated insistence of the NRP on pursuing the 'Who is a Jew?' controversy is a disastrous blow to the vital national and religious interests of the Jewish people at a time of supreme crisis.

The decision cannot but gravely weaken Israel's leadership and unity when these are indispensable assets for the security and survival of the Jewish State and the stability of Jewish life everywhere. Even if, as is likely, the NRP will eventually rejoin the government on finding some face-saving formula, the damage done to Israel's political strength and to the standing and influence of the religious community is incalculable.

To make my own priorities absolutely clear, I added:

All committed Jews are deeply concerned to resolve the 'Who is a Jew?' issue, consistent with our millennial traditions. But a principle of such universal Jewish ramifications should not be determined by political bargaining. Nor is this the time for divisive confrontations which are bound to vitiate Israel's hopes for peace, both externally and internally, and bring religious Jewry into disrepute.

I therefore reiterate my plea, made publicly a few weeks ago, to concentrate all efforts on securing religious instruction and observance at all Israeli schools and to declare a moratorium on all new legislation of religious significance during the present emergency. This would be a major step towards national and spiritual consolidation in these trying times.

A little personal experience may fittingly conclude this odd chapter on the strangest question ever asked in Jewish history. The experience is related here to substantiate my opposition both to the conferment of Jewish status for services rendered to Israel and to the debasement of the Halachah by ritual conversions without a true change of heart.

On 21 July 1973, an Israeli intelligence operation disastrously misfired in Lillehammer, Norway. An assassination team, planning to kill a notorious Palestinian terrorist, mistook his identity and shot an innocent Arab instead. Numerous blunders soon enabled the Norwegian police to arrest six members of the team. Among them was Sylvia Rafael who was sentenced to five-and-a-half-years' imprisonment. She was of South African origin, born to a Jewish father and a non-Jewish mother. In Israel she had evidently taken part in the agitation that such persons of non-Jewish birth should be accorded recognition as Jews without any religious conversion. When she was caught in the ill-fated Mossad operation, it was feared that her case would again inflame public opinion against the religious insistence on conversion. Motivated by this fear, an Israeli rabbi wrote to me on 18 March 1974, urging me to send several basic Jewish books to Sylvia in her Oslo prison. He had already sent her several other books on Judaism from Israel and wanted everything possible to be done to prevail on her to become a proper proselyte. Her conversion would prevent another major conflagration; it might even be a *Kiddush Hashem*. I could not quite see it that way, and replied to the rabbi on 25 March 1974:

I would gladly try to obtain and transmit the volumes you ask for to Oslo in your name. But, frankly, I am not sure that this is the right approach to adopt in this particular case. I fear that the encouragement of such quasi-enforced conversions can only bring Halachah itself into disrepute. If this girl is honest enough to reject the 'hypocrisy' of a conversion by a religious ceremony which affronts her religious or non-religious convictions, I cannot see why we should importune her. ... I would not like her to allege that rabbis in Israel or elsewhere are putting any kind of pressure on her to become what is at best likely to be a nominal convert.

Nine years later, my hunch was confirmed, when I met Sylvia in Oslo – married to the non-Jewish lawyer who had conducted her defence!

Once the proposal to confer Jewish status by purely secular criteria was removed from the Knesset agenda when the new law of 1970 accepted the traditional definition, the 'Who is a Jew?' controversy became practically irrelevant, certainly to a civil legislature, in Israel. The real question that continues to face Israel is not *who* is a Jew, but *what* is a Jew. This question bedevils the entire Jewish people, for the answer will determine who and how many *will* be Jewish in the future.

Few factors will have a more decisive bearing on the answer to this question than the direction which Zionism will take in its fulfilment through Jewish statehood. If Israel drifts further from its Jewish moorings, more and more Jews will be lost as Jews, whether in Israel or in the rest of the world. On the other hand, Jews everywhere will be reclaimed to live as Jews in direct proportion to Israel's return to the Covenant which established the Jewish claim to the Land in the first place. Our faith is invincible in the fulfilment of the Prophetic promise to Rachel, Mother of comfort to our people: 'There is hope for your latter end, says the Lord: and your children shall come again to their own border.' Rachel will as assuredly rejoice at her children's religious homecoming as she rejoices in the wondrous fulfilment of their promised physical return. They will be restored to the soul as well as to the soil of their people.

# Part Three:

# Zionist Studies

# 15

# The Attitude to Zionism of Britain's Chief Rabbis as Reflected in Their Writings*

In many broad respects, the story of the British Chief Rabbinate – and the opposition to it – largely is, or reflects, the history of Anglo-Jewry, at least since Nathan Adler assumed the office in 1845. Indeed, as I have argued in an essay on 'The Evolution of the British Rabbinate': 'In no other country in the world is the overall history of the Jewish community so intimately bound up with the Chief Rabbinate as in Britain. From this office, or in close association with it, or in protest against it, have grown virtually all the major institutions and religious movements in Anglo-Jewry'.[1] This is certainly true of the two Adlers, to whose initiative we owe not only the foundation of such diverse institutions as Jews' College and the United Synagogue, but the highly centralized structure and predominantly traditional outlook of the community to this day. It is equally true of Joseph Herman Hertz, whose dynamic leadership preserved the institutional and religious character of Anglo-Jewry against the mighty buffetings of two World Wars and the Holocaust, which so dramatically changed the face of so many other communities, including American Jewry, during this convulsive period.

This assertion, incontestable as I believe it to be on the internal or domestic front, requires major modification in regard to Zionism. While, as Cecil Roth[2] has pointed out, the role of British Jewry 'in the implementation if not evolution of Zionism in its modern sense' represents a significant contribution to Jewish history at large, the part played in this achievement by the Chief Rabbis was never decisive. Only on a few notable occasions

* Lecture delivered before the Jewish Historical Society of England on 9 May 1979

did their intervention leave some permanent mark on Zionist fortunes in this country, and to some extent on the world Jewish scene.

This generalization is not to say that successive Chief Rabbis did not have some very determined, mostly even passionate, views on Zionism, or that they did not render many most noteworthy services to the Zionist cause. But lest we lose our general perspective in a maze of detail to be presented, it is, I think, important to acknowledge at the outset that their impact on the course of events in Zionist history cannot be compared to their commanding influence on communal life, nor indeed to the influence on the development of Zionism of such Anglo-Jewish lay personalities as Chaim Weizmann, Herbert Bentwich and Herbert Samuel. By and large, all the Chief Rabbis mirrored rather than shaped the popular Jewish attitude to Zionism of their generation, leaving the major thrust in the dynamics of modern Zionism mainly to secular leaders. Even those few spiritual leaders who did leave some indelible imprint on Zionism in this country and beyond were outside the Chief Rabbinate and its jurisdiction. I think in particular of the Kamenitzer Maggid, who inspired the Chovevei Zion movement in the 1880s; Haham Moses Gaster, who bestrode the Zionist scene from Herzl's first public meeting in London, over which he presided, across the First Zionist Congress in Basle, which he attended, to his active role in the diplomatic moves leading to the Balfour Declaration; and the Rev. J.K.Goldbloom, who pioneered Zionist education with effects which outlive him to the present day.[3]

Before I let the Chief Rabbis speak out of their writings, freely interspersed by my own comments, I must make a few remarks on my sources. All the Chief Rabbis left us a sizeable literary heritage. Paradoxically, the most enduring part of it is of no interest to us here, viz., the classic commentaries of the *Nethina Lager* on the *Targum* by Nathan Adler, and on the *Chumash* and *Siddur* by Hertz, as well as his *Book of Jewish Thoughts*. Perhaps I should here add also Brodie's three-volume edition of Jacob Hazzan's *Etz Chaim* and my own *Jewish Medical Ethics* as works which have no bearing on our subject. My source material comes mainly from the volumes of collected writings published by all the Chief Rabbis, with the exception of Nathan Adler, who wrote none, and Hermann Adler, whose *Anglo-Jewish Memories* contains no reference of Zionist interest.

But we have a wealth of relevant material in Hertz's three volumes of *Sermons, Addresses and Studies* and his *Early and Late*; Brodie's *A Word in Season* and *The Strength of My Heart*; and my *Journal of a Rabbi* and *The Timely and the Timeless*. In addition, there are also many tracts and pamphlets by these authors not included in their books, as well as statements recorded by other contemporaries and newspapers, especially the *Jewish Chronicle*, which I have consulted extensively, and which covers the entire period from the election of Nathan Adler in 1844. Obviously, I have also used a number of secondary sources, though I must add that the composite account is by no means complete. But I do hope it provides a fairly balanced survey.

The term 'Zionism' was coined by Nathan Birnbaum in 1890,[4] and we may date the emergence of modern Zionism as a political phenomenon from about that time. That was of course also the year of Nathan Adler's death, and we may therefore be justified in excluding him from our present survey, an exclusion perhaps also justified by my inability to discover any writings of his relevant to Zionism.

But not quite. Some important precedents to political Zionism occurred before 1890. A seminal forerunner was the Chovevei Zion movement founded in the early 1880s in Eastern Europe to promote the colonization of Palestine. Its Zionist fervour soon spread to the West, and a British branch was established in 1885.[5] Its activities were endorsed by Nathan Adler,[6] although by then failing health had compelled him to delegate most of his functions to his son, Hermann, who had been formally appointed as Delegate Chief Rabbi in 1879 and eventually succeeded his father in 1891.

Hermann Adler, despite his subsequent opposition to Herzl's political Zionism, which he dismissed as 'an egregious blunder', remained an ardent supporter of the Chovevei Zion for the rest of his life, presiding over several of its frequent meetings in London.[7]

In fact, he visited Palestine in 1885 on behalf of the Trustees of the Mansion House Fund for the Relief of the Jews in Russia, entrusted with the distribution of £500 for the settlers of Petach Tikvah. While there, his intervention with the Turkish Governor of Jerusalem succeeded in removing a ban on further building operations in that colony, acting on a request received from the famous Rabbi Samuel Mohilever and others.[8] A full report on his visit, as given to the Trustees who had sent him, appeared in the *Jewish Chronicle* of 12 June 1885. Adler's sympathies at that time, including his remarkable call for Jewish tourists to visit the Holy Land, are illustrated by a sermon entitled 'A Pilgrimage to Zion', which he delivered a month later and which was published in *The Jewish Pulpit*, July 1885.

It is not a strange anomaly that in our liturgy we profess so deep an attachment for Palestine? . . . And yet we refuse to bestow even a passing thought on this country. . . . We take a pleasure in journeying to many a land, we gaze with admiration on some half-ruined tower in which there dwelt some lawless evil robber, we are delighted by visiting a spot with which some curious legend is connected. But how small is the number of those who care to wend their way to the land of their fathers, the land of the Bible! . . .

How necessary is it that the system of doles and allowances, which now prevails,

should be altered, and that charitable relief be administered on lines and principles more akin to those which obtain in the civilized West. . . .

Whilst it is our duty to watch that they [the children] be imbued with the
devoted love of our faith and a full knowledge of our law, it must be our care that
they be taught to speak and write the language of the country in which they live,
the elements of general knowledge, and one of the various branches of handi-
craft. . . .

I saw the colonists of Petach Tikvah, Moshav Yehudit, and Rishon leZion dig-
ging the ground, planting the olives, the vines. . . . It would be premature as yet
to speak of the absolute success of these ventures. The opinion of those best informed on the subject is that, whilst it is our bounden duty to assist the existing
settlers to the utmost of our power, it is inexpedient at present to establish new
colonies.

Five years later, his active interest tempered by caution was still in
evidence when he presided at a crowded Chovevei Zion meeting to report
on his visit to Paris to see Baron Edmond de Rothschild about the
colonies in Palestine. The *Jewish Chronicle* account of this meeting,
dated 5 December 1890, records Adler as having 'advised them not to
hurry, and to consider carefully before they took any step'. At this time
the Chovevei Zion movement, at least in the West, was still predominantly a philanthropic organization intended to find and support a haven in
Palestine for destitute and persecuted Jews from Eastern Europe.

In May 1891, the purposes were more clearly defined when a meeting
in London adopted a constitution which included the aims '1. to foster the
national idea in Israel, and 2. to promote the colonization of Palestine
and neighbouring territories by Jews. . . .' This was followed by a lengthy
correspondence in the *Jewish Chronicle* in which some leaders of the
movement claimed and others denied that these aims implied a quest for
a 'Jewish State'.[9] This controversy was not finally resolved until the
Chovevei Zion eventually decided to dissociate themselves from Herzl's
political Zionism,[10] culminating in the refusal even to send a delegation to
the First Zionist Congress in 1897.[11]

The conflict and the prevailing arguments underlying it were well presented by Mr Joseph Prag, presiding at a Chovevei Zion meeting in
London in November 1898:

Two years ago, however, a new light seemed to dawn on Israel with the advent
of Dr Herzl, who advocated the establishment of a Jewish State either in Argentina or in Palestine. But it was soon seen that the idea of a Jewish State embodied
the danger of completely destroying the work to which the Chovevei Zion Association had for years been applying itself, because it set the authorities in Turkey
against Jews, and those who had had experience of colonization work in Palestine

were convinced that the Political Zionist Movement, which advocated immigration upon a vast scale, before any provision had been made for the people, was destined to be attended with dire results.

The quixotic mood of London's organized Zionists at the time was also illustrated by another speaker at the same meeting, Mr Hermann Landau:

We, the Chovevei Zion, are reproached by the Political Zionist Movement for not joining them, and they quote our Prayer-book, wherein we pray daily for our restoration to the Holy Land. This reminds me of a story told during the agitation for the emancipation of the Jews in Germany. A learned Protestant divine asked a Rabbi how he could reasonably expect full German citizenship for his people when, in their daily prayers, they supplicate for the return to their own land. The Rabbi, in his turn, asked the good clergyman whether he believed that the future world would be better than the present. The answer was, of course, in the affirmative. 'That being so,' said the Rabbi, 'you surely do not think of hastening on the happier and better state by committing suicide.' Our Political Zionists are evidently of the opinion that the work of the Chovevei Zion is far too slow and natural. Since they do not apparently believe in our miraculous restoration, for it is by means of a Jewish Bank that they propose to gain this great object, I contend that their method is practically to commit suicide in order to attain their ideal.[12]

That the clash between the Chovevei Zion and Herzl was quite fundamental already emerged two years earlier, when Mr Joseph Prag, in a letter to the *Jewish Chronicle* dated 17 July 1896, stated: 'Dr Herzl's plan is, by his own admission, the result of anti-Semitism. Fear of the nations, the policy of panic, has moved him to devise *his* plan; ours is based upon love for our Land and our people....'

Adler was therefore by no means isolated or unrepresentative in his consistent opposition to Herzl's Zionism. The encounters between these two autocratic leaders soon revealed their personal antipathies as well as their ideological divergencies. On his first visit to London, Herzl records in his *Diaries* (22 November 1895) that the Chief Rabbi 'received me like an old acquaintance'.[13] But by 27 January 1896, Herzl notes: 'The Chief Rabbi has written that he considers the matter impractical and at the same time dangerous. The Chief Rabbi has too comfortable a post to find pleasure in my project. This sort of thing does not bother me.'[14] Herzl suffered similar disappointments in his efforts to enlist the support of other leading rabbis, always betraying a mixture of imperiousness with acrimony. Commenting on the 'changed mood' of Grand Rabbin Zadok Kahn, of Paris, following his initial enthusiasm, Herzl again complains of Zionism being incompatible with comfortable living, this time by French Jews, when he writes in his *Diaries* (18 November 1895): 'Things here go too well with them to admit thought of a change.'[15] But neither Adler nor Zadok Kahn incurred the wrath which Herzl poured on his own Chief Rabbi of Vienna. For several years, Dr Moritz Guedemann had been Herzl's only spiritual mentor and intimate confidant, whom he even consulted while preparing his revolutionary book *The Jewish State*. An entry in the *Diaries* (dated 27 January 1896) reads: 'Guedemann has read the first proofs and writes me in rapture. He believes that the tract will strike like a bombshell, and work wonders.'[16] But within little more than a year Guedemann was disenchanted and firmly joined the anti-Zionist camp, leading Herzl to write (*Diaries*, 17 April 1897): 'Dr Guedemann has published a malicious attack in a pamphlet entitled *Jewish Nationalism*. Obviously at the behest of the local "upper-class Jews". He confines himself to vague, cowardly ambiguities ... I shall answer him – and, following the Machiavellian formula, it will be a crusher.'[17]

I have digressed a little from Adler and his writings, both because Adler's stand on Zionism can only be properly understood in the context of the attitude of his contemporaries, including his European colleagues, and because his actual writings on political Zionism are limited, as far as I could discover, to a single sermon, delivered on 12 November 1898 and published in full two weeks later in the *Jewish Chronicle* under the title 'Religious versus Political Zionism'. Speaking soon after the Second Basle Congress, Adler vindicates his determined opposition by a combination of British patriotism, a denunciation of Herzl's secularism, a disbelief in the practicability of the Zionist programme, and an uncompromising faith that the Messianic solution of the Jewish problem could only be effected by a Divine act of Redemption:

At a congress recently held in Basle, it was resolved that as a means of securing a public legally assured home for the Jewish people in Palestine and Syria, a Jewish Colonial Bank should be founded in this city with a capital of £2 million. The enquiry has been addressed to me. Why do you hold aloof from a movement charged with such great possibilities?

After then quoting in full Jeremiah's charge to the exiles leaving for Babylon (Jer. 29: 1-14), he continued:

A somewhat lengthy text, but one strikingly appropriate to the agitation that has been fanned by the two Basle Congresses. I maintain that, if in the case of the Babylonian Captivity, the termination of which was in sight, the Israelites were bidden to eschew unrest and to await quietly their ultimate restoration, how much more needful is it that we should avoid all precipitate action at the present day, when there is no sign whatever of our hoped-for redemption, no premonition of the promised ingathering. I view the present movement with unfeigned concern, because I regard it as opposed to the teaching of Judaism, as impolitic, as charged with grave peril. I do not identify this movement with Zionism. This agitation has its rise from a brochure published by Dr Herzl two years ago, entitled *The Jewish State*. In this pamphlet, the author, prompted by sentiments of mingled indignation and pity for the degraded condition of his fellow-religionists in many lands, proposed that a Jewish State should be formed. ... The author left it an open question whether Palestine or Argentina should be the country selected for the establishment of this State. But learning that Palestine was the only country which would evoke a responsive thrill from Jewish hearts, Dr Herzl ... fixed upon that land as the proposed seat of the new Hebrew polity. Hence, I contend that it would be incorrect to describe this plan as Zionism, pure and simple. It should be labelled Political, Secular, or Basle Congress Zionism.

Every believing and conforming Israelite must be Zionist ... but our objections to Political Zionism are based on the fact that it is claimed to constitute a solution of the Jewish Question.

Adler also believed the economic obstacles to be insuperable, especially in view of the abandonment of the imperatively needed water supply system for Jerusalem. The whole enterprise would prove a cruel disillusionment to Diaspora investors and Palestinian settlers alike:

We cannot approve of our toiling brethren being asked to place their hard-earned savings in a Jewish Colonial Bank, when there is no guarantee whatever that their investments can prove remunerative. ... Nor can we deem it a kindness to tantalize these trustful people with illusory hopes of their settling in a country where they will all enjoy independence, prosperity and security. (Assuming that the leaders of the agitation will acquire possession of Palestine, who are the persons that would migrate? Not the thriving inhabitants of Western Europe and of the United States, but the unfortunate starvelings that pine in the Russian Pale of Settlement, and the hapless beggars that crowd the Galician villages.)

But we are met with the taunt, It is no wonder that you deprecate the proposed establishment of a Jewish State, you who dwell in peace and comfort on British soil without one to molest you or to make you afraid. But what solution of the Jewish Question do you propose? ... Brethren, we need not quail before this taunt. I make claim for the Jews of England that they have never turned a deaf ear to the plaint of their brethren. We, together with the Jews of the United States, have striven manfully to provide a refuge as far as in our power lay, for the stricken fugitives from the North. And when we refuse our co-operation to the project that has now been formulated, it is not from lack of sympathy but because we regard it as impracticable, as inoperative, as fraught with peril, as calculated to revive the false charges of incivism and lack of loyalty to our native country or land of our adoption, and finally as opposed to the teachings of Judaism.

(As for) the various passages in our Liturgy relating to our restoration ... it is not declared in the Prophetic books that our return to Palestine is to be accomplished by our instrumentality and at the period we desire. It is distinctly announced that our redemption is to be effected by Divine interposition at such time as seemeth good in God's sight. . . .

He concluded: (No man has ever lived fired with a more ardent love for Zion than Sir Moses Montefiore. Again and again he pleaded on behalf of his sorrow-stricken brethren. . . . If ever there was one who, by his commanding influence, might have hoped to regain possession of the Land of his Fathers it was he. But he was not the man to embark on an enterprise so impolitic and chimerical.) I would ask you to be quickened by the religious Zionism that inspired him, that has burned in the hearts of all true Israelites. Religious Zionism urges you, whilst devoting your fullest energy to the service of your country and your community, to labour also for the welfare of the indwellers of the Holy Land, to aid in extirpating pauperism, banishing ignorance, and alleviating sickness. Religious Zionism urges you to labour for the advent of Messianic Times by seeking to discard every racial fault, by endeavouring to realise the Higher Ideals which our religion set before us.[18]

Adler evidently regarded this sermon as his major statement on the subject. For he rendered it into Hebrew and supplied it as his contribution to a book entitled *Or Layesharim* ('Light unto the Righteous'), published in Warsaw in 1900, featuring anti-Zionist speeches and letters by leading rabbinical personalities, including the then Lubavitcher Rebbe,[19] with Dr Adler appearing as the only West European contributor among them.[20] Incidentally, a year later an equally polemical rejoinder of pro-Zionist statements appeared in Vilna under the title *Beyn Or Lechoshech* ('Between Light and Darkness').[21]

Even before his pulpit blast, Adler made no secret of his strong antipathy to Herzl and his ideas. He dismissed Herzl's 1895 London visit, which had aroused such enthusiasm among the Jews of the East End, as 'a fiasco',[22] and at the time of Herzl's second visit in July 1896 he warned the Anglo-Jewish Association at its annual meeting: 'We must be on our guard against fostering fantastic and visionary ideas about the re-establishment of a Jewish State and a Jewish Nation'.[23]

But I could find only scant evidence for the allegation of the *Jewish Encyclopedia* in 1904 that 'In England, several rabbis were inhibited by the Chief Rabbi from preaching on Zionism and the Haham M. Gaster was prevented by the Mahamad of the Spanish and Portuguese Congregation from touching on the subject in his official capacity.'[24] One of Adler's most prominent ministers, the Rev. Simeon Singer, was among Herzl's principal hosts and organizers during Herzl's first two London visits, and continued to support the Zionist leader for several years, from the pulpit and by correspondence, though he too became finally estranged.[25] But on Herzl's death in

1904 Singer and many other leading ministers paid generous tributes to his achievements,[26] while Adler himself was content to write a brief letter of condolence to the Secretary of the English Zionist Federation on learning of 'the terrible tidings'. He 'would have deemed it a great privilege to have delivered the Hesped at the Great Synagogue' if he had not suffered 'from a somewhat severe attack of illness', and he paid tribute to Herzl's 'transcendent abilities ... and the services he has rendered to the Jewish cause'.[27] Instead, the Hesped was given by Gaster, who remained, of course, an irrepressible advocate of Herzl's Zionism until much later when that support was compromised by contentiousness, eventually leading to an open break with the Zionist leadership in Britain until he became President of the English Zionist Federation in 1907.[28]

Nor is there much justice in Achad Ha'am's criticism of Adler for 'having no time for Zionist activities, since he is busy with Shechita problems'.[29] Adler continued to take a live interest in his brand of Zionism, as represented by the Chovevei Zion, and he preached a special sermon at the Hampstead Synagogue for the twenty Maccabean pilgrims before they set out for the Holy Land,[30] as recorded in the *Jewish Chronicle* of 9 April 1897. His charge is again characterized by a somewhat patronizing attitude, when he told the pilgrims:

Brethren, if you desire to be veritable Chovevei Zion, with whom the love of Zion is not a mere rhetorical flourish, you must help to train our Palestinian brethren in habits of self-reliance and independence. You must endeavour that their charitable relief be administered on lines and principles which obtain in civilized Europe.

Political Zionism, however, was anathema to Adler, as confirmed by what was probably his last pronouncement on Zionism. It is a quote from a statement he made on 23 April 1909 to the *Manchester Daily Dispatch*, reproduced by Judge Finestein in an article[31] to which he kindly drew my attention:

Since the destruction of the Temple and our dispersion we no longer constitute a nation; we are a religious communion. We are bound together with our brethren throughout the world primarily by the ties of a common faith. But in regard to all other matters we consider ourselves Englishmen and we hold that in virtue of being Jews it is our duty and privilege to work as zealously as possible for the welfare of England.

Adler, then, clearly belonged to what Herzl contemptuously called the 'Protestrabbiner'.

Here I must add an intriguing postscript before we leave Adler and his era. The term 'Protestrabbiner' was coined by Herzl in an article in *Die Welt* (16 July 1897) to designate the five German rabbis who had signed a letter of protest against Zionism and the Zionist Congress in the name of the 'German Rabbinical Association'. This consisted of two Orthodox and three Liberal rabbis, united in their opposition to Zionism. Seventy years later, a survey published in *Ma'ariv* (16 July 1968) discovered that almost all the children, grandchildren, and great-grandchildren of these 'protest rabbis' had settled in Israel.[32] By contrast, most descendants of the secular founders of Political Zionism, including Herzl and Weizmann, dissociated themselves from Zionist and Jewish life, married out, or even became converts to Christianity. There is surely some lesson to be learned from this amazing paradox.

We may fittingly take leave from Hermann Adler by recording that in his will, published in full in the *Jewish Chronicle* of 18 August 1911, he bequeathed £20 each to the Shaare Zedek Hospital and the Etz Chaim Yeshiva in Jerusalem.

Chief Rabbi Hertz could hardly have been more different from his predecessor, in temperament as well as in the attitude to Zionism. Where Adler's Anglican airs induced a certain disdain for foreign Jews,[33] which no doubt accentuated his estrangement from the Zionism enthusing the East End masses, Hertz, who had never been anything but a foreigner – whether in South Africa, America, or on arrival in England – did not differentiate between the indigenous Anglo-Jews and by now far more numerous immigrants, among whom the Jewish National Idea had already struck firm roots. Indeed, Hertz fought an almost lifelong battle with the Anglo-Jewish establishment, especially over Zionism.

Hertz boldly professed his Zionist beliefs in word and action very early in his ministry. Already during his first incumbency in Syracuse, New York, he published a powerful article fiercely attacking his assimilationist colleagues for their complacent opposition to Zionism. It appeared under the title 'After the Congress – A Résumé and a Retrospect' in *The American Hebrew*, October 1897. Strangely, he did not reproduce this memorable essay in his collected writings, perhaps because in its youthful boisterousness it still lacked the literary grace of which he was to become such an accomplished master in his later years, and it was only fifty years later that it was republished thanks to his son, Samuel, in the booklet *Essays and Addresses* issued in his memory in 1948.[34] 'Zionism as a dynamic force', he writes in the immediate aftermath of the First Zionist Congress, 'is only fifteen years old. But in that short space of time it has built up waste spaces and brought back the hearts of the children to the parents; it has created a greater and more voluminous literature than the entire "reformatory commotion" during 150 years, all the multitudinous and motley revisions of the prayer-book included.' Hailing Herzl alongside Jeremiah and Yehuda Halevi, he passionately extols Zionism as the only answer to rampant anti-Semitism, and then denounces its ecclesiastical opponents with ridicule and venom. A small quotation will convey the flavour of his castigation:

They argue: 'Let them stay in Russia. They have there a mission to perform.' As there seems to be something sanctimonious about this advice, let us look and see who are they who preach thus? Is it fellow-sufferers, who bid them courageously endure for their father's sake? No, for the most part this phrase is on the lips of those who lounge in luxury; who never knew suffering, least of all for conscience sake; to whom martyrdom smacks somewhat of madness; who among other things trade away their Sabbaths and gamble away their Sundays; who have crossed the word 'self-sacrifice' from their vocabulary; to whom self-denial especially for religion's sake is synonymous with devil-worship.

Other Zionist writings in his early years included *What is Zionism?*, a pamphlet issued by the South African Federation in 1901, and 'Herzl – The Leader of the Diaspora', a lecture given in New York in 1904.[35] He was Vice-President of the South African Zionist Federation from 1899 to 1904. He also attended the Fourth Zionist Congress in London in 1904.

Yet, there is no mention of Zionism in the first three important addresses he did include in his published writings. The subject did not feature in his Graduation Address from the Jewish Theological Seminary in New York on 14 June 1894, nor in his Installation Address at the Orach Chayyim Congregation in New York on 13 January 1912, though on that occasion he did decry the

narrow tribalism called '*American* Judaism'. Its watchword . . . runs thus 'America is our Zion and George Washington is our Messiah'. According to this new revelation, a deliberate estrangement from the collective consciousness of the Jewish People and the Jewish Past is held forth as the course of conduct which true Americanism dictates.[36]

Perhaps more surprisingly, he omitted any reference to Zionism even in his Installation Address as Chief Rabbi at the Great Synagogue in London fifteen months later. I consulted Judge Israel Finestein on this, and, among other helpful suggestions he gave me in the preparation of this paper, I am grateful to him for the following comments on Hertz's omission:

The essential theme of his Installation Address was of course the need to raise educational standards. With English Zionism in 1913 divided and in the doldrums, and with the movement as a whole in a trough, it might well have seemed anomalous to introduce Zionism into the address. There was no point in being 'imprudent' for no immediate or relevant purpose. By 1916, a new situation had begun to develop. Seen with the eyes of 1913, there was none of the pervasiveness of later Zionist thought that would have rendered the absence of any reference in his sermon strange. If there was on his part any self-censoring on this occasion, I doubt whether it had anything to do with a *stille* Zionism in his new office, not even at the outset. His Zionism was universally known.

As far as I could discover, Hertz never explicitly referred to the anti-Zionism of his predecessor, whom he altogether mentions but rarely in his writings. But I suspect that he had the contrast between Hermann Adler and himself in mind when much later he wrote: 'In 1918 he [Dr H. P. Chajes] was called to the Chief Rabbinate of Vienna – one of the most important Jewish communities on the Continent. What a tribute to his personality that he, the ardent Zionist, was chosen to succeed Guedemann, the uncompromising opponent of Theodor Herzl and Zionism.'[37] Hertz can have had little doubt that his own election five years earlier represented a similar tribute to his personality. For he had made no secret of his Zionist loyalties, even before the Anglo-Jewish public. I cannot say for certain whether his not infrequent appearances in the columns of the *Jewish Chronicle* – in fairly extensive news reports on his appointments in Johannesburg and New York, in lengthy letters to the editor, and especially in a striking interview with him published on 7 April 1911 – indicate that he already then had his eyes set on the British Chief Rabbinate. That interview certainly exposed him as a confirmed Zionist, though also as a severe critic of the movement's irreligion, which he was often to lambast in similar terms in his later years, when he referred to the 'Hebrew-speaking heathens'.[38] This is what he told his interviewer in 1911:

> As you know, I am a convinced Zionist. . . . I have a word, however, to say about the outcome of the Zionist movement, and that is in regard to that form of Jewish nationalism which is Torah-less and decadent, and at the same time scribbles and dabbles in pure Hebrew. It is the loathing of my soul. Modern Hebrew literature, always anti-rabbinic, has, of late, experienced some anti-religious and pornographic developments. It is not only in biblical antiquity that prophets of Baal used 'Hebrew as a living language'. Many a Nationalist, no less than Reform Jew, sadly needs conversion to Judaism.

Yet his revulsion against the secularization of Zionism never deflected him from supporting its political cause. This support reached its climax in two celebrated letters he wrote in favour of the Balfour Declaration about to be issued.[39] Both showed courage and statesmanship of the highest order. The first was, in his own words, 'my indignant reaction to the attempt by the then leaders of the Board of Deputies and the Anglo-Jewish Association to strangle the Balfour Declaration before its birth'. It appeared in *The Times* on 28 May 1917, and is worthy of reproduction in full:

> I do not propose to advance any arguments contesting the extraordinary statement on Zionism and Palestine which you published on Thursday last, signed by Mr

B.L.Alexander, K.C., and Mr Claude G.Montefiore. But, as Chief Rabbi of the United Hebrew Congregations of the British Empire, I cannot allow your readers to remain under the misconception that the said statement represents in the least the view held either by Anglo-Jewry as a whole or by the Jewries of the Overseas Dominions. Moreover, neither the Board of Deputies nor the Anglo-Jewish Associ- ation – on whose behalf their Presidents signed the document in question – authorized its publication or had an opportunity of considering its contents.

It is indeed grievously painful to me to write this in your influential columns, but I am impelled to do so in the interests of truth and of justice to the communities of which I have the honour and privilege of being the spiritual head.

The second letter was sent to the War Cabinet on 15 October 1917 in response to an official enquiry addressed to him and seven other leading Anglo-Jewish personalities to elicit their views on the proposed draft text of the Declaration. It reads in part:

It is with feelings of the profoundest gratification that I learn of the intention of HM Government to lend its powerful support to the re-establishment in Palestine of a National Home for the Jewish people ... will mark an epoch in Jewish history. To millions of my brethren throughout the world it will mean the realization of Israel's undying hope of a Restoration. ...

The draft Declaration is in spirit and in substance everything that could be desired.

He then suggested, evidently in common with other respondents, a slight amendment in the proposed text (which was adopted), and ended:

In conclusion, I must, as Chief Rabbi, thank the Prime Minister, the Secretary of State for Foreign Affairs, and the members of the War Cabinet for their striking sympathy with Jewish aspirations; and assure them that the overwhelming majority of Anglo-Jewry, as well as of the Jewries of His Majesty's Overseas Dominions, will rejoice with me at this broad humanity and farsighted statesmanship of the men who guide the destinies of the Empire.

Twenty-five years later, this dramatic episode was vividly described by Samuel Landman in the *Essays* presented to Dr Hertz on his seventieth birthday, published in 1942.[40] After Weizmann and others had eventually prevailed on the War Cabinet to consider a Declaration in favour of the Zionist cause, the plan met with bitter opposition by influential Anglo- Jewish notables, led by Edwin Montagu, who was himself a member of the Cabinet. There was also vigorous opposition among Jewish leaders in France, whose government was closely consulted by the British.

In the face of this dilemma – after all, a major objective of the exercise was to rally Jewish support for the Allied cause, then seriously flagging – it was decided to ascertain the views of the eight notables. Interestingly, they excluded Gaster, although the crucial breakthrough meeting between Zionist leaders and representatives of the British government had taken place at his home in February 1917. Of the eight replies, four were favourable, three hostile, and one at best neutral. Hence, Landman is probably right in his assessment that the Chief Rabbi's unequivocal support 'carried the greatest weight. While it would be wrong to underrate the many other factors which helped to weigh down the scale in favour, there is no room for doubt that a negative or even a hesitant reply from Dr Hertz would have severely, if not fatally, prejudiced the chances of the Declaration.'

This was the nearest any Chief Rabbi ever came to actually influencing the course of Zionist history, though even here his role was supportive rather than active, unlike Gaster's, which had exercised a formative influence on Zionism.

I believe Hertz was himself aware that his role fell somewhat short of being decisive or historic in leading to the issuance of the Declaration. In his collected writings, he merely records his two letters, together with brief notes on their antecedents. Thereafter, he never again referred to his intervention, except when he quoted his letter to the War Cabinet at a memorial meeting for Lord Balfour on 1 April 1930, but even then he merely described the letter as expressing 'my own feelings on that occasion'.[41] How different had been his assessment of the crucial part he played in the fight against Calendar Reform during the late 1920s. He told the story himself at length in all its drama in a paper he entitled 'The Battle for the Sabbath at Geneva', delivered before the Jewish Historical Society of England on 16 December 1931, and subsequently published on nearly thirty pages both by the Society and in his own volume of *Addresses*.[42] Had he seen himself in an even remotely similar light regarding the rather more historic Balfour Declaration, he would surely not have left posterity without his account of 'The Battle for Zion'![43]

For Hertz, the Balfour Declaration, in which he retained his faith throughout the erratic course of its implementation by successive British governments, signalled the opening of a new era, promising relief for persecuted Jews and a new glory for Judaism. But enthusiastic and unflinching as he always was in his championship of Zionism, there were limitations both on his visions and on his involvements. He never advocated Aliyah from free countries, nor ever envisaged the Jewish National Home as encompassing more than a tiny fraction of the Jewish people. Immediately in the wake of the Declaration, at a Zionist Demonstration on 2 December 1917, he declared:[44]

Remember the Days of Old. After the proclamation issued by Cyrus, the mass of the Jewish people still remained in Babylon. A mere handful took advantage of the king's decree; and only 42,000 men, women, and children returned to Zion. But compare the contribution to civilization made by these men with that of their brethren who remained in the Dispersion. That handful of Zionists and their descendants, because living on their own soil, changed the entire future of mankind. They edited and collected the Prophets, wrote some of the fairest portions of the Scriptures, formed the canon of the Bible, and gave the world its monotheistic religions. And as in the days of Cyrus, the overwhelming majority of Jews of today will continue to live where they are now, praying and working in absolute loyalty for the land of their birth or adoption, and ever beholding their peace in its welfare. Only a Remnant shall return. But it is the national rejuvenation of that Remnant that will open a new chapter in the annals of the human spirit.

Six years later, he repeated these words in his Opening Address at the Conference of Anglo-Jewish Preachers in 1923.[45]

He was, of course, a religious Zionist, and served as President of the British Mizrachi. Yet his books did not record a single address given in that capacity. Altogether, while constantly stressing the spiritual significance of Zion's restoration, he did not identify with, criticize, or press for any particular religious policies, any more than he took sides on the great political debate between Weizmann and Jabotinsky.[46] In fact, his Zionism remained rather remote from controversies with or over factors any other than unfriendly British policies.

The 'Arab Question', too, never loomed large with him, or indeed with most Zionist leaders until fairly recent times. At a public meeting in the Albert Hall on 12 July 1920, he was content to declare:[47]

I need add nothing on the Arab question to what has been said by the speakers that preceded me. But I should like to remind you of one thing. Within a fortnight, the pious Israelite will observe the Ninth of Ab, and the most beautiful of the prayers of the Ninth of Ab is the sublime Ode to Zion sung by Yehuda Halevi. Legend tells us that in his old age he made a pilgrimage to Palestine, and that in sight of the Holy City he recited his wonderful Ode. At that moment, a Saracen horseman came and rode roughshod over him, mortally wounding him. Ladies and Gentlemen, in the Jewish National Home, there will be no riding roughshod over the Jew – just as there will be no riding roughshod over the non-Jew.

In subsequent writings recording his speeches, the subject is hardly ever touched on again. In 1925, reporting on his first visit to Palestine for the opening of the Hebrew University at another Conference of Anglo-Jewish Preachers, he told his colleagues:[48]

No survey of present-day Israel would be at all complete were it to omit the brightest spot on the Jewish horizon – Eretz Yisrael. It has recently been my good fortune to visit the Holy Land under the most auspicious conditions. I saw the old

*Yishub* under the shadow of the Wailing Wall, and the new Jerusalem stretching forward towards Mount Scopus. I saw Tel Aviv, that unique all-Jewish city, wholly built by Jews, inhabited by Jews, and administered by Jews. ... I saw the Jewish colonies in Galilee, as well as those in Judea. In all of them boys and girls, men and women, *sing* at their work. Religious zealots and fanatic free-thinkers alike rejoice in the redemption of the soil by Jewish labour, and look upon it as the holiest of human duties.

After then referring to his Dedication Prayer at the Hebrew University opening, he continued:

We must, however, face the possibility that these men may not rise to the height of their divine opportunity. They may bring with them from the *galut* a spirit of negation towards Jewish ideas; and, quite unlike their fathers who wept by the Rivers of Babylon, theirs may be the resolve to sing a strange song in the Land of the Lord! Such blind guides in the realm of the spirit would inevitably turn the Hebrew University into an *Akra* of the days of Hellenistic apostasy, into a citadel of assimilation from which a small minority could disintegrate the eternal values of Israel, and decimate the ranks of the Maccabean defenders of Israel's sacred possessions. But even that possibility need not affright us. ... It is the Chalutzim and the Chasidim, the Yemenites and the Bokharans, the Polish Jews and those from Persia, who will redeem and save Eretz Yisrael for us. ... It is the men and women of simple, unquenchable faith, untouched by the poison of rationalism, who are the architects, nay, the very building-stones of our future in the resurrected Holy Land.

Even after the terrible 1929 riots, he was exercised by British policies rᵣ ther than by the Arab problem as such. Thus, in 1932, again addressing a Preachers' Conference, he said:[49]

Alas, we have very little cause for rejoicing. Only a few weeks after we dispersed in 1929, an outbreak of Arab violence against the Jewish population in Palestine resulted in a ghastly butchery of 129 Jewish men, women, and children. The unbelievable happened: under the British flag there took place the worst massacre of Jews in the Holy Land since the Crusades. The conduct of the local authorities before, during, and after those terrible days was, in the opinion of many who are competent to judge, an equivocal one. A Commission of Inquiry was immediately appointed. ... It investigated everything, explained everything, exonerated everybody, and seemed to put the entire blame on the dead victims. A few of the murderers were hanged; but the men who were more morally responsible for inflaming the fanatical mob had not been called to account. These, and their sympathizers among local officials, have since continued their cunning propaganda against the whole Zionist experiment, pointing to the massacre as proof that the Balfour Declaration was impossible of execution, and that Great Britain was accordingly freed from its solemn pledge. ...
However, the spontaneous protest by some of the Empire's leading statesmen ...

that the new policy advocated would constitute a breach of faith on the part of Great Britain led to a modification of the attitude responsible for the Passfield White Paper.

Alas, events in Palestine evoked a similar stand in his New Year Message of 1936:[50]

For nearly five months, the Jews of Palestine have been harried by widespread destruction and murder.... Instead of calling for firm action by the local government to demonstrate the determination to maintain equality of status and rights for the Jewish and Arab populations, voices are clamouring for these dastardly crimes to be rewarded by closing the gates of the Jewish National Home to the Jew.... Certain influences are working for the pledges given to the Jews by Great Britain and the other civilized nations to be repudiated, and for the magnificent Jewish achievement in Palestine in uplifting all sections of land and people to be deliberately ruined.... The success of these machinations would indeed constitute a new Destruction of Judea. Fervently do we trust that these prove idle fears.

The only reference in Hertz's works to the infamous MacDonald White Paper of 1939 is in a small piece entitled 'Jews – 1939', evidently prepared for some year-book. He unreservedly identified himself with the chorus of denunciation, writing:[51]

Jewish Palestine received the White Paper with its forecast of the Jews as a permanent minority in an Arab State with deep dismay, and unanimously rejected it. 'It places the Jewish population at the mercy of the Arab majority' was the declaration of the Jewish Agency, voicing the opinion of Jews the world over. Nevertheless, when the war broke out, Dr Weizmann informed Mr Neville Chamberlain of the readiness of all Zionists to join Great Britain in the defence of civilization.

Even in the darkest days of the Second World War, Hertz proclaimed his faith in Allied victory as well as in a Jewish future in a free Palestine. At a public meeting at Grosvenor House on 8 July 1941, he declared:[52]

We do not forget the cruel disillusionments and heart-rending setbacks of recent decades. But we feel that the miracle of Jewish Palestine – the most outstanding constructive achievement in world affairs of the last half-century – has fully justified our dreams and sacrifices of the past, and will yet prove the salvation of large portions of our hounded European brethren.

Hertz's own records end here. But his most painful battle for Zionism was still to come. When the war was over, with the White Paper still barring refuge in Palestine to the pitiful survivors of the Holocaust, the tensions between Britain and Zionism soon reached breaking-point. So did the tensions between the Chief Rabbi and the leadership of the United Synagogue.

Hertz had never succeeded in carrying the United Synagogue with him into the Zionist camp, though the Board of Deputies had given up its hostility to Zionism long ago, to be eventually controlled by the Zionists. Aubrey Newman, in his official history of the *United Synagogue* written for its centenary, describes Hertz's relations with the establishment in these words:[53]

Despite the close connection between Lord Rothschild and the Balfour Declaration, most of the 'traditional' leaders of Anglo-Jewry were, at best, apathetic, but mostly opposed to Zionist ideas. Hertz, on the other hand, was strongly Zionist and lost little opportunity to preach his ideas. Some organizations of Anglo-Jewry followed him in welcoming Zionism, but the United Synagogue, for one, did not. There were many occasions in these years when the United Synagogue showed itself unwilling, as an organization, to support Jewish settlement in Palestine, and there is no doubt that this, at a time when there was a growing recognition inside the wider Anglo-Jewish community of the importance of the Zionist cause, was yet another issue separating the honorary officers from the bulk of the United Synagogue membership.

But this hardly describes the conflict when it finally exploded. While in 1917 the leaders of the official establishment simply climbed down when Hertz challenged and disowned them, Sir Robert Waley Cohen, still sharing their attitude thirty years later, simply countermanded the Chief Rabbi's instructions telegraphed to his ministers to

Proclaim Sabbath, 6 October [1945] a day of Jewish solidarity with remnants of European Jewry. . . . Jews of England expect government keeping faith in regard to Palestine as only haven of refuge to survivors of Nazi bestiality.[54]

Sir Robert then cabled synagogue secretaries:

The Chief Rabbi's telegram may be misinterpreted as advocating introduction of politics into our religious services. This would be a serious violation of purposes of United Synagogue and of our constitution. Accordingly, please warn your minister . . . vital importance of scrupulously avoiding this grave danger tomorrow. . . .[55]

Even Hertz's death in 1946 did not put an end to the tensions. During the interregnum, Dayan H.M.Lazarus was appointed to act as Deputy Chief Rabbi, and his love of Zion also merits a mention here. For he, too, soon found himself in collision with Sir Robert, and I am indebted to my friend, Norman Cohen, for the following account of it:

Dayan Lazarus had composed a special prayer for the Yishuv and circulated it to ministers. Sir Robert took umbrage and wrote that Dr Hertz would never have sent out such a prayer before clearing the matter with the United Synagogue honorary officers. Lazarus nearly exploded with indignation and wrote back very fiercely, telling Sir Robert that he would not be treated like an office boy!

Norman Cohen adds, significantly:

This was probably the last manifestation of the anti-Zionism of the Grand Dukes, which never recovered from the establishment of the State of Israel.

This leads us to the new era of Israel's independence and of Israel Brodie's Chief Rabbinate – their respective inaugurations separated by only six weeks.

The preface to Brodie's book *A Word in Season* declares:[56]

The outstanding event, the influence which is dominant in practically every address included in this volume is the establishment of the State of Israel, proclaimed in the month when I assumed the tasks of my responsible and sacred office in May 1948.

Yet, surprisingly, his Installation Address on 28 June 1948[57] makes no reference to the Jewish State. Nor do quite a number of other addresses and messages recorded here and in his second volume. Nevertheless, he was a life-long Zionist, more proficient in modern Hebrew than any of his predecessors and most of his colleagues, and a frequent visitor to Israel to the end of his days. He also succeeded Hertz as President of the British Mizrachi.

With Israel becoming so much closer and more central to Jewish life in the Diaspora, it is only natural that his links with the Yishuv and its affairs were far more personal and intimate than Hertz's had been. He was also more critical of its shortcomings. But above all, he was called upon to give initial direction to the religious response to events of Biblical dimensions and significance.

This response, by his own admission, was at first tardy. In his address on Israel's seventh Independence Day, in 1955, the first he recorded, he said:[58]

In previous years on the anniversary of the Day of Israel's Rebirth, we of this community have been tardy at any ample celebration of a demonstrative nature. And there were reasons for the uncertainty and reluctance to give directions on the religious and general character and form of its celebration in this country.... Nevertheless, this year official hesitation about the desirability or manner of the celebration of Independence Day in this country has given way to the overwhelming desire of masses of our people throughout the country to celebrate the Day in a fitting and proper manner. ... The special prayers and readings which this year have been included in the Service on the Sabbath previous to the 5th Iyar, and the special Services such as the one in which we are privileged to participate this evening, are intended to give voice to our sentiments of joy. ...

Other notable innovations relating to Israel which he commissioned or sanctioned included: the Prayer for Israel, introduced in 1949 and featured in the revised edition of the *Authorized Prayer Book* since 1962; the Israel Independence Day Order of Service Book prepared by Armin Krausz and 'approved' by the Chief Rabbi[59] in 1964; and the admission of the Sephardi pronunciation in classrooms, but not at synagogue services, in 1962, modifying an earlier ruling against any change given ten years earlier.[60] Yet, in 1958 he had told a Preachers' Conference:[61]

Within the next few months I propose to consider the wider problem of the Israeli pronunciation in our synagogues and in our schools.

Describing his first visit to the new-born State of Israel at a Preachers' Conference in 1953, he was still overwhelmed by seeing that

The greater part of the people one meets and sees, tinker, tailor, roadmender, taxi-driver, landworker, soldier, policeman, bus-driver, shop-keeper, porter, customs officer, man and woman, boy and girl are Jews; all the ordinary things of life, from pin to anchor, are named, praised, criticized, bought and sold, and delivered with Hebrew words for it all.

Yet, already he saw the shades as well as the light, as he continued:

But one has also to be prepared for the cold douche of reality and disillusionment. Probably that succeeding experience is due to the fact that we employ Prophetic terms and Messianic allusions too literally when we look at the present Israeli scene. If we were to think and speak in basic, concrete terms, while we would still charge them with the wonder and admiration which Jewish achievement must compel, we would also not be blind to difficulties and weaknesses and shortcomings in every sphere of a developing infant state. . . .[62]

His criticisms were usually expressed in rather general terms. Occasionally, he also criticized the critics, though in one curious instance he later retracted his own criticism. In a Pesach broadcast on 5 April 1955, he had said:

I read recently that Professor Einstein is disappointed with the State of Israel because it is not different from other states. I do not know what were its shortcomings that prompted that great man to be disillusioned when he said: 'We had great hopes for Israel at first. We thought it might be better than other nations, but it is no better.' I would prefer to be more charitable with the State which has just begun its career and is in its struggling infancy. . . .[63]

Three weeks later, Einstein having died in the meantime, Brodie started his Israel Independence Day address with these words:

Broadcasting on the eve of Passover, I referred to an interview which the late Professor Albert Einstein was reported to have given to a publisher. . . . After the broadcast, I reflected that however critical and outspoken he might be about Israel and its defects which Israel shared with other nations, Professor Einstein was speaking as one who had espoused the cause of Zionism. . . . Subsequently, we were not surprised to read that Professor Einstein, when asked to amplify the remarks attributed to him, stated that his views had been misinterpreted by the interviewer. Indeed, up to the very last, his thoughts were centred on the preparation of the speech he proposed to make on the occasion of the 7th Anniversary of the Day of Israel's Independence.[64]

In fact, the complaint about Israel's undue urge to be 'normal' like all other nations was Brodie's own frequent theme. For instance, at the Independence Day Service in 1965, he declared:

On sober reflection, however, I sometimes think that in the laudable achievement of normalcy we have tended because of circumstances to become too intensely normal. For example, while I was impressed with the sight of tanks and aeroplanes and the pictures of the latest missiles required by Israel for its defence, and while I felt that in defence of hearth and home the Israeli forces would give a good account of themselves, I was also possessed of sad and bitter thoughts. We are essentially a nation that prefers the paths of peace. . . . We prefer to live by the book rather than by the sword. It is more normal for the Jew, by the teachings of his faith, and by the national experience and suffering of wars and the rumours of wars which punctuate the pages of our history, to promote peace and understanding between peoples, without recourse to the arbitrament of wars. . . . Normalcy is best expressed in spiritual and moral terms.[65]

Brodie rarely involved himself in the major controversies, whether religious or political, which erupted so frequently in Israel and in its relations with the Diaspora. I found no substantial reference to the fierce and interminable debate on 'Who is a Jew?' in his published writings, not even in the many addresses he gave to his British and European colleagues at their regular conferences.

On the agitation for the restoration of a Sanhedrin, he was somewhat ambivalent when he told the Anglo-Jewish Preachers' Conference in 1958:[66]

I recall that at our Conference in 1949, the question of a central religious authority acting as a Sanhedrin was raised and amply discussed. The setting up of a Sanhedrin has had its advocates and vehement opponents. Now that a Jewish State has been brought into being, the time had come, argued some, to see fulfilled such prophecies as 'And I will restore thy judges as at first'. . . . Others felt that these prophecies . . . could not be fulfilled or rather implemented, bearing in mind the circumstances of the legislative supremacy and authority vested in the Knesset, and the qualifications essential for the members of an august, supreme, judicial, and legislative body such as a Sanhedrin. None the less, many rabbis have naturally and increasingly turned to the Chief Rabbinate of Israel for guidance on many points of religious law during the last ten years, and it has become an accepted practice for some communities in the Diaspora to look upon Israel's spiritual leaders as a source of authoritative Law.

He had just attended the festive opening of Heichal Shlomo in Jerusalem, which prompted him to continue his address on a more critical note:

We must not, however, ignore views critical and apprehensive which have been expressed on the role and significance of the [new] religious centre. It has been suggested that the Rabbinic Courts are not independent, first, because the members of the courts are appointed and maintained by the State, secondly, authority of the Rabbinic Courts derives from an Act of the Knesset. Further, there is the fear that Acts of the Knesset or decisions of the High Court may impinge on those spheres of personal status which are now secured to the exclusive jurisdiction of the Rabbinic Courts. . . . I consider this matter of such grave import that I felt it necessary to mention it in this Conference. But the misgiving I have just voiced or any other trends in Israel which may make us apprehensive of a possible weakening of the bonds between Israel and the Diaspora should not prevent us from rejoicing at the extraordinary development of Israel during the last ten years.

On Aliyah, his attitude was also not without some equivocation. One reference to the subject is particularly illuminating. Following a pastoral tour to Australia, he had addressed a Council meeting of the Anglo-Jewish Association in 1952, calling for 'co-operative effort to increase emigration from this country to the Dominions'. In a subsequent address at the Stoke Newington Synagogue Hall, he explained that:[67]

I had in mind not only the material prospects offered in New Zealand and Aus-tralia, nor was I concerned only with prudential and even humanitarian motives behind the generous immigration policies of their respective governments. I was especially thinking in terms of the spiritual and communal contributions which Jews hailing from this country bring to the growing and vigorous countries of the Dominions.

Evidently, this had evoked some criticism, and he continued:

It has been pointed out that my advocacy – with an evangelical tinge – of emigra-tion to the Dominions seems to ignore the mystique of Kibbutz Galuyot associated with emigration to the Land of Israel. That is far from the truth. I have been on record on more than one occasion as a keen supporter of Aliyah from lands of the West. The Aliyah from the West, however, is not a mass emigration. It is qualitative and selective and is prompted by high and noble resolves of the chalutzic motif. . . . We ought to be realists to recognize that the majority of our people are content to continue living in the free communities of the Dispersion. .... We must buttress our Jewish foundations wherever they are, and this applies specifically to the Jewish communities in the British Commonwealth regarded as parts of a larger Jewish community.

I could not discover any further mention of Aliyah in his writings.

But he was forthright in his opposition to Zionist involvement in Jewish education. Addressing a Mizrachi conference on 21 November 1953, he warned:[68]

There is, however, one sphere of Jewish education where it is unnecessary and it may even be harmful for the Jewish Agency to come to the assistance of our community. I am referring to the education of our children. Not a single penny of Jewish Agency funds should be spent on Jewish education whether in Hebrew classes, Talmud Torahs, day-schools, secondary schools, public schools, or kindergartens. ....

I therefore most strongly advise the Zionist organizations and groups who have begun to make approaches, however well-intended, to offer financial assistance to some of our day-schools, to desist. I make the same request to Mizrachi of this country.

He had presumably feared that such support might lead to the setting up of secularist Jewish day-schools. However, an agreement was eventually reached with the Zionist Federation Educational Trust, placing schools it would establish under the religious control of the London Board of Jewish Religious Education, and recognizing the Chief Rabbi as the final arbiter of any dispute. While this agreement has never been operated on these lines, the network of Zionist day-schools, which soon spread in London and the Provinces, was always run on traditional religious lines.

Withal, Sir Israel Brodie's consistently firm support of Israel and Israeli causes induced numerous institutions in Israel to confer high honours on him by the time he retired in 1965, and his recent death was widely mourned in the land he loved so deeply.[69]

In concluding with some account of my own period, I realize that the identity of subject and object must necessarily place subjectivity above objectivity, compromising my critical faculties in the process. This conceded, I will lift from my writings a few events and attitudes I consider significant, with trust in your critical faculties.

Recognizing that times have again changed dramatically, I broke with tradition in several ways, from being the first Chief Rabbi to make a Zionist reference, including a pledge to support Aliyah, in an Installation Address,[70] to my more recent challenge of religious and political policies which I feared might imperil the interests of Judaism and Israel alike.[71] I did not accept the presidency of the Mizrachi, being disinclined as Chief Rabbi to have any political affiliations, and having altogether questioned the continued useful-ness of religious political parties in Israel. I managed at last to draw the United Synagogue establishment more actively into pro-Israel work and the Zionist establishment into massively supporting Jewish education, an in-volvement I welcomed rather than spurned.

This increased activism, reflected in all my writings, was partly generated by the growing centrality of Israel in communal life, as manifested, for instance, by the glaring disproportion of funds raised for Israel and for domestic needs respectively. Another important factor was the alarming escalation of pressures on and inside Israel, and the rapid succession of dramatic events which could not but suck Jewish leaders everywhere into the vortex of the fast-whirling waters of argument and activity.

Within two months of my Installation, the Six Day War was upon us, confronting me with the largest crowd and the gravest challenge I had ever faced. In an atmosphere charged with unprecedented emotion and anxiety, I started my address to the vast rally assembled in the Albert Hall on the first day of the war:[72]

Nearly thirty years ago my illustrious predecessor, Chief Rabbi Dr Hertz, addressed a massed assembly in this very hall to arouse the conscience of the world on the catastrophe which lay ahead for European Jewry. Alas, the cry was too weak and to faint to avert disaster....

We are here this evening to make quite sure that we will not be too weak and not be too late this time. We are not going to have another Holocaust in the martyred history of our people. The hope of two millennia, and the toil and sacrifice of two decades, is not now going to be wiped out in two weeks or two months.

Having been challenged a few days earlier on my response to Israel's predicament by a noted journalist in the national press, I continued:

I make no apology for having called last week ... upon the Anglo-Jewish com-munity to mobilize all its resources in the defence of Israel. Nor will I ever be deterred from doing my religious and moral duty in this moment of our people's anguish by anyone coming forth with the dangerous nonsense of dual loyalties.

Let me try, as plainly as I can, to clear up this diabolical confusion. As a British citizen, England is my country. And as a Jew, Israel is my people. When my father and my mother, my brothers and sisters, are in danger of being murdered, I will defend them whatever their nationality, and if I were not to do so, then my fellow-citizens would have nothing but contempt for me. I am, therefore, overcome with grief, I am sickened to the depths of my heart by the spectacle of some Jews who, having previously betrayed their God and betrayed their religion, are now publicly calling upon their fellow-Jews to betray their people.

I then announced a number of steps I urged the community to take during the emergency, including synagogues being kept open all day for prayer, and the curtailment of personal parties and functions, 'to use the resources that had been set aside for these purposes as contributions to Israel, that it may prevail.'

The Six Day War evoked an enormous response, from individuals and institutions alike. But the United Synagogue had still remained untouched by the new fervour which swept the community. In a comprehensive address to the Council of the United Synagogue on 26 November 1967, later published, I therefore included the following passage :[73]

I believe the United Synagogue as an institution was the only major Jewish institution in this country, or anywhere else, which carried on during the Israel emergency without in some form or another, as a corporate body, responding to the gigantic, historic challenge, although of course members of the United Synagogue, as individuals, all contributed magnanimously. It was then argued, and we saw it in print, that nothing could be done to identify the United Synagogue more closely with the needs of Israel, because there was no provision for doing so in the Constitution of the United Syngagogue. Should it be said that Israel ought not to exist because the Constitution of the United Synagogue does not provide for it?

I want to suggest, and have previously proposed to the honorary officers, that just as we have a Welfare Committee, a Burial Committee, a Youth Committee, and numerous others, the United Synagogue today ought to have an Israel Committee. We ought to have at the highest level a body that seeks identification with Israel, liaison with its affairs, especially the religious affairs of Israel.

Such an Israel Committee was eventually set up, though it still awaits greater drive and support to be really effective.

But the Six Day War also induced a national state of euphoria and complacency. At the same time, the bonds which the war had forged between us and Israel emboldened me to match support with criticism in the partnership with the Jewish State. One of the challenges which particularly beclouded my vision of peace and constantly gnawed at my conscience was the Arab refugee problem and the way in which this was swept under the carpet only to erupt in vile acts of Arab terrorism.

The Jews – no strangers to the problems of the homeless – cannot be indifferent to the plight of the Arabs languishing in wretched camps. Even if we were not responsible for creating this problem nor had it within our power to solve it, I deemed it morally wrong and politically unwise simply to suppress it by the rhetorical 'Who are the Palestinians?'. The absence of Jewish protests at this intolerable human misery, I felt and stated, could only provide others with an excuse for publicizing it through terror. I frequently drew attention to this moral blot,[74] sometimes facing a hail of denunciation for mentioning a subject which was simply taboo in Zionist circles. Already, in my Passover BBC broadcast of 1968 I gave expression to 'my pained rebuke of those who are insufficiently touched by the unspeakable misery and indignity of the refugees – whether Arab refugees displaced from their homes in the Holy Land, or deprived Jews in and from Arab Lands',[75] while in my New Year broadcast the same year I spoke of 'the shattering explosions of terrorist mines ripping peaceful civilians in Israel, and the near-by cries of despair from Arab refugees drained of all human dignity in the world's worst breeding-grounds of hate'.[76] Even at the height of our grief, in the memorial address I later entitled 'The Infamy of Munich' for the slain Olympic Israelis on 11 September 1972, the thought of the refugee problem as the root of our troubles never left me, as I uttered the words:[77]

We are to feel the anguish of all mothers who lose their children, and our Prophets would surely expect us to sense even the grief of the mothers of the evil assassins. They would also expect us not to be insensitive to the enormous human tragedy of hundreds of thousands who still suffer the indignity and deprivation of refugeedom, a fate with which we ourselves are all too familiar.

Then came the disaster of the Yom Kippur War, which once again elicited much intensive activity – and numerous addresses and writings – from me. I viewed the Jewish predicament, soon to be aggravated by the iniquitous United Nations Resolution equating Zionism with racism, primarily as a spiritual crisis. In a wide-ranging lecture on 'The Jewish Destiny – the Spiritual Challenge of the Yom Kippur War', delivered at the Hendon Synagogue on 30 January 1974, I declared:[78]

The spiritual crisis may well trace its origin to the fallacious premises on which the earlier secular Jewish nationalists based their dreams, plans and policies. They, and their successors to the present day, believed that the restoration of Jewish national independence in Zion would solve 'the Jewish problem'. Ignoring the perennial lessons of our history and faith, they sought to turn their backs on our past traditions and the spiritual ingredients in the mystique of Jewish survival, convinced that, if only we had a State like all other nations, we would 'normalize' the Jewish condition. . . . The boon of sovereignty – with a government, an army, a diplomatic corps, universities, and all the trappings of statehood – would make us accepted as an equal among the nations and, by removing the 'abnormalcy' of our homelessness, eliminate anti-Semitism. What an idle dream this was! The Yom Kippur War has shattered this illusion. Jews today are as different, and as lonely, as they ever were. Far from having solved 'the Jewish problem', the Jewish State has highlighted it. . . .

In pursuing the phantom of equality and the mirage of normality rather than the unique goals of our Prophetic destiny, we reversed the flow of national features, of virtues and vices, in our trade of ideas with the nations. Instead of exporting the ideals and values peculiar to the Jewish spirit – the whole range, from humility, moral excellence, and profound faith to the discipline of life trained by the regimen of religious observances – we all too often imported from our exile the base materialism, the social and moral depravities to which we have been exposed. The whole ethos of our national existence became widely contaminated by these alien imports. In the end, the benefits of equality escaped us, as the nations still do not treat us as equals, whilst the liabilities of equality afflict us as we now sadly experience, like all other peoples, rising rates of delinquency, divorce, illegitimacy, social inequality, if not downright discrimination, and many other evils which erode society at large.[79]

I developed this theme further in an address before the Synagogue Council of America on 20 November 1974. Recalling Yitzchak Breuer's comparison of the early German Reform movement with secularist Zionism, I said:[80]

Significantly, the attempt to gain security and acceptance [through individual assimilation] by making us equals came to grief in Germany, the very country where Reform was born to bring us salvation by blurring the distinction between Israel and the nations, whilst the futility of achieving equality through national assimilation became manifest in the Land of Israel, in the very state which was established to end Jewish inequality once and for all, and which now has turned us all into the loneliest people on earth.

I also returned to the Arab refugee problem then, as well as at President Katzir's seminar on 'World Jewry and the State of Israel' held at his residence in Jerusalem the following summer, and subsequently included in a volume of the Proceedings edited by Professor Moshe Davis:[81]

Even if we could do little or nothing to solve the problem, surely as Jews – faithful to our ethical heritage of marked sensitivity to the sufferings of the stranger and the homeless – we should not have left it to gangs of murderous terrorists to draw the world's attention to this stain on humanity. Had we cried out in protest against the intolerable degradation of hundreds of thousands of human beings inhumanly condemned to rot in wretched camps for a generation, had we aroused the world's conscience over a tragedy of such magnitude, we might have prevented the growth of a monster organization which has already destroyed so many innocent lives. Now, with the blessing of the world community, that problem threatens the very existence of Israel more acutely than the Arab armies ever did.

However, other problems besetting the Jewish people preoccupied me rather more acutely. Foremost among them, for instance, were the fearful ravages wrought by the abortion practices in Israel. Again and again, I sought to raise the alarm on the disastrous effects of violating the dictates of Jewish ethics, as I did, I believe for the first time, at the 8th World Congress of the Israel Medical Association in Tel Aviv on 19 May 1970 in these words:[82]

It is estimated that the number of abortions in Israel may now reach 40,000 a year, a staggering figure confirmed to me by sources within the Israel Medical Association – a figure probably more than half the total number performed under the new permissive laws in Britain with twenty times the population of Israel! This means that since the establishment of the Jewish State the better part of one million potential Sabras may have been smothered in their mothers' wombs, making a mockery of the vast resources, energies, and propaganda efforts spent on inducing but a fraction of that number to go on Aliyah from the Western world in response to Israel's grave population needs.

By now, this mass slaughter of the innocents in Israel, posing a security problem graver than any threats of war or terror, may have reached an incredible 80,000 a year, and I have never ceased to focus public attention on this evil. In my book alone, the index features six references to the subject.[83]

Of course, I was no less outspoken in defending Israel from the forces and arguments ranged against it. But I always endeavoured to balance the criticism of others with recognizing our own failings. In my post-Yom Kippur War lecture at Hendon, I put this balance thus:[84]

The specious claim, repeated *ad nauseam*, that territory acquired by war may not be retained even for self-defence and security, reeks of particularly odious hypocrisy when it comes from the lips of Arabs whose vast empires across Asia and Africa were all conquered by the sword. Or from Russia, which still subjugates half of Eastern Europe by annexation and military occupation as a strategic security-belt, or even from France and Britain, whose territorial acquisitions by force, some retained to this day, dwarf all conquests made by Jews in four thousand years of history.

But whatever blame attaches to them and to others for our tribulations cannot invalidate the authentic teaching of Judaism on the philosophy of Jewish history as proclaimed throughout our sacred literature, and as enshrined in the Psalmist's words: 'If only My people would hearken unto Me, and Israel walk in My Ways, I would soon subdue their enemies and turn My hand against their adversaries.'

Nor were my strictures and pleas limited to the secularists. In the same lecture, still under the trauma of the Yom Kippur War, I addressed myself particularly to our spiritual leaders and the religious community generally, with the charge:

In particular, we are summoned to apply ourselves to three distinct tasks: to provide comfort, hope, confidence, and encouragement to those of our people whose faith is tottering in adversity; to explain the meaning of our current tribulations and our response to them in the light of our historical experience and religious insights; and to respond to the intense search for spiritual values evoked by the war, by arousing a massive religious reawakening to restore our people to its timeless purpose and destiny. In addition, in the Diaspora, it is primarily for the religious community and its leaders to stimulate the mass-movement of Aliyah, by re-directing Jewish education to this end; by transferring ever more seminars, schools, and yeshivot to Israel; by sponsoring projects to encourage all school-leavers to spend at least a year in Israel, with the prospect that out of the many thousands going annually, many hundreds will stay; and above all, by cultivating in our youth the faith and idealism which will predispose them to prefer a full Jewish life in Israel, even under conditions of some risk and hardship, to the spiritual hazards of their exilic existence, even in relative prosperity.

Arguing that the religious parties in Israel may have outlived their usefulness, I said on the same occasion:[85]

By and large, the secularists resist the extension of religious power and influence not because of any intrinsic objection to traditional Jewish values, the need for which is now widely recognized, but because they are not prepared to raise the potential threat to the voting strength of their parties, or simply because they see in the religious establishment a force which lacks spiritual qualities and non-partisan appeal. Hence, I believe that, without separating religion from politics, we are not likely to unite Judaism with the Jewish State, which is imperative for the survival of both.

Perhaps the most comprehensive of my Zionist writings – which are, I believe incidentally, more extensive than those of all my predecessors combined – is an article on 'The National Idea – Differing Religious Attitudes', which appeared in the Spring Issue 1977 of *L'Eylah*.[86]

Finally, I come to the most controversial item: the overriding quest for peace as the foundation of my Jewish commitment and my Zionist faith. I dealt with this at some length in my Hendon lecture, which included this passage:[87]

Real peace is a state of mind, rather than an expedient accommodation. Little wonder that the Psalmist speaks not of wanting or loving peace, but of 'pursuing peace', and that in our synagogue usage, when reciting the Prayer for Peace at the conclusion of the *Amidah* and *Kaddish*, we draw back three steps before coming forward again.

Which led me to some comments on territorial concessions:[88]

No rabbinical authority disputes that our claim to a Divine mandate (and we have no other which can not be invalidated) extends over the entire Holy Land within its historic borders and that halachically we have no right to surrender this claim. But what is questionable is whether we must, or indeed may, assert it at the risk of thousands of lives, if not the life of the State itself. Any religious law is set aside . . . if it involves a danger to life . . . . We are halachically compelled to leave the judgement on what provides the optimum security for Jewish life in Israel to the verdict of military and political experts, not rabbis. Included as a major factor in this difficult judgement must also be the overriding concern to preserve the Jewish character of Israel which may clearly depend on the proportion of Jews within the State.

However, I added:

In an altogether unique category is Jerusalem. It enjoys a sanctity of its own, and is the common possession of all Jews, wherever they may live, the gateway of all their prayers, the symbol of all their hopes and, now, happily, also the spiritual heart of Jewish learning, circulating inspiration to the most distant parts of our dispersion. To save life, one can amputate a limb or even excise parts of some internal organ. But not the heart! . . .

We should expect the Jewish title to Jerusalem – now completely free for the first time to the adherents of all faiths – to be recognized by the community of nations in acknowledgement of the people who originally sanctified it, who have maintained an unbroken association with it for 3,000 years, and who have constituted the majority of its inhabitants for the past 150 years.

This line of thinking prompted me, four and a half years later, to write to the *Jewish Chronicle* in support of peace proposals advocated in an editorial, and, above all, as a challenge to the widespread notion that all religious Jews shared the militant stance so vociferously adopted by a few. The letter appeared on 7 July 1978. Its effects – ranging from hysterical attacks to enthusiastic applause – are still reverberating. Some key sentences in that letter were:[89]

Whilst stipulating a period (of at least five years) of genuine peace with *all* Arab States *before* ceding any territory, the proposals would yet break the current deadlock by a firm commitment *now* to meet Arab claims in exchange for convincing proof of peace, supported by other safeguards spelt out by you (border adjustments, demilitarization, and international guarantees).

The likely alternative to an *eventual* withdrawal *on Israeli terms*, holding out some prospect of true peace, [may] be a *speedier* withdrawal *without any returns*, enforced by America as happened in 1956.

The preponderant opinion in Jewish history and literature seems to favour conciliation and peace notwithstanding the cost of territorial sacrifices. Even Joshua and Ezra did not complete the occupation of the entire Land.

Altogether, the battlecry 'not an inch', with its 'all-or-nothing' overtones, evokes ominous echoes of Masada – an episode without parallel in Jewish history and entirely out of tune with Jewish teachings. . . . If such a philosophy had ever been embraced by our people, Jewish history would have ended long ago with national euthanasia.

The attempt to silence dissent and constructive criticism sits particularly ill with a people which cannot forget the awesome price paid for silence in the face of suffering and injustice not so long ago. . . . Rather should we heed the Prophet's cry : 'For the sake of Zion I will not remain mute, and for the sake of Jerusalem I will not be silent.'

I cannot speak for my predecessors, and I do not know whether they would now reaffirm every word they have committed to print. But for myself, and with hindsight, I do not regret what I have written, nor would I wish to make any amendments or deletions. However, I am sure I can speak for all the five Chief Rabbis who have featured in this paper when, in my first comment on the 'Who is a Jew?' controversy made in 1958 and reproduced in my *Journal of a Rabbi*, a controversy on which I was later to take such a lonely stand within the Orthodox rabbinate,[90] I wrote :[91]

As a result of the present conflict, it may now gradually dawn on the Jewish masses everywhere, who are the true defenders of Jewish unity and survival, and who threaten to undermine these values. It is bound to become increasingly clear that only religious Jews will prevent the bonds between Israel and the Diaspora from snapping. They . . . will be recognized as the upholders of Jewish integrity in the future, just as they were acknowledged as the champions of the Jewish heritage in the past. Without them there would be no Judaism today and no Jewish people tomorrow.

## NOTES

1. Immanuel Jakobovits, *The Timely and the Timeless*, 1977, p. 268.
2. Cecil Roth, 'The Anglo-Jewish Community in the Context of World Jewry', in *Jewish Life in Modern Britain*, ed. Julius Gould and Shaul Esh, 1964, p. 101.
3. See Paul Goodman, *Zionism in England*, 1929, pp. 8ff.
4. In his journal *Selbstemanzipation*, 1 April 1890.
5. By Kalman Charles Walrauch ; see Elhannan Orren, *Chibbat Zion Be-Britannia*, 1974, p. 38.
6. See Orren, *op. cit.*, pp. 40, 68.
7. See *e.g., Jewish Chronicle*, 5 December 1890; 25 December 1891; 6 February 1891.
8. See Orren, *op. cit.*, pp. 44ff.

9. See *J.C.*, 12 June 1891 and following issues.
10. See Goodman, *op. cit.*, pp. 13ff.; and *J.C.*, 18 November 1898.
11. The British delegation were known as 'the Delegates of the Foreign Jews in London'; see *J.C.*, 16 July 1897.
12. *J.C.*, 18 November 1898.
13. *The Diaries of Theodor Herzl*, ed. Marvin Lowenthal, 1958, p. 78f.
14. *Ib.*, p. 88.
15. *Ib.*, pp. 74f.
16. *Ib.*, p. 88.
17. *Ib.*, p. 208. Another Chief Rabbi who protested against the Congress, describing its aspirations as 'far from those of Judaism', was Grand Rabbin M.A.Bloch, of Belgium; see *J.C.*, 10 September 1897.

18. *J.C.*, 25 November 1898.
19. *Or Layesharim*, ed. S.Z.Landau and J. Rabinowitz, 1900, pp. 57–61.
20. *Ib.*, pp. 62–68.
21. Ed. A.Miller.
22. See Orren, *op. cit.*, p. 129.
23. *J.C.*, 10 July 1896; see also Goodman, *op. cit.*, p. 13.
24. *EJ*, 12:673. In January 1899 the Elders asked Gaster to keep out of public Zionism and in any event to make it clear that his views were personal; see *J.C.*, 3 February, 1899. But this warning seems to have had no more effect on him than Adler's 'inhibitions' had on his colleagues.
25. On Singer's meetings and correspondence with Herzl, see *Diaries, op. cit.*, pp. 78ff., 94, 130, 174, 176, 179. On his attitude to Herzl and Zionism, see Israel Finestein, 'The New Community 1880–1918', in *Three Centuries of Anglo-Jewish History*, The Jewish Historical Society of England, 1960, p. 116.
26. For the tributes to Herzl by Singer and many other ministers, see *J. C.*, 15 July 1904 and subsequent issues. But no reference to Herzl was made at the first United Synagogue Council meeting following his death; *ib.*
27. *J.C.*, 8 July 1904.
28. In a letter to *The Times*, Gaster identified the 'whole orthodox and realistic Jewry' with the First Zionist Congress; see *J.C.*, 3 September 1897. But soon after Herzl's death Israel Zangwill declared: 'We have no internal strife. Dr Gaster's only follower is Dr Gaster'; see *J.C.*, 11 November 1904. On his erratic relations with the Zionist leadership, see Goodman, *op. cit.*, pp. 11, 21, 25, 43 *et passim*.
29. See Orren, *op. cit.*, p. 101.
30. The pilgrimage consisted of twenty participants, led by Herbert Bentwich and Israel Zangwill, and it had the blessing of Herzl; see Orren, *op. cit.*, pp. 134–136.
31. Israel Finestein, 'Arthur Cohen, Q.C.', in *Remember the Days*, ed. John M.Shaftesley, 1966, p. 297.
32. See *EJ*, 13:1255.
33. *Cf.* Jakobovits, *op. cit.*, p. 270.
34. *Essays and Addresses*, ed. Wolf Gottleib, 1948, pp. 45–50. The editor describes the essay as 'an amazing document of the farsightedness of young Dr Hertz, who already then showed the qualities of the great Jewish patriot and humanist, as we knew him'.
35. For a full bibliography of his writings, see *Joseph Herman Hertz, In Memoriam*, ed. I.Epstein, 1947.
36. J.H.Hertz, *Early and Late*, Addresses, Messages and Papers, 1943, p. 131.
37. *Early*, p. 98.
38. See p. 220 for the expression of similar views.
39. Both letters are reproduced in *Early*, pp. 203ff., with an introductory note by Hertz.
40. Samuel Landman, 'Origins of the Balfour Declaration: Dr Hertz's Contribution', in *Essays Presented to J.H.Hertz*, ed. I.Epstein, E.Levine and C.Roth, 1942, pp. 261–270.
41. J.H.Hertz, *Sermons, Addresses and Studies*, 3 vols., 1938, *Addresses*, p. 370. But see also note 43.
42. *Addresses*, pp. 265–292.
43. However, a letter dated 28 July 1941 addressed by his secretary to the Board of Deputies, asserting the independence of the Chief Rabbinate from the Board, contained the following: 'In 1917, the Board was guilty of what Zionists call "a Great Betrayal of Jewry".... The Chief Rabbi publicly denounced their action, and helped to secure the support of Britain for the promulgation of the Jewish National Home. The verdict of history will surely be that the cause of Jewry was strengthened as a result of the stand taken by the Chief Rabbinate....' (*Early*, p. 234).
44. *Addresses*, pp. 359f.
45. *Ib.*, pp. 110f.
46. Indicative of his 'neutrality' on conflicts within Zionism are the many memorial addresses he delivered and published for Zionist leaders, including Herzl (*Early*,

pp. 119ff), Wolffsohn (in *Zionism: Problems and Views*, ed. P.Goodman and A.D.Lewis, 1916, pp. 38ff.), Bialik (*Early*, pp. 103ff.), Sokolow (pp. 106ff.) and Jabotinsky (pp. 111ff.). These eulogies are all equally laudatory and uncritical. Perhaps the only exception is Israel Zangwill, whom Hertz praised as a 'writer, novelist, wit and dramatist' without mentioning his role in Zionist history (*Addresses*, pp. 376ff.).

47. *Addresses*, pp. 361f.
48. *Ib.*, pp. 134ff.
49. *Ib.*, pp. 187f.
50. *Ib.*, p. 374.
51. *Early*, p. 298.
52. *Ib.*, p. 196.
53. Aubrey Newman, *The United Synagogue*, 1976, pp. 108f. This is the only reference to Zionism in the book. Strangely, it omits to mention that there was a 'United Synagogue Central Keren Hayesod Committee' set up by the Council in December 1927 (see Goodman, *op. cit.*, p. 53). *Cf.* note 26 above.
54. *J.C.*, 5 October 1945.
55. *J.C.*, 12 October 1945.
56. Israel Brodie, *A Word in Season: Addresses and Sermons 1948–1958*, 1959, p. 10.
57. *Season*, pp. 76ff.
58. *Ib.*, pp. 105f.
59. Brodie contributed the Foreword to this volume.
60. See Immaneul Jakobovits, 'The Ashkenazi and Sephardi Pronunciation in Prayer', in *The Timely and the Timeless*, 1977, p. 242.
61. Israel Brodie, *The Strength of My Heart: Sermons and Addresses 1948–1965*, 1969, pp. 162f.
62. *Season*, p. 163.
63. *Ib.*, p. 57.
64. *Ib.*, p. 104.
65. *Heart*, pp. 77f.
66. *Ib.*, pp. 163ff.
67. *Ib.*, pp. 391f.
68. *Ib.*, pp. 373f.
69. The fullest account of Brodie's life and activities, including a wide-ranging list of quotations, is John M.Shaftesley's 'Biographical Sketch', in *Essays presented to Chief Rabbi Israel Brodie on his seventieth Birthday*, ed. H.J.Zimmels, J.Rabbinowitz, and I.Finestein, 1967, p. xi–xxxviii. Strangely, the only reference to Israel is a five-line statement quoted from an address to the Wellington Rotary Club on 12 February 1952, and to education a two-line extract from a speech in Toronto on 3 July 1956 (p. xxix).

70. *Timely*, pp. 53–60.
71. Letter to the *Jewish Chronicle*, 7 July 1978.
72. For the text of the address in full, see *Timely*, pp. 3f.
73. *Looking Ahead*, Address delivered to the Council and District Council of the United Synagogue on 26 November 1967, pp. 6f.
74. *Timely*, see Index, *s.v.* 'Arab refugees'.
75. *Ib.*, p. 153.
76. *Ib.*, p. 155.
77. *Ib.*, pp. 9f.
78. *Ib.*, pp. 20ff.
79. The futility of the early Zionists' dream that Jewish statehood would 'solve the Jewish problem' already exercised me in my fourteenth Israel Independence Day address given at the Fifth Avenue Synagogue in New York in 1962; see I.Jakobovits, *Journal of a Rabbi*, 1966 and 1967, pp. 125f.
80. *Timely*, pp. 105f.
81. *World Jewry and the State of Israel*, ed. Moshe Davis, 1977, p. 289.
82. *Timely*, p. 333.
83. *Ib.*, see Index, *s.v.* 'Abortion in Israel'.
84. *Ib.*, pp. 18ff.
85. *Ib.*, p. 30.
86. *L'Eylah*, published bi-annually by the Office of the Chief Rabbi, vol. 1, no. 3, pp. 6ff. I first discussed these diverse religious attitudes to Zionism in my thirteenth Israel Independence Day address at the Fifth Avenue Synagogue in New York in 1961; see *Journal*, p. 122f. The *L'Eylah* article, as later expanded in *Tradition*, is reproduced in chapter 16 of this book.

87. *Timely*, p. 28.

88. *Ib.*, pp. 32f.

89. On the same date the *New York Times* prominently featured a grossly distorted report on the letter under the provocative banner-headline 'British Chief Rabbi Assails Israel for Hard Line on Mid-East Peace'. It published only three weeks later (27 July) a letter I had submitted immediately (10 July) to correct the report 'attributing words and views to me which I had not expressed'. But by then a furore bordering on hysteria and been unleashed in America, particularly by Orthodox rabbinical, communal and national organizations which generally supported Israel's extreme right-wing political line (which I had not directly attacked) and the 'intransigent stance' by some 'religious elements' (which I had challenged).

90. *Timely*, pp. 199ff. and 215ff.

91. *Journal*, p. 10.

# 16

# Religious Responses to Jewish Statehood*

The centrality of Israel in contemporary Jewish life is bound to be reflected in a journal dedicated to 'Orthodox Jewish Thought' especially since current events and policies in Israel are significantly affected by the pressures of religious groups inside and outside the government, whether 'hawks' like Gush Emunim, Lubavitch and Meir Kahane's Kach demanding greater militancy, or 'doves' like the Agudat Israel holding the balance of power in the coalition insisting on purely religious concessions. Thus *Tradition* (issued quarterly by the Rabbinical Council of America) has lately featured quite a few articles assessing the various religious attitudes towards Zionism and the Jewish State.[1]

* This article, originally published in *Tradition* (Fall, 1982), is concerned solely with the religious attitudes to the Zionist idea and the Jewish State. It does not deal with religious issues arising from Jewish statehood (for example, state–religion relations, religious legislation, 'Who is a Jew?', and the like). Special attention is also given to controversies between the various religious groups, as reflected in their writings.

The sources are limited, with few exceptions, to *rabbinic* writings (not mere statements) supporting or opposing particular views in the light of Jewish religious teachings and to documentation on such writings.

Within these limitations, there is sizeable material on the Neturei Karta, Satmar, Agudah, Lubavitch and of course Mizrachi. *Oz veShalom* has published some rabbinic responsa and opinions, claimed to favour its stand, in several pamphlets and over thirty newsletters (*Ha-Chug Harayoni Medini le-Ziyonut Datit*, Jerusalem), but none of these rabbinic writings specifically support the movement. Nor could I find such material on Gush Emunim (again other than statements, notably by its principal mentor, the late Rabbi Zvi Yehuda Kook), though the extensive politico-halachic writings of Chief Rabbi Shlomo Goren mainly (but never expressly) support its cause. On Kach, too, I am not aware of any rabbinic documentation, apart from the (non-halachic) statements of its founder, Rabbi Meir Kahane.

Some of these contributions are scholarly and dispassionate; others polemical and plainly partisan. But virtually all of them examine, propagate, or rebut only one particular ideology or personal view. What has not been attempted so far is an overall survey of the different religious responses to the restoration of Jewish sovereignty as such and to Israeli policies generally, insofar as they are guided by, or impinge on, religious perceptions. This chapter will enquire into the reasons for these extraordinarily diverse views, ranging from super-nationalism to rabid anti-Zionism, at least in the light of some historical antecedents as well as some inter-group polemics.[2]

Comparing the religious inspiration of the Zionist movement over the ages with the religious reaction to its realization, one is struck by a strange mixture of paradox and ambivalence: the paradox of the movement's religious nurture before its emergence and the indications of widespread religious opposition, or indifference, to it after its fulfilment, and the ambivalence of the still-unresolved, indeed intensifying, diversity of views on the religious significance of the restoration of Jewish statehood. Partly both the paradox and the ambivalence may be due to the discrepancy between the reborn State of Israel and its Biblical blueprint. Perhaps we are unreasonably impatient when we expect in three decades that spiritual consummation which previously took nearly 500 years to evolve – the period separating the Revelation at Sinai, with its constitutional provisions for national and spiritual sovereignty, followed by Joshua's entry into the Land, and the building of the First Temple by King Solomon.

The origins of the Zionist idea are, of course, entirely religious. Many secularists are no less insistent than religious believers on the slogan 'the Bible is our mandate' as the principal basis of our legal and historical claims to the Land. This 'mandate' is itself derived from the purely religious covenant between God and Abraham, a covenant reaffirmed with our people at Sinai and constantly reasserted by our Prophets in the context of Israel's religious purpose and destiny. Through the ages, all our dreams and prayers for the Return to Zion have been religiously inspired. And we prayed not so much simply for *our* return, or the restoration of *our* national sovereignty, as for God's return and the establishment of His sovereignty in Zion. Our Return was merely the means – in the words of our daily prayers – for 'restoring His Divine Presence to Zion'.

Up to well into the nineteenth century, therefore, all Aliyah movements were religious movements – from the pioneering beginnings of Nachmanides in the thirteenth century and the much more significant following of Karo, Luria and others of the mystic school settling in considerable numbers in Safed in the sixteenth century, to the bulk of the immigrants who founded the 'old Yishuv' in the nineteenth century.

Modern political Zionism could never have struck root if it had not been planted in soil seeded and fertilized by the millennial conditioning of religious memories, hopes, prayers and visions of our eventual Return to Zion. Nor could Hebrew have been revitalized as a modern language if religious Jews had not persevered in maintaining its vitality and the reverence for it through prayer and study. In the nineteenth century, religious visionaries like Rabbis Zvi Hirsch Kalischer and Judah Alkalai played as important a role as forerunners of modern Zionism as secular nationalists and humanists like Moses Hess and Leon Pinsker.

To this day, the primary dynamic of Zionism in its truest form remains religious. If we distinguish between positive and negative Zionism, or voluntary and involuntary Aliyah – that is, those *drawn* to Zion simply by the love of the Land and those *driven* there by persecution or by rebellion against the ghettos and their traditions – then such positive Zionism is mainly religiously motivated. Religious Aliyah from the free countries is at least five times as high as the corresponding figure of non-religious Olim.

In the light of these religious dimensions of Zionism – from its origin to the present day – it seems almost incomprehensible that the actual establishment of the Jewish State was greeted with, and still encounters, so much apathy and even downright opposition among large numbers of the religious community. Incredibly, the Arabs, the Vatican and an assortment of anti-Semitic countries are joined only by certain religious sections of our own people in the continued denial of formal recognition to the State of Israel. Since 1967, even the Reform movement has accorded a recognition to Israel which some very Orthodox segments still withhold.

This non-recognition assumes various forms; some more vehement, others more passive; a few more confined and quite a number more widespread. It includes the refusal to sing the *Hatikvah* or to teach modern Hebrew, to support appeals or other projects sponsored by the Israel government or the Jewish Agency, to read the Prayer for the State of Israel, to celebrate Yom Ha'atzmaut, or to concede that Zionism is an integral part of Judaism.

Yet, one must hasten to add, accentuating the paradox, it is out of this element that the Western Aliyah rate is by far the highest, as is the flow of Diaspora students learning at Israeli institutions. Entire communities of various Chasidic sects have transplanted themselves to Israel from America and elsewhere, notwithstanding their opposition to the Jewish national idea in its existing form.

How can we explain or understand this contradiction between the passionate fervour of yearning for the Return and the apparent indifference to its realization; between the hostility to the State and the love for the Land of Israel?[3]

The paradox is equally striking at the other end of the religious spectrum. The most militant form of Jewish nationalism is today also generated out of religious convictions. Indeed, without the fierce idealism of the Gush Emunim settlers in Judea and Samaria, often cheerfully enduring extreme privations, self-sacrifice and perils, the pristine spirit of the early Zionist pioneers would now hardly exist at all. Their intransigence is all the more uncompromising because it is dictated by religious rather than political or military considerations.[4] Their main argument in defying the Israel government, not to mention world opinion, by asserting the claim to Jewish settlement in the entire Land of Israel is precisely that this is required by Biblical precept and halachic imperatives. Other religious groups sharing this radical stance, notably Lubavitch,[5] are likewise motivated by purely religious dictates, though their attitude to Zionism as such, and indeed to the religious significance of Jewish statehood, may vary greatly.

It would be an over-simplification, though not without some substance, to define the various groups by their observance or non-observance of Yom Ha'atzmaut: Those who recite *Hallel* with *Berakhah* (Mizrachi); without *Berakhah* (probably most religious Zionists outside Israel); no *Hallel* and no *Tahanun* (many Agudists); and *Tahanun* (Satmar and numerous other Chasidic as well as yeshivah elements) – with stones thrown (literally or figuratively) at those who say *Hallel* (Neturei Karta) or *Tahanun* (Kahane's Kach).[6] There are inconsistencies and overlaps in this classification.

Some find saying *Hallel* with *Berakhah* quite compatible with being in the Peace Now camp (Oz veShalom). On the other hand, there are *Hallel*-opponents who regard Jews in Israel as being in *galut* no less than in the Diaspora, and are yet on the extreme right of the religio-political spectrum (Lubavitch); whilst other non-Zionists refuse to join the Israeli cabinet, for religious reasons, though they keep it in power by supporting the coalition (Agudah). Again, in many intensive Jewish schools where *Hallel* is officially proscribed, the Aliyah rate among graduates is high (for example, the Hasmonean in London), whilst there are enthusiastic *Hallel*-sayers to whom Aliyah is an ideal for others. The pendulum, hung on the same allegiance to the *Shulhan Arukh*, swings all the way from those prepared to negotiate with the PLO for living under Arab rule (Neturei Karta) to those seeking to expel the Arabs by violence if necessary (Kach).

What unites all religious groups, popular misconceptions and propaganda notwithstanding, is their aversion to a theocratic state[7] as demonstrated by the fraction with the greatest leverage and the most far-reaching religious demands declining to accept cabinet posts (Agudah).

Even more important, what all these groups also have in common (as indeed with most secular Israelis, too) is an indifference to the non-Jewish world often bordering on disdain. This attitude may be quite understandable in the shadow of Western civilization's betrayal of the Jewish people leading to the Holocaust and the growing isolation of Israel in the world community. Nevertheless, this Jewish religious response, now so widespread in the most diverse religious circles, whether Zionist or anti-Zionist, does represent an abrupt disengagement from the universal dimension of Judaism in the tradition of Israel's prophets and sages. Such a withdrawal from 'the mission to the nations', or the concern to promote their moral advance through Israel's example and its good name in their eyes, may be natural for Chasidic or yeshivah elements conditioned to self-containment by the '*galut*-mentality' nurtured in Eastern Europe. But it is surprising that this introspective vision is equally shared even by those whom the Zionist idea inspires with Messianic fervour, since the whole concept of Messianism is after all inseparable from universal salvation and Israel's serving as 'a light unto the nations'.

These common denominators apart, we may discern three principal divisions, each of them of course further ramified by various subdivisions.

First, and historically perhaps most significant, there is the non-Zionist, or more often even anti-Zionist, camp. Its activist heartland is the Chasidic sect of Satmar.[8] Politically, this camp is prodded by the extreme fringe element of the numerically insignificant Neturei Karta,[9] probably counting no more than a few hundred adherents in Israel and a few isolated Diaspora fastnesses.

The antics and fanaticism of these anti-Israel zealots, repugnant to so many Jews, may be limited to these groups. So is their implacable hostility to the 'Zionist heresy' as the incarnation of evil. But their basic philosophy in rejecting the legitimacy of Zionism is shared by a very large and important section of the Orthodox community. Sympathizing with this attitude are virtually all the Chasidic movements,[10] the bulk of what is known as the 'yeshivah-world'[11] (with the notable exception of the Bnei Akivah yeshivot) led by most of today's leading Torah sages, and a considerable segment of the so-called 'Independent Orthodox congregations' – all now experiencing such an extraordinary growth-rate all over the world. For all these, the foundation of Israel was and remains, religiously, a non-event. Together, the members of these groups may well run into several hundred thousand souls, possibly by now in excess of half-a-million. The difference between Satmar, and even most Agudists,[12] who grant a form of *de facto* recognition to Israel, is one of degree and emphasis rather than of fundamentals. They all oppose political Zionism and negate Jewish statehood as a manifestation of religious significance or Prophetic fulfilment.

Their views are, to be sure, well-founded on Jewish literary sources and historical precedents. For instance, they refer to the famous oaths taken by the exiles of Jerusalem at the time of its destruction, and recorded in the Talmud (*Ketubot* 111a), never to reconquer the Land by force, or they point to Rashi's commentary (on Exodus 15 : 14) attributing the massacre of the tribe of Ephraim mentioned in the Book of Chronicles to Ephraim's attempt to anticipate the deliverance from Egypt by a premature and violent escape.[13]

Historical analogies, too, are not hard to find. There is the attitude of Rabbi Yochanan ben Zakkai in coming to terms with the conquering Romans and in opposing the Zealots' resolve to continue the struggle. And there is the scorn with which Rabbi Akiba's colleagues ridiculed his claims for Bar Kochba's Messianic mission in regaining Jewish independence from the Romans. These episodes certainly show that the anti-nationalist line is not altogether alien to the authentic Jewish tradition.

Nor are the numerous anti-nationalist rabbinical leaders and scholars today without predecessors of high eminence at other critical periods in our history. Leanings in this direction may well be found, for example, with a ranking thinker and statesman of the stature of Don Isaac Abravanel, the principal Jewish leader and scholar at the time of the expulsion of the Jews from Spain, and his reliance on a Messiah unaided by human effort. How different the course of Jewish history might have been, as has been suggested,[14] had he directed his fellow-exiles to reconquer or resettle their own land rather than to exchange the exile of Spain for that of Italy, Greece or Turkey in anticipation of the Messianic Redeemer. Even the resettlement of Jews in England some 300 years ago was not unrelated to this line of thinking. Menasseh ben Israel pressed Oliver Cromwell to readmit the Jews on the ground that the coming of the Messiah would be imminent if only the Jewish dispersion were to be completed by its extension to England – *Angleterre*, 'the end of the earth'.

Again, in the nineteenth century, the founder of modern Orthodoxy, Rabbi Samson Raphael Hirsch, strongly affirmed the *galut* as an indispensable means to fulfil the Jewish mission to the nations, and he warned against any idea of a pre-Messianic effort to restore Jewish national sovereignty in the face of Gentile opposition. Indeed, Hirsch may well be regarded as the spiritual father of modern religious anti-Zionism, as a reading of his voluminous works will confirm.[15] Incidentally, distinct overtones of this philosophy can be detected even in the writings and policies of Martin Buber[16] and, for very different reasons, of Isaiah Leibowitz.[17]

Added to the support for their stand which the religious opponents of Zionism draw from Jewish literature and history, is their abhorrence of the secularization of Jewish life. They regard as utterly inconsistent the lofty visions of the Return to Zion by our Prophets and sages with the realities of Jewish statehood today. They simply cannot believe that a secular state can be the fulfilment of Biblical promises and millennial prayers. But it is only fair to stress again that their hostility to Zionism in no way compromises the love of the Land of Israel and often the intense encouragement they give their followers to settle there.

The second important religious response to the national idea takes the exactly opposite line. It is represented by those who believe, with equal conviction, that the cataclysmic events culminating in the establishment of the Jewish State, followed by the reunification of Jerusalem and the Jewish reconquest of the bulk of the historic Land of Israel in the Six Day War, are indeed happenings of the most momentous religious significance in fulfilment of Biblical promises. Consequently, they hail these events as an essential and irreversible part of the final Messianic process – 'the beginning of the Redemption'.[18]

This school of thought finds its main exponents in the Mizrachi movement,[19] though its supporters include many beyond the confines of party lines. Its principal protagonists were spiritual and scholarly giants of the calibre of Rabbi A.I.Kook and Rabbi J.L.Maimon, succeeded by Rabbi I.H.Herzog and other rabbinic immortals of our age. Rejecting the literary and historic evidence produced by their opponents as misleading or irrelevant, they regard the experiences of our times as being without precedent, and they point to the miracle of Israel's rise from the catastrophe of the Holocaust, accompanied by the Ingathering of Exiles, as unmistakable signs that the first acts in the drama of the Final Redemption are at hand.

Naturally, the devotees of this philosophy, too, do not lack literary and historical material to sustain their religious Zionism. Statements in the Talmud and rabbinic literature extolling life in the Land of Israel, and its unity with the Jewish people and faith, are legion. The line of leading sages advocating a mass return to Zion stretches all the way, certainly from Nachmanides to the present time. They also find ample halachic support for the claim that it is a religious duty to engage in war to liberate the Land,[20] to bring it under Jewish control and to promote the corporate expression of full Jewish life through the exercise of Jewish sovereignty. Since the highest aspirations of the Jewish people cannot be achieved without national independence, they regard life in the Jewish State even under non-religious rule as preferable to Jewish exilic existence,[21] however intensive its Jewish vibrancy may be.

All religious nationalists would subscribe to these fundamental tenets. Yet there is today a major difference among them on the extent to which these beliefs must govern or override political considerations. Part of the argument also concerns the applicability of patently Messianic calculations to the contemporary situation and its dilemmas. A considerable and still influential section of the Mizrachi movement, while not questioning the supreme religious significance of Jewish statehood as a forerunner to the promised Redemption, nevertheless acknowledges the reality of factors beyond Israel's control – such as external political pressures, the impact of an ever-increasing Arab minority on the Jewish character of the State, and the claims of Palestinians to some territorial concessions for the sake of peace provided they do not constitute a security risk.[22] Ranking religious leaders inclining to this stance are Rabbi J.B.Soloveitchik[23] and Chief Rabbi Ovadia Yosef.[24]

Leading the fierce opposition to these moderates is the Gush Emunim movement,[25] which has gathered formidable strength since the Yom Kippur War, and which, despite its purely religious motivation, now enjoys widespread support among other ultra-nationalists as well. The late Rabbi A.I.Kook's passionate commitment to Jewish self-redemption in the Land of Israel is frequently cited as a vindication of the Gush Emunim platform today. But careful students of his prolific and inspired writings are inclined to challenge this posthumous invocation of support for a contrived eschatology of confrontation and militancy as alien to his pacific teachings and mellow character.[26]

For others, the battlecry 'not an inch', with its 'all-or-nothing' overtones, evokes ominous echoes of the Masada experience – an episode quite unique in Jewish history. Unique not because of its heroic martyrdom (for which there are ample parallels), but because of the declared preference by an extreme religious sect for a national euthanasia or death with dignity over life under foreign subjection, for which Jewish history has no parallel.[27]

Even more disturbing to the religious and historical sensitivities of many are the Messianic undercurrents of this religious radicalism. The pages of Jewish history are littered with the debris, sometimes the lethal shrapnel, left behind by the explosion of pseudo-Messianic movements, as grim reality dashed with shattering force the high expectations of imminent deliverance they had raised. The bitter wounds inflicted by devastating disillusionment stretch from the collapse of the Bar Kochba rebellion[28] to the fearful aftermath of the Shabbetai Zvi débâcle.

As will be explained in the next part, there is all the difference between Messianic *hopes*, which constitute the very stuff of faith serving our people to prevail over our tribulations, and Messianic *expectations* of impending salvation. Basing national policies or religious guidance on such *assumptions* can lead to catastrophic consequences against which we are forewarned by ample danger signals flashed from the shipwrecks of Messianic disasters spread along the course of our annals for the past 2,000 years.

Finally, between the two poles of intense religious nationalism and anti-nationalism, is a third grouping. Though less vociferous and politically less clearly defined or organized, it may still be most significant numerically. In contrast to the first group, its adherents strongly and unequivocally affirm their commitment to the State of Israel, supporting its institutions and recognizing its religious significance as a wondrous manifestation of Divine favour. They regard themselves as religious Zionists without reservation. Yet they differ from the second group in one crucial respect.

Perhaps this difference can best be illustrated by a critical distinction between the two versions of the Prayer for the State of Israel. The text attributed to the late Chief Rabbi Herzog, which is widely used in Israel and in some Diaspora communities, specifically refers to the State of Israel as 'the beginning of the sprouting forth of our Redemption'. In other words, it authentically declares the Jewish State to be not only the fulfilment of our hopes and prayers, but the incipient phase in the process of the promised 'Redemption', a term used only for the realization of our Messianic aspirations. On the other hand, this phrase is omitted in the text authorized by the late Chief Rabbi Brodie, as it appears in the Singer's Prayer Book and is commonly used in Britain and the Commonwealth communities. This version passes no authentic opinion, or reserves final judgement, on whether or not the present State of Israel is in fact the embryonic nucleus out of which the ultimate Redemption is *bound* to develop, with all its universal ramifications of the Messianic era which form an essential part of Prophetic teaching and Jewish belief.

The difference between these two versions is of course not only of semantic, theoretical or even purely philosophical significance. It marks a fundamental divergence of views on the religious interpretation of present-day events as well as the place of the State of Israel in the perspective of Biblical visions. From this divergence naturally flow some important practical consequences.

If the pre-Messianic character of the State is taken for granted as a *certainty*, whether as an act of faith or of rational conviction, then obviously conscious and deliberate efforts must be made to ensure that all related Biblical prophecies fall into place, and that our national strategy must be based on this assumption. This might, for instance, include the planned liquidation of the Diaspora, or an unconcerned resistance to the pressures of world opinion, safe in the knowledge that the advances towards full Redemption are irreversible. Faith can thus govern pragmatic policies, and risks can be disregarded.

On the other hand, if the pre-Messianic stage of our current experience lies in the realm of *hope*, rather than certainty, then such conclusions may not yet be warranted, and a more 'realistic' approach may be indicated. This more cautious attitude, while it in no way affects the intensity of the commitment to Israel, would of course also cushion our people against the impact of reverses such as we suffered in the Yom Kippur War, and as may yet be encountered before Israel is finally at peace and the promise of Redemption shared by the entire human family.

For the protagonists of this view, the halachic demand 'not to rely on miracles' remains paramount and in contradiction to the widely accepted dictum, first ascribed to Ben-Gurion: 'He who does not believe in miracles is not a realist' as a norm for Israeli policy-making. For them, neither the uncompromising determination with which we assert our national claims, nor the self-reliance on military strength, nor even the simple faith that in the end 'all will be in order', can guarantee ultimate salvation. In their religious perspective, based on faith in the conditional character of the covenant between God and Israel, only religious and moral worthiness can provide such a guarantee, as spelled out in the second paragraph of the *Shema*, by all the Prophets and reaffirmed by the Psalmist: 'If only My People would hearken unto Me, and Israel walk in My ways, I would soon subdue their enemies and turn My hand against their adversaries' (81 : 15).[29]

This survey is confined to examining the different strands of the main religious responses evoked by the rebirth of Israel. It would not be complete, however, without at least cursorily projecting these responses, or their effect, on to the wider Jewish scene in the post-war world.

Even secularists will no longer deny that all these groups within the Orthodox community, whatever their differences, have made enormous contributions to the reconstruction of Jewish life after the devastation of the Holocaust. In fact, they now represent the only true growth element within the Jewish people. Enjoying a disproportionately high birthrate and having achieved, for the first time in modern history, virtual immunity to erosion by assimilation, intermarriage and Yeridah, they alone need no longer feature the question of Jewish survival as the first item on the global Jewish agenda.

This achievement is all the more remarkable when one remembers that, whilst we lost one-third of our people at large in the European catastrophe, Orthodoxy suffered the destruction of perhaps as much as 90 per cent of its strongholds, its citadels of learning, its rabbis and scholars and its vast communities which had been concentrated in Eastern and Central Europe. In the light of this near-annihilation, the regeneration of Torah living and learning in Israel and the Western world, on a scale and of an intensity never previously known in these communities, is nothing short of one of the great wonders of our time and of all time. These colossal advances are beginning to reclaim for Orthodoxy the primacy and influence which had gradually declined ever since the Emancipation.

The contributions of the diverse groups towards this momentous achievement, while perhaps equal in value, are altogether different in substance and size. For the astounding Orthodox resurgence itself, it must be conceded, the non-Zionist element is primarily responsible. Perhaps because they could afford to be more single-minded and were less distracted by other national aspirations, they succeeded in pioneering the creation of networks of schools, yeshivot and seminaries, and in rebuilding the shattered remnants of the Chasidic fraternities (Satmar now have the largest Jewish day-school in the world!). Through their efforts, there are now hundreds of thousands of intensely committed and knowledgeable young people, and entire communities have been rescued from spiritual oblivion.

Religious Zionists may have been junior or later partners in these pioneering enterprises. Their unique contribution is of another order. From their ranks, and more particularly the Bnei Akivah high schools and the Yeshivot–Hesder under Mizrachi sponsorship combining intensive Torah studies with positive nationalism and army service, have emerged a growing breed of young idealists, distinguished by their total dedication, self-discipline and spiritual stature, who have salvaged the honour of religious Jewry and regained widespread respect for their convictions. Their influence on the direction of Jewish affairs, already appreciable, is bound to gather increasing momentum, even – perhaps especially – if this is not expressed simply in political party votes.

Jointly these two segments, though otherwise at opposite poles, have ensured the continuity of Jewish life and strengthened our people's resilience in the face of mounting hostility and international isolation. This feat is all the more noteworthy when set against the collapse of the philosophy of secularist nationalism which for many decades promoted the illusion that the restoration of Jewish statehood would put an end to the abnormality of the Jewish condition, securing the equality of the Jewish people among the nations and the elimination of anti-Semitism.

No effort has been made here to minimize the radical divisions which beset the religious community today in its response to what is certainly one of the most momentous turning-points in our long and chequered history.

Of course, internal dissension, when driven to the point of internecine strife and hatred, and especially when fanned by religious passions, can lead to the most disastrous consequences, as a greater threat to our security than any external enemy. Unless controversy, however bitter, is bridled by mutual tolerance and understanding, the perils of an internal conflagration are real and sinister, as we remember only too well from the 'causeless hatred' which devastated the Second Jewish Commonwealth.

But as long as we maintain a disciplined respect for each other's views and convictions, we have nothing to fear from controversy and disagreement. On the contrary, the dynamics of Jewish thought and life are such as to make diversity, and even constructive conflict, an indispensable ingredient of progress, creativity and vitality. Certainly since Biblical times, we have never responded to the promptings of revolutionary thinking or convulsive experiences with monolithic uniformity. In the tensions generated by debate lies the mystique of Jewish indestructibility and the road to the Preacher's prescription: 'Salvation is in the multitude of counsellors' (Prov. 11 : 14).

## NOTES

1. Isaiah Leibowitz, 'The Spiritual and Religious Meaning of Victory and Might', and 'The Mitzvot, the Messiah and the Territories' (Spring 1969); Norman Lamm, 'The Ideology of the Neturei Karta' (Fall 1971); Emanuel Feldman, 'Israel, Torah and I' (Fall 1975); Hayim Donin, 'Israel, Torah and I: Musings of a Permanent Resident' (Fall 1976); Sol Roth, 'The Right to the Land' (Fall 1977); Uriel Simon and Leon Stitskin, 'The Biblical Destinies – Conditional Promises' (Spring 1978); Shimon M. Glick, 'The Tragedy of Gush Emunim' (Summer 1981); Binyamin Walfish, 'Gush Emunim – Faith and Hope' (Winter 1981). For some other relevant articles in *Tradition*, see notes 15, 20, 22 and 27.

2. There is of course a vast literature of religious polemics on political Zionism. Among the earliest is a collection of anti-Zionist statements and letters by leading rabbis (including Hermann Adler) published under the title *Or Layesharim* (Warsaw, 1900), followed a year later by a book of pro-Zionist rebuttals by similarly eminent rabbis entitled *Beyn Or Lehoshekh* (Vilna, 1901). For a list of other early rabbinical writings against Zionism, see *Bibliographia le-Toldot*

*Am Yisrael*, Zalman Shazar Center, Jerusalem, 5736. The polemical works cited here are confined to current rabbinical arguments between the various religious factions. For a more recent religious attack on Zionism under the mounting pressure of the Holocaust, see Isachar Reichthal. *Em Habanim Semechah*, Budapest, 1943.

3. There is a striking precedent for this apparent contradiction. The beginnings of formal anti-Zionism will always be associated with the '*Protestrabbiner*' – a term coined by Herzl for the five German rabbis (two Orthodox and three Reform) who signed and published a protest letter against Herzl and the First Zionist Congress in 1897. Seventy years later, a survey discovered that almost all the children, grandchildren and great-grand-children of the 'Protest Rabbis' had settled in Israel! (*Ma'ariv*, 16 July 1968, cited in *Encyclopaedia Judaica*, 13 : 1255.) By contrast, few descendants of the secular founders and leaders of Zionism now live in Israel, if they remained Jews at all. There is surely a profound lesson in this irony!

4. On visiting Elon Moreh early in 1981 with a group of European chief rabbis, I asked a leader of that exposed new settlement

overlooking Shechem what motivated these idealists to live there, having defied the Israeli government and experiencing much hardship and danger; was it Israel's security or the determination to assert Jewish claims to all parts of *Eretz Yisrael*? 'Security?' he answered, 'I know nothing about security; I am not a general. We are here solely to carry out our religious duty to occupy the whole Land.'

5. Lubavitch activism on the extreme right of the Israeli politico-religious scene is relatively new. Thus, Israel is not mentioned at all in J. Immanuel Schochet's 'The Philosophy of Lubavitch Activism', in *Tradition* (Summer 1972). For details on the present Lubavitch stand, see *Da'at Torah B'Inyanei Hamatsav b'Erets Hakodesh*, by R. Shalom Dov Wolpo, Kiryat Gat, 1981, based on Talks by Rabbi Menachem M. Schneerson of Lubavitch. For more recent statements, especially on the conflict with the Agudah's Rabbi Eliezer Shach, see also the journal *K'far Chabad*, 1982, nos. 35–37.

The Rebbe's implacable opposition to the Camp David Accord, the surrender of Sinai, and yielding 'an inch or less' of the Land of Israel is based entirely on the Halachah permitting the violation of the Sabbath to protect a Jewish border town even if non-Jews 'come merely to take straw and stubble, lest they capture the city and find it easy to make further conquests' (*Shulhan Arukh, Orah Hayyîm*, 329:6). Later he added the inviolability of the Land's sanctity as a second factor.

Nevertheless, the Rebbe firmly denies that present events indicate the *geulah*, and he considers Jews living inside Israel as being no less in *galut* than those outside (see Talk, published in *She'arim*, 23 April 1980). The Jewish State, he declares, is a haven for Jews and Torah, but 'it has nothing to do with the Redemption or the Beginnings of the Redemption' (*Da'at Torah*, p. 24). Nor does the return of millions of Jews represent the Ingathering of the Exiles which will be realized only after the rebuilding of the Temple in Messianic

times (p. 29). Even the government of Israel embodies no Jewish sovereignty other than Jewish leadership exercised over any large community of Jews (p. 30). The author of *Da'at Torah*, now in its third edition, has lately compiled a further even bulkier volume *Shalom Shalom V'eyn Shalom* (1982), in which he reproduces numerous press cuttings and the like to support the Lubavitch stand and virulently attacks a letter counselling moderation by Rabbi E. Shach.

The anomaly of the anti-Zionism of Lubavitch contrasted with the intransigence on any territorial concessions (only the latter being widely publicized) has generally escaped public attention, though it has occasionally been exposed and challenged. See, for example, Amnon Schapiro, 'Where is the Galut, in Brooklyn or Jerusalem?' in *Amudim*, Adar 5740 (no. 413). See further response to Schapiro's article in *Amudim* 5740, (S.C.)

6. The halachic literature justifying or opposing the various practices is very considerable. For an interesting exchange between Rabbi Mosheh Zvi Neriah (opposing *Berakhah*) and Rabbi Meshulam Roth (favouring *Berakhah*), see *Shanah b'Shanah*, Hechal Shlomo, Jerusalem, 5727. For a fuller discussion of the *Hallel* controversy, see Menachem Kasher, *Hatekufah Hagedolah*, pp. 227 ff., and pp. 9f. (note). Even the Chief Rabbinate of Israel has issued conflicting instructions: whilst Chief Rabbis Herzog and Unterman ruled against reciting the *Berakhah* (Kasher, p. 10), Chief Rabbi Goren insists on it (see his *Torat Ha-Mo'adim*, Tel Aviv, 5724, pp. 576–597). On Meir Kahane's 'Manifesto', see his *They Must Go*, New York, 1981.

7. For a fuller rebuttal of this canard against religious Jews, see my 'The Two Faces of Orthodoxy', in the *Jewish Chronicle*, 25 September 1981.

8. Satmar's anti-Zionism (and the opposition to it) commands some impressive literature. The doctrine is propagated

with intense zeal in two scholarly works by the late Rebbe of Satmar, Rabbi Joel Teitelbaum, *Vayoel Mosheh*, Brooklyn, 5721; and *Al Hage'eulah ve'al Hatemurah*, Brooklyn, 5727. The arguments and conclusions of Rabbi Teitelbaum were refuted with great erudition by the encyclopedic scholar Rabbi Menachem Kasher in *Hatekufah Hagedolah*, Jerusalem, 1968. Kasher's work was in turn vehemently challenged in an anonymous volume of considerable bulk and scholarship, *Kuntres Veha'emet Ed Le'atsmo*, Brooklyn, undated.

9.  For two authentic works in English, see I. Domb, *The Transformation: The Case of Neturei Karta*, London, 1958; and Emile Marmorstein, *Heaven at Bay: The Jewish Kulturkampf in the Holy Land*, London, Oxford University Press, 1969. See also Norman Lamm's article cited in Note 1.

10. The opposition of Chasidic leaders to Zionism goes back to the days of Herzl who failed in several efforts to win their support. See Harry Rabinowicz, 'Herzl and Hasidism', in *Niv Hamidrashia*, Tel Aviv, 1974. However, some renowned Rebbes strongly supported the Return to the Land throughout the Zionist era; see Menachem Kasher, *Hatekufah Hagedolah*.

11. On the association of this ideology with the 'yeshivah-world', see S. Zalman Abramov, *Perpetual Dilemma: Jewish Religion in the Jewish State*, Rutherford, 1976, p. 232.

    A rare (because of the usual indifference) but typical presentation of the 'yeshivah-view' on contemporary issues is the 180-page anonymous book *Beyn Sheshet Le'asor*, 3rd enlarged edition, Jerusalem, 5739. While it advocates the intense love of the Land as unique on account of its holiness, it completely rejects Zionism or any religious recognition of the State, arguing (against the view of the Agudist *Hamodia's* editor) that today's leading Torah sages have in

no way modified the uncompromising opposition of the Hazon Ish and the Brisker Rav at the time of the establishment of the State.

12. 'Agudath Israel, from its inception, approached Zionism in a most negative manner, but the upbuilding of the Land in a most positive manner' (Joseph Friedenson, *A History of Agudath Israel*, New York, 1970, p. 26). At the Third 'Knessia Gedola' (Marienbad, 1937), the 'Moetzes Gedolei Hatorah' declared: 'A Jewish state not based on the laws of the Torah is a denial of our peoplehood ... and threatens our existence as a people.' Yet the Assembly, following a debate raging for three days, finally rejected the Peel Commission Partition plan, since 'the Jewish people cannot possibly compromise ... the boundaries of the Holy Land established by the Creator', but partly also for 'fears about a secular Jewish state' being set up (*ib.*, p. 36).

    Forty-three years later, at the Sixth 'Knessia Gedola' (Jerusalem, 1980), the views on Zionism and Jewish statehood had hardly changed, though the prevailing opinion on territorial concessions was more conciliatory, as expressed in the keynote address by Rabbi Eliezer Shach of Ponevez, the senior Yeshiva dean (reproduced, together with other writings, in his *Michtavim Uma'amarim*, Bnei Brak, 1980). The stance taken at that vast assembly again provoked bitter opposition, particularly by the Mizrachi, as documented in the pamphlet *Lemahutah shel Medinat Yisrael* (following the accusations at the 'Knessia Gedola'), Mizrachi World Center, Jerusalem, 1980.

    Recently the official Agudah stand was most unambiguously proclaimed when its Knesset delegates were instructed by the Council of Torah Sages to abstain from voting for the Golan Annexation Law, despite its coalition commitments. As widely reported in the world Jewish press, Rabbi Eliezer Shach added to the furore this edict created by invoking the commandment 'not to provoke the nations' (Deut. 2:5), arguing that Jews had always survived by submissiveness in the face of Gentile provocation and that the Jewish people had lived without the Golan for 2,000 years and would continue to do so. Instead of godless nationalism only a return to the Torah could assure Jewish existence. The bitter attacks on this defiant statement, especially by Lubavitch, aroused thousands of yeshivah students and their leaders to demonstrate in New York and elsewhere against this challenge to 'authentic Torah opinion' and the 'honour of its sages'.

13. Both these quotations were cited as long ago as 1885 to warn against any violent conquest of the Land by even so pro-Zionist a rabbinical leader as Dr Israel Hildesheimer, the friend and supporter of Rabbi Zvi Hirsch Kalischer: 'Of course, in all these ventures, I considered only the principle of colonization, but never of a seizure of Palestine. No one can sympathize less than I with those 30,000 Ephraimites who wanted to hasten their freedom by storm twenty-three years before the Exodus from Egypt; it must never be forgotten that, according to our sages, one of the warnings given by God to those dragged into captivity was not to press for the end of the exile by force. To pave the way towards the Messianic future in a quiet manner according to human ability is a Jewish duty; beyond this line begins rashness bordering on crime' (Izriel Hildesheimer, *Gesammelte Aufsätze*, ed. Meir Hildesheimer, Frankfurt am Main, 1923, p. 216).

14. See, Benzion Netanyahu, *Don Isaac Abravanel*, JPSA, 1953, pp. 255f. Cf. also Isaiah Leibowitz, *Emunah, Historia ve-Erachim*, Jerusalem, 5742, pp. 102f.

15. Striking illustration is to be found in his commentary on the Fourth Blessing of the Grace-after-Meals: 'When, during the reign of Hadrian, the uprising led by Bar Kochba proved a disastrous error, it became essential that the Jewish people

be reminded for all time ... that Israel must never again attempt to restore its national independence by its own power: it was to entrust its future as a nation solely to Divine Providence. Therefore when the nation, crushed by this new blow, had recovered its breath and hailed even the permission to give a decent burial to the hundreds of thousands who had fallen about Betar as the dawn of a better day, the sages who met at Yavneh added yet another blessing to the prayer for the restoration of Yerushalayim.' (*The Hirsch Siddur*, The Samson Raphael Hirsch Publication Society, Feldheim, Jerusalem–New York, 1972, p. 703).

Hirsch refused Kalischer's plea publicly to endorse the society for the resettlement of Jews in the Land, probably for 'Germano-nationalist' reasons; see Sam N. Lehman-Wilzig, 'Proto-Zionism and its Proto-Herzl: The Philosophy and Efforts of Rabbi Zvi Hirsch Kalischer', in *Tradition* (Summer 1976), p. 65.

For further relevant sources in Hirsch's writings, see 'Samson Raphael Hirsch', in my *The Timely and the Timeless*, London, 1977, p. 254.

16. 'Zion must be born in the soul before it can be created in visible reality.' Protesting against the power of the sword in determining the fate of the Land, he declared: 'The weapons of war may defeat the land; they cannot conquer it; conquest must come from within, as a deed of love.' And again, 'Only he will conquer it who, as did Israel long ago, will turn this land into the habitation of the Invisible One.' These views were in some respects even more anti-Jewish statehood than Satmar's, for they led Buber to advocate his peculiar belief in creating 'a peaceful symbiosis of Jews and Arabs in Palestine as peoples having equal rights in a binational commonwealth'; he saw 'the authenticity of Zion as being tested by Israel's attitude to Ishmael'. See Martin Buber, *On Zion – the History of an Idea*, East and West Library, 1973, pp. viii–ix.

17. See his *Emunah, Historia ve-Arachim,*

Akademon, Jerusalem, 5742. While declaring himself 'a Zionist and a patriot of the State of Israel' (p. 70), he sees the purpose of the State neither in serving as 'a light unto the nations' (which was an assignment given to the Prophets, not to Israel [p. 122]), nor as a salvation from Jewish alienation and insecurity (Jews are safer today in other lands [p. 128]), but simply because 'we are fed up with being ruled by goyim' (p. 129). In fact, he regards the attribution of *value* to the state itself as 'a fascist idea' (pp. 130 and 138), the choice of Israel in the teachings of Yehudah Halevi, the Maharal of Prague and Rabbi Kook as 'a national-racist chauvinism' (p. 132), and any Messianic significance ascribed to present events as misguided and highly dangerous (pp. 102 and 120). Hence, he advocates the complete separation of religion from the State (pp. 127 and 187), and regards *Yom Ha'atsmaut* as purely secular, marking the victory of the modern 'Hellenists' and not the 'Hasmoneans' (p. 70). He also strongly opposes the 'Greater Israel' devotees, as a peril to Israel's security and Jewish character (p. 214).

18. The most comprehensive work presenting the sources and rabbinical authorities supporting the Return to Zion and the Jewish State as part of the process of Redemption is Menachem Kasher's massive *Hatekufah Hagedolah*, Torah Shlemah Institute, Jerusalem, 5769. It includes *Kol Hator* (with an introduction and commentary) containing the views of the Gaon of Vilna on the Beginning of the Redemption.

19. The literature on this mainstream of religious Zionism is too vast and well-known to be listed here. See especially the quarterly *Or Hamizrach*, published jointly by the American Mizrachi and the Torah Education Department of the wzo, New York; and the extensive writings of S. Z. Shragai.

20. They base themselves in particular on the inclusion by Nachmanides of the duty to conquer the Land among the 613 commandments (*Sefer Hamitsvot*, Additional Commandment no. 4), derived from the verse 'And you shall take possession of the land and dwell in it' (Nu. 33 : 53, see also Nachmanides, *a.l.*). But Maimonides does not list this commandment, since 'it applied only in the days of Moses, Joshua and David and at a time when [the people of Israel] were not exiled from the land' (*Megillat Esther* on *Sefer Hamitsvot, loc. cit.*). Rashi likewise interprets the verse (ib.) differently. A similar argument concerns the borders of the Land. While Rashi explains that these are detailed in the Torah to indicate the area within which the special laws dependent on the Land's holiness are applicable (on Nu. 34 : 2), Nachmanides takes these borders to show the extent to which the Jewish conquest of the Land is obligatory, whilst the special laws apply to any territory under Jewish occupation even beyond these borders (on Deut. 11 : 24). Once again, Rashi as well as Maimonides clearly dissent from the opinion of Nachmanides. See also A. Newman, 'The Centrality of *Erets Yisrael* in Nachmanides', in *Tradition*, Summer 1968.

Leibowitz (*Emmunah*, etc. p. 119) regards Nachmanides as the *only* authority to declare settlement in the Land to be a positive commandment, and he dismisses this view as 'belonging to religious folklore'. But numerous scholars hold that the view of Nachmanides is widely shared, with slight variations, probably even by Maimonides. See Israel Schepansky, *Eretz Yisrael be-Safrut Hateshuvot*, Mosad Harav Kook, Jerusalem, 1978, vol. 3, p. 2 (note). The first 111 pages are devoted to rabbinic responsa on the subject, many based on the opinion of Nachmanides.

21. So expressly Rabbi Eliezer Yehudah Waldenberg, *Tsits Eliezer*, Jerusalem, 5723, vol. 7, no. 48:12, cited in Schepansky, *op. cit.* p. 95.

22. For a comprehensive halachic study on the return of the Occupied Territories

(generally favouring moderation), see J. David Bleich, 'Judea and Samaria: Settlement and Return', in *Tradition* (Summer 1979), pp. 44. The hard line arguments against the Egyptian peace accord and any territorial concessions are presented by Chief Rabbi Shlomo Goren, 'Beyn "Heskem Shalom" le-Shalom Emet', in *Or Hamizrach*, New York, Tevet 5740.

23. On his philosophy of religious Zionism in general, see his *Kol Dodi Dofek* in *Hadat Vehamedinah.* Tel Aviv, 5724; and *Hamesh Derashot*, Jerusalem, 5734. Although on record as stating that he would surrender even the Western Wall to save a single Jewish life, he has lately taken no public stand on peace and the territories. Remarkably, the known moderate attitudes of this acknowledged leader of modern Orthodoxy in America are not shared by most of his disciples, now comprising the principal personalities of the modern Orthodox rabbinate in America.

24. See his *Hahzarat Sh'tahim me-Eretz Yisrael bimkom Pikuah Nefesh*, in *Torah Shebe'al Peh*, no. 21, Jerusalem, 5740.

25. For a summary of rabbinic as well as other views for and against this movement, see Moshe Kohn's thirty-six page pamphlet *Who's afraid of Gush Emunim, The Jerusalem Post.* See also Introductory note, above. Rabbi Zvi Yehudah Kook's statement is featured in *Shanah b'Shanah*, 5728. See also Note 1.

26. Altogether, Rabbi Kook's vision of the Jewish State far transcended the political or even cultural aspirations of the Zionist Organization which he strongly criticized for its hankering after European culture and nationalism. While constantly emphasizing the unique character of Israel, he could conceive of the restoration of Jewish sovereignty only as conterminous with universal redemption, to be achieved through the impact of Israel's spiritual regeneration on the whole of mankind. He firmly believed – with a faith which some of his latter-day disciples might dismiss as

naïve – that Jewish independence would be regained by an enlightenment campaign to convince the world that its salvation would flow from Israel's national resanctification (in fact, he founded a movement, 'Degel Yerushalayim', to promote this objective), rather than by reliance on political action and propaganda. See Benjamin Ephrah, 'Israel's Politics in his Teachings', in *Harayah: Kovetz Ma'amarim Bemishnat Maran Harav Avraham Yitzchak Kook*, ed. Yitzchak Raphael, Mosad Harav Kook, Jerusalem, 5726.

27. This judgement clearly conflicts with the conclusion reached by Shubert Spero ('In Defense of the Defenders of Masada', *Tradition* (Spring 1970), who argued 'that the action of the defenders of Masada was not at variance with the teachings of the Talmud'. Dismissing the views of other scholars (cited in the article) who held the mass-suicide to be 'contrary to the Jewish tradition', and finding nothing 'baffling' in the silence of the Talmud on Masada, since it is 'not a systematic chronicle of historical events', Spero supports his claims by referring to the Talmud's approval of the mass suicide of 400 children 'who feared torture and immoral usage they faced in captivity' and to the self-inflicted martyrdom of entire Jewish communities in the Middle Ages. But halachically and historically one can hardly compare martyrdom to avoid torture, immorality or apostasy with suicide to escape from foreign domination. I would rather agree with 'the brilliant Orthodox historian', Y. I. Halevy, whom Spero quotes strangely with approval: 'The opinion of the rabbis was to wage war against Rome so long as the matter remained within the realm of the possible. Only after they realized that ... all hope of victory was lost, did they decide *to salvage what could be salvaged*' (my italics). For further contributions to this debate in *Tradition*, see Bernard Hiller, 'Masada and the Talmud' (Winter 1968), Louis I. Rabinowitz, 'The Masada

Martyrs According to the Halachah' (Fall 1970); Zvi Kolitz, 'Masada – in the Light of Halachah' (Summer 1971); and Sidney B.Hoenig 'Historic Masada and the Halachah' (Fall 1972).

28. The relevance of the Bar Kochba revolt to the contemporary situation has lately been re-examined in a little book which provoked a stir and much heated debate in Israel and beyond. Prof. Yehoshafat Harkavi (*Betokef Hametziut*, Van Leer Institute, Jerusalem, 1981) argues that Bar Kochba, far from being hailed as a national hero, should be seen as having inflicted one of the greatest disasters in Jewish history. The challenge of the Romans in an uprising which never had a chance of permanent success led to the oppression of Jews and Judaism, and to the destruction of Jerusalem, on a scale far more devastating than the defeat under Titus sixty-five years earlier when a measure of Jewish self-government and religious freedom were still tolerated under Roman domination. The gravamen of Harkavi's charge lies not in Bar Kochba's Messianic pretensions, nor the catastrophe in the post-Messianic disillusionment, but in the futility and lack of realism in engaging the Romans in a conflict which could not be won and instead was bound to wreak unprecedented havoc on the Jewish people. See also pp. 136f. above.

29. For a fuller exposition of this view, see 'Israel – Sanctuary or Asylum', in my *The Timely and the Timeless*, 1977. See also my 'Israel, Religion and Politics', in *L'Eylah*, Office of the Chief Rabbi, London, Autumn 5741; and 'The Jewish Purpose – A Reassessment', in *L'Eylah*, Spring 5741.

# Epilogue

I concluded the narrative part of this book about five months ago. Between then and my writing of this Epilogue, early in April 1984, much has happened. I resisted the occasional temptation, and made no further public statements which might have set off renewed controversies. Events clearly spoke louder and argued more convincingly than any pronouncements of mine could have done.

Sadly, my fear that 'the action in Lebanon may not achieve its objectives' (already expressed in my *Times* article of 7 July 1982) proved an understatement. The nightmare turned into a catastrophe. Instead of a peace partner, Lebanon became a base for renewed terrorist outrages deep inside Israel; Syria emerged from its mauling as the ascendant Arab power in the region; the humiliated PLO leader, Arafat, basked in new friendships in Cairo and Amman; and the Palestinian problem stubbornly refused to be buried in the rubble of Beirut and Tripoli.

These reverses set a whole chain of events into quick motion. Menachem Begin resigned, simply fading away from the Israeli scene, with both Jewish national fervour and bitter divisiveness at an all-time high. The coalition maintained its precarious majority under the new leadership of Yitzchak Shamir. Next to be hit was the economy; it was suddenly convulsed under the weight of a prolonged war costing a million dollars a day, plus the soaring security and settlement expenses to keep a hostile population beyond the 'green line' under Jewish rule. Finally, the parliamentary majority collapsed. What broke the government's back were the straws of three defectors comprising a tiny religious splinter party.

Linked with all or most of these events was the partnership between politics and religion, each making the other more radical. Religious militancy helped to encourage the Lebanese adventure from the beginning.

Many rabbinic articles endorsed the 'Peace for Galilee' action, arguing that, although launched as a preventive war, it belonged to the halachic category of a religiously 'obligatory war', not an 'optional war' (which could only be waged under very limited circumstances).

The government responsible for this war came to and stayed in power through the support of the religious parties, and it came to grief when one of these withdrew its support, again for reasons quite unconnected with any moral issues.

The cost exacted by this alliance from the religious parties was high enough, as expediency prevailed over principle. The anti-nationalist Aguda sustaining the most ultra-nationalist policies ever pursued in the history of Zionism and Israel is but one example of a spiritual force being frittered away for the manipulation of power. But even more damaging than the cost of this marriage of convenience were the 'gains'. Sordid deals traded political support for financial and legislative favours. The majority could not but nurse a feeling of oppression and exploitation when a minority used its balance of power to impose not only highly divisive policies shattering any consensus, but heavily subsidized settlement programmes, massive subventions to religious institutions, and coercive laws which non-believers could hardly appreciate.

Anti-religious feeling was further stirred up by Jewish religiously agitated terror groups operating against Arab targets, and by ugly confrontations over Sabbath desecration, bones found in archaeological digs, the exhumation of a non-Jew buried in a Jewish cemetery, and various other flashpoints liable to incite internal strife. Indeed, President Herzog himself, during a much-acclaimed visit to London towards the end of March, publicly stated that the bitter rift between the religious and non-religious segments of the population was his greatest worry and the country's gravest danger.

To me, even more disturbing were other by-products of this unholy partnership. The moral conscience of the Jewish people has been all but despiritualized, transferred from its traditional custodians, and virtually monopolized by the secularist masses and their spokesmen. When over 10 per cent of Israel's Jews, aroused by moral qualms over the war in Lebanon, participated in what must have been proportionately the largest spontaneous demonstration ever seen anywhere, there were few rabbis among the protesters, and certainly none of the better-known religious leaders who constantly summoned mass demonstrations against some isolated desecration of the Sabbath or of some suspected graves.

Worse still, ideals such as peace, conciliation, tolerance, sympathy for the sufferings even of one's enemies, and simple faith in the eventual triumph of human understanding – all so deeply rooted in the Jewish tradition – were virtually obliterated from the religious vocabulary of virtues. This religious insensitivity to Jewish moral values continues to baffle and trouble me to no end.

In my desolation over this disengagement of Judaism from its moral imperatives, I find little comfort in a somewhat parallel anomaly characterizing the post-war world at large. I adverted to this paradox in my Lambeth Interfaith Lecture delivered on 25 October 1983:

> Perhaps in this age of constant moaning over declining morals and mounting perils we should occasionally also recognize some very solid advances towards social justice and human brotherhood registered in our lifetime at a speed and on a scale unprecedented in all the thousands of years of man's tortuous evolution before we were born. The dismantling of colonialism leading to the emergence of scores of newly freed nations, the rise of the welfare state providing care for the sick and the aged and the workless and the poor where they previously had to endure complete destitution and abandonment, the instant communications of the media we so often decry and which yet can rouse millions to protest against injustices perpetrated against others thousands of miles away, the emphasis on human rights now upgraded as a major international concern – all this represents momentous progress in the cultivation of a social conscience....
>
> All these ideals of compassion, equality, freedom and brotherhood are basically the essence of religious teachings and aspirations.... We may therefore have expected the major forward thrusts of the moral conscience in society to have been generated primarily by religious forces....
>
> Yet nothing of the sort did in fact happen. The role of religion and religious leadership proved to be only marginal in the advances I have mentioned. For instance, it was the technological wonder of television rather than the spiritual marvels of religious faith which moved countless people in Europe and America to care about the scourges of hunger in Biafra, or apartheid in South Africa, or war in Vietnam, or desperate want in underdeveloped countries....

I acknowledged that 'religious leadership readily reacted to these changes in social awareness'. But I had little doubt that 'all this progress can hardly be attributed to religious initiatives . . .', and that even

> the main thrust in the substantial improvement of interfaith relations . . . has been a part of the overall drive towards better human relations, with its far more pronounced emphasis on human rights as a universal phenomenon in the secular world, rather than the other way round.

The parallel between Jewish and other religious phenomena may not be limited to their relative impotence in moral pioneering. At the opposite pole, there may also be certain similarities in religious tendencies towards political radicalism – whether in the form of Moslem fundamentalism or Christian revivalism on the one hand, or Jewish militancy on the other.

But these parallels can be misleading. The limits of the analogy lie in the distinctive interplay between religion, land and people in Judaism. Just as the attachment of Moslems to Mecca or Catholics to Rome cannot be compared to the Jewish yearning for Jerusalem, which extends to physical residence or even burial there, so is the fusion of faith, race and nationhood unique among Jews. The bond of a common peoplehood, itself a supreme religious factor, transcends all their sectarian divisions.

This explains such apparent contradictions as religious anti-Zionists sustaining a supernationalist government, or religious parties strictly opposed to any theocracy (even refusing cabinet posts) constantly pressing for religious legislation in a secular parliament, or Jews severely critical of Israeli policies and staunchly loyal to their own country yet supporting Israel without reservations.

These anomalies characterize the mystique of the Jewish people and their wondrous survival in the distant and not-so-distant past. They also lend realism to the faith that the common purpose and identity uniting the Jewish people will prevail over the centrifugal forces of fragmentation and divisiveness. This faith is further vindicated by the experience that in Israel the only thing to be expected is always the unexpected.

Yet, at the present time the dangers of polarization and extremism leading to major reversals in Jewish fortunes are acute and ominous. I remain unshaken in my belief that the key to stability and progress, certainly to the on-going realization of the Zionist dream, lies above all in restoring Israel's spiritual visions. To achieve this, as well as to preserve Israel's unity, two main impediments must be removed: the politicization of the religious elements and the secularization of the rest.

My principal challenges therefore continue to be directed in the first place to my own rabbinical fraternity, urging them to renounce both political partisanship and religious coercion if they want to be effective. As I told the congregation at the special Sabbath service at London's Marble Arch Synagogue in honour and in the presence of President Herzog on 31 March 1984:

The only formal or official protocol which unites a President with a Chief Rabbi is that they must both stand above party politics. Indeed, the Israel presidency puts to the test what rabbis should have learned long ago: that in a democratic society moral influence is exerted not by authority or legislation but by the power of persuasion and example.

In the same sermon I also stressed the special responsibilities of Israel's secular leadership. I related again how Chaim Weizmann, on being sworn in as Israel's first President, turned to his present successor's sainted father, the

Jewish State's first Chief Rabbi: 'My installation restores Jewish political sovereignty in succession to the kings of Judah and Israel; your task is to resume the heritage of the Hebrew Prophets, to provide the moral opposition and spiritual challenges to the political establishment.' And I continued:

Admittedly, in the intervening thirty-five years, the two respective roles assigned by Weizmann in that remark have been fulfilled by Israel's presidents more than by the rabbinical establishment. But, what Weizmann, the secularist, did not appreciate was that this dichotomy of king and prophet, representing the political and spiritual powers in opposition to each other, was itself quite un-Jewish: the prophets opposed the kings only when they fell short of their Jewish constitutional obligations. Ideally, the kings of Israel themselves were to combine political statecraft with leadership by the principles of the Torah which was to accompany them at all times.

Readers patient enough to reach these pages will not be surprised that the latest events and their escalation of external and internal perils have only reinforced the views I consistently expressed over the years. In the light of the grave anxieties as well as of the high hopes now stirring our people, I remain as committed as ever to the following propositions which sum up the imperatives of faith and action as I see them:

*On the Jewish purpose*

*There can be no Zionism without Jews, and no Jews without Judaism.
*The Jewish purpose cannot be to prevent our own destruction, and 'Never Again!' cannot replace purposeful Jewish living as its principal dynamic.
*Anything less than Israel's uniqueness renders the Jewish State dispensable and Jewish survival meaningless.
*Other countries may compete with Israel as a refuge of safety for Jews; but none can offer a comparable haven of Jewishness. This will determine both the Aliyah and Yeridah rates: those who seek a full Jewish life will come; those who care only for security and prosperity will leave.
*This applies in particular also to Soviet Jews: if the slogan is only 'Let My People Go', they may go – but hardly to Israel. Only by adding 'Let My People Live', by making equal efforts at turning them first into Jews inside Russia, will they afterwards prefer living as Jews in Israel to escaping elsewhere.

*On anti-Semitism*

*More to be feared than anti-Semitism is the fear of anti-Semitism if that fear becomes the major cause of Jewish identity and activity.

*More important than to fight anti-Semites is to win respect among non-Jews to prevent their becoming anti-Semites.

## On extremism and peace

*Militancy or radicalism in religion and politics alike cannot but further intensify the tensions between Israel and the Arabs and exacerbate the divisions within Israel, eventually reaching some breaking-point in war or civil strife.

*As in physics, every action produces an equal and opposite reaction: intransigence on one side breeds intransigence on the other, and likewise moderation. The vicious cycle of violence and hatred cannot be broken until one side begins to welcome instead of scorn signs of moderation on the other, thus setting the process of de-escalation in motion.

*A smaller and more intensively Jewish Israel is both safer and more ideal than a greater Israel in which the Jewish majority and its Jewish ethos are increasingly at risk.

*To believe that there will never be an accommodation with the Arabs is the counsel of despair and destroys any prospect of peaceful co-existence.

*Neither religious discipline nor national sovereignty can be permanently imposed by force on hostile majorities. Such force must in time disaffect the ruled and brutalize the rulers.

## On religion in Israel

*Without the antagonism created by religious politics and coercion, the hunger for Jewish values would have made the majority of Israel's Jews loyal, or at least sympathetic, to Torah ideals long ago.

*The less coercive religious legislation there is, the more religious Jews will be.

*The separation of religion and party politics is inversely proportional to the union of religion and the Jewish State.

## On security through moral strength

*Military strength cannot guarantee Israel's security indefinitely; only moral superiority can. Hence the call for 'double standards' is to be welcomed both as a non-Jewish tribute to Jewish moral excellence and as an insurance of Jewish survival.

*Logic and history alike dictate that for the Jewish people to prevail against incomparably superior odds in the long run, moral worthiness will matter more than any physical factors.

*Such a return to Jewish values would give Israel demographic strength through large families and high Aliyah rates; internal cohesion through uniting the country in a common purpose; external respectability as a model society; and an eventual accommodation with the Arabs through moral sensitivity for Palestinian sufferings and aspirations compatible with Israel's security.

*Israel's moral fibre cannot withstand constant erosion by the denial of traditional Jewish education to two-thirds of all children, by progressively replacing idealism with materialism, and by encouraging sole reliance on military strength.

*To reverse these trends by cultivating Jewish virtues must therefore become Israel's prime objective. 'And all the peoples of the earth shall see that the Name of the Lord is called upon you; and they shall respect you' – this is today a political no less than a religious truth. So is the assurance: 'If only My people would hearken unto Me, and Israel walk in My ways; I would soon subdue their enemies, and turn My hand against their adversaries.'

## Postscript

Shortly after the completion of this Epilogue, while on a pastoral visit to Australia and New Zealand, I was shocked to read one morning that Israeli life had been ruptured by Jewish terrorist cells which had been uncovered about to blow up a number of Arab buses and also places of worship deemed holy by the entire Arab world.

Unlike the group of American Orthodox rabbis who took advertising space in the *Jerusalem Post* and casuistically sought to exonerate the perpetrators as 'guilty of no moral crime', the distinguished President of Israel roundly denounced them as guilty of 'an act of lunacy and treason'.

The accused were religious zealots loyal to Gush Emunim. Their misguided idealism spurring them on to defiling the Holy Land by the shedding of innocent blood – albeit in retaliation for earlier Arab acts of terrorism – provides the ultimate QED for the major thesis of this book: the fearful realization that nothing menaces Israel and Judaism more than the explosive compound of religious and political extremism detonated by the fuse of Messianic fervour.

Conversely, physical, moral and spiritual security can only be restored by heeding the sage dictum in the *Ethics of the Fathers*: 'By three things is the world preserved: by truth, by justice and by peace.'

# Glossary

(all terms, except one, are Hebrew)

| | |
|---|---|
| Agudat Israel | Non-Zionist Orthodox movement, represented as ultra-Orthodox party in the Knesset |
| Ahavat Yisroel | Love of fellow-Jews |
| Aliyah | Lit. 'going up' – immigration of Jews to Israel |
| Baal Koreh | Public reader of Scriptures in synagogue |
| Bachad | Religious Zionist movement for the training of agricultural settlers in Israel |
| Berakhah | Benediction (recited before fulfilling a religious precept) |
| Beth Din | Ecclesiastical court |
| Bnei Akivah | Religious Zionist youth movement |
| Chabad | Philosophy of Lubavitch movement, often used as synonym for the movement |
| Chalutzim | 'Pioneers' – agricultural settlers in Israel |
| *Chillul Hashem* | Desecration of the (Divine) Name; disgracing reputation of Jewish people |
| Chovevei Zion | Pre-Zionist movement supporting Jewish settlements in Palestine, founded *c.*1880 |
| *Galut* | Exile, Jews in Diaspora |
| Gush Emunim | 'Block of the Faithful' – a militant group of religious Zionists promoting Jewish settlements in the whole of the Biblical Land of Israel |
| Haftarah | Reading from Prophets in synagogue |
| Halachah | Authentic norms of Jewish law |
| *Hallel* | Psalms of praise recited in festival liturgy |
| *Hatikvah* | National Anthem of Israel |
| Hesped | Memorial eulogy |
| *Ivrit* | Modern Hebrew |
| *Kiddush Hashem* | Sanctification of the (Divine) Name; enhancing reputation of Jewish people |

| | |
|---|---|
| 'Kotel' | Lit. 'the wall', referring to remnant of Western Wall enclosing Solomon's Temple in Jerusalem |
| Maftir | Concluding part of Sabbath reading from Pentateuch in synagogue |
| Medinah | State |
| *Mitzvah* | Religious precept; good deed |
| *'Nachtasyl'* | Lit. 'refuge for the night' (German), term used (by Max Nordau) for scheme considered by Herzl to settle hundreds of thousands of persecuted Russian Jews in a Jewish state in Uganda, pending their eventual move to Palestine. |
| Omer | Forty-nine-day count between Passover and Pentecost |
| Shechita | Ritual slaughter |
| Tahanun | Propitiatory prayer (not recited on festive days) |
| *Tallit* | Prayer-shawl with 'fringes' (see Nu. 15: 37–41) |
| Tisha B'Av | Ninth of Av; anniversary fast for Destruction of Temple in 586 BCE and 70 CE |
| Torah | Lit. 'teaching', applied to the Five Books of Moses, or to traditional Judaism generally |
| Torah Va'Avodah | Religious Zionist Labour movement (junior Mizrachi) |
| Yerida | Lit. 'going down' – emigration of Jews from Israel |
| Yeshiva | Talmudical college |
| Yishuv | Jewish community in Palestine before 1948 |
| Yom Ha'atzmaut | Israel Independence Day |

# Index

Bachad, 3, 8

Balfour Declaration: & Biblical tradition in Britain, 21, 157–9; as dawn of Messianic era, 7; the 'full-stop', 129; & Gaster, 210; & Hertz, 220–22, 224, 226, notes 240

Baltimore Board of Rabbis, 84

Bar Ilan University, 26, 32, 77, 95, 103, 147, 150–51

Bar Kochba, 67, 132, 136–7, 248, 250, 260n

Baron, Salo W., 156–7

Bauer, Prof. Yehuda, 163

Begin, Menachem: *Al Ahram* on, 90; on anti-Semitism, 170; Beirut investigation, 116; meeting with author, 103–4; policies & personality, 59–73, 71–4, 179; resignation, 261; & 'Who is a Jew?' controversy, 194, 200

Beirut massacres, 110–14, 115–16, 182

Ben–Gurion, David: condemns Moyne assassination, 50; memorial tribute to, 49; & Peel Commission, 157, 159; & roots of Zionism, 131; sayings of, 147, 252; & Sinai campaign, 12, 63; & 'Who is a Jew?' controversy, 16, 193, 198

Bentwich, Herbert, 210

Berlin, Sir Isaiah, ix, xiii

Berman, Julius, 115–16

Berman, Yitzchak, 115

Bermant, Chaim, 87, 178

*Beyn Or Lechoshech*, 216, 240n

Birnbaum, Nathan, 131, 211, 239n

birth rate & birth control, *see* abortions, population trends

Blanch, Dr Stuart, Archbishop of York, 121

Bloch, Grand Rabbin M.A., of Belgium, 239n

blood donation units, 21, 35

Bnei Akivah, 3, 132, 145, 247, 253

Board of Deputies, of British Jews: on Balfour Declaration, 220–21, 226, 240n; on Six Day War, 35

*Boston Jewish Advocate*, 84

Breuer, Yitzchak, 162–3, 235

Britain: Biblical tradition, 157, 170; reaction to author's 'luncheon' views, 86–7; struggle against in Palestine, 5;

*see also* Chief Rabbinate in Britain

British Council of Churches, 114

British Immigrants' Association (Hitachdut Olei Britannia), 94–5, 147, 155, 158

British Zionist Federation, 42

Brodetsky, Professor S., 50

Brodie, Sir Israel, Chief Rabbi: & Conference of European Rabbis, 26; installation of, 7, 19; & 'Jacobs Affair', 18; Prayer for State of Israel, 251; travels, 32; on Zionism, 210, 227-31, notes 241, 251

Brondesbury Synagogue, 8

Buber, Martin, 131, 146, 248

Burg, Dr Y., 79, 203

Callaghan, James, 72

Camp David Accord, 62–3, 71, 99

Carrington, Lord, 93–4

Carter, President, 63, 67, 71

Casper, Chief Rabbi Bernard, 84–5

Central Conference of American Rabbis, 81

Chasidism & 'yeshivah world', 132, 245, 246–7, 253, 256n

Chief Rabbinate in Britain: attitudes to Zionism (lecture), 191–2, 209, 242; author's travels & conferences, 32–3; 'cabinet', 22; dichotomy of office, 174; election of author as Chief Rabbi, 18–19; *see separately* Chief Rabbis Adler, Hertz & Brodie

Chief Rabbinate of Israel: Conference (1974), 52–3; relationship of author with, 75–6; *see separately* Chief Rabbis Goren, Herzog, Kook, Unterman & Yosef

Chovevei Zion, 158–9, 210–13, 217; notes (Orren) 239 & 240

Christian attitudes, *see* Jewish-Christian relations

Cohen, Isaac, Chief Rabbi of Ireland, 24

Cohen, Norman, xii, 226–7

Cohen, Sir Robert Waley, 226–7, 241n

Cohen, Chief Rabbi Shear Yashuv, 109, 117

*Concepts of Judaism* (Breuer), 162–3

Conference of Anglo-Jewish Preachers, 151, 223, 224, 240n, 241n